Economics and Environment

Economics and Environment

Essays on Ecological Economics and Sustainable Development

David Pearce

Professor of Economics, University College London and Associate Director, Centre for Social and Economic Research on the Global Environment, University College London and University of East Anglia, UK

Edward Elgar

Cheltenham, UK • Northampton, MA, USA

Published by
Edward Elgar Publishing Limited
Glensanda House
Montpellier Parade
Cheltenham
Glos GL50 1UA
UK

Edward Elgar Publishing, Inc.
6 Market Street
Northampton
Massachusetts 01060
USA

A catalogue record for this book is available from the British Library

Library of Congress Cataloguing in Publication Data

Pearce, David W. (David William)
Economics and environment : essays on ecological economics and sustainable development / David Pearce.
Essays written over the course of the author's career—'Some are reprinted, with modifications, from previous publications, but many are printed here for the first time'—P. 1.
Includes bibliographical references.
1. Environmental economics. 2. Sustainable development.
I. Title.
HC79.E5P369 1999
333.7—dc21 98–46611
CIP

ISBN 1 85278 772 4

Printed and bound in Great Britain by Biddles Ltd, Guildford and King's Lynn

Contents

Figures

Tables

Acknowledgements

In an academic career of over 30 years my debts to others are understandably too many to list comprehensively. To those with whom I have worked most closely I owe a special debt of thanks: Mick Common and Kerry Turner in particular. The most formative influence on my life, however, was one schoolteacher, Merlyn Rees as he then was and Lord Merlyn-Rees as he is now. Merlyn taught the virtues of plain speaking and I have never regretted taking on that attribute, though I am aware that it sometimes makes some people uncomfortable.

To Edward Elgar go my apologies for delaying this volume far too long and thanks to him for being so patient.

I dedicate this volume to Daniel and Corin, inheritors of our environment and fine young men, and to my mother who did not live to see the grandchildren she wanted so much, or her son a Professor.

I am indebted to various colleagues for allowing me to reprint some of their work: David Ulph for Chapter 16 on the social discount rate, Giles Atkinson for Chapter 6 on capital theory and sustainability, Giles Atkinson and Kirk Hamilton for Chapter 7 on sustainability indicators, Kerry Turner for Chapter 13 and Tom Crowards for Chapter 9.

Finally, Mikki Byskup revised my poor wordprocessing and put it all into final form: profound thanks are due.

DWP

The publishers would like to thank the following who have kindly given permission for the use of copyright material.

Blackwell Publishers Ltd for article: 'The role of carbon taxes in adjusting to global warming', *Economic Journal*, **101**, July 1991.

CAB International Ltd for article: 'Global environmental value and the tropical forests: demonstration and capture', in *Forestry, Economics and the Environment*, V. Adamowicz *et al.* (eds), 1996.

Cambridge University Press for articles: 'Measuring sustainable development: progress on indicators', *Environment and Development Economics*, **1**, 1996;

'Assessing the social rate of return from investment in temperate zone forestry', in *Cost Benefit Analysis*, 2nd edn, R. Layard and S. Glaister (eds), 1994.

Elsevier Science b.v. for articles: 'Capital theory and the measurement of sustainable development', *Ecological Economies*, **8** (2), 1993; 'Particulate matter and human health in the United Kingdom', with Tom Crowards, *Energy Policy*, **27**, July 1996; 'Packaging waste and the polluter pays principle: a taxation solution', with Kerry Turner), *Resources, Conservation and Recycling*, **8** (1/2), 1993.

IPC Magazines for article: 'Economists befriend the earth', *New Scientist*, 18 November, 1998.

Kyklos for article: 'The limits of cost–benefit analysis as a guide to environmental policy', **29**, 1976.

John Wiley and Sons Ltd for article: 'The social incidence of environmental costs and benefits', in *Progress in Environmental Planning and Resource Management*, T. O'Riordan and R. K. Turner (eds), 1980.

Every effort has been made to trace all the copyright holders but if any have been inadvertently overlooked the publishers will be pleased to make the necessary arrangements at the first opportunity.

Introduction: ethics, economists and the environment

This volume contains a selection of essays on the linkages between economics and the environment. Some are reprinted, with modifications, from previous publications but many are printed here for the first time. A few are jointly authored and I am grateful to my co-authors for allowing their work to be represented here.

In the late 1960s, when I was at Southampton University, I started, with a few colleagues, a UK 'Environmental Economics Study Group'. Our meetings rarely attracted more than a half dozen academics, but they were lively sessions and we had a sense that we were doing something new. Those were exciting times. The 1960s social revolution had brought into question the so-called 'materialist' way of life. This questioning in turn generated volume after volume of 'anti-growth' literature, declaring that economic growth was either feasible but not desirable or infeasible. That debate has not gone away and some of the essays in this volume comment on the central features of the argument: the concern with 'lifestyle', with sustainability and with the extent to which we can trust the economic system to warn us in advance of impending problems. My interest in matters environmental never went away, but the late 1970s and early 1980s saw a move to Aberdeen in Scotland where the driving force was the oil industry. Hence a substantial part of my writing then was about the economics of oil and gas, both in the rich and poor countries. None of those essays is reprinted here but, self-evidently, energy economics and environmental economics are close relations. Making my final move to UCL in 1983 rekindled the desire to work once more directly on issues in environmental economics. UCL has proved to be a fertile ground: its whole ethos is one of high profile excellence and departmental devolution. This backdrop enabled the creation of a joint venture with the International Institute for Environment and Development with the creation of the 'London Environmental Economics Centre'. LEEC was in fact the place where Ed Barbier, Anil Markandya and I wrote *Blueprint for a Green Economy* in 1988. It first appeared as a rather weighty report to the UK Department of the Environment who were then asking themselves exactly what 'sustainable development' meant for the UK economy. Besides LEEC, which lasted several years, UCL was the spawning ground for the UK's first ever taught graduate course in environmental economics. Finally, in 1991 we founded CSERGE which continues to this day. These events serve to show that in the space of two decades, the highly limited interest shown by academics and others in environmental economics had become, effectively, big business.

I make no secret of my own concern for the fate of the natural world, nor for seeing economics as a means to an end, namely avoiding, or at least minimizing, the destruction of habitat and wildlife. With many others, I share the belief that in conserving and enhancing the natural world we conserve and enhance human well-being. A lifetime working in developing countries, and often the poorest developing countries, underlines for me the vital link between human welfare and the natural environment. Whatever efforts are made to divorce the population from its reliance on the natural properties of the soil, its biomass and water, the reality is that for many decades to come, and whatever the promise of biotechnology, a vast portion of the world's population will rely directly on natural resources. Conserving those resources has to be both a humanitarian aim, and an obligation to the very many people who value those resources for other reasons. In the richer world the link is no less important: the experience of nature has become critical as a defence against the apparently ever increasing threats of violence and indifference, threats that seem to have their genesis in the retreat from nature and the substitution of wholly human-created experience. There is often a harmony between the concern for the natural world and concern for humanity. But concern for the environment does not have its sole justification in the role it plays in human well-being. Indeed, I have to be honest and say that the human orientation is not my dominant motive. Like others, I believe in trying to protect other species and their environment for their own sakes. While some seem to regard the continued presence of *Homo sapiens* as some kind of ethical imperative, I do not share that view. Viewed against the workings of Nature as a whole, human beings are indeed 'puny', as Lynne Margulis has said.

Nonetheless, relegating human wants and desires to an inferior position in favour of what some philosopher-king declares is good for us, is unacceptable. As some of the essays argue, there is a disturbing indifference to the ordinary mortal and to democratic processes in the writings of so many so-called environmental philosophers. Of course, what individuals and governments want is not always consistent with conservation. If that were true we would not have so many environmental problems. In many situations there is therefore an inevitable trade-off between human well-being and environmental conservation. It is the economic perspective that promises to help us make better and informed choices about the nature of that trade-off. To date, conservation has not stood much of a chance. The fact that so much of the value of conserved resources is not marketed means that, when faced with competition from marketed products, conservation loses out. By imparting economic value to the natural world, we can ensure a more 'level playing field' between conservation and development. This message is still understood by too few 'opinion makers', but probably the most foolish opponents of environmental economics are those who, reading little about the subject and understanding even less, claim that it is all 'unethical' and that some form of radical moral revolution *alone* will save the environment. The reader should not be surprised, therefore, to find some of the essays in this volume addressing those critics directly. Probably the single most important observation one can make about the economics–environment link is that if we wish to save the world's environments we can only do so by modifying and reforming the way we manage the world economy and national economies. That single observation places economics at the heart of what we might term 'practical environmentalism', i.e. getting significant improvements in conservation and environmental quality put into real-world policies. Simply put, we are more likely to conserve biological diversity, protect the rainforests, the ozone layer and the global atmosphere through economic policies than we are by other means. This is not meant to suggest that 'non-economic' actions are unimportant: campaigns, protests, appeals to conscience, political lobbying are all important. But the biggest improvements are to be had through modifications in economic policy, as a number of the essays in this volume demonstrate.

All economic decisions affect the environment, and so the way to improve the environment is to change the way in which those economic decisions are made. In general, the ways in which those decisions should be modified have been well developed in the economics literature. Indeed, the tools of analysis have been available for a long time – most of them emanate from neo-classical welfare economics. It is the application of those concepts to environmental problems that has been most fruitful and this, by and large, describes the content of environmental economics. Nonetheless, I am not a slave to 'neo-classicism', although some people seem to think so. In particular, I am not convinced that we live in a world of smooth substitutability between natural resources and the other inputs to economic activity. I did not believe that back in the 1960s and I do not believe it now. But the neo-classical framework is productive and offers insights to policy that are of immense value. The current focus, for example, on creating property rights in environmental assets, on creating markets, designing economic incentives and removing perverse subsidies, all emanate from the neo-classical position. Those who criticize neo-classicism suffer an 'all or nothing' syndrome, an incapacity to take what is good from a given approach and to reject what is bad. For them, it is either all bad or all good.

My argument, then, is that some environmentalists are missing an opportunity if they set themselves against economics as such, for it can be their most powerful ally. But that does not mean that there are no problems with environmental economics. There are other sources of criticism. One major source of criticism is that environmental economics still treats the world as if it consists of self-centred human beings, devoid of altruism and moral principle. Worse, economics generally seems to elevate this description of human behaviour to the level of prescription: this is how the world should be and the allocation of resources should respond to self-interest. In this sense, economics is, the argument goes, immoral because its underlying morality is that what is good for the self-seeking individual is good for society as a whole. This is an understandable line of criticism, but it is simplistic. Economics does not, for example, always assume that resources should be allocated according to individual wants: there is a sizeable literature on the economics of fairness and justice, including inter-generational justice. Even where self-interest is assumed, a great deal of economics is devoted to the resolution of conflicts between the self-interested. Few economists believe in wholly unfettered free markets. Most would claim a central role for enlightened intervention, for limits to human greed, but they would warn that the opposite assumption to consumer sovereignty, the well-motivated, representative and benign government, is just as much an artificial construct. Anyone who has worked with government will know that they are frequently confused, often ignorant – especially in the sphere of environmental policy – and generally unimaginative. If we deny the rights of individuals to seek their own ends, and perhaps to destroy themselves in the process, we have to be equally vigilant about self-serving governments. It would of course be nice if the world was full of other-serving good citizens. There is indeed a vast reserve of good citizenry about. But to rely on it, or on governments to stimulate it, is to waste effort. The only practical approach is to manipulate self-interest in the interests of the higher good, and in so doing continually to ask who has the right to judge the behaviour of others. The 'moral standpoint' against economics is often a thin disguise for saying that people don't count, only some self-appointed expert does. There is therefore another theme in these essays: the construction of environmental economics on the basis of minimum regulation, on 'mutual coercion, mutually agreed upon' as Garrett Hardin put it.

The other line of criticism of environmental economics is perhaps more interesting, even though it embraces some of the concerns of the moralists. This is the emergence of a still hazy and ill-defined subdiscipline of ecological economics. Environmental economics is, by and large, neo-classical in its construction. There is a belief in the standard conceptual structures – utility maximization, profit maximization, substitutability in consumption and in production. Ecological economics parts company in a number of ways. There is certainly a basic questioning of utility maximization, not in the sense of describing the world but certainly in the sense of saying that what is, ought also to be. As we indicated above, that questioning has its own problems and there is a detectable non-democratic streak in ecological economics. There is a justifiable questioning of the fact of substitutability. Environmental economists have probably spent too long thinking of natural resources as being typified by copper or oil, and too little thinking of ecological processes and cycles as 'capital'. There is no real substitute for many of the life support functions of the natural world, and hence there are limits to the neo-classical interpretation of the world. That said, as these essays show, there is immense practical policy-influencing power in the neo-classical model. The impatient desire for a 'new' or 'alternative' economics to replace it should be contained less we lose the influence that can be exerted to conserve natural environments through the use of that model. The opposition likes nothing better than a confusion of experts. But there are some valuable insights in ecological economics and, to that end, I have included an essay on the subject here.

My main concern, then, is to convey a message that will be familiar in most of my writing. Intellectually justified or not, moralism will not save the world for human beings or for other species. I doubt if human motivation has ever changed much and the only way to serve environmental goals is to adapt that motivation so that what is good becomes what humans find in their own collective self-interest. That means finding solutions that make all parties feel better off with the solution than without it. The approach is pragmatic and focuses on the design of incentives. If it doesn't work, we can be sure that nothing else will.

Part 1 of the volume produces papers on the issue of 'valuation' and ecological economics. Putting money values on people's preferences (not 'on the environment' as those who misread economics claim) is a significant part of environmental economics, but by no means all of it. One could, for example, go a long way with environmental economics thinking without once addressing the issue of valuation. Valuation is also controversial, as these essays show. Chapter 1 deals with the philosophical criticisms of economic valuation. If there is any one message to emerge from that chapter it is that environmental philosophers ignore the elementary concept of opportunity cost. By invoking the 'rights' of Nature and the ethical beliefs of individuals they do a part service to us all, but sadly they fail to see that rights are not independent of cost, since what is spent defending one set of rights could have been spent defending another set. What it costs to protect a wetland, say, could have been spent on hospitals or schools, both uses reflecting rights. As Chapter 1 suggests, part of the problem lies in a lack of real-world context for so many of today's philosophers, although, to be fair, modern philosophers are far more real-world than when I took a philosophy degree some thirty years or so ago. Chapter 2 is reprinted not because it says anything profound but because, when it was published ten years ago, it gave rise to more incoming mail and calls than anything else I had written before. As reprinted here it appears somewhat dry. When printed in the *New Scientist* it was accompanied by some brilliant artistry and diagrams that did so much to give it appeal. Like Chapter 1, Chapter 3 has not been reprinted before. It deals with the emerging paradigm of 'ecological economics'. One of the paradoxes of modern science is that, as fast as we get one coherent world view, we demand that something takes its place. That is for the good of science, but it can be disastrous for the object of concern, in this case the environment. The problem arises because, rather than apply what we know or believe will work, we are too busy rushing off to pronounce that the previous paradigm is dead and a new one lives. But there are some vital features in ecological economics that are perhaps more a matter of emphasis than fundamentals, and these are discussed in Chapter 3. Chapter 4 is an early paper on the 'limits' of cost–benefit analysis. One of the continuing debates in environmental economics is the compatibility, or otherwise, of concepts like 'critical loads' – a concentration or deposition of pollution below which no biophysical damage is done – and cost–benefit outcomes. Typically, cost–benefit analysis would dictate some optimal level of damage greater than zero, so that cost–benefit and critical loads would appear to be incompatible. Chapter 4 suggests that once a longer-term, dynamic look is taken, critical loads become a long-run optimum. Note that this is what ecological economists are effectively saying now. For those who spend their time labelling me as a 'neo-classical', we might note that I was writing on the subject of neo-classicism and ecological economics before many of these critics had sat before a computer screen.

Part 2 of the volume deals with sustainable development. While many economists have been and are suspicious of the concept, it has been an effective stimulator of some rethinking in environmental economics and, perhaps more importantly, of environmental action. Nonetheless, in terms of the literature it has come to mean all things to all men. The essays in Part 2 try to give some coherence to the way in which some of us have come to define sustainable development and to measure it. Chapter 5 has been specially prepared for this volume and deals with the underlying theory. Chapter 6 was the first attempt at introducing a measure of sustainability based on the idea of 'genuine savings', essentially the excess of the resources that a nation or a company would put aside to cover the depreciation on assets. In this case, however, environmental assets are treated just like any other set of assets, so that environmental damage and resource depletion are fully integrated into our measures of economic progress. In effect, what Giles Atkinson, Kirk Hamilton and I developed as the genuine savings rule is a reworking of 'green' national income measures, but with far more policy meaning than green national product figures can convey. Getting the original article published was quite problematic because it appears to espouse the 'weak sustainability' concept whereby all forms of capital asset are substitutable (see Chapter 3). As we show in Chapter 7, however, it is a test that many countries fail. Moreover, and seemingly not appreciated by those who focus on 'strong' sustainability alone, all sustainability rules require weak sustainability as a prior test. The genuine savings measure was presented at a seminar at

Resources for the Future (RFF) in Washington where I was, effectively, howled down and told to go away and think again. It is salutary that the World Bank adopted the measure and extended it to include net appreciation of human capital, publishing a genuine savings indicator for over one hundred countries. Our efforts have been fully vindicated.

Chapter 7 surveys the state of the art in sustainability indicators, or, rather it surveys the approaches that are rooted in a theory of sustainability. Unfortunately, so many 'indicators' with the title of sustainability indicators are nothing of the sort, but simply measures of environmental change.

Chapter 8 is there simply to provoke those who seem to think that phrases like 'sustainable consumption' are helpful in the sustainability debate. If sustainable consumption means changing the *pattern* of production and consumption away from polluting to less polluting technologies and products then, of course, this is nothing more than what economists have been saying for decades. An environmental tax, for example, is simply a means of changing consumption and production patterns. But it is clear that many of those who advocate 'sustainable consumption' think it means reducing absolute consumption *levels*, usually only in the North countries. The implications of this for the South would actually be disastrous, but, as the chapter argues, it is not in any event a policy option open to governments. This chapter has not previously been published, although part of it was presented at a Norwegian conference (where I was privately asked by a senior official if I was serious), and part of it was prompted by discussions at the World Commission on Forests and Sustainable Development.

Part 3 of the volume illustrates how some aspects of environmental economics can be applied to real-world problems.

Chapter 9 shows how environmental economics concepts can be applied to an 'every day' problem such as air pollution from particulate matter. Epidemiological relationships are used to establish the effects on health of given concentrations of pollutants. These effects are then 'monetised' to produce a total health damage for the United Kingdom. Such exercises are still rather uncertain, partly because the epidemiology is not clear and partly because we still lack adequate European studies of what people are willing to pay to avoid damage to their health. That picture will change and, with it, perhaps the conclusions of Chapter 9 will change too. In the meantime, it does the best we can with the information available. Chapter 10 looks at forestry in the UK from a multipurpose standpoint. Forestry still suffers from centuries-old traditions of forest science as being all about timber and optimal rotations and thinnings etc. Like so many environmental assets, forests are multifunctional and need to be managed as such. They regulate climate, protect watersheds, fix carbon, provide recreation, and so on. Chapter 10 shows how some of these functions can be monetized to estimate a broader rate of return than that to timber alone.

Unfortunately, the answers still look bad for UK forest planting when measured against the government's 'test' discount rates. But that tells us more about erroneous thinking in government on the issue of discounting than it does about forestry. Chapter 15 in fact shows us that UK 'official' discount rates are far too high.

Chapter 11 takes the same theme of multipurpose forestry but puts it in a tropical context. It defines the functions of forests and says what we know about their economic values. This is the process of 'demonstrating' value. But saying what a forest is worth in economic terms is of limited help. We must also show how those values can be 'captured' by forest-owning countries and, often more importantly, by local communities. Exactly the same issue of demonstration and capture is applied to African wildlife in Chapter 12. Wildlife management regimes vary substantially. Some countries have opted for low price, mass 'ecotourism' with consequent damaging effects on the health of their wildlife. Certainly, the measurement of carrying capacity for tourists is something we still know too little about. Other African nations have effectively reaped the rents from unique wildlife by charging high prices and keeping tourism under stricter control.

Chapter 13 looks at how one might devise an economic instrument for the control of packaging waste. For good and bad reasons, many governments have targeted packaging as an environmentally damaging sector of economic activity. In reality, packaging rarely even figures in opinion polls about serious environmental problems, rightly in my view. Nonetheless, it is a fertile field for the application of environmental taxes and other measures and Chapter 13 shows to devise a product tax that varies with waste at source, with recycling, and with environmental impact. Taxes of this kind have in fact been introduced in several countries.

Chapter 14 addresses an issue that was popular in the 1970s but which 'died' in the 1980s only to return with a vengeance in the 1990s under the guise of 'environmental justice'. Essentially, we ask who actually suffers from environmental damage and who pays for its mitigation. Popular opinion has it that the environment is a 'luxury good', one that we demand only when we are rich. This idea has even been furthered by modern constructions such as the 'environmental Kuznets curve' which purports to show that environments get worse at low levels of economic development and then get better as a certain average income is surpassed. Whatever the merits of the environmental Kuznets curve, Chapter 14 was an early challenge to this presumption. I could find little or no evidence that environment was a luxury good and, interestingly, very recent work, building on the paper in Chapter 14, has confirmed this finding.

Chapter 15 challenges the official view in the United Kingdom on discount rates. Rates of 6% and 8% in real terms are recommended for public agencies.

Yet the rationale for these numbers appears, at best, to rest on a mistaken reading of the literature. Rates of 2–4% would seem far more rational.

Chapter 16 attempts to do something that is very common in the USA but not in Europe. It tries to see what evidence we have for the efficiency or otherwise of European Union environmental Directives. The disturbing finding is that few past Directives were subject to any form of rigorous appraisal. Using what information we can, we show that some very costly Directives are hardly likely to pass a cost–benefit test.

Part 4 of the volume deals with global environmental change. Arguably, the real difference between the environmental economics of twenty and thirty years ago and the environmental economics of today is the development of analysis to deal with the 'global commons'. Issues such as global warming, ozone layer depletion, biological diversity loss, forest loss and so on have both localized and global impacts. Securing solutions is all the more difficult because of the need for international agreements. Finding solutions that are consistent with each party being better off with the solution than without it is complex and, in the end, it may be necessary to 'buy off' the losers.

Chapter 16 is relatively simplistic. The aim is to show that there are 'alternative paradigms' for environmental management and that communication between the holders of different views could be facilitated by the simple diagrammatic comparison adopted.

Chapter 17 actually addresses the monetization issue. For reasons ill understood by casual commentators, the damage assessment chapter for the 1996 Second Assessment Report of the IPCC caused considerable controversy. Only a few seemed to object to the idea of monetising the damages. Indeed, the most vociferous critics resorted to their own, rather fanciful, attempts to place different monetary values on the damage. The controversy stemmed from a concerted campaign by a handful of people who thought, allegedly, that one should not use different 'values of statistical life' for different people in different parts of the world. As it happens, one could have used some world average to get to essentially the same conclusion as we did for the IPCC, i.e. the damage numbers would not have changed much. But given that values of statistical life are in fact aggregations of individuals' valuations of risk, it must be obvious that those valuations are not in fact the same in any one country or across different countries. The motivations of those who shouted loudest or who behaved in a juvenile fashion almost certainly had nothing to do with a concern for the poor or the vulnerable. The disturbing fact, however, was the espousal of their cause by people who should know better, including several people who joined in the criticism while simultaneously admitting, quite openly, that they had not read the 'offending' material. Chapter 17 therefore reprints one of around ten papers produced by my colleagues and I after the IPCC 1996 assessment.

Chapter 18 concerns carbon taxes. It was written in 1990 and it shows how quickly things have changed. Since the essay was written the Framework Convention on Climate Change was introduced in 1992; carbon taxes have actually been introduced in several European countries; and even the United Kingdom has begun the move towards fiscally neutral environmental taxes, though not in the energy sector. The idea of fiscal neutrality is itself interesting. Those who oppose it point to the obvious potential for inefficient taxes as revenues are earmarked for specific uses which may well not be the socially most efficient ones. Those who support them point to the need for the electorate to see where their money is going and to approve of the direction. It seems likely that sectoral taxation, as with transport, will have to adopt earmarking if the public is to swallow the now painful measures needed to put the transport sector right.

PART 1

Ethics, Ecological Economics and the Environment

1. Valuing the environment[1]

1.1 A BEGINNING: VALUES AND MOTIVATIONS

I shall begin with what I think is a reasonable assumption, that we share a common concern for the environment and that we wish to do something constructive to reduce the rate of environmental degradation and resource loss. This common concern affects a large and varied group of individuals whose motivations for what I shall loosely call 'conservation' are themselves very varied.

A common distinction is that between 'anthropocentric' and 'ecocentric' values, between those who see value as being necessarily 'of' people 'for' the environment, and those who see value as being 'in' nature and independent of people. Broadly speaking, this distinction also coincides with that between 'instrumental' value and 'intrinsic' value (Rolston, 1994). While these distinctions are useful for pedagogic purposes, they are in fact fuzzy. In expressing *my* (instrumental) value for nature, I may be motivated by a concern for the intrinsic value of nature. That is, I may be expressing instrumental value but in so doing I am also acting *on behalf* of nature, giving it a voice that it otherwise would not have. This compromise approach is what some have called 'weak anthropocentrism' (Norton, 1987). The values are necessarily expressed by a *valuer*, namely myself, but the prospect exists that at least part of the value so expressed represents a stewardship or representational motive. Indeed, since nature and species do not have voices that permit them to count in any conflict between conservation values and non-conservation values, this valuing on behalf of nature is important. Whereas instrumental values may be reducible to some logical form such as 'I like koala bears but not water buffalo', weak anthropocentrism affords the water buffalo more of a chance in any conflict of values because I say 'I don't like water buffalo but they have rights to existence, or intrinsic value'.

This weak anthropocentrism is important in the world of environmental and ecological economics. The external image of economics is that it assumes a set of human preferences motivated solely by self-interest in the sense of strict anthropocentrism. Crudely put, people are greedy. This image reflects a *partial* truth: people are greedy. But people also have other motivations for their actions and economists have been slow to explain that those motivations are also part of human decision-making and part of economics. As a result, economics has been caricatured in the environmental philosophy literature. Holmes Rolston, for example, clearly has this false image of economics:

> In the market per se, people operate in self-interest. There it is rational to be efficient, get the most for your money, make the most profit. Within economics, that is the meaning of rationality (Rolston, 1994, p. 156).

In much the same vein, for example, Tim Hayward declares that the problem of modern economics is that it has lost its roots in the Greek word *oikonomia*, the management of the household for the wider good, and has instead absorbed *chrematistics*, the maximization of short-run gain (Hayward, 1995, p. 92).

But that is not the meaning of economic rationality and economists must either be very bad communicators, or philosophers must be very bad at understanding economics. Economic rationality is certainly about maximizing something, let us call it well-being, but there is nothing in economics that says my well-being has to depend solely on what I consume. My well-being may depend on your level of well-being and on the well-being of my family, my relatives, my neighbours, cats and dogs, and the state of the world environment too. In turn, economists' attitudes to the long run tend to be coloured by how individuals behave with respect to intertemporal choice: any 'short-termism' is not imposed by economists, but reflects what they observe. Once we are in the domain of normative economics, however, there is nothing in economic doctrine that says economists have to take a short-term view.

These rather basic misconceptions would not matter very much but for the fact that critiques of economics and environmental economics are built up on the basis of this straw man. One suspects that the age-old confusion between economics as commerce, and economics the science has not yet gone away. Clearly, both sides have to try harder.

1.2 THE NATURE OF ECONOMIC VALUE

A critical step in the economic calculus is that between a preference for something and a willingness to pay to secure it. That is how markets work, and in affording economic values to environmental assets, functions and processes the economist is taking what are often, but far from always, non-market phenomena and simulating willingness to pay for those phenomena. Put another way, even though markets do not exist, the economist attempts to derive economic values *as if* markets exist. The extent to which this process reflects the hypothetical varies. For example, to calculate the impact of low level ozone on crop productivity and then to value the resulting losses at market prices is one example of economic valuation that is barely divorced at all from real-world markets: indeed, it relies on the real-world market for the resulting values. On the other hand, to measure willingness to pay to conserve, say, the spotted owl may involve an essentially hypothetical process of asking people what they *would be* willing to pay for conservation of the owl *if* some market could be established to channel funds into conservation. This is the methodology known as 'stated preference' and instances of it include contingent valuation, contingent ranking and conjoint analysis (see Bjornstad and Kahn, 1996). Such hypothetical approaches are deliberately hypothetical: they have their justification in the fact that there often is no market in which to elicit willingness to pay. But they need not be unrealistic. To see this, suppose we choose a different label for this process and instead of calling it stated preference we call it 'market research'. Market research is familiar and widely used. It does not differ in essence from hypothetical valuation, though it may differ in form (Hanemann, 1995). It may also be tested for realism by applying it to assets where real willingness to pay can also be measured, or by applying it to contexts where quite different procedures for inferring willingness to pay are available.

In between the reality and direct observability of market valuations and the hypothetical reality of market research lies a range of approaches that rely on the fact that markets exist but in indirect form. The price of houses is, we know, affected by environmental amenity neighbourhood noise, air pollution, visual disamenity and so on. Individuals have therefore expressed their willingness to pay for peace and quiet, for clean air and for amenity by reflecting those characteristics of property in their decisions to buy property. That willingness to pay then influences the price of the property. Much the same goes for willingness to pay for recreational amenity where individuals' willingness to pay may be derived from the travel expenditures they make; for risk reduction where individuals pay for protective measures or receive wage compensation for risk, and so on. There are, then, sets of 'surrogate markets' which indirectly afford economic value to unmarketed environmental assets. In this way, the economist is able to build up sets of economic values, based on willingness to pay which is in turn based on individuals' preferences stated or revealed in hypothetical or real markets. This process is not without problems, and we return to some of these shortly.

We can now re-emphasise an important feature of the economic approach. It is entirely consistent with weak anthropocentrism. My motivation for being willing to pay positive sums for the conservation of an environmental asset may be wholly self-centred: I may want the asset for myself now (current use value) or in the future (option value) and for no-one else. But it is also possible that my motivation derives from wanting the asset to be available for my children or generations to come (bequest value) or from wanting the asset to exist in its own right (existence value). In expressing or revealing my economic values I may be speaking on my behalf, or on behalf of my family, on behalf of society in general, or on behalf of future generations. It has been argued that hypothetical questionnaire approaches to willingness to pay contingent valuation elicit not self-interested preferences but 'warm glow' or 'moral satisfaction' (Kahneman and Knetsch, 1992). Even if true, this is not an argument for calling such values 'non-economic' – see Harrison (1992). It is not essential that my preferences be motivated by pure self-interest for them to qualify for economic relevance, a point that has been made fairly often in the economics literature from Arrow (1951), through Becker (1993), to Hanemann (1996).

Of course, it should also be accepted that intrinsic value may also be a motive for *not* being willing to pay to conserve the environment. A few contingent valuation surveys have found that a minority of respondents have indicated intrinsic value as their motivation while simultaneously being unwilling to pay anything at all for conservation (Stevens *et al.*,1991; Freeman, 1994; Hanley *et al.*, 1995). Thus, the Stevens *et al.* study suggested that 70% or more of respondents agreed with the statement 'all species of wildlife have a right to exist independent of any benefit or harm to people'. Yet around 60% of respondents refused to pay anything, and 25% of these said wildlife values should not be measured in dollar terms. The objects of value in this study were salmon, bald eagles, wild turkeys and coyotes. Seventy per cent of respondents in the study by Freedman, of white-backed woodpeckers in Sweden, suggested that rights to existence defined their motivation for positive willingness to pay. The Hanley study also suggested that some 23% of respondents were unwilling to trade-off conservation of Caledonian pinewoods against money. But these studies could be criticised for not making the trade-off context as real as possible. Interestingly, a later study by Hanley and Milne (1996) found that 99% of respondents thought that wildlife and landscape have a right to exist. But this percentage fell to 49% when it was suggested that conservation costs money and jobs, and to 19% when the cost was translated to be 25% of the respondent's income. While the authors of this study see the remaining 19% as a salutary reminder that not all individuals are willing to trade-off conservation against other things, we might equally point out that 80% of respondents lost their belief in a rights-based approach as soon as the reality of trade-offs was presented to them. Rights, it seems, may be easily assigned and defended when they cost nothing, a finding that game theorists have known for some time. Small wonder that politicians make pious speeches about some international agreement when the agreement merely confirms a path of activity that would have been pursued anyway. It would also be interesting to see how such studies fare in contexts where the respondents depend for their livelihood on a particular land use. Yet these are the contexts where most of the world's biodiversity is being lost.

We must acknowledge the concerns that the small but growing literature on 'lexical' preferences poses – preferences in which no trade-off is apparently allowed. But it remains the case that economic values must not be identified and equated with selfishness: that is too narrow a reflection of how preferences are formed. And it is preferences, not their motivations, that determine economic values.

1.3 LABELS

This confusion about economics as advocacy of pure self-interest is a general warning against the disease that might be called 'labelitis' which appears to be endemic in environmental discourse. Labelitis is a process of classifying and labelling individuals and 'schools of thought', sometimes regardless of the potential for wearing more than one label at a time, sometimes without understanding the philosophical foundations for particular outlooks – as the economics example showed – but mainly with the aim of compartmentalising everyone so that they can be damned for being in some compartment different to one's own. Labels become terms of abuse. Taking the journal *Environmental Ethics* as a leading example of a forum for philosophical investigations into moral discourse on the environment, the first impression is that environmental ethicists suffer from an extreme form of 'labelitis'. Thus a criticism of one well-known paper by philosopher Jim Cheney takes him to task for positing:

> a radical epistemological break between a deluded modernism – characterised as foundationalist, essentialist, colonising and totalising – and a contextual postmodernism (Smith, 1993).

This is apparently a very serious matter because it means that Jim Cheney's postmodernism allies him with 'economic humanism' which in turn appears to have something to do with markets and economic value, and that, clearly, is the enemy since it is a common theme in many of the essays in *Environmental Ethics*. I suspect that 'economic humanism' is a catch-all for what I am calling the approach based on economic values, and what others call 'reformist environmental economics' (Hayward, 1995) or even 'ecological modernisation' (Redclift, 1996). If it is, then, as we have seen above, what the critics are criticizing is a parody of what economists actually say.

The second impression is that environmental ethics as a philosophical discipline is not particularly useful in the practical fight to save natural environments. My personal motives for defending the environment arise from (a) a belief that the environment is extremely useful for human beings, where being useful includes giving us all cause to wonder and admire its beautiful complexity; (b) an empathy with other species which I know feel pain and pleasure and which pain and pleasure has a similar Benthamite moral standing to the pain and pleasure of human beings; and (c) because the entire environmental edifice is so mysterious that I do not want to assume I know for sure what environmental destruction will do to us or our descendants. Any set of beliefs entails a commitment to action. A commitment to action can take many forms. It could consist of political action, it could consist of a moral crusade to change minds, it could consist of changing behaviour regardless of whether minds are changed. But it is difficult to make it consistent with intellectualising in an academic journal and adopting a private language not shared with many others and, above all, not shared by those who make the decisions to allow environments to live or die. In case I seem unduly harsh on environmental philosophers, let me say at once that this private language disease is also shared by a great many economists and, for that matter, a great many academics. But it is particularly important in this context because it inhibits action.

Now, it could be that environmental philosophers do not wish to be particularly useful or action-oriented, but that is not the way many of them write. Moreover, I think we have other evidence for the suggestion that environmental philosophy does little that is practical for the environment (indeed, by absorbing the energies of clever individuals it must contribute to environmental destruction since their energies would be better directed elsewhere).

Writing in the same journal, *Environmental Ethics*, Michael Bruner and Max Oelschlaeger ask why it is that

> ecophilosophy has not . . . effected consequential societal change (Bruner and Oelschlaeger, 1994).

Their answer is worth quoting in full because it bears on the credibility of those who argue that the only true way forward is to change people's minds, to alter the way we view nature, to develop a new ethic of environmentalism. If Bruner and Oelschlaeger are right, then the *exclusive* focus on changing mindsets rather than behaviour is fiddling while the Rome of Nature burns. They write:

> environmental ethics . . . is a specialised form of discourse that less and less resembles the prose found in Leopold's *Sand County Almanac*, and more and more revolves around either arcane discussions of such issues as ethical monism, moral considerability, intrinsic value, and the like, or discussions among contending factions in ecophilosophy (ecofeminism, deep ecology, social ecology, and so on). However, in order for discourse to promote social change, it must achieve a hearing before a large audience. By this criterion, environmental ethics has not been effective discourse (p. 383).

They continue:

> The scandal of philosophy, since the beginning, has been that no two philosophers ever agree about anything an overstatement, to be sure, yet close to the mark in environmental ethics;

and

> How can lay publics place faith in environmental ethics when ecophilosophers have no faith in one another – when they produce an endless string of arguments demonstrating that so and so is wrong, dazed, bemused, or even crazed? Most recent issues of *Environmental Ethics* contain at least one essay, written by someone representing one particular kind of ecophilosophy, showing how some other kind of philosophy offers an inadequate foundation for or account of environmental ethics because of conceptual confusions, blunders of logic, mysticism, mean spiritedness and so on. . . One must wonder, ultimately, just what it is that is at stake: academic reputations, promotions, power, or actually effecting changes in human behaviour that lead toward sustainability . . . *Perhaps it is more important for ecophilosophers to be useful, that is, help society move itself toward sustainability, than anything else* (pp. 384/5, our emphasis).

Perhaps Bruner and Oelschlaeger are being unfair on their colleagues who occasionally do foray into the real world of harsh environmental concerns. Pursuing the same journal in search of papers that dealt with reality, I noticed an essay addressing the problem of conservation of the Amazon rainforest, by Eric Katz and Lauren Oechsli (1993). This essay promised to provide a non-anthropocentric rationale for saving the Amazon rainforest. They launch an attack on the economic approach to conservation, arguing that we simply do not know what the economic benefits of conservation actually are. This perhaps reflects a fairly understandable ignorance of the economics literature demonstrating that we know rather a lot, but certainly not everything, about the economic value of rainforests. As we shall see shortly, this attribution of economic value to tropical forests and ecosystems generally is rather important.

Katz and Oechsli's non-anthropocentric justification for conservation proceeds as follows.

First, they assume that a non-anthropocentric justification for conservation exists. It is not, they say, part of their purpose to provide that justification.

Second, since it exists, we would have a moral obligation to conserve the Amazon rainforest, 'not for the human benefits resulting from this preservation, but because we have an obligation to nature and its ecosystems' (p. 57).

Third, to offer justification for simply asserting that obligations exist, Katz and Oechsli draw a parallel with a hypothetical example of two businessmen, Smith and Jones, who debate the share of profits in a business deal. We then learn that the deal involves the murder of a third person, Green. Once we know this, the issue of the right way to share profits disappears, for the moral obligation not to murder Green is transcendent: it is morally far more important.

Fourth, given these obligations, 'questions of trade-off and comparison of human benefits, and questions of justice for specific human populations, do not dominate the discussion'. Other values have not disappeared, they are simply insignificant relative to the moral obligation to conserve nature. As they say:

> It is unfortunate that this direct obligation to the rain forest can only be met with a cost in human satisfaction – some human interests will not be fulfilled (p. 58).

There we have it. The argument is breathtaking, for the human interests that may be at stake, and indeed are at stake in the Amazon case, are the livelihoods of many hundreds of thousands of poor farmers and their families. This reveals an indifferent understanding and appreciation of the issue. Simply asserting that it is wrong to destroy rainforest, the Smith–Jones–Green example reveals a rather shaky understanding of what is at stake with tropical deforestation.

Yet, if the analogy is pursued, these poor farmers are in cahoots with the rich in a plan of murder, since Green is the Amazon forests.

1.4 ON COST

I would argue that the unreality of much environmental ethics is somewhat worse than this. In most discussions it is difficult to find even a mention, let alone a discussion, of economic cost. There are two aspects to the cost concept. The first is that conservation often involves a money cost. The second is that, once we recognize that much species loss arises from competing land uses, as explained below, conservation involves a forgone benefit, namely the economic value of the land in some alternative use. The sum of these two components is what the economist refers to when speaking of 'opportunity cost': the thing that is sacrificed when undertaking a course of action. It is important to understand this concept since it is the very cornerstone of economics. Any cost is a foregone benefit since the resources that make up cost could have been used elsewhere. But forgone benefits embrace potential rights or obligations: the right to a livelihood, the obligation to work to secure such livelihoods for the poor and for the disenfranchised. And as long as the money spent on conservation could have been spent on reducing risks to, say, human life elsewhere, existence itself is at stake. If, therefore, we ceased to speak of cost as if it was just money, and spoke instead of foregone rights, obligations, lives and livelihoods, which is what opportunity cost means, we would be reminding ourselves that any discussion of rights of or obligations to Nature is a discussion about conflicts of rights and obligations.

As long as the world has finite resources, be it money or land, conservation will involve opportunity cost. And if opportunity cost contains embedded rights and obligations, conservation will offend those rights and obligations. That does not mean conservation should lose out. There are three ways in which conservation can be advanced:

a. by seeking out contexts in which the conflict does not arise – the so-called 'win win' situations;
b. by ensuring that conservation has higher value than the thing it competes with; and
c. by declaring that we will seek only to sacrifice some 'lower order' wants and desires rather than higher order obligations and rights.

1.5 'WIN WIN'

There are contexts in which opportunity costs are low or even zero. So called 'win win' situations cry out to be exploited first simply because they entail little conflict of rights. Examples abound. Much air pollution is related to the consumption of fossil fuels. There are huge wastes of fossil fuels the world over because of a failure to price energy correctly. The lower the price the more fuel is squandered, the more pollution there is. Yet we know that annual fossil fuel subsidies in the world approximate some $230 billion, around four times the annual total official aid from North to South. Reducing the subsidies would not just improve the environment but would release valuable government finance which can be used to reduce problems of poverty. Extended to water, forests, and agriculture, world-wide subsidies may well be $1 trillion, or about 5% of the entire world's income. Clearly, the scope for this kind of win win solution is vast.

But win win situations, important as they are, carry few ethical problems with them: if no-one loses and if nature gains, we have a positive sum game. Such contexts are important but not particularly interesting from the environmental values standpoint.

1.6 ADDRESSING THE REAL WORLD: WHY EXTINCTION OCCURS

The second option is to confer high economic value on conservation. To understand the importance of this approach, let me offer a generalised explanation for environmental degradation. It will be necessarily limited for we know that causation varies from issue to issue, and from location to location. Nonetheless, it is important to grasp the essentials of a general theory of causation for without that understanding any policies we devise will almost certainly fail, and I include in that judgement policies that take the form of declaring the act of destruction to be morally wrong. We can illustrate the real world issue by looking at species and ecosystem extinction.

Two sets of factors may give rise to extinction in the traditional economic theory of resource extinction (Gordon, 1954; Clark, 1973a, 1973b, 1990). The first is the property rights regime: the set of institutions and rules governing ownership and access to a natural resource. Regimes may be 'open access', common property, single private owner, or single state owner. Open access differs from common property in that the former regime has no owners and hence no rules for restricting or managing access to the resource. Common property regimes involve sets of rules and regulations limiting access and 'harvesting' rates, these rules being enforced by communal law or communal custom. Under single ownership, access is restricted to any outsider not part of the ownership regime, and the community in question is now a private organisation or the nation state. Fairly self-evidently, the greater the restrictions on access the less the harvesting effort applied to the resource and hence the more likely it is that resource stocks will be large. With open access, however, effort is unconstrained until the newest new entrant finds that resource stocks have depleted to the point where his effort is only just rewarded by the extra revenues obtained from the sale of the extracted resource: the 'zero rent' point. In itself, then, open access does not generate extinction of the resource because further entry beyond the open access equilibrium does not occur. As long as the costs of harvest are positive, some of the resource is left intact, though with low sustainable yields. Nonetheless, population dynamics are ill understood and hence the risk of extinction is higher the lower are the stocks. It is quite possible, therefore, for open access to create the conditions in which harvest levels give rise to stock levels that are below minimum viable sizes. This will be especially true in contexts where minimum viable size is influenced by family or group dynamics, as is the case for some land-based animals. Removing critical family members may render the remaining population non-viable. Note also that, while common property regimes are far more likely to protect the resource against extinction, common property tends itself to be vulnerable to external influences, including human population growth which places pressure on the regime to continue managing the resource in the interests of the whole community.

Particular combinations of cost of harvest and resource price will also make the open access situation more risky still. Suppose that technological change occurs such that the costs of effort are reduced substantially. Suppose too that the resource attracts a higher price, so that, for the same level of effort, total revenue increases. This 'high price, low cost' combination appears to fit certain land-based species well, e.g. elephants. Ivory prices can be very high and the use of vehicles and high velocity rifles makes costs low. Such a combination provides greater incentives for rapid reduction of the resource.

The first cause of extinction on this traditional model, then, is the property rights regime, with open access having the highest risk of extinction for the species, and common property having a far lower but non-zero level of risk. Species attracting exotic demand, such as for ivory, and being subject to advances in technological change which reduce effort costs are particularly at risk.

The second cause of extinction in the traditional model arises in the single owner, profit-maximizing context. Whereas extinction under open access can be regarded partly as the outcome of ignorance about population dynamics and partly the outcome of a failure to comprehend the risks inherent in unrestricted access, extinction under single ownership can be the outcome of deliberate planning. The high price, low cost combination no longer threatens the species because such a combination implies large profits from sustainable uses of the resource. It is when the picture is changed from the (essentially unrealistic) static one to a more dynamic context that the risks arise. The essential condition for dynamic profit maximization is that the biological growth rate of the species stock should equal the single owner's discount rate, the rate at which the owner 'discounts' the future because of a preference for benefits now rather than benefits later. The growth rate of the resource is effectively the rate of return on the resource. It then follows fairly obviously that if this rate of return is less than the rate of return the single owner can get by investing elsewhere the resource will be run down to zero. It will pay to 'mine' the resource to extinction.

Again, the analysis is suggestive since slow growth species will almost automatically be at risk on this model: their 'own rate of return' will be low. And this is how it tends to be in practice. Elephants, rhinoceros and whales are endangered while most (but not all) species of deer or seals are not.

Until recently, it was assumed that this traditional model applied to all species, whether fish (the original focus of the theory) or land-based species without much adaptation. Hence the analysis has tended to be in terms of property rights regimes, the price/cost ratio, and the discount rate/own growth comparison. For an application to the African elephant, see Barbier *et al.* (1990).

Swanson (1994) has set out the important adjustment required to the traditional model once the resource in question is land-based, an adjustment that radically alters the policy implications of the traditional model. Swanson's argument is rooted in the fact that land-based biological resources are assets that are subject to human management: they are part of an 'asset portfolio'. Moreover, whereas fisheries can be argued to have low opportunity costs – there are few competing uses of the seas – this is categorically untrue of land-based biodiversity. This is because land-based biodiversity depends on a base resource, the land itself, and this land does have alternative uses. The most obvious conflict is between land for conservation and land for 'development' uses such as agriculture. The critical point here is that whereas marine resources may be depleted because their growth fails to exceed the harvester's discount rate, in the land-based case they may be depleted because the returns from conservation fail to compete with the returns from land conversion to agriculture, roads, urban expansion, etc.

The second feature of the Swanson model is that whereas marine resources have a (generally) fixed carrying capacity, this is not true of land-based resources. Carrying capacity is no longer a 'given': it is something that is determined by choices about the level of base resources allocated to biodiversity.

There are two ways of seeing the differences in the traditional and Swanson model. The first consists of a contrast between the conditions for maximizing profit from resource harvesting. In the Clark model what is being maximized is the difference between revenues from the sale of the fish and the costs of harvesting them. In the Swanson model what is being maximized is the difference between the proceeds of sale and the sum of the costs of 'harvest' and the foregone return to the alternative use of the land. Put another way, the net benefits of land-based conservation have to be greater than the total opportunity costs of conservation, i.e. the foregone net returns from developing the land. This is also the condition set out by Pearce and Moran (1994) in their review of the rates of return to biodiversity conservation.

The second way of viewing the difference between the two models is to look at the policy implications. Taking the elephant example again, the traditional model blames high prices for ivory for the decline of elephant populations. The Swanson model suggests the very opposite, i.e. that ivory prices need to be kept high to encourage investment in sustainable management of elephant populations. As a further illustration, the range states that invested in elephant conservation in a significant way were the southern African states – South Africa, Botswana, Zimbabwe and Namibia. These were the states where ivory sales were (largely) controlled and authorized, and where elephant populations grew dramatically. States that 'underinvested' in elephants, including even a country like Kenya where the tourist value of the elephant was high, were the ones that lost elephants to poachers.

The insights from the Swanson model are therefore important. It is not enough to take the property rights regime as given, as in the traditional model of extinction. For the property rights regime is a matter of choice and management. It is incorrect to cite open access, say, as a 'cause' of environmental degradation, for the question should be why open access is allowed to prevail. Put another way, why has an open access state not invested in changing the rights regime so as to allocate the base resource – land of suitable characteristics – to biodiversity?

Once it is understood that biodiversity is competing with alternative uses of the land a systematic analysis of the fundamental causes of extinction can be developed. First, population growth becomes immediately relevant because population growth simply intensifies the conflict as humans demand 'niches' to occupy as residences or as locations for cops, roads, etc. Second, if markets in the 'products' of biodiversity are non-existent, the rate of return to conservation will almost certainly fail to compete with the rate of return to the alternative uses of land. Biodiversity is doomed. It is in the creation of markets for biodiversity that hope for conservation resides. While this conclusion offends the instincts of many environmentalists, we have to consider the possibility that a preoccupation with moral obligations to, and rights of, other species reinforces the fate of biodiversity by diverting attention both from the real, underlying causes of species loss, and by avoiding the reality of effective action. Unwittingly, then, the 'deep ecologist' and even those of a paler shade of green may be contributing to the demise of biodiversity. This is a strong conclusion but one that has to be faced up to once we secure a closer understanding of the economic dynamics at work. Thus, bans and moral outrage serve to 'disinvest' value in biodiversity: they take economic value away, when what is required is the investment of economic value in conservation through more and better markets for the sustainable output of conservation practices.

The causes of biodiversity loss then lie in three broad areas:

a. population growth which leads to more and more of the base resource, land, being converted to non-conservation uses. Here it is important to understand some of the dynamics of population change. Taking central estimates, the phenomenon of 'population momentum' means that the developing world's current population of 4.5 billion cannot be prevented from rising to 7.3 billion by the year 2100. It may well rise further to just under 10 billion, roughly double the existing global population. Policy has the capacity to act on the range 7.3 to 10 billion. It can do little or nothing about the rise to 7.3 billion. Hence we are dealing with a world in which, allowing for the developed world population, we shall have around twice as many people in just 100 years time;
b. the failure to ascribe economic value to biological diversity and the failure to establish markets in which that economic value can be appropriated for conservation purposes;
c. government actions, such as subsidies to land clearance, clear-felling of forests and to agriculture, which simply exaggerate the rate of return to the developmental uses of land, thus further biasing the equation against biodiversity.

1.7 THE PRIMACY OF ECONOMIC VALUE

We now have the justification for doing what we can to ascribe economic value to natural assets. For we live in a real world in which natural assets are supported by a base resource which is the subject of competing forces. That base resource is land and its ecological characteristics. Competition for this resource will intensify as population unavoidably and irreversibly increases, perhaps by

100% and certainly by 60% of current levels. That is the real-world context and no amount of wishful thinking will make it otherwise. Enunciating moral values about the sanctity and rights of, or human obligations to Nature, may motivate our politicians to find their consciences and sit up and take notice, but it will do little to alter the incentive structures that generate environmental degradation. Nor can we resolve conflicts over land use by simply declaring one user to be 'right' and the other 'wrong'. For whatever choice we make about land use involves a cost: if we develop the land the cost is the foregone value of conservation. If we conserve the land, the cost is the forgone benefit of development. In both cases, those sacrifices involve offence to moral principles. Economic cost is not a matter of 'mere money', nor a reflection purely of some motive declared base and inferior by an elite, but a matter of rights and obligations and moral value too. Moral views that imply conservation values are 'above' or superior to those other values leave us with a world of frustrated demands that sooner or later will destroy the resource. And this much has now been understood by much of the conservation movement who no longer speak of outright prohibition of land use, but who speak instead of sustainable use.

But the essence of sustainable use is that the battleground is an economic one in which the economic value of sustainable use must be shown to exceed the economic value of destruction. More than this, this superior economic value must be *appropriated* by those who make land use decisions – whether a national government or a local farmer. We have to demonstrate economic value, and we have to capture it. Demonstration and capture is the sequence for conservation. And capture involves the creation of markets that realize individuals' willingness to pay for conservation. The ways in which capture can be pursued are discussed extensively in Pearce (1995).

1.8 HIGHER- AND LOWER-ORDER RIGHTS AND OBLIGATIONS

We have established that there is enormous scope for win win actions that avoid, though not entirely, the kinds of conflicts that seem to permeate the literature of environmental ethics.

We have sought to establish that the second action, attaching economic value to environmental assets, and appropriating that value through markets and bargains, also has potentially immense scope for saving environmental assets.

The third dimension of action is to acknowledge that all cost is opportunity cost and opportunity cost embodies potential rights and obligations, but to argue that not all the beneficial uses of money have equal value. What this argument says is that we should target *certain* expenditures and divert them to conservation because those expenditures have lower value. In concrete terms, we say that we should not consider the cost of conservation because any cost would only have been spent on armaments or TV dinners, videos and computer games. This is essentially Malnes' argument about 'vital needs' (Malnes, 1995). I have some sympathy with this argument but I suggest it offends another right and one that some people hold very dear, including myself. This is the right to pursue our lives without an excess of moralizing about how we should pursue our lives. In so doing, we acknowledge that in pursuing what others see as 'trivial pursuits' we impose a cost because what we spend could have been allocated to the protection of some other right. This, for some people, is what the values debate is all about: it is about a hierarchy of wants, needs, rights and obligations. But it is the *process* of securing the hierarchy that creates the problem, for it may be secured only by imposition. And imposition offends the right to self-determination and personal freedom.

This view of a hierarchy of wants and desires has currency in some political philosophy circles where it is argued that the human well-being concept as interpreted in economics is not relevant at all, i.e. social decisions should not be based on economic well-being. As Mark Sagoff puts it:

> The question we must ask is whether 'welfare' has anything to do with happiness, well-being, or any goal that appeals to common sense, morality, law or culture (Sagoff, 1993; see also Sagoff, 1988).

This is a curious view even in a rich-world context. It argues that 'quality' of desires is more important than 'desires' *per se*. The danger in such a view is that it quickly becomes elitist. A declares B's preferences to be of 'low quality' and therefore inadmissible. A knows better and best. Yet the appropriate strategy in a world where quality of desires matters is education and persuasion. It cannot be the disenfranchisement of the illiterate and the non-aesthetes because they do not qualify as having the 'right' desires. Sagoff's response to this would be that no-one is being disenfranchised. When individuals express votes for or against something in terms of their willingness to pay, the motive for their votes is self-interest. When they express votes in a political context they are voting as 'citizens', expressing views and opinions, and taking into account concerns of justice and the common good as well as their self-interest. Since the environment should be the subject of citizen preferences not self-interested preferences, using willingness to pay as a criterion of value of environmental assets is an example of a 'category mistake' – predicating of one concept another logically unrelated concept.

But this argument is extremely fragile. First, it is not at all clear that political votes are necessarily non-self-interest votes. Second, and as discussed above, willingness to pay votes are consistent with any number of motivations, including so-called citizen preferences. Third, the case for taking the environment out of the economic value context has not been made. And as we shall argue shortly, the case for including it in the economic value context is very powerful. Leaving it to political votes is, of course, what we have always done, and yet we find ourselves arguing for significantly more, not less, environmental action. We cannot say the economic approach has failed, because it has barely been tried. We cannot perhaps say the political approach has failed in any outright sense, but I suspect we would not be having this series of lectures if we thought it had succeeded.

Incidentally, it is interesting to note Sagoff's language. Preferences are 'arbitrary inclinations'; 'Socrates dissatisfied [is] better off than a pig satisfied' and even, 'libertarians see no reason to distinguish mainstream environmental economics from socialism' and 'giving people what they 'would' choose, not what they do choose – is also characteristic of collectivist planning' ! (Sagoff, 1993). Economists Vatn and Bromley (1994) also come close to this kind of preference imposition:

> the challenge is one of specifying the conditions for discourse over what is worth valuing by individuals – and why that is so (p. 139).

Is imposition a necessary outcome? Clearly, we could engage in a process of persuasion that itself does not offend some other principle, such as democracy, a moral lesson that some single-cause environmentalists have still not learned, or do not wish to learn. The problem then is practicality. We seek to 'change mindsets', secure a moral revolution, secure spiritual change as the hope for the environment. If we truly want conservation then we are logically obliged to weigh the chances that action of this kind will achieve results in a timely manner, and by timely I imply that there is not 'world enough and time' to do what is necessary. Have the 'environmental revolutions' of the last three decades really changed things? It is difficult to say without knowing what the counterfactual historical record would have looked like, but it is surely correct to say that the environmental groundswell has contributed to making things less worse than they otherwise would have been. But the issue here is whether such moral opinion is enough on its own to change the world. Each individual must decide for themselves on this issue, but I venture the view that reliance on moral change alone is an incoherent approach that fails to address the driving forces of environmental change. Declaring things to be wrong will not make those forces go away, especially when they are as powerful as the need for a livelihood.

1.9 STRATEGIC VALUES

As indicated previously there is no necessary incompatibility between economic and moral view. My moral concerns may well be embodied in my willingness to pay, and, indeed, are very likely to when the object of valuation is something that necessarily benefits all. But suppose we accept that the real-world stage for environmental conflict is a world where economic values prevail. Isn't the argument that we must therefore confer economic value on conservation simply a strategic argument? Are we not saying that the game being played is one we do not like but have to accept. Having to accept it does not make the case for ascribing economic values morally right. There are several responses to this view.

First, suppose the case for economic valuation is only a strategic one. What this could mean is that we have more chance of conserving nature by using this argument than by using the purely moral point of view. I suspect that is true, and it certainly accords with my own experience of practical advice on conservation. But, a moment's reflection suggests that, as long as we are operating in a world of strategy, we should use *all* arguments to hand, provided none of them is wholly morally offensive. Unless the economic approach is so morally offensive, it seems odd for so much effort and energy to be spent by critics of environmental economics in rejecting an approach that could serve the very end that the critics supposedly want – more, not less, conservation.

Second, is the economic approach really morally offensive? It certainly raises some apparently awkward issues.

For example, individuals' willingness to pay (WTP) is partly a function of the level of information the individual has. If he or she is not informed, the resource may go to extinction and that, to many, seems wrong. But that is not an argument for rejecting economic values. It is an argument for informing people of risks and benefits. It is sometimes suggested that environmental assets may be significantly 'distant' from individuals' familiarity and experience (Freeman, 1986; Vatn and Bromley, 1994). While this qualification applies to stated preference techniques, such as contingent valuation, it is far from clear that it applies to other procedures of economic valuation which often involve some mix of expert assessment – e.g. the relationship between air pollution and crop loss – and individuals' valuations. Information is also important for valuing market goods as well. Where information is deficient, for example with infrequent purchases such as housing, information markets emerge. To some extent, contingent valuation functions in this way – it supplies information to the respondent. In that respect it could be held to be superior to inferred valuations from behaviour in other markets, such as travel expenditures. This suggests that economic valuation will function more successfully the better the information. But lack of information is not an argument for rejecting WTP approaches. It is an argument for better information.

A second problem is that willingness to pay is partly determined by ability to pay – by income and wealth. Is willingness to pay therefore not an unfair calculus for conservation? Such arguments are often made. They sound a little hollow against a moral view that declares something to be wrong regardless of the sacrifice to others whose very livelihood may depend on a particular land use. As it happens, it is possible to adjust willingness to pay measures to reflect some 'average income' if that is needed. But given that the unfairness is thought originally to derive from an unfair distribution of income, it is never very clear why those who oppose willingness to pay on these grounds do not seek a wholesale change to the distribution of income through fiscal measures. Put another way, the argument is not one against willingness to pay but against the underlying distribution of income.

A third problem is that the economic approach is incomplete. It is quite true that efforts to ascribe economic values have been limited, particularly in the context of biological diversity. It is argued that it excludes 'system functions' such as life support functions. These values are variously described as 'primary value' (Gren *et al.*, 1994) and even the 'glue' of the system. Here there does seem to be a problem. It has close similarities to the informational issue, but it differs in that the information issue rests on individuals being ignorant but others having knowledge, whereas the 'primary value' argument says that neither individuals nor the experts really know what the true functions of some or even all environmental assets are. It is then more an argument about uncertainty than information. The 'glue' is then a condition for the existence of other values, it is in that sense prior to other values. However, if the primary value argument is an argument about uncertainty of values, then the proper approach is to incorporate the uncertainty in the analysis. It need not be an argument for rejecting economic values as such, but rather one of adjusting values to reflect precaution. There must be some sympathy for a view that says, while such extensive ignorance prevails, some kind of precautionary approach is required. Of course, if the 'glue' value is present across all environmental assets, it offers little assistance in the choice context. Arguments of this kind, however attractive on paper, fall foul of the reality test introduced earlier.

Of all the criticisms, this 'uncertainty of function' problem is the most important for economic valuation. Brief reflection will show that it will also be problematic for *any* choice approach. It is not therefore a criticism that is peculiar to economic valuation alone, but is a weakness of all decision-making procedures. It is here that the greatest challenge to research and pragmatism lies.

1.10 CONCLUSION

There are many actions that can be taken which will benefit the environment and for which there is no particular need for philosophizing or quantification, economic or otherwise. The actions involve the removal of economic distortions that have as one of their incidental impacts the destruction of the environment. The scope for action is huge.

Once these low-cost solutions have been exhausted we are faced with what is left, for one can only hazard a guess that even with the removal of economic distortions, much will remain to be done. The defining characteristic of this area for policy is the sheer unfairness of the competition between nature and economic development as it is currently practised. That competition is played out mainly in terms of land use change, though we should not forget the growing competition for our coastal zones and, soon, the oceans. Development does have moral justification because it meets the needs of a rapidly growing global population and because it meets the aspirations of individuals. Its social return is measured in money terms. To compete, nature must be demonstrated to have economic value, and that economic value must be captured through the creation of institutions that feed that economic value to those who make land use decisions. The idea that development and environment need not conflict at all, perpetuated in some interpretations of 'sustainable development', is, in this respect, fanciful.

The problem with so much environmental philosophy is that it is worked out in an intellectual vacuum, seemingly divorced from an adequate understanding of what the world is like and why nature is losing the fight for conservation. The force of arguments about intrinsic values, lexical orderings, obligations and rights has limited appeal in the harsh world of inescapable choice. How nice it would be to declare, at a stroke, that our obligations to nature involve no conflict with other rights and obligations. But they do and, in the limit, the notion of economic cost is there to remind us that such conflicts are not rare side issues but are endemic and pervasive to the world in which we live. From that there is no escape.

We considered the issue of a hierarchy of wants, of some wants being less valid than other wants and, of course, all societies declare some goods, such as education, to be higher-order goods. Personal freedom could then be compromised if individuals genuinely do not want to be educated. But education fits within the aspirations of most people: rather than being inconsistent with personal freedom it is, of course, something that enables personal freedom to be realized. The environmental opportunity cost argument is also less relevant, but not irrelevant, because we know that basic education (as opposed to education in environmental issues) may well be one of the most powerful weapons in reducing environmental damage. The social, as well as the individual, rate of return to education is high. The issue, then, is whether environmental goods have the same features as education, of being something that we simply should provide regardless of preferences. Against this I have argued that it is dangerous to ignore the conflict of values that may arise, that if, for example, the only way of providing those goods is through some personal revolution in lifestyle, that revolution should not be a matter of one moral elite imposing its will on the rest of society. Moreover, if the call for such lifestyle change is to be made, it has to be made on the basis of far more persuasive arguments than we have so far.

That is an issue of empirical argument, not morality. And, I have suggested that simply declaring environment to be some sort of 'merit good' fails to address the underlying causes of environmental loss, and that much of the environmental movement already acknowledges that in its advocacy of sustainable use practices as opposed to outright protection.

The final issue is therefore one of tactics and strategy. We should not assume that because there is a problem there must be a solution. It is almost certainly too late already for much of Nature. But we can save a great deal and probably the supreme moral obligation, the ultimate categorical imperative, is to do what we can. That means firing from all barrels of the conservation gun. Some arguments will fail. There will be others. How foolish we would be to put all our moral eggs into one moral basket, only for the moral of the story to be that we found the perfect argument, but too late to save the world.

NOTE

1. This essay was originally given as a public lecture in the University of Cambridge, March 1996.

REFERENCES

Arrow, K. (1951), *Social Choice and Individual Values*, Wiley, New York.

Barbier, E., Burgess, J. Swanson T. and Pearce, D.W. (1990), *Elephants, Economics and Ivory*, Earthscan, London.

Becker, G. (1993), Nobel lecture: the economic way of looking at behaviour, *Journal of Political Economy*, **101**, June, 385–409.

Bjornstad, D. and Kahn, J. (1996), *The Contingent Valuation of Environmental Resources: Methodological Issues and Research Needs*, Edward Elgar, Cheltenham.

Bruner, M. and Oelschlaeger, M. (1994), Rhetoric and environmentalism, *Environmental Ethics*, **16**,(4), 377–96.

Clark, C. (1973a), Profit maximisation and the extinction of animal species, *Journal of Political Economy*, **81**(4), 950–61.

Clark, C. (1973b), The economics of overexploitation, *Science*, **181**, 630–4.

Clark, C. (1990), *Mathematical Bioeconomics*, second edition, Wiley, New York.

Freeman III, A.M. (1986). On assessing the state of the art of the contingent valuation method of valuing environmental changes, in R.G.Cummings, D.Brookshire and W.Schulze (eds), *Valuing Environmental Goods: an Assessment of the Contingent Valuation Method*, Rowman and Allenheld, Totowa, NJ, 148–61.

Freeman III, A.M. (1994), *The Measurement of Environmental and Resource Values*, Resources for the Future, Washington, DC.

Gordon, H. (1954), The economic theory of a common property resource: the fishery, *Journal of Political Economy*, **62**, 124–42.

Gren, A.-M., Folke, C. Turner, K. and Bateman, I. (1994), Primary and secondary values of wetland ecosystems, *Environmental and Resource Economics*, **4**(1), February, 55–74.

Hanemann, W.M. (1995), Contingent valuation and economics, in K.Willis and J.Corkindale (eds), *Environmental Valuation: New Perspectives*, CAB International, Wallingford.

Hanemann, W.M. (1996), Theory versus data in the contingent valuation debate, in Bjornstad and Kahn (1996), 38–60.

Hanley, N. and Milne, J. (1996), *Ethical Beliefs and Behaviour in Contingent Valuation*, Discussion Papers in Ecological Economics, Department of Economics, University of Stirling, 96/1.

Hanley, N., Spash, C. and Walker, L. (1995), 'Problems in valuing the benefits of biodiversity protection', *Environmental and Resource Economics*, **5**, 249–72.

Harrison, G.W. (1992), Valuing public goods with the contingent valuation method: a critique of Kahneman and Knetsch, *Journal of Environmental Economics and Management*, **22**, 57–70.

Hayward, T. (1995), *Ecological Thought: an Introduction*, Polity Press, Cambridge.

Kahneman, D and Knetsch, J. (1992), Valuing public goods: the purchase of moral satisfaction, *Journal of Environmental Economics and Management*, **23**, 248–57

Katz, E and Oechsli, L. (1993), Moving beyond anthropocentrism: environmental ethics, development and the Amazon, *Environmental Ethics*, **15**(1), Spring, 49–59.

Malnes, R. (1995), *Valuing the Environment*, Manchester University Press, Manchester.

Norton, B. (1987), *Why Preserve Natural Variety?*, Princeton University Press, Princeton, New Jersey.

Pearce, D.W. (1995), *Blueprint 4: Capturing Global Value*, Earthscan, London.

Pearce, D.W. and Moran, D. (1994), *The Economic Value of Biodiversity*, Earthscan, London.

Redclift, M. (1996), *Global Environmental Values*, Lecture in Cambridge University series on Environmental Values, Corpus Christi College.

Rolston III, H. (1994), *Conserving Natural Value*, Columbia University Press, New York.

Sagoff, M. (1988), *The Economy of the Earth*, Cambridge University Press, Cambridge.

Sagoff, M. (1993), Environmental economics: an epitaph, *Resources*, Spring, No.111, 2–7.

Smith, M. (1993). Cheney and the myth of postmodernism, *Environmental Ethics*, **15**(1), 3–18.

Swanson, T. (1994), The economics of extinction revisited and revised: a generalised framework for the analysis of the problems of endangered species and biodiversity losses, *Oxford Economic Papers*, **46**, Supplementary Issue, 800–821.

Stevens, T., Echeverria, J. Glass, R. Hager, T. and More, T. (1991), Measuring the existence value of wildlife: what do CVM estimates really show?, *Land Economics*, **67**(4), November, 390–400.

Vatn, A. and Bromley, D. (1994), Choices without prices without apologies, *Journal of Environmental Economics and Management*, **26**, 129–48.

2. Economists befriend the earth[1]

Economics, the dismal science as Thomas Carlyle called it, is not generally regarded as a friend of the Earth. Economic progress destroys and modifies natural environments, and appears to make the quality of the environment a dispensable item in the pursuit of raising living standards. The image of economics as the science that legitimizes this process is outmoded and false. All economists would accept that if development and environment have to be traded off against each other, we should surrender environmental assets only when our decision is fully informed about the economic value and functions of those assets. In other cases, environment and economic development are complementary goals: they are not in conflict. In many developing countries, especially the poorer ones, the prospect of long-term development depends on the careful management of natural resources such as pasture, water, fertile soil and forest.

An alliance of economics and the natural sciences, especially the life sciences, offers the best hope for sustaining economic progress in the developing world. Research efforts towards this goal over the past 20 years are now coming to fruition. There is already an established subdiscipline of environmental economics that, until recently, largely confined itself to the rich nations of the world. Development workers now plan to use it to resolve some of the problems of developing nations. Our understanding of the physical linkages within environmental systems, although still hazy in many respects, has advanced considerably. Quantification is difficult but, for example, there are clearer indications of how cutting down forests causes soil to erode and rivers and estuaries to silt up, how ground water behaves, and how land becomes desert. Environmental economists focus on the interface between environmental systems – characterized by these often complex physical links – and the workings of the economy. The result is a complete transformation of the directions in which economic policy might go. For example, we know that changing agricultural prices affect the farmer's decision about how much and what to grow. As prices rise, farmers tend to grow more, although how far the response is one of substituting higher-value crops for lower-value ones, and how far the higher prices encourage an overall increase in crops, is much less certain. Less certain still is how the farmer's response affects natural resources. Output may increase because farmers use their land more intensively. Intensive use may be based on the application of inorganic fertilizers, pesticides and modern machinery, or on technology that is more traditional – organic fertilizer from animals and crop residues, contour ploughing and terracing to retain water in the soil and so on. Alternatively, farmers can grow more by expanding the area they keep under cultivation – extensive cultivation. The impact on natural resources varies according to the action the farmer takes.

In poorer countries, the opportunities for increased intensive cultivation are limited. But expanding the area under cultivation can mean clearing forested land or moving on to hilly land whose slopes are unsuitable for sustained agriculture. Both activities contribute to the degradation of natural resources. An initially simple economic prescription, that raising the prices that farmers get for their produce will expand output, incomes and the standard of living, becomes a far more complex issue. It is essential that economists understand this chain reaction from prices to natural resources better if interventions by policy-makers are to be beneficial on a sustainable base. Once this is done, manipulation of economic policy becomes a flexible and powerful means of influencing the use of resources. This is just one of the areas where environmental economists are playing an important role in what is a change of emphasis in development planning.

International agencies have led much of the rethinking that applies environmental economics to the problems of developing countries. The World Bank, often the target of criticism from environmentalists over loans for major projects that squander resources, has produced some of the most impressive work – e.g. *Environment, Growth and Development*, the World Bank's statement of its new environmental philosophy. The Asian Development Bank has sponsored similar work to emphasize the importance of considering the effect on the environment when planning projects for investment. More recently, the African Development Bank devoted a whole issue of its Annual Economic Report to the role that environmental economics can play in designing developments. Several research and advisory institutions now specialize in environmental economics for developing countries, notably the World Resources Institute in Washington, the East–West Center in Hawaii, the London Environmental Economics Centre, and the Centre for Social and Economic Research on the Global Environment.

While there are many points at which environmental economics can enter the dialogue about policy between aid donors and recipient countries, between governments and non-governmental organizations, and within governments, one fruitful area for the development of practical guidelines is the appraisal of projects for investment. Because environmental damage does not often show up – immediately anyway – in international markets, it is tempting to think of it as being less real, and less important, than the costs and benefits of an investment that are easier to identify and measure. For example, researchers are more likely to assess the worth of investment in a hydroelectric dam in terms of the electricity it will generate, the water produced for irrigation, and the construction and operating costs. Yet a large dam entails social costs: it may displace many people, and can damage the environment. Agricultural land and forests are flooded, agricultural land downstream is lost as silt previously deposited to enrich the soil remains in the reservoir, coasts erode as silt no longer protects land in deltas, waterborne diseases increase, there are effects on the levels of ground water and so on.

What is needed is a method of counting all the costs and benefits, regardless of whether they show up in the final prices of products when they reach consumers or not. The fact that environmental effects tend not to show up in such markets is no reason to lower their status in economic appraisal. Integrating the social and environmental costs of projects at the stage of investment puts them on the same footing as the gains in productivity from irrigation, or the value of the electricity generated by hydropower.

There are two ways to analyse investment projects that have significant environmental effects. The first is to build into the analysis a requirement that any environmental damage is somehow cancelled out by ensuring that the project is debited with the necessary expenditure to restore the environment or to create environmental benefits elsewhere. A dam, for example, that contributes to deforestation could be debited with the cost of a similar level of afforestation elsewhere. Clearly, carried to the extreme of replacing each and every natural asset destroyed, such an approach would stifle all economic progress. More widely interpreted as a general requirement that development projects forming a package of aid or policy should contain specific measures aimed to rehabilitate the environment, the approach is very much in keeping with the philosophy of sustainable development. Sustainable development focuses on the need to maintain environmental capital such as soils, forests, ground and surface waters, because of the role that it plays in long-term development. This approach has a pedigree in economic theory, but has not yet entered into the more general development of environmental economics. It is one of the areas that researchers must pursue. The second approach requires that we make every effort to place economic values on the environmental damage done. If, when the value of this damage is added to the costs of building the dam, the total outweighs the benefits of irrigation and electricity, then the dam should not be built. This overall approach, somewhat more traditional in terms of the evolution of economic thought, underlies many sets of guidelines. It places a heavy burden on the analyst's ability to attach economic values to environmental damage.

Valuing environmental damage in units of money is simply the obverse of valuing the benefits of environmental improvement. If soil erosion costs £*X* million a year, then measures to restore the fertility of the soil will yield benefits of £*X* million a year. In the same way, the damage done by deforestation will, generally speaking, be the benefit of afforestation. The techniques of valuing damage and benefits have occupied environmental economists for more than

20 years. Most of them have been developed in the developed world where markets tend to function more freely than in the developing world. For example, even though we have no market in the control of air pollution, we do know that pollution affects house prices. By careful analysis, it is possible to separate out the part of a house price that is due to improvements in the quality of air and, again with careful interpretation, we can relate this to the value of cleaner air expressed in economic terms. In this way, although the absence of markets in pollution creates complexities, the link between pollution and property prices permits us to derive a value. The fact that housing markets in developing countries rarely function freely is not an overwhelming obstacle to the use of these indirect approaches. Some developing countries, for example, have well-developed markets in land. Economists can, in some circumstances, use changes in the value of land arising from improvements in the environment to measure the environmental benefit. If they cannot use land values, they can often look at the productivity of land. For example, Nepal has lost many of its forests. It also suffers from soil erosion brought about by the demands of a rapidly growing population caught in a vicious circle of poverty and environmental degradation. Planting and managing young trees improves the quality of pasture, shrubland and grazing – the keys to sustainable development. A project sponsored by the Asian Development Bank aimed to produce a plan to manage some 30 000 hectares of land. The land was to support improved pasture for growing fodder, improved grazing, and some was for forests managed for timber and fuel. To obtain a measure of economic benefit, the researchers first had to estimate the productivity of each class of land with the improved management, and to compare it with the productivity of the land without improvement. For grazing, the researchers estimated how many animals a hectare of land could support. They could then determine the milk yield and value the milk at market prices. They also estimated the yield of dung from the animals and valued it by calculating the cost of the equivalent amount of fertilizer. Similarly, they could value the yields from pasture at the market prices for fodder and timber, and also put price on fuel. By estimating the differences in productivity between the various uses of the land, the researchers show that, even ignoring more complex benefits such as reduced soil erosion, the project paid its way.

There are other approaches to valuing the environment, such as simply asking people what they are prepared to pay to prevent damage or to restore any damage done. This approach, far more sophisticated than it sounds, has been effective in the US and in some European countries. Environmental economists in the US estimated, for example, that improving the visibility in the Grand Canyon area by cutting down air pollution could be worth as much as $7 billion per year. This is the result of asking people what they were willing to pay for better visibility. These benefits compare with the costs of reducing pollution of some $3 billion per year, making clean-up more than worthwhile. Again, it is likely to have limited use in the developing world and could appear absurd in the poorest countries. But under some circumstances, it is possible to use the cost of restoring land or other resources as measures of benefit. Thus, the cost of avoiding the need to restore the quality of the soil can be a measure of potential benefits of preventing the degradation of the soil. The logic here is, that by preventing erosion in advance, planners could save the costs of restoration. We need to express some caution about this view. By implicitly assuming that soil restoration is worthwhile, the approach assumes that benefits outweigh costs, something that investment appraisal is supposed to find out. It seems more likely that we shall understand the economic cost of soil erosion by looking to soil scientists and agronomists for the indicators of losses in the productivity of crops due to erosion, and then placing economic values on the crops by using their market values.

To estimate the economic cost of environmental degradation it is also important to understand how people react when they face scarcity. In Ethiopia, clearance of forests, the demand for fuel, drought and war caused a shortage of fuel. This diverted animal dung from the lands, where it was used to fertilise the soil, to the stove: people dried and burnt it as a cooking fuel. In Ethiopia, however, artificial fertilizers are scarce, so the diversion of dung to fuel has a cost that can be expressed as the loss of future fertility of the soil. The simple answer seems to be to grow more trees for fuel. But rural afforestation occupies land that could be used to grow crops. We need to understand the relative costs and benefits of each course of action. By looking at the economic value of dung, researchers at the World Bank showed that rural afforestation has very high economic rates of return. The idea was that growing trees specifically for firewood would displace dung as a fuel and divert it back to the land as an organic fertilizer. Economists suggested that the gain in dung as a fertiliser was a measure of the benefits of afforestation. But how much is dung worth? Dung can be valued in three ways: at the price in the market when sold as a fuel; at what it would cost to replace with artificial fertilizer, and the value of additional output in crops obtained by using dung as a fertilizer. In 1983, for example, these values were $50 to $100 a tonne for dung as fuel, $20 a tonne for fertilizer and $60 to $90 a tonne for extra crops. The farmers' decision to sell the dung is rational – they generally get more for it than they gain in increased yields of crops. If trees are grown for firewood, we can measure the benefit of replanting land with trees as the value of the dung diverted back to the land as fertilizer. Researchers at the World Bank showed that dung had to be worth above $4 for afforestation to pay. Economically, there is no contest. Rural restoration of forests pays handsomely.

Whatever the merits of one particular approach, there are important reasons why we must secure a better feel for the economic value of environmental damage. Planning in developing countries rarely has an environmental dimension. Ministries of finance and economic planning make the critical decisions, not ministries of wildlife and tourism. This may be as it should be, but the failure of economic planners to understand the role played by environment in the development process will, as much of our environmental economics tells us, be a failure to secure sustainable development. The only way to get the environment onto the economic agenda is to demonstrate that the environment matters to the economy. This has to be the priority for the science of environmental economics. The rest, including a more rational appreciation of environmental functions and values, will follow.

NOTE

1. This short article originally appeared in *New Scientist* in November 1988. It was intended as a book review but grew a little. It was aimed at the general reader, not the economist. It is included here as an aperitif for the remaining essays. Minor corrections have been made.

3. Economic valuation and ecological economics[1]

3.1 INTRODUCTION

I do not know whether ecological economics is a new paradigm or, as my colleagues Kerry Turner, Charles Perrings and Carl Folke argue, a somewhat different perspective (Turner *et al.*, 1996). In the grand order of things, I am not sure that it matters much which it is. But it clearly matters in the narrower sense of how academics and others use their talents and energies. Arguments about 'labels' – about pigeonholing individuals and their thoughts – clearly occupy a great deal of space in the journals and it is a legitimate question as to whether that time and energy would not be better spent applying what we know to what has to be done to save what we can of the Earth's environment. Indeed, that is the perspective I want to emphasize. A great many environmental economists are fairly passionate about environmental conservation, but it has never been a qualification for being an environmental economist that such a passion be shared or demonstrated. Perhaps we will find that ecological economists are more passionate, more caring. If they are, then they are surely duty bound to reflect on the ways in which their science – however it develops – can contribute to conservation. And in reflecting on how to help they must also be duty bound to make their contributions realistic, to look at how policy may be changed in the real world rather than the world of textbooks and journals, coffee bars and conference rooms. I do not want to be misunderstood. I would go to great lengths to defend the right of us all to investigate what subjects we like, without political or ideological interference and without having to look over our shoulders to appeal to some pressure group, some received wisdom or some form of political or ideological correctness. Without the pure theorist, without the original thinkers, without unconstrained free thought, human endeavour is doomed. But there are real problems to be solved and after much of a lifetime working in and with policy-makers all over the world, I can tell you that those real problems need your skills and abilities, your energies and your actions. Let me express the hope then, that ecological economists will take time to dwell on those problems and offer solutions, perhaps expending less energy in classifying and labelling and damning those who do not fit some neat category or, worse, who do not wear the right label.

In what follows I shall focus on some real-world implications of ecological economics and, in particular, on whether there are implications for the monetary measurement of human preferences – economic valuation. There are many ways in which ecological economics may change the emphasis we give to issues in environmental economics, but valuation is not only controversial, and hence more interesting, but it is also, as I hope to demonstrate, fundamental to an action-oriented ecological economics.

3.2 SOME DIFFERENTIATING CHARACTERISTICS OF ECOLOGICAL ECONOMICS

It is worthwhile exploring some of the characteristics claimed for ecological economics to see whether they are likely to survive what I shall call a 'reality test', a test that requires us to say what it is that we would do in policy terms that we do not already do or that we do not already know about. In keeping with my defence of pure research, I do not argue that reality tests are the sole test of what should and should not be emphasized in ecological economics (or any other branch of science). After all, what is remote now may be of great value later: knowledge is not always perceived as being immediately useful. But many will share my perception that those real-world problems cannot wait for consensus or the full development of a science, with all the uncertainties that entails. It is a matter of balance.

In what follows I use some of the characteristics identified by Turner *et al.* (1996), while accepting that others may have different views about both the list of differentiating characteristics and the priorities within the list.

Economy–Ecology Interaction

The first of these characteristics concerns the extent to which economic and ecological processes are modelled as one whole. Turner *et al.* claim this is more a feature of ecological than environmental economics. Here I suspect they do not adequately reflect the extent to which environmental economics has absorbed the early mass balance, general equilibrium nature of environment and economy interactions. It is now more the rule than the exception to try to model the hydrological impacts of, say, deforestation when some overall change in the allocation of environmental assets is at stake. In many other contexts, the focus is on very small changes to the prevailing allocation of resources and here I think it is difficult to argue that going beyond the partial equilibrium approach has much justification. Put another way, real-world policy contexts sometimes call for modelling of wider economy–environment interactions and sometimes do not. The limitations in the real world for developing and applying such models usefully have much more to do with their lack of a high profile in environmental economics. That practical limitation will be equally applicable to ecological economics. I doubt therefore that ecological economics can claim the simultaneous analysis of interacting systems as their differentiating feature.

Complexity and Thresholds

The second characteristic identified by Turner *et al.* is more interesting and concerns the fact that the interacting systems being analysed are complex and perhaps non-linear. Such systems may behave in a non-smooth fashion when exposed to stresses and shocks. We might expect thresholds and chaotic behaviour in such contexts. If there are thresholds, then there are immediate implications for environmental standard setting, economic instruments and economic valuation. It could be argued, for example, that 'optimal' standards must never exceed the threshold, that any pollution or resource quota scheme must always have quotas less than those corresponding to threshold damage and that valuation is a largely irrelevant exercise because marginal damage at the threshold will always be infinite. Some of these issues are explored in Perrings and Pearce (1994). It is important to distinguish between the existence of thresholds and the behaviour of ecosystems if the thresholds are exceeded. In some cases we might expect chaotic behaviour, e.g. that ecosystems 'flip' and change their very nature. In others, we may expect gradual ecosystem change consistent with continuous damage functions.

In the real world the extent to which thresholds and discontinuities characterize ecological systems is unclear. Ecological and environmental economists are necessarily concerned with concepts of damage, whether defined in physical terms or monetary terms. In the physical dimension, our knowledge of dose–response functions, i.e. the relationships between environmental insults and environmental responses, suggests some functions are linear with thresholds, others are non-linear with thresholds, and some are linear with no thresholds. For example, the very concept of a 'critical load' as developed in the science of acid rain damage (see Posch *et al.*, 1995) defines a threshold below which depositions of acidic pollutants, either singly or in combination, do no physical damage to receiving ecosystems. The ecosystems in question are soils and freshwaters. An analogous concept of 'critical level' relates to ambient concentrations and their effects on crops, natural vegetation and forests. Critical loads and critical levels research suggests, then, that ecosystem damage thresholds do exist, lending some support to the notion in ecological economics that thresholds are important.

On the other hand, what the damage function for depositions and concentrations above these thresholds looks like is very unclear: the science has focused on the thresholds rather than the function. Accordingly, little light has been cast on the linearity, non-linearity issue. In contrast to ecosystem impacts, there appear to be no thresholds if the damage in question relates to human health and, say, particulate matter concentrations, or acidic pollutants and buildings. Interestingly, then, the issue has become one of defining 'acceptable' levels of exposure and economists of all persuasions will recognize in that phrase the essential trading off of costs and benefits.

Valuation remains germane in both the threshold and zero thresholds contexts. In the latter it is a matter of defining acceptable standards. In the former ecosystem transformation cannot itself be assumed to have infinite damage costs unless (a) the new equilibrium is demonstrably worse than the old one, (b) discount rates are zero, and (c) the benefits of ecosystem transformation do not accrue to future generations or accrue to them but are regarded as being non-substitutable for the ecosystem function.

Critical loads analysis has been fundamental in the development of real-world policy on acid rain. For example, the Second Sulphur Protocol signed in Oslo in 1994, and which covers the whole UN Economic Commission for Europe region – i.e. basically Western Europe and the new economies in transition – has as its long-term aim the achievement of critical loads, i.e. no depositions of sulphur in excess of critical loads in any part of the region. In practice, critical loads will not be achieved. Technically, they cannot be achieved across 100 per cent of the region because there will always be some areas where critical loads are exceeded however much sulphur is reduced. More importantly for real-world policy, the sharp rise in the marginal abatement cost curve means that the cost of going to critical loads is extremely high for the final sulphur reductions required. It is significant that the Second Sulphur Protocol does not have as its practical aim the achievement of critical loads but a 60 per cent reduction in the 'exceedance' of actual depositions over critical loads. Now, deliberately accepting levels of damage that are known to create physical changes to ecosystems may set off a dynamic feedback mechanism which we discuss below. If it does, then the negative consequences of that feedback effect are essentially being traded off against the opportunity cost of the resources that would be needed to reduce those effects. Once the trade-off is acknowledged, then we have entered the world of valuation. There is, in essence, no escape from the phenomenon of opportunity cost in a finite world, a self-evident proposition one would think, but one that seems sometimes to be forgotten.

If ecological economics wishes to stress thresholds and the behaviour of systems when thresholds are exceeded, then, what real-world experience we have suggests that (a) there may indeed be thresholds in some cases but not in others, and (b) that damage beyond the threshold may or may not be characterized by non-linearities. This suggests two cautions. The first is that it would be unwise to build a science on the basis of limited rather than general ecological behaviour. This amounts to a call for more and better information, without denying in any way that thresholds exist. The second is that thresholds *per se* do not make a significant difference to the kind of static analysis familiar to environmental economists, but do suggest the importance of analysis dynamic behaviour, i.e. what happens if the system's functions themselves change as environmental insults proceed, and the costs and benefits of that dynamic change. Put another way, it cannot be assumed that dynamic change is always for the worse. This brings us to the issue of dynamics.

Dynamics

The presence of dynamic feedback effects from pollution are not new issues to environmental economists. The dynamic consequences of exceeding thresholds were explored, albeit simplistically, in my 1976 *Kyklos* paper (see Chapter 4), the purpose of which was to demonstrate that static cost–benefit optima were not necessarily consistent with dynamic optima once ecological feedback mechanisms were accounted for (Pearce, 1976), and in a host of theoretical papers in the context of fairly conventional neo-classical economic growth theory (e.g. Forster, 1973; 1975; 1977; Barbier, 1989). The issue that emerges of central importance from these papers is the central role played by the discount rate in ensuring 'optimality', a result that also pervades the more general models of optimal economic growth in the face of exhaustible resources and cumulative pollutants (Dasgupta and Heal, 1979). The basic conflict appears to be between optimality defined conventionally as some present value criterion and sustainability in the sense of development paths that preserve the capacity of future generations to be at least as well off as current generations. Optimality and sustainability are not necessarily consistent, a result present in the neo-classical growth literature, and reinforced more recently by others – see for example, Pezzey (1989). Whether we hive these contributions off and regard them as forerunners of ecological economics seems to me to be a fairly arbitrary decision. The fact remains that systems dynamics are not a novelty for environmental economists, although we can argue about how successful environmental economics has been in modelling the complexity of such effects.

The Precautionary Principle

In terms of the real world, dynamic externality does offer some support for zero externality environmental objectives depending in part on how we approach uncertainty (see below), how we see the substitutability between forms of capital (see below), and how we formulate the overall social objective function. Ignorance of dynamic ecosystem effects suggests caution, non-substitutability suggests that present value optimality may be even more at variance with sustainability, and intergenerational equity dictates that sustainability be given a higher policy profile. It is interesting, therefore, that if we collapse these concerns into some form of 'precautionary principle' just such a principle, ill-defined or not defined at all, permeates recent environmental policy statements in some areas. How far we can say that the adoption of such principles in practice is a vindication of ecological economics is, however, a different issue. Thus, Article 130r of the Maastricht Treaty requires that European Community environmental law be based on the precautionary principle, while simultaneously calling for benefit–cost appraisals of policies. The two may be consistent if a 'safe minimum standards' interpretation is allowed: there should be a presumption in favour of not harming the environment unless the opportunity costs of that action are, in some sense, very high. This can be contrasted with the typical cost–benefit rule to the effect that the benefit cost ratio should be greater than unity.

The UK Government's espousal of the precautionary principle certainly implies that it is applicable only where the costs incurred in adopting it are low:

> The precautionary principle applies particularly where there are good grounds for judging either that action taken promptly *at comparatively low cost* may avoid more costly damage later, or that irreversible effects may follow if damage is delayed (UK Government, 1990, para.1.88).

Clearly, on these interpretations, adoption of the precautionary principle could be expensive. If the benefits forgone are substantial and new information reveals that the measure turns out not to have been warranted, then there will be a high net cost to precaution. On the other hand, if new information reveals that precaution was justified, nothing is lost. This suggests that some balancing of costs and benefits still must play a role even in contexts where the precautionary principle is thought to apply.

If the precautionary principle is interpreted as implying something like safe minimum standards, then the question arises as to the need for economic valuation of environmental costs and benefits. But whatever rule is adopted it will imply an economic value. Safe minimum standards, for example, effectively says that the avoidance of environmental damage is worth the sacrifice of the economic benefits from the environmentally damaging activity. It is still necessary to have some idea of the cut-off point: when is the forgone cost so large that it justifies environmental damage?

Weak and Strong Sustainability

It seems likely, though as far as I can see, far from necessary, that environmental economists will favour weak sustainability over strong sustainability, and that ecological economists will favour strong sustainability. Weak sustainability requires constancy of the *aggregate* of all forms of capital, while strong sustainability requires that both the aggregate be non-declining and that natural capital be non-declining. The crux of that choice, as is now well known, rests on the extent to which environmental and man-made assets are substitutable. This, I suggest, is an empirical issue, though it could be a matter of faith or even preference-based values if one thinks that environmental assets should all be very highly priced. It is difficult to have much sympathy for 'deep ecology' views that confer rights to existence on everything, for such an approach falls foul of the unavoidable concept of opportunity cost. If everything has a right to exist, then all choice is severely constrained and there will be high costs for conservation. But costs are forgone benefits, and forgone benefits are other sets of rights. If I spend whatever I have to conserve a forest, that expenditure is lost to say the health service or even the defence industry. The rights of others to health care, or education, or defence are compromised. Just as risk analysts are more than used to talking of 'risk risk' analysis, so it is time that philosophers came to terms with the notion of opportunity cost. It rarely seems to figure in their discourse. As long as this remains the case, they must surely fail the real-world test we spoke of earlier.

Some writers have criticized the weak sustainability approach which assumes substitution (see for example, Victor *et al.*, 1994). Some of these criticisms are curious. First, they suggest that one should not focus on weak sustainability because it creates a sense of comfort to the effect that the environment can be dispensed with. It is hard to understand why such a discussion should preclude advocacy of strong sustainability by those who believe in it. More to the point, the preliminary evidence on weak sustainability indicators shows the potential for surprise: a large number of economies fail the weak sustainability test and if they fail that they are likely to fail any strong sustainability test (although not necessarily so) – see Atkinson *et al.* (1997). Second, it is suggested that monetary indicators of constant capital fail because they use market prices rather than externality-adjusted prices. But the whole point of valuing capital is to value the externalities. Whether this is done by applying shadow prices to marketed outputs or by valuing the externality, e.g. air pollution, directly, is immaterial. Moreover, if prices are irrelevant, constant natural capital has no meaning either since it is unclear what numeraire would be used to 'value' the stock of natural capital. The critics also seem conveniently to forget that strong sustainability is a two-part requirement: not only must natural capital be constant but so must the aggregate stock. Otherwise we would regard an economy with ever increasing natural assets as sustainable, regardless of whether knowledge is lost and buildings decay. The real issue is surely about what is and what is not substitutable, and why. Oddly, in criticizing weak sustainability Victor *et al.* (1994) actually admit that no review of such substitution possibilities exist.

It would be unfortunate, then, if ecological economists were to reject analysis of weak sustainability on such flimsy grounds.

Diversity, Stability and Resilience

A more sophisticated argument for ignoring the costs of precautionary action arises in the context of biodiversity conservation. Ecologists speak of the resilience of ecological systems – the ability of those systems to withstand stress and shocks. While it is a disputed proposition in ecology, there is some evidence to suggest that resilience increases with system complexity, and complexity can be measured by biological diversity. In that way, the more diversity there is, the more resilience there is and hence the more sustainable the system is. Turner *et al.* (1996) place considerable emphasis on the resilience issue. Since resilience is a characteristic of systems, any optimization procedure that neglects the overall health of the ecosystem will fail to account for the dynamic effects identified previously and hence is likely to be inconsistent with sustainability. An optimization procedure based on individuals' preferences could easily produce such neglect. It follows that the standard forms of economic valuation, based on monetised preferences, are extremely risky. Individuals, it is argued, do not value system effects.

These are serious arguments and I doubt if it is possible to sit comfortably on either side of the fence with respect to them at the moment. Let me raise some issues.

First, the evidence linking diversity and resilience is limited. There is some evidence that uniformity – the opposite of diversity – is producing non-resilient economic systems. The work of Peter Hazell (Hazell, 1982, 1984, 1989) shows clearly that cereal output, while growing through time, is experiencing larger and larger variations about the mean trend. One of the factors hypothesized to explain this lack of resilience is the uniformity of the crops grown so that a larger and larger stock is at risk from ecological stresses and shocks. Prakash and Pearce (1993) show that the coefficient of variation of output is higher for high yielding crop varieties in Karnataka in India than for other crops. Over time, the Hazell work suggests that there is less and less resilience in the sense that the coefficient of variation actually increases with time. Perrings and Pearce (1995) suggest a link between the sustainability-as-resilience argument and the weak/strong sustainability approach. They suggest that future choice sets can only be (at least) as large as they are now if biodiversity is maintained. Biodiversity must itself be non-declining through time which, if the diversity–resilience link is accepted, means non-declining resilience through time. Increasing coefficients of output variation, then, are prima facie evidence of declining resilience and hence declining sustainability.

The problems with this view are that, as Perrings *et al.* (1995) acknowledge, it is more of a research agenda than a policy-relevant statement of immediate use. The diversity–resilience link is, for example, disputed, although the extent to which it overlaps with the diversity–stability link is unclear. At best the diversity–resilience link suggests further support for the precautionary principle and for 'strong sustainability', but it still does not confront the valuation issue adequately. It is tempting to argue that it suggests that biodiversity be maintained regardless of the cost of doing so. As we see shortly, those costs could be significant and are also likely to impinge most on the livelihoods of those whose lives are already most vulnerable. If diversity and resilience are essential for sustainability, what we have to face, then, is that sustainability and well-being of the poor now are not compatible.

The second issue arising from the resilience discussion follows immediately from the first. What role does it imply for individuals' preferences in policy towards sustainability? In fairness to ecological economics, raising this question at such an early stage of development of thought is perhaps a little unfair. Nonetheless it is important to signal the obvious concern that 'maintaining natural capital stocks' or 'maintaining biodiversity' are rules that, because they will conflict with human wants now, are likely to require the overriding of those wants. The risk is some tyranny of decision-making in the name of sustainability. It is at least legitimate to ask first whether we can have such constraining rules together with democracy, and, if not, whether sustainability is worth the sacrifice of preference-based value systems. I venture the perhaps paradoxical personal view that human freedom is more important than human survival, a view some Gaian philosophers might agree with.

Third, and perhaps offsetting the gloom of the second issue somewhat, is it possible for preference-based value systems to be rescued in a world of ecological limits? Those who believe that monetary preference measurement techniques are incomplete because they ignore system functions, or 'primary value', may well be arguing not for the overthrow of human preferences as the basis for decision-making but for better and more information. Not only is there nothing in stated preference techniques that precludes me answering questions as a local or even global citizen, but market-based techniques could be argued to be consistent with values of system functions since they invariably involve some mix of expert assessment of dose–response linkages rather than individual preferences alone. This suggests a challenge both for ecological economists who may be concerned at the moral implications of overthrowing preference-based techniques and for advocates of monetary valuation who must improve or develop techniques so that they capture better system functions and values.

3.3 ACTION-ORIENTATED ECOLOGICAL ECONOMICS

Let me now illustrate the necessity of economic value in a world where biological diversity is being lost. If ecological economists are right and diversity is a critical asset that should not decline, and that is to have practical relevance, then we must understand why biological diversity is declining. The immediate reason for most diversity loss is land use change (Brown *et al.*, 1993; Swanson, 1994). Land use change occurs in the main because the economic value of the changed land use exceeds the economic value of the existing land use. Most land use change is from forest to agriculture and pasture. Why is the existing value of forests less than that for agriculture or pasture? The answer is fairly self-evident. It is because the many ecological functions of forests, from biodiversity and carbon store, to wildmeat supply and watershed regulation, are not marketed, and because many of the land conversions are subsidized. In a world in which economic values play no part, we might decide that these are unfair rules to play by and that conservation should not have to demonstrate its economic viability over and above the alternative land use. But that is not the real world and, more to the point, as world population grows inexorably, it will increasingly not be the world in which we live. Biodiversity therefore competes economically with agriculture, or it disappears, which is exactly what is happening now. The benefits of land-based conservation have to be greater than the total opportunity costs of conservation, i.e. the foregone net returns from developing the land. This is also the condition set out by Pearce and Moran (1994) in their review of the rates of return to biodiversity conservation.

In equation form, the fundamental equation for the conservation of wildlife becomes (ignoring the time dimension):

$$[B_{\mathrm{C}} - C_{\mathrm{C}} - (B_{\mathrm{D}} - C_{\mathrm{D}})] > 0$$

where

B_{C} = the benefits of conservation

C_{C} = the direct costs of conservation (e.g. monitoring, policing)

B_{D} = the benefits of some alternative use of the land, i.e. ‘development’

C_{D} = the costs of the alternative use of the land.

What this very basic equation underlines then is that biodiversity is competing with other uses of the land and unless biodiversity is invested with economic value it will be depleted, providing the essential economic rationale for the sustainable use approach to conservation.

Let us illustrate this in the context of African wildlife (see Chapter 12). First, we know that wildlife ranches, which conserve significant biodiversity, can often secure higher financial rates of return than cattle farming, which is not consistent with diversity. If markets functioned freely, the policy conclusion would be to leave markets to function freely. Wildlife would be saved in those contexts where the alternative use of land is for cattle. But we know that markets do not function freely, so the policy conclusion is first to remove distortions and then let markets get to work.

But we also have some evidence that wildlife conservation can impose net costs on an economy. Norton-Griffiths and Southey (1995) suggests that Kenya, for example, secure a GDP gain of only $40 million per annum from wildlife tourism against an opportunity cost of $200 million if the land was devoted to agriculture. Of course, it would be nice to have the agricultural output shadow priced for any externalities such as soil erosion and water contamination, but one suspects the result would not be changed. So far, economic valuation seems to have worked against wildlife, not for it. But what is relevant, of course, is the total willingness to pay of all visitors for wildlife experience. Moran (1994) suggests that total willingness to pay for game park experiences is over $400 million. This is not directly comparable to the $40 million GDP because the latter accounts for costs and for leakages in terms of foreign claims on receipts. Nonetheless, the $400 million represents a potentially 'capturable' sum of money. The first phase of policy then is to 'demonstrate' this value and that requires economic valuation techniques, in this case contingent valuation and travel cost procedures. The second phase involves 'capture' which means securing as much of the $400 million as possible and then also ensuring that a fair proportion of that goes to the people whose land values would be higher if the land was devoted to agriculture rather than wildlife. Capture mechanisms are various and include the raising of visitor prices to revenue-maximizing levels, something that is easier to do with an idea of what the demand curve looks like rather than on a trial and error basis. Economic valuation, of course, provides the demand curve estimate. Other capture mechanisms could involve debt-for-nature swaps, transferable development rights, joint implementation, grants from the Global Environment facility, and so on.

If markets in the 'products' of wildlife are non-existent, the rate of return to conservation will almost certainly fail to compete with the rate of return to the alternative uses of land. Hence it is in the creation of markets for wildlife products that hope for conservation resides. This conclusion still offends some traditional conservationists and their argument would be that wildlife should not have to compete. The alternative economic use of designated conservation land should simply be declared unlawful. The problem with this approach is that it invariably leaves the incentives for converting the land entirely unaltered. This results in increasing frustration over time, and in the inevitable and familiar problem of erosion of protected areas. Put another way, since the demand for the developmental use of land is unaltered, that demand will still exert a formidable pressure on conservation land. The only ways out of this impasse are either to compensate those who lose from conservation, or to provide positive incentives for them to participate in conservation.

Following on from the last, community participation and the sharing of conservation benefits with local communities becomes an integral part of any sustainable conservation plan. It is not just that participation is right in itself, but that it is a condition for successful economic intervention. Ascribing economic value to wildlife is not enough: those who otherwise have an incentive to thwart conservation plans must be able to capture at least some of that value. Otherwise, their incentive structure remains unaltered. This is important in the context where, from the community's standpoint, wildlife has no economic value, and doubly important when it has negative economic value because it destroys crops or threatens human lives and livestock. That applies as much to snow leopards in Nepal as it does to elephants. Capturing value involves the establishment of property rights in the wildlife resource, e.g. that the local community collects revenue from the sustainable utilization of wildlife whether that utilization is consumptive or otherwise. Note also has to be taken of the needs of local communities since wildlife cannot substitute for other assets at all times: an obvious example is the need for draught cattle in subsistence communities, so that 'blanket' removal of cattle would deprive farmers of a 'technology' that cannot be provided by wildlife.

Finally, not only do bans and moral outrage leave the fundamental forces causing wildlife loss largely unaffected, they also serve to 'disinvest' value in biodiversity: they take economic value away, when what is required is the investment of economic value in conservation through more and better markets for the sustainable output of conservation practices. Part of the problem with the conservationist argument that calls for 'the killing of demand' for wildlife products is that it ignores the supply side of the picture, the competition for land.

In summary, the economic analysis of wildlife conservation suggests a several tiered approach to policy:

a. demonstrate economic value;
b. ensure that this economic value is capturable, i.e. that institutions and markets exist which turn this economic value into a flow of real benefits;
c. ensure that part at least of this flow of real benefits accrues to those whose livelihoods are affected by the continued existence of the wildlife and who would benefit from the sacrificed land use;
d. avoid, wherever possible, conservation practice which bans or prohibits the utilization of wildlife products. Such bans take economic value away from the wildlife and render it an asset with limited economic value and thus less capable of competing against alternative land uses;
e. where such bans appear to be essential, ensure that compensation is paid to those who lose.

Here, in a nutshell, is why economic valuation is important. At worst it provides one more argument for conservation, though we must always be ready to acknowledge contexts where it might fail to do this. At best, it may be the only argument that has realistic potential for saving wildlife and biodiversity.

3.4 CONCLUSIONS

Perhaps the real distinction between ecological and environmental economics lies not in the individual characteristics discussed above – all of which have been addressed in one form or other in the recent history of environmental economics – but in the 'packaging' or 'bundling' of these characteristics. It is not the characteristics themselves but their combination that produces the challenge.

There clearly is much to debate in ecological and environmental economics. The outcome of the brief discussion above can best be summarized by saying that the science of ecological economics rests as yet on very limited foundations for there to be what some have called a 'foundational debate' (Norton, 1995). The danger is that effort will be made to create such a debate, whether it is justified or not. The cost to the environment of such a debate could be substantial. Contrary to widespread belief among non-economists, economists are not very powerful, and, among economists, environmental economists are perhaps the least powerful. But that does not mean they do not have powerful arguments. I believe they do and I believe that a more concerted effort to speak about what we know and are reasonably sure of could make a difference to the real world of conservation. Nowhere is that effort more important than in demonstrating that conservation can yield economic values greater than those it must compete against in an unavoidably harsh and real world of economic choice.

NOTES

1. Originally presented as a plenary address to the European Society for Ecological Economics Inaugural International Conference – 'Ecologie, Societie, Economie', University of Versailles, Guyancourt, France, May 1996.
2. It is more complex than this. Given population growth the requirement is that *per capita* stocks should not decline or that the rate of technological progress should not be less than the rate of population growth.

REFERENCES

Atkinson, G., Dubourg, R., Hamilton, K., Munasinghe, M., Pearce, D.W. and Young, C. (1997), *Measuring Sustainable Development: Macroeconomics and the Environment*, Edward Elgar, Cheltenham.

Barbier, E. (1989), *Economics, Natural Resource Scarcity and Development*, Earthscan, London.

Brown, K., Pearce, D.W., Perrings, C. and Swanson, T. (1993), *Economics and the Conservation of Global Biological Diversity*, Working Paper No.2, Global Environment Facility, Washington DC.

Dasgupta, P. and Heal, G. (1979), *Economic Theory and Exhaustible Resources*, Cambridge University Press, Cambridge.

Forster, B. (1973), Optimal consumption planning in a polluted environment, *Economic Record*, **49**, 435–545.

Forster, B. (1975), Optimal control with a nonconstant exponential rate of decay, *Journal of Environmental Economics and Management*, **2**, 1–6.

Forster, B. (1977), Consumption–pollution trade offs, in J.D.Pritchard and S.Turnovsky (eds), *Applications of Control Theory in Economic Analysis*, North-Holland, Amsterdam.

Hazell, P. (1982), *Instability in Indian Foodgrain Production*, Research Report No.30, International Food Policy Research Institute, Washington, DC.

Hazell, P. (1984), Sources of increased instability in Indian and US cereal production, *American Journal of Agricultural Economics*, August, 302–311.

Hazell, P. (1989), Changing patterns of variability in world cereal production, in J.Anderson and P.Hazell (eds), *Variability in Grain Yields: Implications for Agricultural Research and Policy in Developing Countries*, Johns Hopkins University Press, Baltimore, 13–34.

Moran, D. (1994), Contingent valuation and biodiversity: measuring the user surplus of Kenyan protected areas, *Biodiversity and Conservation*, **3**, 663–84.

Norton, B. (1995), Evaluating ecosystem states: two competing paradigms, *Ecological Economics*, **14**, 113–127.

Norton-Griffiths, M. and Southey, C. (1995), The opportunity costs of biodiversity conservation in Kenya, *Ecological Economics*, **12**, 125–39.

Pearce, D.W. (1976), The limits of cost benefit analysis as a guide to environmental policy, *Kyklos*, **29**, Fasc.1, 97–112.

Pearce, D.W and Moran, D. (1994), *The Economic Value of Biodiversity*, Earthscan, London.

Perrings, C., Mäler, K-G., Folke, C., Holling, C and Jansson, B.-O. (1995), Biodiversity, conservation and economic development: the policy problem, in C.Perrings, K.-G. Mäler, C. Folke, C. Holling and B.-O. Jansson, *Biodiversity Conservation*, Kluwer, Amsterdam, 3–21.

Perrings, C. and Pearce, D.W. (1994), Threshold effects and incentives for the conservation of biodiversity, *Environmental and Resource Economics*, **4**, 13–28.

Perrings, C. and Pearce, D.W. (1995), Biodiversity conservation and economic development: local and global dimensions, in C. Perrings, K.-G Mäler, C. Folke, C. Holling and B.-O. Jansson, *Biodiversity Conservation*, Kluwer, Amsterdam, 23–40.

Pezzey. J. (1989), *Economic Analysis of Sustainable Growth and Sustainable Development*, Environment Department Working Paper 18, World Bank, Washington, DC.

Posch, M., de Smet, P., Hettelingh, J.-P. and Downing R.J. (1995), *Calculation and Mapping of Critical Thresholds in Europe*, National Institute of Public Health and the Environment, Bilthoven, The Netherlands.

Prakash, T.N and Pearce, D.W. (1993), *Sustainability as Resilience: Measuring Sustainable Development*, Centre for Social and Economic Research on the Global Environment, University of East Anglia and University College London, mimeo.

Swanson, T. (1994), *The International Regulation of Extinction*, Macmillan, London.

Turner, R.K., Perrings, C. and Folke, C. (1996), *Ecological Economics: Paradigm or Perspective?*, Centre for Social and Economic Research on the Global Environment, University of East Anglia and University College London, mimeo.

UK Government (1990), *This Common Inheritance: Britain's Environmental Strategy*, CM 1200, Her Majesty's Stationery Office, London.

Victor, P., Hanna, E. and Kubursi, A. (1994), *How Strong is Weak Sustainability?* Ontario Ministry of Environment, mimeo.

4. The limits of cost–benefit analysis as a guide to environmental policy[1]

4.1 INTRODUCTION

This chapter explores the limits to the applicability of cost–benefit analysis to pollution problems. The emphasis is on conceptual limitations and not practical problems. For anyone familiar with the complexities of empirically estimating shadow prices for environmental goods, it seems safe to say that the practical limitations exceed the conceptual ones. In part, the empirical difficulties arise because of limited information and because of the relative novelty of seeking to evaluate, in monetary terms, environmental goods and bads. Whether the problems arising from this 'newness' in the art of valuation will persist is arguable: there is always a tendency, perhaps based more on faith than experience, to suppose that more research and more time will solve many of the outstanding difficulties. But some of the difficulties arise because of a further tendency which has no justification, namely, to assume that, because environmental improvement requires resource inputs, and because environmental goods clearly are the object of varying degree of preference intensity, the conceptual basis of cost–benefit analysis is applicable, without modification, to environmental policy. It is this latter assumption that this paper questions.

4.2 A TAXONOMY OF POLLUTION

We first establish a classificatory framework within which certain features of pollution can be distinguished. These features will be shown to have implications for policy towards pollution abatement.

In order to establish a taxonomy we utilize the concept of the assimilative capacity of the environment. Environments are capable, in varying degrees, of receiving waste matter, degrading it, and converting it to nutrients which then 'feed' the occupants of an ecosystem. This conversion process takes place for many wastes. Still other wastes are converted so as to render them harmless to species even if the converted product is not itself required as an input to the ecosystem. The capacity of any system to carry out these functions we call the system's assimilative capacity. This capacity then depends on the size and functioning of 'degrader populations' such as the bacterial occupants of water systems. We shall see later that crucial differences in pollutants can be defined according to whether or not those pollutants have counterpart degrader populations or whether, if counterpart populations exist, the effect of pollution is to itself destroy the degrading capacity. For some wastes there is no counterpart degrader population so that wastes accumulate. Other wastes have counterpart degrader populations but the nature of the effects of pollution depend on both the quality and quantity of waste relative to the size of assimilative capacity. These correspondences are investigated more thoroughly shortly.

Initially, we shall consider assimilative capacity in a static sense only. That is, we shall develop a taxonomy that does not allow for the fact that environmental assimilation itself has a time dimension. Wastes are emitted to receiving environments and are then degraded over time unless the capacity of the system to degrade wastes is itself impaired. A late section of the paper assesses the implications of giving assimilative capacity a dynamic dimension. Essentially, it will be argued that it makes little difference to the outcome of the analysis.

To the concept of assimilative capacity we add that of 'biological effect'. Quite simply, we observe whether or not a pollutant generates some biological change in organisms in the receiving environment. These effects may be change in human health, species mutation, changes in cell metabolism, and so on. Mellanby (1972) has in fact declared that anti-pollution policy should be guided solely by biological criteria: 'I believe that we should try to prevent any pollutant reaching a level where any biological reaction can be demonstrated [. . .] even if this reaction has not been shown to be harmful' (Mellanby, 1972, p. 4). Our taxonomy of pollution tries to allow for biological effects.

Finally, we need the concept of an 'economic effect' of pollution. This we define in the conventional way in terms of whether or not a negative external effect (external cost) is present. We need only remember that externalities are defined with respect to sufferers' utility functions, so that any physical measure of pollution may be positive without any externality being present: if people do not care about biological changes in species (or, indeed, in themselves) no 'economic' effect can be said to exist. We shall see, however, that it will be necessary to investigate the implications of those pollutants which do damage health but only after lengthy time periods – the so-called 'invisible' pollutants.

We now consider these three concepts – assimilative capacity, biological effect and economics effect – in two contexts. The first context is that where the volume of waste emitted to the receiving environment is less than that environment's assimilative capacity. We immediately suppress this context by our prior assumption that the assimilative process is (virtually) instantaneous, so that the ecosystem degrades the waste without biological or economic effect. We relax this assumption later.

The second context relates to an excess volume of waste residuals over assimilative capacity. In this context we shall further distinguish situations in which there exists a counterpart degrading capacity (assimilative capacity > 0) and those where that capacity is effectively zero because no counterpart populations exist. We can then classify pollutants and pollution contexts in terms of biological and economic effects. Figure 4.1 shows a taxonomy in the form of a 'pollution tree' based on these concepts. In the diagram W = volume of waste, A = assimilative capacity, B = biological effect, E = economic effect.

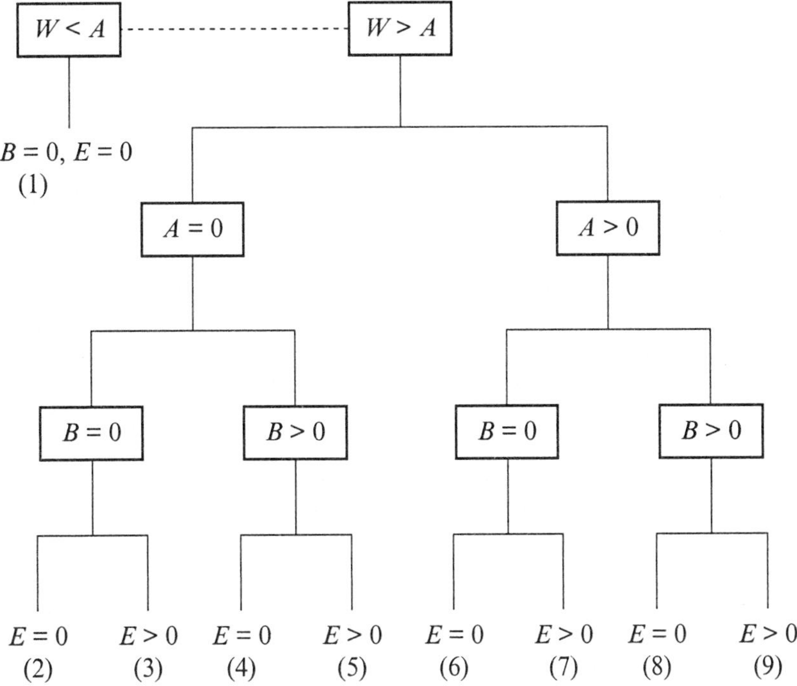

Figure 4.1 A pollution 'tree'

4.3 ANALYSIS OF THE TAXONOMY

We can now look at each of the final categorizations.

Box (1): for the moment this context is not subject to further analysis since, *ex hypothesi*, it defines a situation in which neither biological nor economic effects are present.

Box (2): this category would involves a waste residual which, when disposed of, has no counterpart degrader population (A = 0), has no biological effects (B = 0) and no economic effects (E = 0). It is clearly irrelevant for policy purposes and, indeed, appears to be an 'empty box' altogether.

Box (3): in this case $A = 0$, B = O but E > O. An example would be glass bottles. No degrader population exists to convert the waste, but, equally, biological effects are not present. On the other hand, waste bottles tend to be aesthetically offensive so that an externality may well be present. Category (3) is directly relevant to policy in so far as this externality is present and the cost–benefit approach would be appropriate as a means of determining the optimal level of waste. Indeed, category (3) defines the classic externality problem. Numerous caveats still apply. The use of cost–benefit analysis does not mean that only an approach in which compensating variations are summed will give the right answer. The philosophy of cost–benefit analysis is consistent with any number of valuation procedures – see Nash *et al.* (1975a, 1975b). Also a cost–benefit approach in which pollution control costs are weighed against damaged cost saved will not produce a Pareto improvement if imperfectly competitive conditions prevail – see Pearce (1974b).

Box (4), *Box* (5): here we observe a possible divergence between biological and economic criteria. Biological effects are present in both cases but in (4) no externality appears present. As such, cost–benefit would dictate a status quo policy whereas biological criteria, as advocated by Mellanby, for example, would indicate that avertive action should be taken. The difficulty with the status quo solution is that E may be zero solely because individuals are unaware of the biological effects of pollution and, if they were aware, would take avertive action. That is, some situations in which $E = 0$ are in fact situations where, *ex post*, $E > 0$.

An excellent example of this problems of 'awareness' is cadmium. Essentially, cadmium particles are highly toxic but only after they have accumulated unperceived to particular threshold densities in human organs, the thresholds varying with body weight and, in any event, being rather imprecise (Nobbs and Pearce, 1976). Most cadmium concentrating in the human body is ingested and only some is inhaled. As such, cadmium reaches the body via food and water. $A = 0$ for cadmium so that waste cadmium accumulates as a stock in the environment. Its toxic effects are numerous. It is certainly implicated in renal dysfunction and is on the list of suspects for hypertensive conditions, including cardio-vascular disease. In massive doses its effects are dramatic, as with the so-called 'itai-itai' disease one of the features of which is osteomalacia – a softening and eventual collapse of the skeletal structure of the body.

Now, if we know this much, albeit with wide margins of uncertainty, why should it present problems for cost–benefit analysis? Awkward empirical issues such as valuing health and life apart, the essential problem that arises with these pollutants where $A = 0$ and $B > 0$ is that the damage they do arises from a (by and large) non-reducible stock and hence only incremental damage arises from the flow of pollution. In addition, and as noted above, we must rely on some social learning process to prevent the cadmium stock rising further since, because of the unperceived cumulative nature of the pollutant, individuals cannot be relied upon to take avertive action. To see the difficulty of looking at the problem in cost–benefit terms we can try to construct a control cost-damage cost diagram such as that widely applied to other pollution problems. This is done in Figure 4.2.

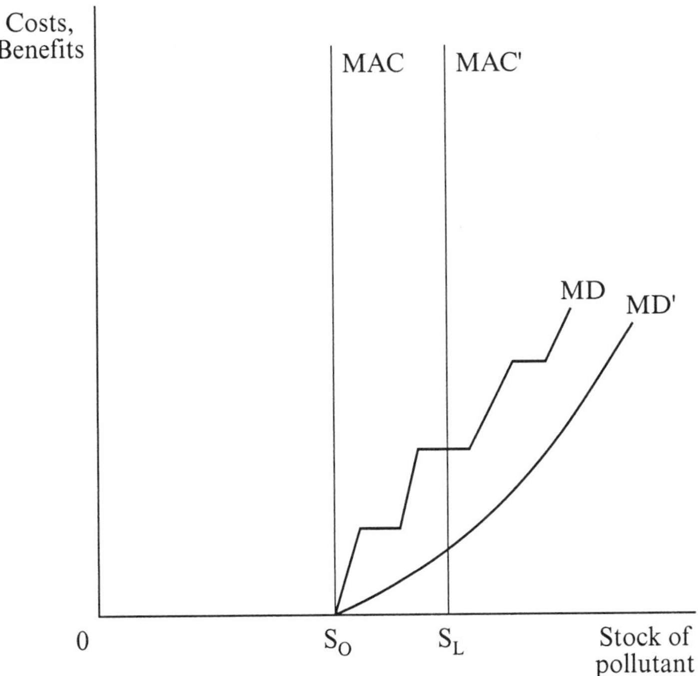

Figure 4.2 Stock pollutants

Whereas the conventional pollution abatement cost/damage function diagram relates costs and benefits to the flow of pollution, the relevant variable in the case of cadmium is the stock of pollution. The flow variable can then be introduced by considering movements along the horizontal axis to the right since the existing stock is generally non-reducible. The damage function presents serious problems of interpretation. If life and health are afforded finite values, if we know the probabilities of damage, and if we adopt a present value approach to perpetually repeatable expected damage, then the marginal damage function might appear as MD in Figure 4.2. The stepwise nature of the curve reflects the fact that damage tends to be related to threshold levels of pollution, although the variability of response to cadmium intake is more likely to make MD a smooth function such as MD'. More important than the shape of MD, however, is the fact that movements along MD can take place only in a rightwards direction: there is little or no option to move down MD simply because there is little or no option to reduce the stock of cadmium in the environment. But critical to the cost–benefit approach to pollution is the requirement that the pollution variable be controllable in any direction. It follows that one essential feature of the cost–benefit approach is missing in the context of those $A = 0, B > 0$ pollutants such as cadmium.

To reinforce this conclusion, consider the marginal abatement cost function (MAC). Since the stock of pollution is non-reducible, MAC must be vertical and must have its origin coincident with that of the MD function. That is, if we take any stock situation such as point O in Figure 4.2, MAC must intersect the horizontal axis at S_O. But S_O is in no way an optimum even though MAC = MD, the conventional requirement for maximizing net social benefits. For if we consider a move to, say, S_1, the MAC curve will shift rightwards with a new origin at S_1 thus indicating that S_1 is also optimal. Indeed, any level of pollution stock in Figure 4.2 could be judged optimal by the simple application of a cost–benefit rule.

Of course, if the stock of pollution is non-reducible it can be held to be analogous to unavoidable fixed costs; bygones are bygones. The only variable subject to control is the flow of pollution – i.e. the rate at which we move up MD in Figure 4.2. Marginal abatement costs corresponding to this increment will then be finite and an apparent 'optimum' result of decisions about the flow of pollution. On this view, the initial stock situation is always irrelevant to the decision about additions to that stock: each initial point corresponds to some unavoidable cost situation. Whereas cost–benefit analysis cannot be applied to the stock context, it can be applied to the flow context. Since both MD for the flow (the slope of MD in Figure 4.2) and MAC for the flow will tend to be 'well behaved', additions to the stock will always be justified. It is worth noting that this result will be reinforced by the existence of positive discount rates which, if MD is construed in present value forms, will ensure that MD itself does not rise very steeply.

Applied in this way, then, cost–benefit becomes a mechanism for shifting the costs of pollution forward in time to future generations and it is clear that there are anomalies in its use in contexts such as boxes (4) and (5) in Figure 4.1. This problem of burden shifting is discussed more fully in Nash (1973).

Box (6); *Box* (7): these categories appear to be 'empty boxes' again simply because the $W > A$ context must entail reductions in A so that we can expect $B > 0$

to be the general rule. A situation in which $W > A$ and $B = 0$ appears to be precluded.

Box (8); *Box* (9): on the face of it, these categories fit the cost–benefit framework. If $W > A$ then reductions in A can be thought of as a cost to be set against the benefits from the joint products of pollution, namely, goods. However, as argued in earlier papers (Pearce, 1974a, 1974b; see also Common 1974a, 1974b) this presumption is not warranted when we consider the externality in a dynamic ecological context. The argument may be summarized with reference to Figure 4.3. The top half of the diagram shows a waste generation function $W(X)$ where X is physical output of goods. $W(X)$ is shown such that $W'(X) > 0$. Also shown is A, the receiving environment's assimilative capacity, assumed fixed at A_0 initially. A later section considers the implications of giving A a time dimension.

The lower half of Figure 4.3 measures costs and benefits against output of goods, X. B' is to be thought of as a marginal net private benefit curve – i.e. marginal private benefit less marginal private costs. In the case of a firm, for example, it would be a marginal profit curve. Curves C'_0, C'_1, C'_2 are marginal

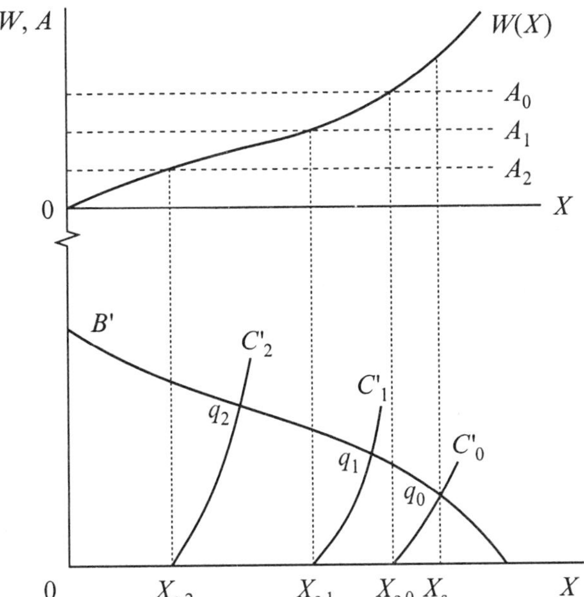

Figure 4.3 Dynamic externality 1

external cost curves. If we consider C'_0, we see that it has its origin at $X_{e,0}$ which corresponds to the situation in which $W(X) = A_0$. That is, we assume externalities cannot occur until $W > A$. This reflects our current assumption of (virtually) instantaneous environmental assimilation, an assumption we relax in a short while. (In fact C_0 could begin to the right of $X_{e,0}$ if $B > 0$ but $E = 0$ in the neighbourhood of $X_{e,0}$. But reworking of the argument will show that such a situation merely reinforces the conclusions.)

Now, given an initial context where $A = A_0$, $W > A$ and $C'_0 > 0$, we have a Pareto optimum at q_0 with output level X_S. This is what cost–benefit analysis would dictate. But we should now be able to see that such a situation is ecologically unstable. Essentially, a $W > A$ context will result in a reduction in A as the counterpart degrader population is reduced in size. We can show this by shifting A_0 downwards to A_1. But, if no corrective action is taken – i.e. the output level remains at X_S – W exceeds A to an even greater extent and the process begins again and can end only by total destruction of the environment's assimilative capacity. Even if there is a social response, however, the dynamic process noted above is not prevented. If A_0 moves to A_1 we can expect C'_0 to move to C'_1, reflecting the fact that W now exceeds A at lower output levels. C'_1 will also tend to be steeper than C'_0 since the ratio of W to A is now increased. (This change in slope is absent in Pearce, 1974a and 1974b). If a Paretian adjustment is made, q_1 becomes the new 'optimum'. But q_1 is also unstable since $W > A$ and a further shift in A to A_2 will occur. The corresponding external cost curve now becomes (at best) C'_2 and a new 'optimum' of q_2 is dictated. Again, the situation is ecologically unstable, and, if continuous Paretian adjustments are made, zero output is the convergent solution. It is worth noting, however, that if $X_{e,0}$ had been adopted as a policy objective at the outset, dynamic externality situation could have been avoided.

What cost–benefit analysis fails to do, then, is to acknowledge a particular aspect of externality – the impact of any apparent optimum on ecological stability. If, on the other hand, ecological stability had been introduced as a constraint of the form $W > A$, the dynamic externality problem would have been avoided. However, since such a constraint dominates the solution, there seems little point in a cost–benefit calculus to determine the prior optimality of the $W = A$ output level (Pearce, 1974a, 1974b).

4.4 ASSIMILATIVE CAPACITY AS A TIME-RELATED PROCESS

The salient weakness of the 'dynamic externality' model developed in Section 4.2 is its failure to acknowledge environmental assimilation as a time-related process. That is, waste emitted to the environment will be degraded over a period of time unless, as we saw, some defined capacity level of assimilation is exceeded. During the process of assimilation, some negative externality is likely to appear. We now investigate the implication of this feature of the assimilative process.

Figure 4.4 repeats the essentials of the dynamic externality diagram. However, we now distinguish two categories of externality. Those external costs that occur during the process of assimilation we shall call 'assimilation process externalities' or, simply, 'process externalities'. By definition, these externalities relate to situations in which $W > A$, and hence are ephemeral. Since the process of assimilation can be accompanied by reductions in degrader populations, we may also find temporary shifts downwards in the A function in Figure 4.4. However, the essential fact remains that, since $W > A$, such reductions must eventually be restored.

By contrast, those externalities which relate to $W > A$ contexts are associated with permanent reductions in A thus generating the dynamic process noted in earlier sections. Figure 4.5 shows the distinguishing features of the two categories of externality. Following Common (1974b) we refer to the second category as

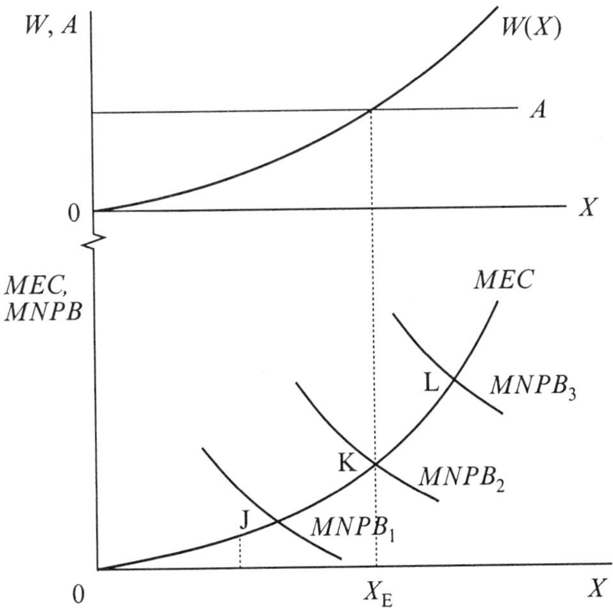

Figure 4.4 Dynamic externality 2

'dynamic externality'. Returning to Figure 4.4 we see that MEC can now be thought of as comprising two sections. Section OK refers to the process externality and the arrow shows that, over time, this externality must disappear (subject to a modification discussed below). The section to the right of K refers to the dynamic externality element. Whereas process externalities are associated with temporary changes in A (see top of diagram), dynamic externalities are associated with permanent reductions in A.

	Category of externality	
	Process	Dynamic
Context	$W < A$	$W > A$
Time path of $A(t)$	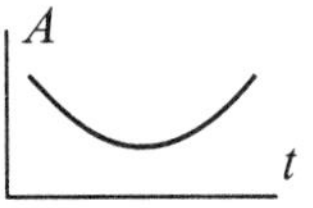 A, t	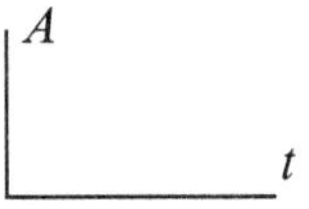 A, t
Time path of total external cost (for given time flow of X)	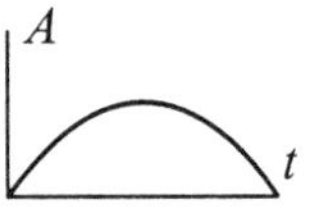 A, t	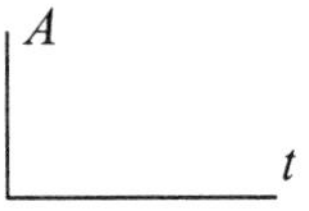 A, t

Figure 4.5 Categorizing externalities

What we have now to consider is whether the presence of process externalities alters the relevance of the dynamic externality process noted in previous sections. It will be recalled that, given the assumptions stated, Pareto output levels gave rise to continual degradation of the environment as far as this category of pollutant is concerned. Figure 4.4 shows their marginal net private benefit (*MNPB*) functions. If $MNPB_1$ operates we clearly have no problem since the Pareto optimum, if set with respect to the process externality 2, will lie at J and we are in the $W > A$ context. This adds nothing to our earlier conclusions because output levels do not exceed assimilative capacity levels.

If $MNPB_2$ operates we have a Pareto optimum at K which corresponds to X_E, the maximum output level consistent with unchanged levels of ecological stability. Hence it is possible for Paretian regulation of output levels to be compatible with ecological stability, contrary to the conclusions of the earlier sections of this paper and those of Pearce (1973, 1974a, 1974b). This possible compatibility is noted in Common (1974a, 1974b). $MNPB_3$, on the other hand, fails to meet the requirements for avoiding the ecological destabilizing process and our previous analysis applies.

Consequently, we can argue that private benefit functions giving Pareto optima at points along OK, but excluding K, do not detract from our earlier conclusions since no ecological destabilizing process occurs as a result of process externalities. Benefit functions producing optima to the right of K fit the picture previously established.

This leaves us with a benefit function such as $MNPB_2$ which produces a Pareto optimum output coincident with X_E. However, we have to ask whether there is anything in $MNPB_2$ which is likely to make it more likely to occur than benefit functions like $MNPB_3$. The answer is in the negative – it can only be by chance that $MNPB_2$ occurs. Our previous conclusions are therefore altered only to the trivial extent that fortuitous event makes $MNPB_2$ the relevant function rather than any other. We conclude that the dynamic externality process remains intact.

4.5 CONCLUSIONS

There is a sense in which, if we construe it as a technique in which all advantages and disadvantages are evaluated, cost–benefit analysis will, subject to arguments about its underlying value judgements, always dictate the 'right' answer. But such an argument advances us nowhere, for what we have tried to show is that there are conceptual problems in applying cost–benefit to pollution issues and that these problems are not of the kind that can readily be accommodated by some modification to cost–benefit itself. Arguably, the problem of dynamic externality in the context of $W > A$ is one more instance of static analysis failing to identify a dynamic optimum, and no more than this. Even at this level, however, it is suggested that the problem raised is an important one. Moreover, it raises the issue of whether a cost–benefit calculus is needed in such a context since physical information alone will identify the optimum. For stock pollutants such as cadmium, mercury, lead and perhaps polychlorinated biphenyls, the cost–benefit approach appears positively irrelevant. But if cost–benefit is, at the very least, misleading for these cases it leaves us with contexts in which W is less than A such that the dynamic externality problem does not arise, and those $A = 0$, $B = 0$ contexts where externality does occur. That is, as long as biological effects are (genuinely) absent, cost–benefit is as good a tool as any other, and perhaps a superior one, for determining optimal levels of waste disposal. Where the context takes on dynamic externality features of where biologically harmful pollutants cumulate, cost–benefit should give way to standard setting based on a caution attitude to epidemiological and other physical information.

NOTE

1. Reprinted with minor amendments from *Kyklos*, **29**, 1976.

REFERENCES

Common, M. (1974a), *Pollution, Pareto Optimality and the Ecological Gap*, University of Southampton, *mimeo.*

Common, M. (1974b), *Pollution: The Dynamic Consequences of Static Externality Correction*, University of Southampton, mimeo.

Mellanby, K. (1972), *The Biology of Pollution*, Edward Arnold, London.

Nash, C.A. (1973), Future generations and the social rate of discount, *Environment and Planning*, **5**(4), 611–17.

Nash, C.A., Pearce, D.W. and Stanley, J.K. (1975a), Criteria for evaluating project evaluation techniques, *Journal of the American Institute of Planners*, March, 83–9.

Nash, C.A., Pearce, D.W. and Stanley, J.K. (1975b), An evaluation of cost–benefit analysis criteria, *Scottish Journal of Political Economy*, **XXII**(2), 121–34.

Nobbs, C.A. and Pearce, D.W. (1976), The economics of stock pollutants: the example of cadmium, *International Journal of Environmental Studies*, **8**, 245–55.

Pearce, D.W. (1973), An incompatibility in planning for a steady state and planning for maximum economic welfare, *Environment and planning*, **5**, 1–7.

Pearce, D.W. (1974a), Economics and ecology, *Surrey Papers in Economics,* 10, July.

Pearce, D.W. (1974b), Fiscal incentives and the economics of waste recycling: problems and limitations, in *Fiscal Policy and the Environment*, Institute of Fiscal Studies, London.

PART 2

Sustainable Development

5. Sustainable development

5.1 THE POLITICAL RELEVANCE OF SUSTAINABLE DEVELOPMENT

Few concepts have attracted so much political, popular and academic attention as that of 'sustainable development'. While politicians are adept at embracing high-sounding objectives – especially when they are so loosely defined as to be consistent with almost any form of action (or inaction) – it is significant that 'sustainable development' now figures as a goal in dozens of national environmental policy statements and in the opening paragraphs of 'Agenda 21', the massive shopping list of world actions adopted at the Earth Summit in Rio de Janeiro in June 1992. Agenda 21 states:

> In order to meet the challenges of environment and development, States decided to establish a new global partnership. This partnership commits all States to engage in a continuous and constructive dialogue, inspired by the need to achieve a more efficient and equitable world economy, keeping in view the increasing interdependence of the community of nations, and that sustainable development should become a priority item on the agenda of the international community (United Nations Conference on Environment and Development, 1992, para.2.1).

Whatever it means, therefore, sustainable development has become a high profile objective. But what is it that the world's politicians have committed themselves to aspire to?

5.2 DEFINING SUSTAINABLE DEVELOPMENT

While it is a popular pastime to collect different and incompatible definitions of sustainable development, inspection of the words and of their origins suggests that *defining* sustainable development is really not a difficult issue. The difficult issue is in determining what has to be done to achieve sustainable development, assuming it is a desirable goal.

Slightly expanded, what is being referred to is sustainable economic development. The term 'sustainable' is not open to much dispute: it means 'enduring' and 'lasting' and 'to keep in being'. So, sustainable development is economic development that lasts. Economic development could be narrowly defined in traditional terms as real GNP per capita, or real consumption per capita. Alternatively, it could be broadened to include other indicators of development such as education, health and some measure of the 'quality of life,' including human freedom. One such exercise is to be found in the United Nations Development Programme's 'Human Development Index' (HDI) (UNDP, 1992). This combines measures of sub-goals – literacy, life expectancy and GDP – to provide an index of relative achievement, i.e. a score which is defined in terms of a country's position relative to other countries. Since the index is then an average of the relative achievements in each of the three main sub-goals, there is an implicit assumption of substitutability between the different components. More education might be at the expense of GNP for example. For current purposes, the definition of 'development' does not matter much, although it is a legitimate source of investigation not least because 'development' is a value word that invites any number of interpretations which could proliferate to the point where 'sustainable development' is then meaningless. The economist would generally prefer to substitute per capita 'utility' or 'well-being' as the indicator to be sustained.

Sustainable economic development now becomes fairly simply defined. It is non-declining consumption per capita, or GNP, or whatever the agreed indicator of development is. And this is how sustainable development has come to be interpreted by most of the economists addressing the issue (see for example – Maler, 1990; Pezzey, 1989; Pearce *et al.*, 1990). The merits of this definition are, first, that it accords with the intuitive idea that the meaning of words is to be found through observation of common usage of those words, and, second, it is consistent with, though not identical to, the most widely used definition in the report that made the term so popular. That report is the World Commission on Environment and Development's report in 1987 on North–South relations and the global environmental problem (WCED, 1987). There it is declared that:

> Sustainable development is development that meets the needs of the present without compromising the ability of future generations to meet their own needs (WCED, 1987, p. 43).

Substituting a development indicator for 'needs' makes the equivalence of non-declining well-being and the WCED definition fairly complete, but, as we shall see, the WCED had a specific purpose in selecting the term 'needs'. Notice also that defining sustainable development is not the same thing as searching for the necessary and sufficient conditions for achieving it.

For how long sustainable development should last is of course open to debate. The context of sustainable development has always been that of intergenerational equity. Thus the time horizon must be a few generations at least, but it will not be infinity. We might appeal to some 'coefficient of concern' to set some pragmatic limit on how far into the future we should look. Casual observation indicates that people care for at least their children and grandchildren. Few probably look ahead much further than that. So, we might take, say, 100 years as a minimum time horizon. Of course, if individuals now already integrate future concerns into current actions and choices, there is little reason to elevate 'sustainability' as a source of concern. It will automatically be taken care of. But, as Page (1977) observed, the kinds of bequests to future generations that emerge from the existence of 'overlapping generations' reflect what he calls 'selfish altruism' whereby the well-being of an individual now (W_0) is determined by consumption now and consumption by future generations over some time horizon, i.e.:

$$W_0 = f(C_0, C_1, C_2, \ldots, C_T)$$

But a unit of consumption going to generations 1,2,...,T would have less value than a unit of consumption going to generation 0 because generation 0 is the arbiter of value. The weighting applied to generate this result is in fact the weighting that arises from generation 0's time preference, i.e. the discount rate. (More strictly, the discount rate relevant to the choice of consumption today versus consumption tomorrow is the consumption rate of interest which has the form $CRI = eg + p$, where e is the elasticity of marginal utility of consumption, g is the projected growth rate in real consumption, and p is 'pure time preference'. p reflects the rate at which well-being is discounted – it is the 'utility rate of discount'.) If we seek to maximize W_0 we are, by definition, maximizing the well-being of the current generation. It can only be by accident, then, that selfish altruism would ensure future levels of well-being at least equal to those of the current generation. We cannot appeal to selfish altruism to guarantee the sustainability of development.

5.3 OPTIMAL GROWTH AND SUSTAINABLE DEVELOPMENT

Economists looking at the theory of economic growth have tended to work with utilitarian assumptions. This means that an 'optimal' path of future consumption is traced out by setting up the problem in the following form:

$$\text{Maximize } \_{0,\infty}\ U(C_t).e^{-\delta t}.dt$$

where U is utility, C is real consumption per capita, and δ is the utility discount rate. A number of commentators have remarked on the oddity of this formulation for it implies that future utility should be discounted. When tomorrow comes we shall experience the same feelings as today. There is no apparent reason for discounting future utility, although there may be good reasons to discount future consumption if we can feel assured that future consumption will be higher than today (Page, 1977; Georgescu-Roegen, 1979).

It is well known that maximization of this present value function can produce paths of real consumption per capita over time which may or may not be 'sustainable' in the sense defined above (Dasgupta and Heal, 1979; Page, 1977; Pezzey, 1989). Figure 5.1 illustrates some of the possibilities and the annexe to this chapter provides a formal derivation of the rules. In Figure 5.1 it is seen that two of the three consumption paths obey the sustainability requirement and one does not. The numbers on the curves correspond to the numbered notes below. The following results emerge, where s = rate of discount and r = marginal productivity of capital:

1. If the resource base consists of non-renewable resources only ($r = 0$) and there is no discounting ($s = 0$), then the optimal consumption path is also a constant consumption path and is therefore consistent with sustainable development as defined above.
2. If the resource base consists of exhaustible resources only ($r = 0$) and there is a positive discount rate ($s > 0$), then the optimal consumption path is not sustainable. Consumption declines over time.
3. If the resource is renewable ($r > 0$) and there is no discounting ($s = 0$) then optimal consumption rises over time. This is consistent with sustainable development.

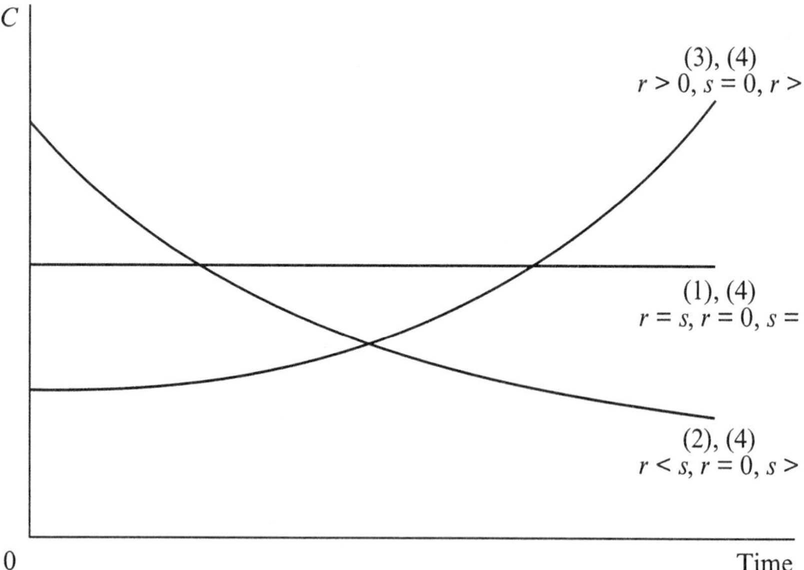

Figure 5.1 Consumption paths

4. Where there is both positive natural capital productivity and positive discounting, then, as might now be expected, the result depends on the relative size of s and r. If $r = s$, we get constant consumption. If $r > s$ we get rising consumption over time, and if $r < s$ we get falling consumption over time.

The overall conclusion is clear, and is familiar from other work (see, especially, Dasgupta and Heal, 1979 and Pezzey, 1989). The consistency of optimal growth and sustainable growth depends very much on the relationship between the productivity of the resource base and the social discount rate. It also depends on the parameter of the elasticity of the marginal utility of consumption – b in the annexe. This elasticity can be thought of as an index of a generation's aversion to inequality over time. But, as Dasgupta and Heal (1979, chapter 10) show, the time path is dominated by the value of the discount rate when $r = 0$ (the non-renewables case) and by the productivity of capital (the renewables case). The higher the discount rate the more is sustainable development at risk from the deliberate planning of 'optimal' growth. The lower the discount rate, the less is the risk of 'optimal extinction' for future generations. Given that economies are not likely to be on optimal consumption trajectories anyway, the conclusion is probably strengthened if we compare actual consumption paths and sustainable development paths. As Dasgupta and Heal put it in the context of non-renewable resources:

> A positive rate of time preference tilts the balance overwhelmingly against generations in the distant future. This alone is a powerful result; it indicates that 'Utilitarianism' with a positive rate of impatience can recommend what can be regarded as ethically questionable policies (Dasgupta and Heal, 1979, p. 299).

Figure 5.1 appears to give some comfort about the present value criterion, i.e. maximizing present values is consistent with sustainability provided $r > s$. Moreover, if we wish to engage in strict sustainability – the constant consumption path in Figure 5.1 – it can be achieved by setting the discount rate equal to the marginal product of capital. Contrary to the criticisms of discounting, then, it can actually be consistent with sustainable development, a result demonstrated in the literature of the 1970s even if the language was not quite the same (Page, 1977; Dasgupta and Heal, 1979).

The problem is that actual economies do not work this way. In the real world there are strong forces at work which are likely to force the market value of s to be above the value of r. In the economist's perfect world s and r are brought into equilibrium and a path like (1) in Figure 5.1 could come about. Provided society maximizes some intertemporal welfare function and is operating at the boundary of an intertemporal production possibility frontier, $s = r$ (for a simple demonstration, see Pearce, 1986, Chapter 4. Also, see Figure 5.2 below). But there are many distortions that are likely to force market rates to be above the 'true' marginal product of capital. The existence of income tax is just one (Baumol, 1968). For the private sector to invest it will require a rate of return greater than r if it is to pay r to its shareholders. Very simply,

$$m = r/(1 - t)$$

where t is the rate of income tax and m is the rate that must be earned on capital in order to pay shareholders r. The value of m must therefore necessarily be greater than the value of r. Another reason for thinking r is less than m is that r will tend to be a riskless rate due to the ability of society in general (through government) to pool the risks of individual projects both across many projects and across a whole population (Arrow and Lind, 1970). We can also argue that the relevant value of r or s is that rate which takes the welfare of future generations into account, whereas the revealed value of m is likely to be more short-term in orientation. That is, we require a 'citizen's' rate of discount rather than some average of individual discount rates (Sen, 1967). Alternatively, the well-being of future generations can be regarded as a public good as far as members of the current generation are concerned: it is something that each of us cares about. But since any improvement in future well-being brought about by my actions also benefits you, that future well-being is a public good. The level of investment and savings that takes place now because of individualistic decisions will therefore be less than it would have been if a collective decision was made to invest. The fact that the level of investment ought to be higher than it is, means that the social discount rate is below that produced by market forces (Marglin, 1963).

These considerations suggest that an economy can easily be tipped into a consumption path like (2) in Figure 5.1, although we have not yet considered the role to be played by technological progress or population change. But the analysis above has also suggested that sustainability can be more guaranteed if the 'true' value of r could be determined and used as the discount rate ($r = s$) case. This still leaves a special problem – if an economy is heavily reliant upon non-renewable resources, $r = 0$ and any positive discounting will give the result that $r > s$ with a consequent tendency to non-sustainability. We address these issues below.

5.4 FINDING THE DISCOUNT RATE

We have so far assumed that sustainable development is best defined in terms of a per capita consumption path that is constant or rising over time. Figure 5.2 presents a highly simplified construction in which TT' is the transformation frontier between consumption now and in the future (*Cc* and *Cf*, respectively).

SSc and *SSf* are intertemporal welfare functions whereby *SSc* is biased towards the preferences of current generations and *SSf* is biased towards future generations. All points where $Cf = Cc$ must lie on the 45° line, so that strict sustainable development means locating at X and a more general sustainable development zone is shown by the shaded area. If the welfare function is *SSc* we get the 'wrong' discount rate which can be read from the slope of the tangent at Y. The slope of TT' is in fact (1 plus) the marginal product of capital, and the slopes of *SSc* and *SSf* are the equal to (1 plus) the rate of time preference (see Pearce, 1986). Since the slope of the tangent at X is less than the slope of the tangent at Y, it follows that the discount rate that needs to be used to achieve a sustainable development consumption path is below the rate that would be used if resources are allocated according to present-oriented preferences. Economic efficiency demands that society move from a point such as A to a point like Y on the production possibility frontier. Sustainable development considerations demand that the move be from A to X where consumption is equalized (the diagram assumes population has not grown between the two periods). The relevant discount rate becomes the marginal product of capital at X, i.e. the future marginal product of capital once the equity consideration has been built into the maximization problem.

Note that Figure 5.2 reveals a major problem with sustainable development. In order to get to X rather than Y the implication is that current consumption

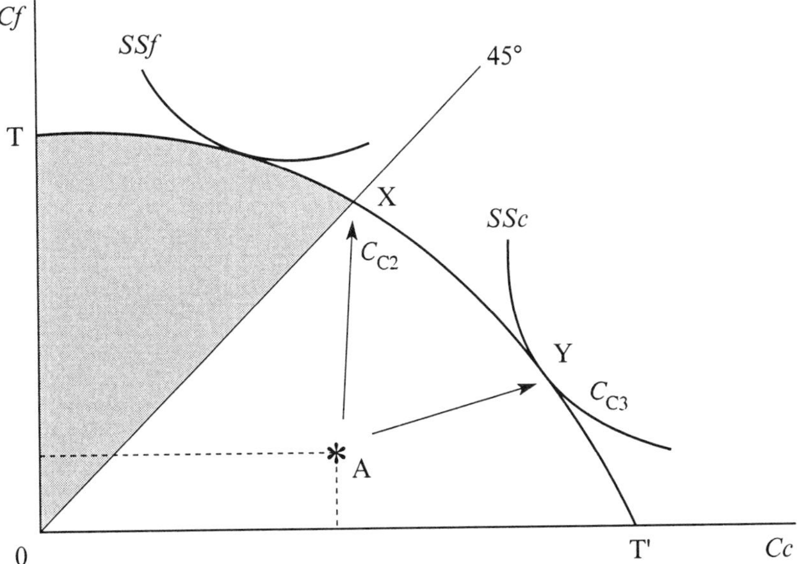

Figure 5.2 Discounting and sustainability

must be less than it otherwise would have been (C_{C2} rather than C_{C3}) – there is a forgone benefit for the current generation, though not a deterioration in well-being relative to the starting point. But, if the starting point is Y, the move to X means an actual reduction in well-being. And this seems to be what concerns critics of the idea that policies should aim for non-declining future well-being. It is that the policies required to do this will actually work to the detriment of existing generations, either in the sense of forgoing current consumption or, in the extreme, actually reducing consumption now. This will especially be true, the critics argue, if, in order to achieve sustainable development, it appears necessary to invest in low productivity assets. Environmental assets may appear to be in that category. As Nordhaus puts it:

> The shame of the current generation in America is, contrary to much popular opinion, that we have probably overinvested in seductive areas like pollution control and military R&D while under-investing in dull areas like training, equipment, and applied research. Our national investment strategy is long in plants and mortars and short in plant and mortar (Nordhaus, 1992, p.37).

But there are several problems in arguing the view that investment in the environment is 'low productivity'. First, environmental investments account for a very low proportion of GNP in most countries. Table 5.1 gives some illustrative statistics.

Table 5.1 Pollution abatement expenditure as a percentage of GDP and gross investment (1989/90)

	PAC/GDP	PAC/GrossI
France	0.9	1.2
Germany	1.6	3.5
Japan	1.3	2.9[a]
Netherlands	1.5	2.3
UK	1.4	na
USA	1.5	3.4
incl.households	1.8	na

Note: [a]1988

Source: OECD (1992, p. 9).

It is difficult to believe that current generations have distorted their investment policies significantly by spending under 2% of their GDP on allegedly low productivity environmental investments. (For comparison, military expenditures in 1987 were: France 3.7%; Germany 2.8%; Japan 1%; Netherlands 2.9%; UK 4% and the USA 5.8% (UNDP, 1992, Table 41)). Nor is there persuasive evidence that environmental expenditures are low productivity. It is arguable that the benefit–cost ratio for the Clean Air and Water Acts in the 1970s in the USA is about unity and could be above or below (Portney, 1990), but it is well known that the policies there have been inefficient in opting for high cost technology-based standards, thus deflating the benefit–cost ratio unnecessarily. In the developing world, there is ample evidence that investing in environmental improvement can generate very high returns (Anderson, 1987; Pearce and Warford, 1993). And, of course, rates of return to environmental expenditures may well appear low or negligible if the unit of account is measured as increments to the conventionally recorded GNP. That, as we now know, is a misleading indicator of human well-being.

Offsetting these observations to some extent is the potential for environmental policy to be misdirected and hence for it to cost an 'unreasonable' amount. Much depends on how the environmental policy is put in place. It is well known that environmental policy based on market-based instruments is likely to be more efficient than one based on traditional 'command and control' measures (Tietenberg, 1991; Pearce and Brisson, 1993). Moreover, the market-based approach has the potential to generate government revenues through environmental taxes or the auctioning of tradeable permits. Once these revenue effects are allowed for there is the potential for offsetting the revenues with reductions in other taxes which inhibit enterprise and effort – the so-called 'double dividend' effect (Pearce, 1991). In this way, environmental policy need not have any significant output or employment effects, and may indeed be beneficial to them (for a review of the evidence see Pearce, 1993). But the reality is that environmental policy is still cast in the old fashioned command and control mode. As an illustration, Europe's Second Sulphur Protocol, signed in 1994, seeks the long-run aim of securing 'critical loads' for sulphur deposition. A critical load is essentially a zero damage point and this could be held to be wholly consistent with that view of sustainable development that requires economies to be constrained by physical requirements such as renewable resource harvest rates less than regeneration rates and waste disposal rates less than assimilative capacity (Pearce, 1976). But simulations of the costs of achieving critical loads using add-on control technology (basically flue gas desulphurization equipment) suggest heavy costs of the order of 0.5–2.0% of GDP for most European countries (Klaassen *et al.*, 1992). This is for a single pollutant and bears comparison with the costs of all pollution abatement of around 1.5–2% of GDP quoted previously. Yet many alternatives exist for the control of sulphur emissions including energy conservation and fuel switching. Misdirected environmental policy can therefore be unnecessarily expensive.

All this suggests that the fears of sustainable development as an instrument for depressing current and immediate future standards of living are generally, but not totally, lacking in foundation. Most of the concern must be that those who oppose sustainability as a goal can readily derive support from the unnecessarily exaggerated costs of inefficient environmental policy. One problem here is that a significant number of those who advocate sustainable development are, indeed, 'anti-growth' (Daly, 1991). The suspicion that the sustainable development advocates are therefore explicitly or implicitly seeking a reduction or forgoing of current standards of living is understandable. Unfortunately, it unfairly lumps together the anti-growth and pro-growth sustainable development advocates. For, while the theoretical analysis has tended to become somewhat preoccupied with constant consumption paths, sustainable development is not only quite consistent with rising incomes and consumption but, we would argue, requires rising incomes and consumption. The modification is that, as far as possible, the growth should itself be sustainable. While that may seem not to add much to what the growth models of the 1970s produced, the fact is that the net present value criterion for deriving 'optimal' policies has been absorbed into policy thinking without the necessary caveats about their potential for non-sustainability being recognized.

But, the critics are right to draw attention to a potential trade-off between future and current well-being. The issue then becomes one of the relative importance of 'sustainability' versus the other objectives of society. Perhaps the sustainable development literature does often read as if sustainable development is some 'higher order' moral principle. It must be met first regardless of the costs it might impose in terms of sacrificing other objectives. As Nordhaus puts it:

> All of the complications arise because the sustainability criterion reifies a particular objective (the non-declining development vector) and demotes all other objectives below that one (Nordhaus, 1992, p. 11).

But it is more likely that what the literature is doing is emphasizing sustainability because it has been neglected in the past. In turn, that neglect arises from the widely shared belief that no-one needed to worry about sustainability in the past. Only now that apparent global risks exist which could reduce the well-being of future generations has the need for thinking about sustainability emerged. To get sustainability 'onto the agenda' then, it is necessary to give it high profile.

Perhaps one way of achieving a perspective is to ask what we would do if we had to choose a known non-sustainable consumption path versus a sustainable path with lower consumption. My guess is that we would probably prefer the non-sustainable path if the time horizon to 'collapse' was 500 years but not if it was 50 or even 100 years. If so, what this suggests is that sustainability is a perfectly legitimate concern if there is a real risk that it cannot be achieved over a 'reasonable' time horizon, but that it ceases to be a concern if the time horizon is distant. In the latter case, humankind's eternal optimism that 'something will turn up' dominates, along with our inability to forecast the distant future (that is, no-one believes forecasts of 'collapse' 500 years hence). If this is right, then sustainability ought not to be a 'super-moral' principle, but one more moral principle which vies for attention along with concern for the poor now, human freedom etc. Certainly, it is not at all clear why sustainability should be an irrelevant moral concern. There is nothing irrational about our moral obligations to identifiable and even non-existent future generations (Broome, 1992).

The extent to which we should worry about sustainable development thus depends on two things:

a. the seriousness of any trade-offs between sustainability and other social goals;
b. the seriousness of any risk to sustainability.

It is fair comment to say that the advocates of sustainable development have not so far sought to look at the costs and benefits of sustainability, a failing that may have been partly generated by one of the messages of the Brundtland Report (WCED, 1987), namely that we can have economic growth and environmental quality without an apparent trade-off. On the seriousness of the risk, the evidence is surely mounting that some societies are increasingly non-sustainable and that identifying that non-sustainability would not have come about but for the search for indicators of sustainability. We do not pursue the point here – see Cruz and Repetto (1992) for a case study of the Philippines, and Chapter 6 of this volume.

Another way of seeing the relevance of future capital productivity for the choice of social discount rate is provided by Maler (1990). What follows is a further simplification to capture the essential ideas.

Suppose there is man-made capital, denoted K, and a non-renewable resource, denoted R. There are two periods reflecting two generations, 0 and 1. If generation 0 decides to reduce the stock of R_0 in order to enjoy more consumption C_0, then it will reduce the consumption possibilities of generation 1 since the resource stock declines and is therefore not available to the next generation. In order to ensure that generation 1's consumption does not decline – the sustainability criterion – generation 0 must compensate generation 1 by increasing the stock of K so that generation 1 inherits more capital.

This compensation requirement can be written:

$$\mathrm{d}I_0 . F_{1K} = \mathrm{d}R_0 . F_{1R} \tag{5.1}$$

The left-hand side of (5.1) is the gain in period 1 and is equal to the change in investment in period 0 necessary to compensate period 1 multiplied by the marginal product of capital in period 1. Equation 5.1 can be rewritten:

$$\mathrm{d}I_0 = \mathrm{d}R_0 .\ F_{1R}/F_{1K} \tag{5.2}$$

The right-hand side is the loss in period 1 due to the reduction in the non-renewable resource and is equal to the change in the resource stock in 0 multiplied by the marginal product of that resource in period 1 (i.e. what it would have yielded in period 1).

The net change in consumption in period 0 is then:

$$dC_0 = dR_0 . F_{0R} - dI_0 \tag{5.3}$$

and is made up of the gain brought about by the extra extraction of the natural resource less the extra investment required to compensate period 1. Substituting (5.2) in (5.3) gives:

$$dC_0 = dR_0 . [F_{0R} - F_{1R}/F_{1K}] \tag{5.4}$$

which can be rewritten

$$dC_0 = dR_0 \ [F_{0R} - F_{1R}/\{1 + (F_{1K} - 1)\} \tag{5.5}$$

Now, $F_{1K} - 1 = r$, the marginal product of capital – 1, or the social rate of discount as given by the productivity of capital. Note that it is the marginal product of capital in period 1 that is relevant, not the productivity in period 0; and that it is the productivity of capital that gives rise to discounting in this context, not the rate of time preference.

Hence [5.5] can be written as:

$$dC_0 = dR_0 . [F_{0R} - F_{1R}/(1 + r)] \tag{5.6}$$

which is then the decision rule for generation 0. Sustainability is ensured if the change in consumption in period 0 equals the benefit from the use of the natural resource in 0 less the costs which equal the discounted value of the forgone future productivity of the resource.

Now consider the substitutability issue. If substitution possibilities between K and R are very small, then F_{1K} would be small and F_{1R} would be very big. Hence F_{1R}/F_{1K} would be large and, from (5.4), dC_0 would be negative. That is, development is not sustainable if resource use now involves resources which cannot be substituted for by K, or which have a low elasticity of substitution.

5.5 SUSTAINABLE DEVELOPMENT AND NON-RENEWABLE RESOURCES

The discussion suggests that optimal consumption paths will risk being unsustainable if, in practice, discount rates are above the marginal productivity of capital. But what does the productivity of capital mean if the capital in question is a non-renewable resource? Strictly, it is zero. Hence, given positive discount rates, an economy dependent upon non-renewable resources would appear to be inherently unsustainable. But this need not be so as long as certain behaviour is followed.

Solow (1974) showed that an economy could achieve a constant level of real consumption over time if the Hotelling efficiency rule, namely that an exhaustible resource should be depleted in such a way that the undiscounted value of its rental (or royalty) should rise over time at the rate of interest, is maintained and certain conditions were met:

a. the elasticity of substitution between natural and man-made capital is greater than unity, or
b. the elasticity of substitution is equal to unity and the share of man-made capital in GNP is greater than that of natural capital, or
c. technical change is such that it outweighs the effect of the discount rate.

Similar results are obtained in Stiglitz (1979). Adding pollution and population change to the model results in a more general and intuitively reasonable requirement that, for non-declining consumption per capita:

> (positive output effects of technical change) > (negative output effects of pollution, population growth and discounting).

Hartwick (1977, 1978a, 1978b) has shown that if the Hotelling rule is honoured and the rents from the exploitation of the non-renewable resource are reinvested in man-made capital then, under certain conditions, this policy will generate a constant stream of consumption, (which means a constant stream of per capita consumption if population does not change). Investing the rents is 'Hartwick's rule' and it suggests that it is feasible, in principle anyway, to generate a path of consumption that is consistent with sustainable development even if there is an initial reliance on a non-renewable resource.

Finally, Solow (1986) has shown that Hartwick's rule is consistent with holding the stock of capital intact and treating consumption as the interest on that stock. It is this interpretation that has given rise to the view that the condition for sustainable development is that overall capital stocks should be constant or rising – the so-called 'constant capital' rule. Clearly, this rule needs modification to allow for technological change. A falling capital stock can sustain a growing per capita consumption level if the capital becomes more productive in the future due to technological progress, which may be 'embodied' in the capital, or 'disembodied' in that it occurs independently of the rate of accumulation of the capital stock. Offsetting this is that such technological progress is needed anyway to offset rising population growth (see below). Nor is all technological change benign, as the example of chlorofluorocarbons (CFCs) serves to remind us.

But there are several restrictive conditions to achieve the sustainability results of the Hartwick–Solow models.

First, the result holds only if there is a greater than unitary elasticity of substitution between natural and man-made capital, or unitary elasticity and the share of man-made capital exceeds that of natural capital. The elasticity of substitution (σ) is unity if the production function is of the Cobb–Douglas form, i.e.:

$$Q = aK_m^{\alpha}.K_n^{\beta}.$$

Then, σ is given by $(K_m/K_n)^*/(P_n/P_m)^*$ where * refers to 'proportionate change in' the two ratios and P is the price of the relevant input. In common language, it must be comparatively easy to replace natural capital with man-made capital (and vice versa). In the Hartwick–Solow models this is achieved by working with Cobb–Douglas production functions. But other forms of the production function do not permit this result. Thus, in a Leontief world, the elasticity of substitution is zero. Constant elasticity of substitution production functions (CES functions) are not consistent with the first law of thermodynamics since the CES function permits the average product of natural capital to rise indefinitely as the ratio of man-made capital to natural capital rises.

What, in practice, do we know about substitutability between man-made and natural capital? Surprisingly little. Brown and Field (1979) report elasticities of substitution (σ) for a limited number of natural resources as shown in Table 5.2.

Table 5.2 Elasticities of substitution

σ between:	Steel	Aluminium	Copper	Paper
N and K_n	4.5	3.0	15.1	1.9
K_m and K_n	3.0	3.4	9.4	6.0
K_m and L	1.0	1.4	0.6	0.8

Notes: N = labour; K_n = natural resources, K_m = man-made capital.

Source: Brown and Field (1979, p. 241)

These estimates would appear to be comforting since those involving natural resources all indicate easy substitutability of capital for natural resources ($\sigma > 1$). The problem, however, is that concerns about intergenerational unfairness do not relate to the concerns over the scarcity of resources such as iron ore, pulpwood or non-ferrous metals. The literature on the empirical measurement of scarcity has indeed focused on these resources (see Barnett and Morse, 1963; Hall and Hall, 1974). Recent studies of real price trends tend to confirm the view that these natural resources are not 'running out' if real price can be regarded as an indicator of scarcity (Ozdemiroglu, 1993). But the issue is not metals or even energy. It is the receiving capacity of natural environments – absorptive capacities for carbon and trace chemicals – and the supply of biological diversity that gives the greatest cause for concern. Ecologists tend to see these as primary characteristics of the natural world, for which there are no real substitutes. In essence, these are the life support systems as we know them. If this is correct, then the natural resource scarcity literature does not help us in determining the sustainability or otherwise of current consumption paths. We have no idea of the elasticity of substitution.

The second problem with the growth model approaches is that sustainable development as non-declining per capita consumption generally breaks down in the Hartwick–Solow world if the rate of technical change is less than the rate of population growth. We say 'generally' because growth models tend to assume that production functions are characterized by full employment of labour. Hence increased population growth expands the labour supply and therefore expands output. In this way, population growth might actually work to the advantage of sustainability. It has also been argued that population change acts as a stimulant, not a deterrent, to technological change (Boserup, 1981). But it is difficult to confer much credibility on such a general characterization of the link between population growth and output. While there are undoubted examples of population change being associated with economic growth, it is clear that only modest growth rates of population are consistent with sustainable development. The general verdict of one major review of the subject was:

> . . . the evidence . . . points overwhelmingly to the conclusion that population growth at rapid rates common in most of the developing world slows development (World Bank, 1984).

As far as technological change being stimulated by population change, more recent research suggests that the effects of rapid population change on natural resource availability generally may well outweigh the effects on technological change in agriculture, the original subject of the Boserup thesis (Lele and Stone, 1989).

The measurement of technical change is problematic, but let us take it as 2–3% per annum for the world as a whole. The rate of world population growth is currently 1.6% per annum. This suggests that, globally, there may be no real problem even if population growth is regarded as 'all bad' for sustainable development (see also Peer, 1991). But at the regional and national level the conclusion is far less rosy. Sub-Saharan Africa has an overall rate of population growth of some 3% and certainly a lower rate of technical change. A significant number of countries have population growth rates above 3%. This raises the possibility that one indicator of sustainability could be as simple as population change itself. Solow himself states:

> At the simplest level, no path with constant consumption per person may be permanently maintainable, unless the rate of technological progress is large enough compared with the rate of population growth (Solow, 1986, p. 145).

The annexe to this chapter extends the results of the simple model to show the links between capital productivity, discounting, population and technical change.

5.6 RESOURCE CONSERVATION IN THE CONTEXT OF UNCERTAINTY

The economic growth models suggest that sustainable development is feasible provided we can be sure that there is a good degree of substitutability between natural capital and labour and/or man-made capital and population growth is not a problem. If this cannot be assured we may be able to fall back on technical change provided (a) it can outpace population change, (b) it is fairly systematically benign and (c) it can replace what otherwise appear to be 'essential inputs' to economic systems which we identify here as the primary or life support functions of ecological systems. (On the links between 'essentiality' and sustainable consumption paths see Dasgupta and Heal (1979) and Stiglitz (1979).) The difficulties for the optimists lie in the role of population change as a threat to sustainable development, and in the unknown elasticity of substitution between what I have elsewhere called 'critical capital' (Pearce *et al.*, 1989).

Uncertainty about the value of the elasticity of substitution should be one reason for a cautious approach to natural capital conservation. And that uncertainty must remain as long as we are ignorant about the workings of global and local ecosystems. Elsewhere I have suggested other reasons for biasing decision-making more in favour of natural capital (Pearce *et al.*, 1990). They include, on the production side:

a. the fundamental asymmetry of the two types of capital with respect to reversibility: once certain critical capital stocks are lost they cannot be reintroduced. That is generally not true of man-made capital; and

b. the unknown scale of effects from loss of critical natural capital, particularly where thresholds are thought to be present – witness the divergent views about the effects of global warming.

As various writers report, e.g. Dasgupta (1982), the combination of irreversibility and uncertainty should make us more cautious about depleting natural capital. And on the consumption side:

c. the apparent 'loss aversion' that arises when certain natural resources are depleted (Kahnemann and Tversky, 1979). It is significant that the resources that appear to produce this phenomenon take the form of amenity and wildlife rather than copper and aluminium. Essentially, this loss aversion suggests non-substitutability in utility functions.

What this adds up to is a 'constant natural capital' rule where there is, however, a legitimate debate about which natural capital assets are to be included. It seems clear that it should include biodiversity and the basic biogeochemical cycles that support life. It is clear that it should not embrace many of those assets that we traditionally term 'natural resources' – metals and energy for example. But in between is the hazy and uncertain area of resources that may serve critical functions (phytoplankton) and those that appear in both the critical and inessential categories (coal as an abundant resource, and as a source of global pollution). The rule has close similarities with the 'safe minimum standards' rule of Ciriacy-Wantrup (1952) which requires a cautious approach to conservation – conserve unless the social costs of conservation are very high.

ANNEXE: DERIVING OPTIMAL CONSUMPTION PATHS

The formal mathematics of optimal growth can quickly become complex. This annexe uses only calculus in a very simple model to derive the basic equations. It follows Page (1977) with modifications and extensions.

The problem is:
Maximize

$$\Sigma_{1,N}\, U(C_t)(1+s)^{-t} \qquad \text{(A5.1)}$$

subject to

$$C_t + I_t = (1+r)I_{t-1} \qquad \text{(A5.2)}$$

where U is utility, C is consumption per capita, I is investment; r is the rate of return on investment (the marginal productivity of capital), and s is the rate of time preference. Output in any one period is then a function of investment in the previous period.

Form the Lagrangean:

$$L = \Sigma\{U(C_t)(1+s)^{-t} + \lambda_t[(1+r)\mathrm{I}_{t-1} - C_t - I_t]\} \tag{A5.3}$$

to obtain the first-order conditions:

$$\delta L/\delta C_t = U'(C_t)(1+s)^{-t} - \lambda_t = 0 \tag{A5.4}$$

and

$$\delta L/\delta I_t = (1+r)\lambda_{t+1} - \lambda_t \tag{A5.5}$$

From (A5.4) we have:

$$U'(C_t) = \lambda_t(1+s)^t \tag{A5.6}$$

and hence

$$U'(C_0) = \lambda_0(1+s)^0 = \lambda_0 \tag{A5.7}$$

and from (A5.5) we have:

$$\lambda_0 = \lambda_t(1+r)^t \tag{A5.8}$$

Combining (A5.5), (A5.6) and (A5.7) we derive:

$$\frac{U'(C_t)}{U'(C_0)} = \frac{\lambda(1+s)^t}{\lambda(1+r)^t}$$

and hence:

$$U'(C_t) = U'(C_0)(1+s)^t(1+r)^{-t} \tag{A5.9}$$

We can now derive a set of conditions for differing combinations of s and r. When $r = 0$ we have non-renewable resources, i.e. the marginal product of natural capital is zero. The four cases are then:

	$s = 0$	$s > 0$
$r = 0$	[**1**] $U'(C_t) = U'(C_0)$	[**2**] $U'(C_t) = U'(C_0)(1 + s)^t$
$r > 0$	[**3**] $U'(C_t) = U'(C_0)(1 + r)^{-t}$	[**4**] $U'(C_t) = U'(C_0)(1 + r)^{-t}(1 + s)^t$ If $r = s$, case [**4**] reduces to case [**1**]

To see what results [**1**] to [**4**] imply for consumption paths, assume that marginal utility ($U'(C_t)$) is given by

$$U'(C_t) = aC_t^b$$

where b is the elasticity of the marginal utility of consumption function. Equation (A5.9) can now be written:

$$aC_t^b = aC_0^b\ (1 + r)^{-t}(1 + s)^t$$

or

$$(C_t/C_0)^b = (1 + r)^{-t}(1 + s)^t$$

If $b = -1$ this reduces to

$$C_t/C_0 = (1 + r)^t/(1 + s)^t \tag{A5.10}$$

Then result [**1**] becomes

$$(C_t/C_0) = 1 \text{ or } C_t = C_0$$

Result [**1**] produces a constant per capita consumption path, consistent with sustainable development defined as non-declining consumption per capita. However, while consumption is constant, the finite resource is fixed in size and must therefore be being depleted. Constant consumption cannot last very long unless the ratio of consumption overall to resource use is rising – the economy gets more and more efficient at using the fixed resource.

Using the same simplifications, result [**2**] becomes

$$(C_t/C_0)^{-1} = (1 + s)t$$

so that $C_t = C_0/(1 + s)^t$. Optimal consumption declines exponentially over time and this path is not consistent with sustainable development.

Result [**3**] is derived in the same way and produces:

$$C_t = C_0(1 + r)^t$$

so that consumption rises over time, which is consistent with sustainable development.

Result [**4**] involves positive discount rates and positive capital productivity where:

$$C_t/C_0 = (1 + r)^t/(1 + s)^t$$

so that, if $s = r$, we obtain result [**1**] again. If $s > r$, consumption *declines* over time, which is inconsistent with sustainable development. If $s < r$, consumption *rises* over time.

Equation (A5.10) can be further modified to allow for population change. C_t/C_0 can be written as $(1 + g)^t/(1 + n)^t$ where g is the rate of growth of aggregate consumption and n is the rate of growth of population. Hence (A5.10) becomes:

$$\frac{(1+g)^t}{(1+n)^t} = \frac{(1+r)^t}{(1+s)^t} \qquad \text{(A5.11)}$$

This can be approximated by

$$g = r - s - n$$

so that if $r > (s + n)$ optimal aggregate consumption grows and if $r < (s + n)$ optimal aggregate consumption falls.

Provided population growth itself does not stimulate increased output (see text), the effect of population growth is to make sustainable growth more difficult to achieve since capital productivity must now exceed the discount rate plus the rate of population change. A similar reasoning can be applied to technical change to show that it will make sustainable growth easier to achieve.

REFERENCES

Anderson, D. (1987), *The Economics of Afforestation: a Case Study in Africa*, New Series Occasional Paper No.1, World Bank, Washington DC.

Arrow, K.J. and Lind, R.C. (1971), Uncertainty and the evaluation of public investment decisions, *American Economic Review*, **60**, 364–78.

Barnett, H.J. and Morse, C. (1963), *Scarcity and Growth: The Economics of Natural Resource Scarcity*, Johns Hopkins Press, Baltimore.

Boserup, E. (1981), *Population and Technical Change: a Study of Long Term Trends*, Chicago University Press, Chicago.

Broome, J. (1992), *Counting the Cost of Global Warming*, The White Horse Press, Cambridge.

Brown, G.M. and Field, B. (1979), The adequacy of measures for signalling the scarcity of natural resources, in Smith, V.K. (ed.), *Scarcity and Growth Reconsidered*, Johns Hopkins University Press, Baltimore, 218–48.

Ciriacy-Wantrup, S.V. (1952), *Resources Conservation: Economics and Policies*, University of California Press, Berkeley.

Cruz, W. and Repetto, R. (1992), *The Environmental Effects of Stabilisation and Structural Adjustment Programs*, World Resources Institute, Washington DC.

Daly, H. (1991), *Steady State Economics*, Island Press, Washington DC.

Dasgupta, P. (1982), *The Control of Resources*, Basil Blackwell, Oxford.

Dasgupta, P. and Heal, G.M. (1979), *Economic Theory and Exhaustible Resources*, Cambridge University Press, Cambridge.

Georgescu-Roegen, N. (1979), Comments on the papers by Daly and Stiglitz, in Smith, V.K. (ed.), *Scarcity and Growth Reconsidered*, Johns Hopkins University Press, Baltimore, 95–105.

Hall, D. and Hall, J. (1974), Concepts and measures of natural resource scarcity with a summary of recent trends, *Journal of Environmental Economics and Management*, **11**, 363–79.

Hartwick, J.M. (1977), Intergenerational equity and the investing of rents from exhaustible resources, *American Economic Review*, **67**, 972–4.

Hartwick, J.M. (1978a), Substitution among exhaustible resources and intergenerational equity, *Review of Economic Studies*, **45**, 347–54.

Hartwick, J.M. (1978b), Investing returns from depleting renewable resource stocks and intergenerational equity, *Economics Letters*, **1**, 85–8.

Kahnemann, D. and Tversky, A. (1979), Prospect theory: an analysis of decisions under risk, *Econometrica*, **47**, 263–91.

Klaassen, G., Amann, M. and Schupp, W. (1992), *Strategies for Reducing Sulfur Dioxide Emissions in Europe Based on Critical Sulfur Deposition Values*, International Institute for Applied Systems Analysis, Laxenberg, Austria, mimeo.

Lele, U. and Stone, S. (1989), *Population Pressure, the Environment and Agricultural Intensification: Variations on the Boserup Hypothesis*, MADIA Discussion Paper 4, The World Bank, Washington DC.

Maler, K. (1990), *Sustainable Development*, Stockholm School of Economics, Stockholm, mimeo.

Marglin, S. (1963), The social rate of discount and the optimal rate of saving, *Quarterly Journal of Economics*, **77**, 95–111.

Nordhaus, W. (1992), Is growth sustainable? Reflections on the concept of sustainable economic growth, Paper for the International Economic Association, Varenna, Italy, October.

OECD (Organisation for Economic Co-operation and Development) (1992), *Pollution and Abatement and Control Expenditure Survey 1992*, OECD, Paris.

Ozdemiroglu, E. (1993), *Natural Resource Scarcity: a Study of the Price Indicator*, Centre for Social and Economic Research on the Global Environment, University College London and University of East Anglia, mimeo.

Page, T. (1977), *Conservation and Economic Efficiency: An Approach to Materials Policy*, Johns Hopkins University Press, Baltimore.

Pearce, D.W. (1976), The limits of cost–benefit analysis as a guide to environmental policy, *Kyklos*, **29**, 97–110.

Pearce, D.W. (1986), *Cost Benefit Analysis*, Macmillan, Basingstoke.

Pearce, D.W. (1991), The role of taxes in adjusting to global warming, *Economic Journal*, **101**, 935–48.

Pearce, D.W. (1993), *Economic Values and the Natural World*, Earthscan, London.

Pearce D.W., Barbier, E. and Markandya, A. (1990), *Sustainable Development: Economics and Environment in the Third World*, Edward Elgar, London and Earthscan, London.

Pearce, D.W. and Brisson, I. (1993), BATNEEC: The economics of technology-based standards, *Oxford Review of Economic Policy*, **9**(4), Winter, 24–40.

Pearce D.W., Markandya, A. and Barbier, E. (1989), *Blueprint for a Green Economy*, Earthscan, London.

Pearce, D.W. and Warford, J. (1993), *World Without End: Economics, Environment and Sustainable Development*, Oxford University Press, Oxford.

Peer, H. (1991), An inquiry into the nature and causes of the wealth of planet Earth, in F. Dietz, R. Van der Ploeg, and J. Van der Straaten, *Environmental Policy and Economy*, North Holland, Amsterdam, 61–74.

Pezzey, J. (1989), *Economic Analysis of Sustainable Growth and Sustainable Development*, Environment Department Working Paper No.15, World Bank, Washington DC.

Portney, P. (1990), Air pollution policy, in P. Portney (ed.), *Public Policies for Environmental Protection*, Resources for the Future, Washington DC, 27–96.

Sen, A.K. (1967), Isolation, assurance and the social rate of discount, *Quarterly Journal of Economics*, **81**, 112–24.

Solow, R. (1974), Intergenerational equity and exhaustible resources, *Review of Economic Studies*, Symposium, 29–45.

Solow, R. (1986), On the intergenerational allocation of natural resources, *Scandinavian Journal of Economics*, **88**(1), 141–9.

Stiglitz, G. (1979), A neo-classical analysis of the economics of natural resources, in V.K. Smith (ed.), *Scarcity and Growth Reconsidered*, Johns Hopkins University Press, Baltimore, 36–66.

Tietenberg, T. (1991), Economic instruments for environmental regulation, in D. Helm (ed.), *Economic Policy Towards the Environment*, Blackwell, Oxford, 86–110.

UNDP (United Nations Development Programme) (1992), *Human Development Report 1992*, Oxford University Press, Oxford.

WCED (World Commission on Environment and Development) (1987), *Our Common Future*, Oxford University Press, Oxford.

World Bank (1984), *World Development Report 1984*, Oxford University Press, Oxford.

6. Capital theory and the measurement of sustainable development: an indicator of 'weak' sustainability[1]

(with Giles Atkinson)

6.1 INTRODUCTION

Victor (1991) has performed a valuable service in reviewing the main theoretical issues in the debate concerning sustainable development. We share his conclusion that the concept of 'natural capital' does not adequately conceptualize the economy – environment linkage. Only a comprehensive 'ecological economics' can do that and we do not believe that a coherent body of thought has yet emerged. Nonetheless, the building blocks are there, and in the spirit of Kuhnian interpretation of scientific advance, we argue that the forces bringing them together are most likely to emerge by forcing existing paradigms to account for environmental problems. In our view, the natural capital concept is doing that very successfully.

Although Victor's paper was concerned with developing 'sustainability indicators', none was presented. In this brief paper we outline a conceptual approach to sustainable development which *does* result in a sustainability indicator. We give provisional results for 18 countries. A more detailed approach is given in Pearce and Atkinson (1992). This work is part of an ongoing research project.

6.2 A SAVINGS RULE

We begin with an intuitive rule for determining whether a country is on or off a sustainable development path. To do this we adopt a neo-classical stance and *assume* the possibility of substitution between 'natural' and 'man-made' capital (respectively, K_N and K_M) in the sense described by Victor (see Solow, 1986). We then assert that an economy is sustainable if it saves more than the *combined* depreciation on the two forms of capital. That is,

$$Z > 0 \text{ iff } S > (\delta_M + \delta_N) \quad (6.1)$$

where Z is a sustainability index, S is savings, δ_M is the value of depreciation on man-made capital, and δ_N is the value of depreciation on natural capital. Dividing through by income (Y) we have,

$$Z > 0 \text{ iff } (S/Y) > [(\delta_M/Y) + (\delta_N/Y)] \quad (6.2)$$

The resulting savings rule is then expressed in readily familiar ratio components. The United Nations System of National Accounts (SNAs) and the World Bank World Development Reports provide data for S/Y and δ_M/Y. The final component δ_N/Y, is discussed separately below. We refer to this as a *weak sustainability* rule since it allows for unconstrained elasticities of substitution between K_N and K_M. As Victor notes, this is not the position of the 'London School' which stresses more the limitations on substitutability. Victor's discussion of the London School is limited to the outline in Pearce and Turner (1990), but much more extensive expositions are to be found in Barbier *et al.* (1990) and Pearce *et al.* (1990). But here we are concerned with focusing on a weak sustainability indicator.

6.3 MEASURING δ_N

As Victor notes, the London School and others face problems of measuring natural capital. However, he greatly exaggerates the problems of monetization. Pearce and Atkinson (1992) assembled estimates of national environmental damage and resource depreciation for 18 countries. Details of sources can be found there. We emphasize that (a) valuation is complex, but no less so than for many other components of modified national income accounts; (b) the valuation we use is market price based, e.g. crop output loss due to soil erosion, thus avoiding the more controversial valuation procedures such as contingent valuation (in which, however, we believe). These estimates are shown in Table 6.1 in the form of δ_N/Y.

6.4 A WEAK SUSTAINABILITY INDICATOR

Inequality (6.2) can be used to derive a weak sustainability indicator of the form,

$$Z_1 = (S/Y) - (\delta_M/Y) - (\delta_N/Y). \quad (6.3)$$

By using percentages, Z_1 produces a deviation measure from borderline or marginal sustainability. The higher is any negative value of Z_1 the greater the 'effort' needed to get back to sustainability relative to national income.

An alternative is:

$$Z_2 = S - \delta_M - \delta_N \qquad (6.4)$$

where Z_2 is measured in absolute currency units. It may be preferred if, for example, a measure of aid flows to secure sustainability is required.

Table 6.1 Testing for sustainable development

	S/Y	– δ_M/Y	– δ_N/Y	= Z_1
Sustainable economies				
Costa Rica	26	3	8	+15
Czechoslovakia	30	10	7	+13
Germany (pre-unif.)	26	12	6	+8
Hungary	26	10	5	+11
Japan	33	14	2	+17
Netherlands	25	10	1	+14
Poland	30	11	10	+9
USA	18	12	4	+2
Marginally sustainable				
Mexico	24	12	12	0
Philippines	15	11	4	0
Unsustainable				
Burkina Faso	2	1	10	–9
Ethiopia	3	1	9	–7
Indonesia	20	5	17	–2
Madagascar	8	1	16	–9
Malawi	8	7	4	–3
Mali	–4	4	6	–14
Nigeria	15	3	17	–5
Papua New Guinea	15	9	7	–1

Note: An economy is sustainable if it saves more than the depreciation on its man-made and natural capital.

Table 6.1 reports Z_1 for 18 countries. The results are preliminary and should be treated as such. They suggest, however, that even on a weak sustainability rule many countries are unlikely to pass a sustainability test. Some of the countries failing the test are as one would expect: Madagascar, Ethiopia, Mali for example. Indeed Mali fails to satisfy a condition of a positive savings ratio. Some are surprises. Mexico is only marginally sustainable despite a relatively high savings ratio. For the USA, the values shown in Table 6.1 are for the year 1981. This emphasizes the essentially static nature of Z_1 at the present stage. It should be noted that the US savings ratio has fallen from the level indicated here during the remainder of the 1980s; hence if the values of δ_M and δ_N remained constant over these periods, then other things being equal, Z_1 would become negative indicating non-sustainability. This is in contrast to the other developed countries for which results are shown: Germany, Netherlands and Japan.

6.5 CONCLUSION

Victor (1991) sets out a challenge to ecological economists to develop sustainability indicators (SIs). We have shown how the challenge might be taken up on the basis of a sustainability savings rule, the collation of existing resource depreciation data on which the appropriate measurement of Z_1 is ultimately dependent. The sustainability requirement we have used is a weak one. Underlying this is an assumption that environmental degradation is consistent with sustainability provided certain rules are followed (for an example see Hartwick, 1990). Much of the ecological literature denies the existence in reality of the substitution possibilities required to underpin such rules (Pearce and Atkinson (1992) provides a fuller discussion of these objections). A strong sustainability indicator would evolve identifying and measuring 'critical' natural capital such that any positive depreciation would be a sign of non-sustainability. With Victor, we believe that natural capital measurement may not be able to capture all the economic functions of ecological systems. But we argue strongly that efforts to monetize the values of those functions advances the development of an ecologically based economics.

NOTE

1. Reprinted from *Ecological Economics*, **8**(2), 103–8.

REFERENCES

Barbier, E.B., Markandya, A. and Pearce, D.W. (1990), Environmental sustainability and cost–benefit analysis, Environmental Planning, **22**, 1259–66.

Hartwick, J.M. (1990), Natural resources, national accounts, and economic depreciation, *Journal of Public Economics*, **43**, 291–304.

Pearce, D.W. and Atkinson, G.D. (1992), *Are National Economies Sustainable? Measuring Sustainable Development*, Centre for Social and Economic Research in the Global Environment (CSERGE), Working Paper 92–11, University College, London.

Pearce, D.W., Barbier, E.B. and Markandya, A. (1990), *Sustainable development*, Earthscan, London.

Pearce, D.W. and Turner, R.K. (1990), *Economics of Natural Resources and the Environment*, Harvester Wheatsheaf, London.

Solow, R.M. (1986) On the intergenerational allocation of resources, *Scandinavian Journal of Economics*, **88**, 141–9.

Victor, P.A. (1991), Indicators of sustainable development: some lessons from capital theory, *Ecological Economics*, **4**, 191–213.

7. Measuring sustainable development: progress on indicators[1]

(with Kirk Hamilton and Giles Atkinson)

7.1 AIM OF THE CHAPTER

In this chapter we briefly survey the operational meanings attached to the concepts of sustainable development and environmental sustainability. We then contrast two apparently consistent characterizations of sustainability. The first, 'strong sustainability' (SS) derives more of its foundations from ecological science than does the second, 'weak sustainability' (WS). Nonetheless, both SS and WS are informed by ecology as we show. The fundamental distinctions between SS and WS are: (a) that the former denies to a greater or lesser extent, substitutability between natural assets and other assets – human and manufactured assets; and (b) SS stresses 'discontinuity' and 'non-smoothness' in ecological systems and hence in the economic damages to which ecological impairment gives rise. (The conventional environmental economics literature addresses this issue in terms of non-convexities. See Baumol and Oates (1988) and Burrows (1979).) In effect, SS has at its starting point ecological imperatives and this dictates the subsequent form of economic analysis. By contrast, WS begins with standard assumptions in economics and this in turn shapes the form in which ecological and environmental concerns are evaluated.

The choice between SS and WS, we argue, has to do with issues of fact about the world in which we live. Since the facts themselves are uncertain, choosing between SS and WS will invariably depend on attitudes to behaviour under uncertainty. In terms of indicators of sustainability, different indicators are relevant to the two paradigms as illustrated in Figure 7.1. The SS paradigm dictates indicators that focus primarily on ecological assets, functions and processes. In turn, such indicators tend to stress 'limits' to the deterioration of ecological assets. In this respect, the SS paradigm has common elements with the earlier *Limits to Growth* literature; see Meadows *et al.* (1972). Indicators in this category include:

a. measures of resilience, most of which have yet to be developed. One suggestion involves indicators of biological diversity, since resilience is assumed to be a function of diversity (Arrow *et al.*, 1995; Common and Perrings, 1992). For agriculture-dependent systems, an indicator of yield variability may also be relevant – see below;

b. measures of carrying capacity, e.g. incorporating supply/ demand ratios for resources;
c. 'distance to goal' approaches in which deviations of ambient concentrations from sustainability 'targets' are aggregated to derive an overall performance indicator (Hammond *et al.*, 1995). The green national accounting counterpart of this is offered by Hueting *et al.* (1992) and is couched in terms of the costs of reaching these goals.

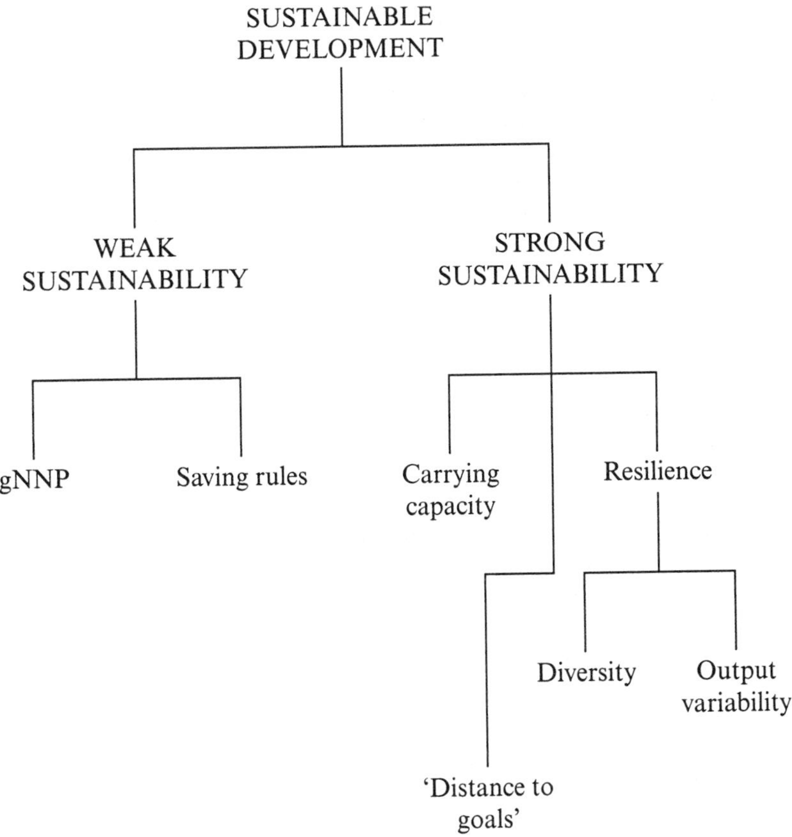

Figure 7.1 Sustainability paradigms

The WS paradigm, on the other hand, emphasizes the substitutability of manufactured and natural assets and hence focuses on aggregate measures such as:

a. 'green' national income;
b. genuine savings.

In the main, these indicators are intended to measure environmental performance at the national level, but it is as well to note in passing that the distinction between WS and SS also affects microeconomic indicators, in particular, it affects cost–benefit measures. See Barbier *et al.* (1990) and von Amsberg (1992).

7.2 SUSTAINABILITY MODELS

Economists have pursued a rigorous, though by no means complete, interpretation of sustainable development (SD). SD is defined as some indicator of human well-being which does not decline over time (Pearce *et al.*, 1989; Pezzey, 1989). The indicator of well-being is not discussed here but could be some suitably modified measure of per capita real national income, making due allowance for existing unmeasured components such as environmental services (see Hamilton, 1994). At this point there is no significant divergence between WS and SS. Both paradigms broadly accept this definition of SD. The approaches are differentiated with regard to the conditions required to satisfy the achievement of SD. Taking the capital base as the means whereby future well-being will be sustained, this implies some form of conservation or maintenance of capital as a condition for SD. This 'constant capital' concept underlies the contributions of Solow (1986) and Maler (1991).

The basic debate about sustainability models relates to the conditions set for the capital stock. In strong sustainability, SD is achieved by conserving certain components of the natural capital stock, as well as setting a constraint of non-decline in the overall stock of capital. In weak sustainability the operative constraint is the overall stock of capital since all forms of capital are assumed to be substitutable. Although natural capital is a form of wealth whose services contribute to well-being it has no 'special role' as such in this scheme. In terms of indicators, then, SS will tend towards environmentally focused measures, supplemented by a weak sustainability measure, while WS will focus on assets generally, with no special highlighted measure for natural capital. Expressed this way, the *information* required for SS and WS indicators is the same: both have to have measures of natural capital to be operative, and both have to measure other capital assets as well. Non-substitutability is alleged to give rise to aggregation problems (see Faucheux *et al.*, 1994): natural capital has to be measured separately to human and manufactured and in non-comparable terms. But the 'constant capital' rule can be preserved even in this context since SS requires that each index be non-declining (assuming also that natural capital can be aggregated). The 'capital aggregation' problem if it exists at all, is not therefore fatal for sustainability indicators.

For exhaustible resources the optimal growth path is not sustainable if resources are essential for production and the pure rate of time preference is positive; if the elasticity of substitution between produced assets and natural resources is less than 1 then the constant utility path is infeasible (see Dasgupta and Heal (1979, Chapter 10) or Hamilton (1995a).) The degree of substitutability is therefore critical in determining whether WS is possible with exhaustible resources. If the elasticity of substitution is greater than or equal to 1 then 'savings rules' that investment in produced assets should offset the value of resource depletion, provide a test of sustainability.

Strong sustainability is not, strictly speaking, about elasticities of substitution that are equal to 0, since this would imply that capital and resources must be used together in fixed proportions. The essential idea underlying SS is that a given amount of a resource must be preserved intact, in order that it may continue to provide critical services. This could be conceived in two ways: (i) some amount of the resource is to be conserved, in which case there is only the residual that can be exploited; or (ii) the resource does not need to be kept intact, but if the stock size falls below a certain critical level then catastrophic consequences result.

For case (i) consider the tropical rainforest. If preserving some quantity of the rainforest is considered to be critical for the long-term well-being of humanity, the effect of this preservation is to reduce the quantity of forest that can be considered to be an economic resource. Other things being equal, therefore, the effect of the strong sustainability policy will be to reduce the quantity of harvest that can be carried out sustainably from the remaining stock. This will have the effect, under standard assumptions about the production function, of increasing the price of the resource – a different mix of natural resource and produced capital inputs into production will therefore ensue. However the savings rule, as applied to the non-conserved stock, will still be the determinant of sustainability, because the savings rule is concerned with the *change* in the real value of stocks rather than with the *absolute size* of the stocks.

The key indicators for this living-resource economy operating under a SS regime will be twofold: are stocks of critical natural assets declining? and are genuine savings rates persistently negative? A positive answer to either of these questions would be an indication of unsustainability.

Case (ii) might be an upland forest, where exploitation beyond a certain point leads to catastrophic losses, as a result of soil erosion for instance. Here an optimal resource tax that is a function of both the size of the remaining stock and the level of harvest can be designed to ensure that the long run steady state stock is greater or equal to the critical stock size. Again the savings rule determines sustainability.

The effect of these sorts of quantitative restrictions is to reduce the present value of consumption that would be attained if the restrictions did not exist. This is only an apparent decline in welfare, however, because of the significant welfare losses that would result if the strong sustainability regime is not followed. The key point is that savings rules provide essential indicators of sustainability whether SS or WS is the development paradigm.

7.3 THE SUSTAINABILITY PARADIGM AND ITS MEASUREMENT

In the WS world there is nothing special about the environment as such. However, this does not permit overly rapid depletion of non-renewable resources or imply that environmental degradation does not matter. In the latter case these actions involve a loss in future well-being unless accompanied by adequate compensation in the form of investments in alternative forms of wealth. In the case of say air pollution, compensation must be equivalent to the social costs of emissions (see below). The SS paradigm requires arguments to the effect that environmental assets are special, i.e. do not have practical substitutes. Pearce *et al.* (1990) present candidate arguments:

a. Irreversibility: manufactured capital can be created, destroyed and created again in ways in which are not true of natural assets (especially living species). While the creation of a manufactured or new technology may be deemed to be an adequate compensation to future generations for an irreversible transformation of a natural asset, this assumes that we have perfect knowledge of future relative prices (Hamilton, 1995b). If future generations value nature much more highly then such compensations will be either unfeasible or inadequate. Some human capital may also be characterized by irreversibility attributes – e.g. indigenous knowledge embodied in social custom.
b. Uncertainty: there is extensive uncertainty about the workings of ecological systems and hence about the consequences of impairing the functionings of those systems.
c. Scale: the existence of thresholds and discontinuities may well result in large-scale damage once thresholds are exceeded.

The combination of (a) to (c) would dictate a 'precautionary approach' to the degradation of natural capital (Dasgupta, 1982) and hence something akin to a SS rule.

If these differing notions of sustainability are to have operational consequences, then measures of progress towards sustainable development are required. As Hammond *et al.* (1995) note, indicators can ideally both quantify and simplify complex phenomena for decision-makers. Below we therefore explore the types of indicator that have been proposed for measuring weak and strong sustainability.

7.4 INDICATORS OF WEAK SUSTAINABILITY

A good illustration of the theory of indicators based on weak sustainability is provided by the literature on 'green' national accounts (see, for instance, Hartwick, 1993; Maler, 1991; and Hamilton, 1994). This work arises from a concern that economic indicators such as gross national product (GNP) do not reflect the depletion and degradation of the environment and so may lead to incorrect development decisions, in much the same way that cost–benefit analyses that do not include the values people place on the environment may yield poor investment decisions. Some basic results from this theoretical work are set out below.

If we assume a simple economy in which a single composite good is produced by production function $F(K,L,R)$, and that this good can either be consumed or invested, then we wish to maximize the present value of utility for an aggregate utility function $U(C,E)$, where C represents consumption and E the level of services provided by the environment. K and L are (manufactured) capital and labour, respectively, and R is the harvest of resource from a stock S that grows by an amount $g(S)$. Environmental services are negatively related to the level of a stock X of pollution in the environment, which dissipates naturally by an amount $d(X)$ and is augmented by pollution emissions related to the level of production, $e(F)$.

From this maximization problem we obtain the following expressions for the basic national accounting aggregates (see Hamilton, 1995c, for details):

$$GNP = F(K,L,R) = C + I$$
$$NNP = C + I - r(R - g) - p(e - d)$$

Here I is investment, r is the net resource rental rate and p is the marginal social cost of pollution emissions. If the notion of 'consumption' is extended to include the value of environmental services E, then a broader measure of economic welfare (MEW) is:

$$MEW = C + I - r(R - g) - p(e - d) + vE$$

where v is the price consumers would be willing to pay for a unit of environmental service. As expected, v can be expressed as the ratio of the marginal utilities of consumption and environmental services,

$$v = \frac{U_{\mathrm{E}}}{U_{\mathrm{C}}}$$

While these green measures of net national product are important, in the sense that they are truer measures of income, their direct policy implications are limited. As argued in Hamilton (1994), the shifts in the level of income entailed by 'greener' measures of income do not, of themselves, suggest any policy consequences, while the policy signals from the growth rates of greener income, as compared with growth rates in traditional income measures, are likely to be equivocal. Pearce and Atkinson (1993) concentrate instead on adjusted savings measures, while Hamilton (1994) develops the concept of genuine savings. In the context of the green accounting aggregates just presented, we may define this as:

$$S_{\mathrm{g}} = I - r(R - g) - p(e - d)$$

That is, genuine saving is a measure of net saving which accounts for the depletion of natural resources and the accumulation of pollutants. There are two important ways in which ecological processes enter this measure. First, growth of living resources is an addition to both NNP and genuine savings, so that management of natural resources that increases their total growth can be considered to be a form of wealth creation. Second, the natural dissipation of pollution stocks is also wealth-creating, in the sense that there is a decreasing liability in the national balance sheet in the form of pollution stocks.

The models of green national accounting presented above ignore geography for the sake of simplicity, but the question of transboundary pollution is clearly important in the case of air pollution. Without developing extensions to the formal model, the following line of argument is offered. First, regarding adjustments to income, an extension of the *polluter pays principle* to the domain of national accounting seems appropriate. This means that the estimates of the unit marginal social costs of pollution in a given country should include all costs, including those in other nations. These unit marginal costs should then be multiplied by the total level of emissions in that country. The argument for this treatment of transboundary pollution in the case of savings rules is, if anything, even stronger. Some portion of a given country's total savings should, at least notionally, be set aside in order to compensate the recipients of the pollution emitted and transferred across international boundaries (Hamilton and Atkinson, 1995). Opposite adjustments to income and saving have to be made when resources are traded internationally (Asheim, 1986, 1994; Hartwick, 1994), i.e. upward adjustments for resource exporters (and corresponding downward adjustments in the case of resource importers). This assertion rests upon the validity of a number of assumptions. In particular, if a country is a price-taker *vis-à-vis* international markets then the standard Hotelling–Solow rule should apply.

Genuine saving measures have proven to be important empirically, as evidenced by Figure 7.2 for sub-Saharan Africa. The topmost curves on this figure represent standard national accounting identities: gross investment less the value of net foreign borrowing equals gross saving; and deducting the value of depreciation of produced assets from gross saving yields net saving. Genuine saving then is the result of deducting the value of resource depletion and the value of pollution emissions (limited to carbon dioxide in Figure 7.2) from net saving.

The welfare significance of genuine saving is that persistent negative genuine savings rates must lead to non-sustainability, in the sense that the level of welfare of the country will eventually decline (Pezzey, 1994; Hamilton and Atkinson, 1995). Figure 7.2, which aggregates many of the countries of sub-

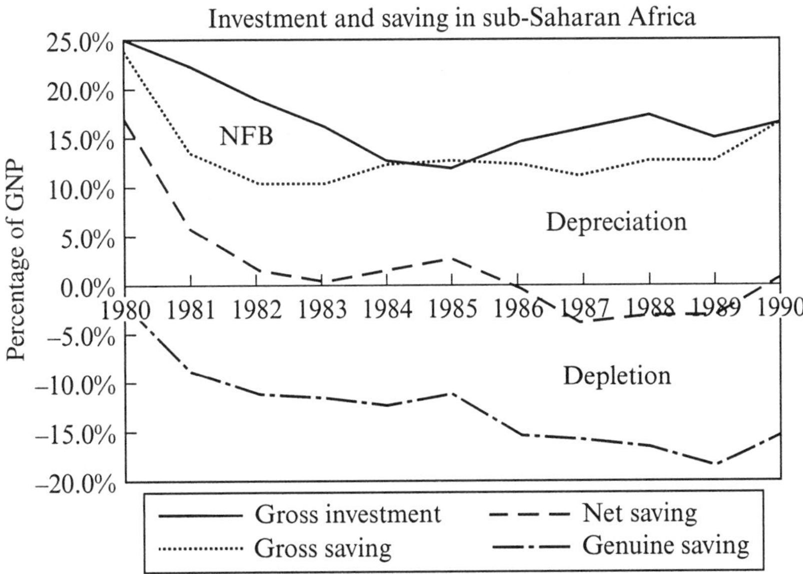

Note: NFB – net foreign borrowing

Figure 7.2 Genuine savings

Saharan Africa, therefore says that not only was Africa's economic performance poor over the 1980s, as suggested by standard economic indicators, but that the situation with regard to future well-being is even worse. Sub-Saharan Africa has been dissipating its wealth, both human-made and natural, at a significant rate over this decade.

What are the policy implications of low and even negative genuine savings? It could be argued that for countries with low income and, *ex hypothesi*, high discount rates, 'mining' natural resources is a perfectly rational response to economic circumstances – this is certainly plausible for countries where the preponderance of the economy consists of subsistence activities. Genuine saving calculations simply emphasize in quantitative form what is already known in qualitative form. The fact remains, however, that many policy-makers are unaware of resource 'mining' in this context. As it happens, the policy implications of genuine savings measures are richer than this.

With regard to natural resources policy, there is the question of whether royalties are being captured by governments, so that there is no incentive for over-exploitation, and whether resource access and tenure regimes, particularly with regard to living resources, do not also encourage excessive harvest rates. There is the related issue of the investment of resource rents, whether in infrastructure or education, a key component of sustainable development policy. And there are the broader issues of macro- and microeconomic policy that play important roles in establishing savings levels.

Simply stating that resource rents should be invested and not consumed, or that investment must offset broader environmental degradation costs, is not sufficient as a policy prescription, however. Equally important is the *quality* of investment. While each unit of savings should be put to its most productive use in principle, in practice many investments, especially in developing countries, have been wasteful. And while public investments have traditionally been in physical infrastructure, it is important to recognize that investment in human capital is one of the surest ways to increase future well-being (see, for instance, World Bank 1995, Chapter 8).

7.5 INDICATORS OF STRONG SUSTAINABILITY

More stringent requirements based on stronger conditions for achieving sustainability will result in a different set of indicators. Indicators of strong sustainability have been suggested by ecological economists. They represent a loosely assembled body of ideas, and in common with other dissenting schools, the most notable unifying theme is a mistrust of neo-classical (environmental) economics, in particular the perceived inability of mainstream economists to integrate ecological imperatives into their analysis. However, some progress is being made in defining ecological economics (see, for example, Perrings and Turner, 1995). Furthermore, Arrow *et al.* (1995) identify two core elements of research in ecological economics: carrying capacity and resilience.

Carrying Capacity

The notion of a carrying capacity is drawn from biology. It states that a given area can only support a given population of a particular species and at this upper limit – the carrying capacity – population will have reached its maximum sustainable level. In order to apply this concept of a saturation point to human populations we have to consider not only the level of population, but also the level of economic activity. Furthermore, the composition of economic output can vary significantly adding a further complication. Inevitably, in developing an indicator a number of brave assumptions have to be made. Some attention has been given to estimates of global carrying capacity especially where these calculations are well below existing population levels or wildly in excess of predicted stationary levels (see, respectively: Ehrlich, 1992; and Simon and Kahn, 1984).

More usually within ecological economics, carrying capacity is defined in terms of exceeding limits – to be set by ecological criteria. In moving to actual indicators of carrying capacity we require a more detailed specification of these ecological limits. Usually, these consist of 'sustainability constraints' with respect to commercial or environmental resources: for example, pollution should not exceed the assimilative capacity of the environment; harvest of renewable resource should not be greater than natural growth. (It is more difficult to think of an appropriate constraint governing the use of non-renewable resources on these terms where growth is by definition zero.) Underlying these constraints is the goal to maintain the stock of *each* resource intact. If the definition of sustainability is non-declining human well-being, then what is argued is that human well-being is decreased unless *all* specified ecological constraints are observed.

Carrying capacity indicators tend to be extremely pessimistic regarding judgements about technology: i.e. the ability of people to expand the carrying capacity of the earth (Cohen, 1995). For example, Ehrlich (1992) speculates that, at industrialized levels of economic activity per capita, the level of global population that would not exceed carrying capacity thresholds is two billion, about one-third of the *prevailing* population. Although the genuine savings rule also assumes constant technology the framework underlying the savings principle does at least allow for substitution between assets. In the carrying capacity schema each asset is to be maintained intact and presumably the scale of economic activity or population is set by whichever constraint is reached first, as suggested by Rees and Wackenagel (1992). This is known as Liebig's Law and implies that,

$$CC = \min CC_i$$

In effect, those who favour carrying capacity indicators are arguing that there is zero substitutability between assets. The difficulties in resolving this argument are well known. Empirically speaking, little is known about what might constitute *critical natural capital*: i.e. those environmental assets for which few or no substitutes exist (Pearce *et al.*, 1994). While lack of substitutability may be an appropriate characterization of some classes of environmental assets, it is asking too much to argue that this is true of all such assets. Neither is it the case that limiting factors will remain the same over time (Cohen, 1995).

A variant of this empirical approach to carrying capacity is to link population levels to very simple indicators of resource use. The commonly cited examples are land use for food production, fuelwood production and water use.

Table 7.1 Fuelwood availability and sustainable populations in Africa

Country	Sustainable population in 1990 (actual population in parentheses) (millions)	Sustainable population in 2000 (predicted population in parentheses) (millions)
Algeria	4 (25)	4 (31)
Burkina Faso	4 (9)	3 (12)
Chad	4 (6)	4 (7)
Ethiopia	37 (51)	36 (67)
Gambia	> 1 (1)	> 1 (1)
Kenya	14 (24)	14 (31)
Madagascar	16 (12)	15 (16)
Malawi	2 (9)	2 (11)
Mali	8 (9)	7 (12)
Morocco	9 (25)	9 (30)
Nigeria	138 (96)	132 (128)
Senegal	6 (7)	6 (10)
Sudan	21 (25)	21 (33)
Tanzania	16 (25)	15 (33)
Tunisia	> 1 (8)	> 1 (10)
Uganda	2 (16)	2 (22)
Zimbabwe	10 (10)	9 (12)

Sources: Adapted from Atkinson (1993); Population data: World Bank (1994).

Table 7.1 provides an illustration of estimates of carrying capacity populations with respect to fuelwood availability in Africa. These estimates are based on FAO data on fuelwood demand (production) and fuelwood supply (regeneration). Obviously, if the ratio of demand to supply is greater than unity, then current rates of harvest must be unsustainable. The carrying capacity estimate simply links this information to data on population levels in 1990 and projected levels in 2000. The estimates also take in account the ecological concern that persistent rates of overharvest will *reduce* the sustainable yield and therefore population, over time. Hence, Nigeria's estimated sustainable population is 138 million in 1990. Yet by the end of the century this is predicted to fall to about 132 million. Owing to population growth over that period the estimate predicts that Nigeria's population may well be unsustainable by 2000, at least in terms of a fuelwood constraint. It is worth noting that Nigeria has oil resources but that pressure on fuelwood resources persists owing to the lack of suitable refineries (Armitage and Schramm, 1989). All of the countries described in Table 7.1 are either unsustainable in 1990 or are predicted to be unsustainable by the year 2000. Some of these are not surprising, being countries located in typically arid North Africa with few forest resources. Pressure on forest resources in other countries such as Malawi has been well documented elsewhere (see, for example, Pearce and Warford, 1993).

Arrow *et al.* (1995) have argued that carrying capacities are not fixed or static in the way that ecological economics has in the main considered them. Thus, the maximum sustainable population (MSP) is given by:

$$MSP = \frac{Annual\ Resource\ Yield}{Minimum\ per\ Capita\ Requirement}$$

MSP can be raised by mining the stock where the resource is renewable but this is clearly unsustainable. On the other hand, 'yields' can be increased by technological change in the case of renewable resources, and depletion profiles can be extended by technology in the case of non-renewable resources. Substitutes may also be found (e.g. kerosene or biomass charcoal for fuelwood). In addition, interactions between various carrying capacity constraints are seldom considered (Cohen, 1995). More importantly, carrying capacity calculations have limited relevance when trade is possible since the scarce resource can be imported in exchange for another asset in which the exporting nation has a comparative advantage. Neither do these indicators address the measurement of progress in protecting critical natural assets. At best they might be thought of as simple poverty measures that introduce the notion of sustainable use of resources.

It is therefore difficult to pin down the concept to any single meaningful indicator. Instead, Arrow *et al.* (1995) propose that a more general indicator be employed such as that set out by Vitousek *et al.* (1986). This describes pressures in terms of how much Net Primary Productivity (NPP) human beings currently appropriate as an indicator of human appropriation of ecosystems under a variety of scenarios. Note that this indicator is not couched in terms of a population carrying capacity, although implicit judgements concerning such a limit may need to be inferred if we are to suggest what levels of appropriation are to be considered excessive.

Resilience

Many ecological economists have come to interpret sustainability as resilience along the lines introduced by Charles Holling (Holling 1973, p. 12). Resilience determines the persistence of relationships within a system and is a measure of the ability of these systems to absorb changes and still persist. In turn the *degree of resilience* of the system determines whether ecological productivity (e.g. ecosystem functioning) is largely unaffected, decreased either temporarily or permanently or, in the extreme, collapses altogether, as a result of stress or shock (Conway and Barbier, 1990). *Stresses* are small and predictable changes such as increasing erosion and salinity. However, while small these forces can have large cumulative effects. *Shocks* on the other hand are relatively large, temporary and unpredictable such as, for example, a new crop pest or a rare drought. For a discussion of these topics see Conway and Barbier (1990). A system that is unable to respond is, in some sense, unsustainable if the stresses and shocks are themselves not capable of control, or, for some reason, are unlikely to be controlled. In turn, capability for response to stress and shocks is usually, but not necessarily, thought to be correlated with diversity of capital, either in the sense of a wide portfolio of natural and produced assets, or a wide portfolio of natural biological assets (Holling, 1973; Conway 1985, 1992; Common and Perrings, 1992).

A measure of the degree of resilience could be interpreted as an indicator of the *degree of sustainability* of the system. However, it is less clear what this means for the sustainability of human development. In the green national accounting literature this link is provided by models that connect changes in human welfare to resource depletion and environmental degradation. These result in alternative measures to GDP (e.g. measures of economic welfare) and lead directly to a notion of genuine saving. Hence, green accounting tells us how resource and environmental issues are linked to sustainable human development. The task for the resilience school is to provide a similar link between changes in resilience and sustainability in this way. Although Common and Perrings (1992) have offered one such possible interpretation based on measures of biodiversity, this preliminary work is not yet suggestive of a set of feasible indicators, although standard measures of species diversity and keystone species are clearly candidates as we discuss below.

It is clear that resilience is not something that can be observed directly and so the search for indicators leads in the direction of measuring *inputs* that are thought to contribute to resilience, or the *outputs* that are believed to be affected by changes in resilience. Examples of the former are indicators of biodiversity. If resilience is positively related to biodiversity – as Common and Perrings (1992) and Arrow *et al.* (1995) tentatively suggest – then indices of diversity might be a useful input-based indicator of resilience in ecosystems. The ecology literature offers many such measures (Krebs, 1985) and a useful summary of information about species and habitat diversity is provided in World Conservation Monitoring Centre (1992).

But problems remain. The first of these, as noted above, is that it is not at all obvious how given measures of diversity-resilience maps into sustainability. A related problem is the absence of any clear baseline to assess the degree of sustainability using these indicators. The genuine savings approach outlined in Section 7.4 has a natural measure of the degree of sustainability, since zero genuine saving defines the borderline between sustainability and non-sustainability. Zero or 'low' diversity would appear to qualify for low sustainability on a diversity measure, but there is no obvious scaling involved. Unless our criterion is to be non-declining diversity, when does sustainability become threatened on a diversity index?

Even if non-declining diversity (say, from existing levels) is to be our benchmark there is a second problem of an empirical nature in that where available, data are often constrained to a single point in time, whereas the relevant measure for sustainability purposes is the change in diversity, not the amount of diversity.

Finally, meaningful interpretations of the data if they did exist are often unclear. For example, the appropriate spatial scale of the index is not simple to define. Finally, indicators based on ecological economic resilience need significant effort before they are suitable for indicating SS. However, measures of resilience have more appeal than the carrying capacity approach in that indicators of biodiversity are stressed as central to the measurement problem and many would now agree that diversity is a critical natural asset (see Schulze and Mooney, 1993). However, as we have seen, practical indicators of biodiversity fall short of what we require to measure sustainability. For these reasons, we argue that resilience, while attractive from an ecological economics standpoint, has, at the moment, little to offer for the development of indicators.

NOTE

1. Reprinted from *Environment and Development Economics*, 1996, **1**: 85–102. An earlier version was presented at the Resource Policy Consortium Symposium, Washington D.C., June, 1995.

REFERENCES

von Amsberg, R. (1992), *Sustainability and Project Evaluation: Case Studies*, University of British Colombia, mimeo.

Armitage, J. and Schramm, G. (1989), Managing the supply and demand for fuelwood in Africa', in G. Schramm, and J.J. Warford, *Environmental Management and Economic Development*, World Bank, Washington DC.

Arrow, K., Bolin, B., Costanza, R., Dasgupta, P., Folke, C., Holling, C.S., Jansson, B.-O., Levin, S., Mäler, K.-G., Perrings, C. and Pimentel, D. (1995), Economic growth, carrying capacity and the environment, *Science*, **268**, 520–21.

Asheim, G.B. (1994), The concept of net national product in an open economy, paper presented to the International Symposium on 'Models of Sustainable Development. Exclusive or Complementary Approaches of Sustainability?', Universite Pantheon-Sorbonne, Paris, March 1994.

Asheim, G.B. (1986), Hartwick's Rule in open economies, *Canadian Journal of Economics*, **86**, 395–402.

Atkinson, G. (1993), *Carrying Capacity as a Measure of Sustainability*, Centre for Social and Economic Research on the Global Environmental (CSERGE), University College London and University of East Anglia, mimeo.

Barbier, E., Markandya, A. and Pearce, D.W. (1990), Environmental sustainability and cost–benefit analysis', *Environment and Planning A*, **22**, 1259–66.

Baumol, W. and Oates, W. (1988), *The Theory of Environmental Policy*, second edition, Cambridge University Press, Cambridge.

Burrows, P. (1979), *The Economic Theory of Pollution Control*, Martin Robertson, Oxford.

Cohen, J.E. (1995), Population growth and Earth's human carrying capacity, *Science*, **269**, 341–8.

Common, M. and Perrings, C. (1992), Towards an ecological economics of sustainability, *Ecological Economics*, **6**(1), 7–34.

Conway, G. (1985), Agroecosystem analysis, *Agricultural Administration*, **20**, 31–55.

Conway, G. (1992), Sustainability in agricultural development: trade-offs with productivity, stability and equitability, *Journal for Farming Systems Research and Extension*, **4**, 37–48.

Conway, G. and Barbier, E. (1990), *After the Green Revolution: Sustainable Agriculture for Development*, Earthscan, London.

Dasgupta, P. (1982), *Control of Resources*, Basil Blackwell, Oxford.

Dasgupta, P. and Heal, G. (1979), *Economic Theory and Exhaustible Resources*, Cambridge University Press, Cambridge.

Ehrlich, P. (1992), Ecological economics and the carrying capacity of Earth, paper presented at the 2nd Meeting of the International Society for Ecological Economics (ISEE), Stockholm, 3–6 August 1992.

Faucheux, S., Froger, G. and O'Connor, J. (1994), The costs of achieving sustainability: the differences between 'Environmentally Corrected National Accounts' and 'Sustainable Income' as information for sustainability policy, Cahier de C3E, Paris.

Hamilton, K. (1994), Green adjustments to GDP, *Resources Policy*, **20**, 155–68.

Hamilton, K. (1995a), Sustainable development, the Hartwick Rule and optimal growth, *Environmental and Resource Economics*, **5**, 393–411.

Hamilton, K. (1995b), *Measuring Progress Towards Sustainable Development*, Issue paper for OECD Group on Economic and Environmental Policy Integration, Paris.

Hamilton, K. (1995c), *National Wealth and Sustainable National Income*, CSERGE, University College London and University of East Anglia, mimeo.

Hamilton, K., and Atkinson, G. (1995), Valuing air pollution in the national accounts, presented to the London Group on National Accounts and the Environment, Washington DC, March 1995.

Hammond, A., Adriaanse, A., Rodenburg, E., Bryant, D. and Woodward, R. (1995) *Environmental Indicators*, World Resources Institute, Washington DC.

Hartwick, J.M. (1994), Sustainability and constant consumption paths in open economies with exhaustible resources, paper prepared for the AERE Conference, Boulder, Colorado, 5 June 1994.

Hartwick, J.M. (1993), Notes on economic depreciation of natural resource stocks and national accounting, in A. Franz and C. Stahmer (eds.), *Approaches to Environmental Accounting*, Physica-Verlag: Heidelberg.

Holling, C.S. (1973), Resilience and stability of ecological systems, *Annual Review of Ecological Systems*, **4**, 1–24.

Hueting, R., Bosch, P. and de Boer, B. (1992), Methodology for the calculation of sustainable national income, *Statistical Essays*, **M44**, Central Bureau of Statistics, Voorburg.

Krebs, C.J. (1985), *Ecology*, third edition, Harper Collins, New York.

Maler, K.-G. (1991), National accounts and environmental resources, *Environmental and Resource Economics*, **1**, 1–15.

Meadows, D.H., Meadows, D.L., Behrens, R. and Randers, A. (1972), *Limits to Growth*, Universe Books, New York.

Pearce, D.W. and Atkinson, G. (1993), Capital theory and the measurement of sustainable development: an indicator of weak sustainability, *Ecological Economics*, **8**, 103–8.

Pearce, D.W., Atkinson, G. and Dubourg, W.R. (1994), The economics of sustainable development, *Annual Review of Energy and Environment*, **19**, 457–74.

Pearce, D.W., Barbier, E. and Markandya, A. (1990), *Sustainable Development*, Earthscan, London.

Pearce, D.W., Markandya, A. and Barbier, E. (1989), *Blueprint for a Green Economy*, Earthscan, London.

Pearce, D.W. and Prakesh, T.R. (1993), *Sustainability as Resilience*, Centre for Social and Economic Research on the Global Environmental (CSERGE), University College London and University of East Anglia, mimeo.

Pearce, D.W. and Warford, J.J. (1993), *World Without End: Economics, Environment and Sustainable Development*, Oxford University Press, Oxford.

Perrings, C. and Turner, R.K. (1995), Paper presented at the European Association of Resource and Environmental Economists conference, Umeå, July 1995.

Pezzey, J. (1994), *The Optimal Sustainable Depletion of Non-Renewable Resources*, University College London, mimeo.

Pezzey, J. (1989), *Economic Analysis of Sustainable Growth and Sustainable Development*, Environment Department Working Paper No. 15, World Bank, Washington DC.

Rees, W. and Wackenagel, M. (1992), Appropriated carrying capacity: measuring the natural capital requirements of the human economy, paper presented to the International Society of Ecological Economists Conference, Stockholm, August 1992.

Schulze, E.-D. and Mooney, H.A. (1993), *Biodiversity and Ecosystem Functions*, Ecological Studies, Vol. 99, Springer-Verlag, Berlin/ Heidelberg.

Simon, J. and Kahn, S. (1984), *The Resourceful Earth*, Blackwell, Oxford.

Solow, R.M. (1986), On the intergenerational allocation of exhaustible resources, *Scandanavian Journal of Economics,* **88**, 141–9.

Vitousek, P., Ehrlich, P., Ehrlich, A. and Matson, P. (1986), Human appropriation of the products of photosynthesis, *Bioscience*, **34**(6), 368–73.

World Bank (1994), *Population and Development*, World Bank, Washington DC.

World Bank (1995), *Monitoring Environmental Progress*, Environmentally Sustainable Development, World Bank, Washington DC.

World Conservation Monitoring Centre (WCMC) (1992), *Global Biodiversity: Status of the Earth' s Living Resources,* Chapman and Hall, London.

8. Economic growth and 'sustainable consumption'[1]

8.1 WHAT DOES SUSTAINABLE CONSUMPTION MEAN?

Extensive confusion surrounds the concept of 'sustainable consumption'. That confusion has partly arisen because of the loose wording of Chapter 4 of *Agenda 21* which speaks of 'sustainable consumption', 'sustainable consumption patterns', and 'lifestyle changes' without defining any of them. The waters are further muddied by reference to the 'optimisation of resource use' and the 'minimisation of waste' without reference to the meaning of optimization, or to any concept of cost.

To shed some light on the problem we first need to distinguish between consumption and the consumption of materials and energy, and the assimilative capacity of the environment to deal with waste. Consumption involves the use of goods and services to meet current wants. The extent to which materials, energy and assimilative capacity – we subsequently use the term, 'resources' to embrace all three – are used up in the act of consumption depends on the ratio of resource use to production and consumption. To take the simplest example, the amount of energy used to produce $1 of consumption – the 'energy intensity of consumption – is an example of such a ratio. The reason that the distinction is important is that consumption can rise while the ratio of resources to consumption can fall at the same time. The extent to which total resource use rises then depends on whether the ratio falls faster than the level of consumption rises.

For the most part, the thrust of *Agenda 21* is that the world needs to raise consumption while reducing resource use. Thus, para. 4.9 of Chapter 4 of *Agenda 21* calls for consideration of 'how economies can grow and prosper while reducing the use of energy and materials and the production of harmful materials'. But some people have wrongly concluded that what is needed is a reduction in consumption. We need to understand why this is not just a misinterpretation, but a serious mistake which, if acted upon, would make the populations of the developing world significantly worse off.

First, reducing consumption can only come about either (a) by raising the fraction of income that is saved for future consumption (investment), or (b) by reducing incomes generally. The savings fraction is open to manipulation by governments through the taxation system or through control of the incentives to save (e.g. interest rates). Control of the overall rate of change of income in the economy ('economic growth') is not by and large under the control of governments, although there is undoubted scope for lowering economic growth over the short term through sheer mismanagement.

Would either path contribute to an improvement of the well-being of the developing world? If savings are increased, some of the increase could be diverted to foreign aid. That would be a transfer of income from North to South, and there are good reasons for supposing that such additional transfers are justified. If incomes are reduced in the North, this does nothing for the South, and is very likely to make them worse off. This is because the 'lost dollar' of consumption in the North does not magically reappear in the South. Not generating it in the North simply means it is not generated at all. Moreover, in so far as some of the consumption in the North spills over into demand for the products of the South, the South is worse off since it loses a market. Sacrificing economic growth, then, means making both the North and the South worse off – this can hardly be the intention of those who advocate 'sustainable consumption'.

There are good reasons to reduce resource consumption by reducing the ratio of resource use to consumption. But we again need to be clear that making those changes in the ratio will not automatically improve the well-being of the South. Suppose, for example, the North reduces its ratio of energy use to consumption, as it has done for a very long time in fact. Clearly, this conserves exhaustible energy resources for a longer period than would otherwise be the case. But 1 tonne of oil not consumed now by the North does not become 1 tonne of oil that can be consumed by the South. Simply making a resource available does not confer on anyone the power to consume it. That power only comes about through the generation of income, and that means economic growth. Put another way, then, if the North conserves one tonne of oil it does nothing for the economic growth prospects of the South. Of course, if the North's resource consumption falls significantly, resource prices could fall. This would benefit the South if the South imports the resources in question. But it will make the South worse off if they export the resource. Ironically, those who call for reductions in the North's consumption are invariably those who complain about low commodity prices on world markets. The two goals may well be inconsistent.

The only exception to this rule is if we believe that the future growth prospects of the South are going to be constrained by the absence of resources. That is possible, but not very likely, at least as far as the supply of materials and energy is concerned. Growth prospects have far more to do with the pursuit of sensible domestic policies and careful development aid. There is a legitimate sense in which conservation of resources by the North will help the South. It is increasingly apparent that the really scarce resources are not materials and energy, but the receiving capacities of our environments. These are damaged through the use of materials and energy, as exemplified by ozone layer depletion, global warming, ocean pollution, etc. Since the world shares these global common resources damage done by their consumption is shared by everyone, North and South alike. Indeed, there is evidence to suggest that the South will suffer disproportionately more from some types of global environmental damage (Fankhauser, 1993).

Even if it is the North that suffers significantly from global environmental damage, the South would still lose since the North would be highly likely to divert resources away from aid towards mitigating the damage in the North.

Finally, reducing resource consumption will of course reduce the environmental impacts in the North itself. Such improvements are unlikely to have a significant effect on the environments or real incomes of the South, but they clearly have their own justification. That is, it makes sense for the North to reduce resource use out of the North's own self-interest.

Agenda 21 speaks interchangeably of changing consumption and changing consumption *patterns*. (It also speaks illogically of 'very high consumption patterns'. A pattern cannot be high or low.) But the two are quite different. Consumption can change without the pattern – the product composition of demand – changing, and the pattern can change without the overall level of consumption changing. If our interest is in reducing resource consumption, as we argued above it should be, then changing consumption patterns away from resource intensive products to less resource intensive products will help achieve the desired effect. From a policy standpoint, however, the kinds of measures that need to be adopted will be the same. They will be characterized by measures that penalize high resource intensive activities and which therefore make other less resource intensive activities more attractive.

It follows from the above, that care needs to be taken when interpreting the loose wording of *Agenda 21*. If it is interpreted as an old-fashioned call for less economic growth in the North, then it is a mischievous and irresponsible interpretation. Sacrificing economic growth will do nothing to improve the well-being of the South. It is far more likely to make things worse.

Nor do we have any guarantee that reducing growth of consumption in the North would be any more 'sustainable' than current levels. By fostering unemployment and social unrest it could easily be less sustainable. The evidence for that is fairly obvious from the recent experience of recession. Making consumption *sustainable* involves far more complex policies than *Agenda 21* contemplates. It involves not just the 'decoupling' of consumption and resource consumption, but the re-investment of rents from the exploitation of natural resources. Space forbids that we address this issue here – see Pearce and Atkinson (1993), Pearce *et al.* (1994).

8.2 SOME REFLECTIONS ON ANTI-GROWTH

While one might expect the 'economic growth' debate to have gone away since the exchanges of the 1970s, it has not. It is worth reflecting, therefore, on some of the problems of adopting an 'anti-growth' stance.

What is economic growth? However it is defined in some of the popular literature, economic growth is measured as an increase in per capita GNP (or GDP, it does not matter) measured in real terms. GNP is a measure of the monetary value of goods and services in the economy, mainly, but far from exclusively, traded goods (thus, public health services are included in the GNP and their 'output' is measured by the cost of providing those services). It is well known that GNP does not measure the flow of all goods and services, e.g. housewives' activities. We know it does not measure, adequately anyway, the flow of environmental goods and services nor the depreciation of environmental assets. We might therefore embrace a 'green' measure of GNP (or more strictly green Net NP, or 'gNNP'). But being for a measure of gNNP does not entail being against economic growth since we could favour improvements in gNNP and these could include increases in conventional GNP.

One reason we might want to be against economic growth is that we might think economic growth causes environmental degradation. If it does, then controlling economic growth should reduce that degradation. Even this position needs careful qualification. Economic growth might, for example, be a cause but there might be other causes as well and the other causes might be more important. Giving up, or reducing, economic growth might also be seen as incurring a social cost for many people who actually like the benefits of economic growth. Unless they are to be disenfranchised in some way, this means that we need to trade this social cost against the social cost of, for example, forest loss. Even if we take this to extremes, for example, by arguing that forest loss involves 'huge' social costs, even the end of the world as we know it, some people would argue that the social cost of interfering with individuals' rights to choose (to go to hell if they want) are also 'huge'. Finally, it all assumes we *can* control economic growth, on which more below.

As a first step, then, we should find out if economic growth causes forest loss. The only scientific way of getting any 'handle' on this is to see if economic growth is statistically associated with environmental degradation. Brown and Pearce (1994) test this proposition for tropical forests, for example. They conclude that there is at best only a weak association of income growth and deforestation: out of seventeen different studies, four show a positive link (higher income means higher deforestation), three show a negative link (the opposite of the 'growth hypothesis') and the remainder find no statistical association. Less than 25% of the studies find a positive association. Of course, this is not conclusive and one wants to see many more studies. But, the evidence as it stands does not support the 'growth hypothesis' for tropical forests. Notice that the 'poverty causes deforestation' is not borne out either (a negative association being found in three of the seventeen studies). We might have variants of these propositions: perhaps growth causes deforestation when people are poor and reduces it when they are rich. This is the so-called 'environmental Kuznets curve' relationship that seems to exist for some conventional pollutants such as particulates and SOx. But there appears to be little evidence for this curve (an upside down 'U' curve) for deforestation.

The discussion could end here: if there is no statistical association there can be no causal link (unless it works through other variables, but econometric studies should pick this up). But let us suppose there is a link and then conduct a thought experiment. Given a link, should we then reduce GNP growth? There are some reasons why not.

a. As noted above, reducing rates of economic growth causes loss of human well-being. More dramatically, we know that it is associated with social issues such as unemployment. So, we have the trade-off referred to above, and the evaluation of that trade-off is not obvious.
b. We know for sure that there are other causes of deforestation and environmental degradation. So, if we pick on growth as the culprit and ignore the others this would be dyslexic policy indeed. But we might argue that focusing on the other causes is likely to yield major reductions in deforestation and perhaps without the distress caused by reducing economic growth. The candidate causes are many: removing price distortions, land tenure and resource rights, credit access, investing in sustainable agriculture, raising agricultural productivity outside the forest areas, extension, etc. So we may not even need to reduce economic growth: it would be odd to invite everyone to punish themselves when it might not be necessary.
c. We have assumed throughout that economic growth is a policy variable, it is something that we can change. But is it? What we are interested is long-term growth, not the kind of growth that preoccupies governments with their worries about short-run interest rates, budget deficits and inflation. A chart of UK GDP at constant prices 1885–1987 actually shows a fairly straight line when the GDP axis is expressed in logarithm form, i.e. a constant rate of economic growth (Liesner, 1989). The implied average rate of growth is 1.8%. This appears to be above that for England in the 18th century, perhaps 0.4% p.a. at the beginning of the 18th century and over 1% at the end. Now, we could take this to mean that growth has come 'under control' in the 20th century where it was not in the 18th. It is arguable, but I doubt it. Looking at it another way, there was economic growth in the 18th century when it seems legitimate to argue we did not know how to manage the economy in

any sophisticated manner and, indeed, when there were no public regular statistics on GNP anyway (GNP is very much a recent invention).

d. Continuing with the thought experiment, suppose we decide that growth is something we can change. Consider the 'modern' theory of economic growth which says that it is due mainly to 'endogenous' technical change, technical change embodied in capital, including R and D, education, etc., i.e. giving special emphasis to 'human capital'. If this approach is correct, then to *lower* economic growth means lowering technical change, reducing education, etc. Some would argue that this is a strange way to tackle an environmental problem, not least because we have good reason to suppose that increasing education is one of the 'best' ways of solving environmental problems.
e. Now suppose growth does cause environmental degradation, and that we are indifferent to the ways in which we control growth (e.g. by reducing education, and this seems unlikely). What matters presumably is *global* growth, i.e. the growth of the world economy, or, at least, the growth of all countries with forests. But even if one nation can control its growth rate, the chances that all countries would agree to control growth rates are small – I would actually say zero.
f. Finally consider what the growth hypothesis is: it is that the change in GNP is the thing causing the problem. But GNP is a flow concept, so it is not just the growth of this flow that should be the focus of attention, but the flow itself. We should not be worrying about increments to GNP, we should be trying to reduce GNP. While there are some intellectual antecedents of this view, the practical question is whether there is anything sacred about 'zero' economic growth. On the basis of the thought experiment, the answer has to be 'no': we should drive GNP down, who knows, even to zero! Once we argue for zero growth we are logically involved in arguing for negative growth. At the very least, the strategic argument says we do not stand a chance.

All this suggests that we have neither a scientific nor a strategic case for being against growth in order to save the forests or probably any other environmental asset. There has to be another way and that surely requires us to focus on the many real causal factors at work. That will give us a menu of practical measures that we can fairly safely advocate.

What of population growth? Here the picture is different. The statistical studies do suggest a population/deforestation link, and we can think of many good arguments for reducing population growth that have nothing to do with forests. Put another way, we are not 'dictating' the preferences of others (though some argue this) by formulating a view that 'they' should have fewer children for the sake of the world's environment. The argument is more sensibly put as informing everyone of the personal benefits of reduced family size: health, education for example. But we still need to caution against high expectations in this area too. For we will not prevent the world's population reaching 7–8 billion, regardless of what we do now. The policy arena relates to the difference between, say, 8 billion and 10 or 12 billion. That is worth fighting for but it will not save the forests on its own.

8.3 CONCLUSIONS

Focusing on anti-growth is not just unhelpful, it diverts attention away from real policies that stand a chance of success. A focus on the quality of growth is surely correct, however. To that end, we can hope for a growth process directed at meeting basic needs – improving education, health and personal well-being, and having more, not less, environmental goods. But the process of growth matters too and we risk interfering with basic freedoms when we tell people what they should and should not want. Ultimately, they must decide.

NOTE

1. Part of this chapter was read as a paper to the Government of Norway Symposium on *Sustainable Consumption*, Oslo, January 1994. The remainder was prepared as an internal note for the World Commission on Forests and Sustainable Development in 1997.

REFERENCES

Brown, K. and Pearce, D.W.(eds.) (1994), *The Causes of Tropical Deforestation*, University College London Press, London.

Fankhauser, S.(1993), *Greenhouse Economics and the Cost of Global Warming*, Centre for Social and Economic Research on the Global Environment, University College London.

Liesner, T. (1989), *One Hundred Years of Economic Statistics*, Economist Publications, London.

Pearce, D.W. and Atkinson, G. (1993), Measuring sustainable development, *Ecodecision*, **9**, June, 64–6.

Pearce, D.W., Atkinson, G. and Dubourg, R. (1994), What is sustainable development?, *Annual Review of Energy,* **19**, 457–74.

PART 3

Applied Environmental Economics

9. Particulate matter and human health in the United Kingdom[1]

(with Tom Crowards)

9.1 INTRODUCTION

Substantial interest has been generated in the links between human health and air pollution in the UK. Several pollutants in particular have been singled out for special attention: particulate matter, ozone – a secondary pollutant formed from the effects of sunlight on volatile organic compounds (VOCs) and nitrogen oxides (NOx), and benzene. This paper focuses on particulate matter. Particulate matter came to the fore with an article in the *New Scientist* (Bown, 1994) which claimed that 10 000 people per annum are dying prematurely because of PM_{10} emissions, mainly from car exhausts. This estimate was based on the work of US epidemiologists, especially Joel Schwartz at the US Environmental Protection Agency and Douglas Dockery of Harvard University (Dockery *et al.*,1992, 1993; Pope and Dockery, 1992; Pope *et al.*,1992; Schwartz and Marcus, 1990; Schwartz, 1991a, 1991b, 1993a, 1993b, 1994; Schwartz and Dockery, 1992a, 1992b; Schwartz *et al.*, 1991, 1993). For more recent evidence see Xu *et al.* (1994) and Pope *et al.* (1995). In this paper we set out a general model of air pollution and health, following the pioneering work of Ostro (summarized in Ostro, 1994), and then focus on particulate matter. We estimate the monetized social costs of exposure to total particulate matter concentrations and the benefits to be obtained by making marginal reductions in PM_{10} emissions. The results suggest that the social costs of particulate matter emissions in the UK are substantial and that substantial benefits could be secured from their reduction, even disregarding the associated benefits that tend to accrue from the kinds of policy measures that would be needed (e.g. reductions in noise and congestion from traffic restraint). In particular, PM_{10} emissions are closely linked to road transport and the control of the transport sector therefore becomes a matter of priority for environmental and health policy. A more complete picture of the links between transport and social cost is provided in Maddison *et al.* (1996). Our findings are similar, but somewhat larger in scale, to those of Small and Kazimi (1995) for California.

9.2 THE UNDERLYING MODEL

Health effects (H) are related to ambient air quality by

$$dH_i = b.POP_i.\, dA_j \tag{9.1}$$

where d $=$ change in
H_i $=$ health effect i
b $=$ slope of dose response function
POP_i $=$ population at risk from health effect i
A $=$ ambient air quality
j $=$ jth pollutant

Ambient air quality is related to emissions either through some diffusion model or through an approximation involving a relationship such as

$$dA_j/A_j = dE_j/E_j \tag{9.2}$$

where E = emissions.

Equation (9.2) says that an $X\%$ change in emissions is associated with an $X\%$ change in ambient concentrations.

Each health effect, H_i, has a unit economic value P_i so that

$$P_i.dH_i = P_i.\, b.POP_i.\, dA_j \tag{9.3}$$

and the sum of damages, D, from pollutant j is:

$$D_j = \Sigma_i\, P_i.dH_i \tag{9.4}$$

b in equation (9.1) is the slope of the dose–response function (DRF). The DRF could begin at some threshold value below which no damage is done. No firm evidence for thresholds for air pollutants appears to be available. For this reason a working assumption is that the DRF begins at the origin. However, this working assumption is clearly open to further analysis.

9.3 PARTICULATE MATTER DOSE–RESPONSE FUNCTIONS

Health damage appears to be related to particulate matter of less than 10 microns diameter, i.e. PM_{10}. Particulates are associated with a wide range of respiratory symptoms. Long-term exposure may be linked to heart and lung disease. Particulates may also carry carcinogens into the lungs.

Concentrations of particulate matter are measured in various ways, as total suspended particulates (TSP), sulphates and 'British Smoke' (BS) (or just 'smoke'). One problem is that the various measures need to be converted into units of PM_{10} since it is PM_{10} that is implicated in health damage. Ostro (1994) suggests the following conversions (all in $\mu g/m^3$):

$$PM_{10} = 0.55 \text{ TSP} \tag{9.5}$$

$$\text{Sulphates} = 0.14 \text{ TSP} \tag{9.6}$$

hence

$$\text{Sulphates} = 0.25 \text{ PM}_{10} \tag{9.7}$$

$$\text{BS} \approx \text{PM}_{10} \tag{9.8}$$

The relationship in (9.5) is confirmed by Desvousges *et al.*(1993). The equivalence in (9.8) appears to be disputed, with some authorities claiming that there is no direct link between BS and PM_{10} and others claiming that there is a link but a more complex one than is suggested by the simple equivalence in (9.8). The conversion problem arises because of different ways of measuring particulate concentrations. The British approach has been to use the black smoke method whereby air is drawn through a filter. The darkness of the stain is then measured and is calibrated to indicate concentration. The darkness of the stain varies by the type of particle and what is in dispute is the link between this measure and those obtained by gravimetric techniques which essentially measure the weight of the particulate matter on the filter paper. Gravimetric approaches have been used in the UK only recently (see below).

Based on a meta-analysis of DRFs, Ostro (1994) concludes that the consensus DRF for *mortality* from particulate matter is

$$\%\text{d}H_{\text{MT}} = 0.096.\text{dPM}_{10} \tag{9.9}$$

where $\text{d}H_{\text{MT}}$ is the (central estimate of the) change in *mortality*. The coefficient makes due allowance for other compounding factors such as smoking.

Equation (9.9) says that a 1 $\mu g/m^3$ change in PM_{10} concentrations is associated with a 0.1% change in mortality, or a 10 $\mu g/m^3$ change in PM_{10} concentrations is associated with a 1% change in mortality. The DRFs surveyed by Ostro include those in the work of Dockery, Schwartz and others. Upper and lower bounds for equation (9.9) are given as:

$$\%dH_{MT} = 0.130.dPM_{10} \tag{9.10}$$

and

$$\%dH_{MT} = 0.062.dPM_{10} \tag{9.11}$$

To get the absolute change in mortality then, we require:

$$dH_{MT} = b.\ dPM_{10}.\ CMR.\ POP.1/100 \tag{9.12}$$

where b = 0.062, 0.096 and 0.130 respectively for lower, central and upper bounds; and CMR is the crude mortality rate. The factor of 100 converts from percentages to absolute numbers.

The measurement problems relate to what exactly the concentrations of PM_{10} are in the UK, since it is a measure of particulate concentration only recently introduced; what the population at risk is; and what the CMR is for that population. Somewhat surprisingly, all three issues cause difficulties for estimating the health–particulate matter link. This may explain some of the variety of views concerning the importance of particulate matter pollution in the UK.

Not all particulate matter is 'anthropogenic' – some arises as a natural background level (dust etc.). It is assumed here that 70% of PM_{10} in urban areas has an anthropogenic origin. In terms of assigning damages to anthropogenic sources, then, dPM_{10} in the above equations is taken to be 0.7 of average PM_{10} concentrations.

9.4 DEFINING URBAN AREAS IN ENGLAND AND WALES

A major problem lies in the estimation of 'urban' populations and deaths. The Census definition of an urban area is 1000 people or more. As a result, using Census data to estimate urban population (and thereby urban deaths) results in an urban population of 90% of total England and Wales population. The *New Scientist* article (Bown, 1994) states that 'Government figures show that some 68 per cent of people live in urban areas.' We have been unable to reproduce this figure from any combination of the available data. Table 7 from the OPCS 1981 *Preliminary Report for Towns* gives a list of towns with population of 50000 or more. Summing these populations gives an urban population of 52% of the total.

Schwartz/*New Scientist* appears to take the number of deaths for those towns for which PM_{10} data are available from *Key Population and Vital Statistics* (KPVS) 1992. These are derived from local authority boundaries, and attribute a higher population to each town than does the 1981 *Preliminary Report for*

Towns. However, Brimblecombe (1994) suggests that PM_{10} is likely to spread somewhat from its original source (although subject to decreasing concentration), so using local authority data (as per the *New Scientist*) which encompasses some less populated outskirts of towns might not be unreasonable. Quoting Dockery *et al.* (1993, p. 1758), 'Long-term transport and large-scale mixing of combustion products play a large part in establishing the levels of sulphate and fine-particulate air pollution. Therefore, concentrations of sulphate and fine particles are relatively uniform within each of these communities.'

Bentham (1994) suggests that perhaps the most practical measure of urban population (and deaths) would be from the 'Area Aggregates' in KPVS. He has investigated the density of population for the various aggregates, and has found that population density is considerably higher for the categories of 'Greater London', 'Metropolitan Districts', and 'Non-metropolitan Districts: Cities' (area aggregates 0–4), than for other aggregates. Using these area aggregates to define urban areas, the proportion of urban population is 44% of total population. Clearly, the choice of definition of urban population (and thereby deaths in urban areas) will influence the results significantly.

If the lowest, and possibly the most reasonable estimate of the proportion of urban population is used, that of area aggregates, the need to assume a constant death rate throughout all regions is avoided since mortality rates are available for each of these areas specifically. This latter assumption is implicit in the *New Scientist* article when multiplying total deaths in England and Wales by the percentage of urban population (at 68%). Note that the urban population here is *residential* and hence excludes commuters who would naturally be exposed.

The following calculations are based on deaths in urban areas as defined in aggregate areas 0 to 4 (representing 44% of total population in 1992), but the calculation can be easily re-run using a different figure for urban deaths/population.

9.5 ESTIMATING DEATHS ATTRIBUTABLE TO PM_{10}

Annual (arithmetic) average concentrations of PM_{10} in England and Wales in 1993 are available only for Birmingham, Bristol, Cardiff, Leeds, Liverpool, London and Newcastle (AEA Technology, 1995). These data are reproduced in Table 9.1.

The average figure for these seven cities in 1993, applying weights to measures of PM_{10} is 28.5μg/m^3. However, there is little difference for these 1993 figures between averaging with or without using population weights (producing an annual average of 28.3 μg/m^3 without using the weights). The estimate of 28.5 μg/m^3 compares directly with the average figure calculated in the *New*

Scientist ('for every city', which seems to mean seven of them) of approximately 28 μg/m^3.

Table 9.1 *PM_{10} concentrations in England and Wales*

Town	PM_{10}	Population	Population × PM_{10}	PM_{10}	Population × PM_{10}
Birmingham	26	1009.1	26236.6	26	26236.6
Bristol	27	396.6	10708.2		
Cardiff	31	295.6	9163.6	26	7685.6
London	29	6904.6	200233.4	30	207138.0
Leeds	27	721.8	19488.6		
Liverpool	29	479.0	13891.0		
Newcastle	29	281.7	8169.3	28	7887.6
Sum		10088.4	287890.7		248947.8
Average	28.29[2]		28.54[1]	27.50[2]	29.32[1]

Notes:
All PM_{10} figures are average annual concentrations in μg/m^3, and population is in 000s.
[1] Average urban PM_{10} concentration, weighted by the size of population associated with the relevant PM_{10} reading.
[2] Average urban PM_{10} without population weighting.

Using the figure of 28.5 μg/m^3 for average urban PM_{10} concentration, along with total urban deaths in 1992 of 243707 (based on KPVS, area aggregates data), and a dose–response function of 0.096% increase in all-cause/all-age deaths for every 1 μg/m^3 of PM_{10} (see Equation (9.9) above) total deaths in 1993 in England and Wales attributable to PM_{10} exposure are: 28.5 x 243707 x 0.00096 = 6668 deaths in 1993. The upper and lower bounds, using the coefficients of 0.00062 and 0.00130 are 4306 and 9029 deaths, respectively.

The central estimate may be compared with the figure in the *New Scientist* of 10 000 deaths. The above figure is lower essentially due to the lower estimate of annual urban deaths (243 707 instead of 377 000). Using the *New Scientist* annual urban death figure would mean multiplying the above estimate by 1.55 to give a central figure of 10 314 deaths. The *New Scientist* figure can therefore be replicated, and the fundamental issue is the relevant urban population. However, these estimates relate to *all* PM_{10}, regardless of source. If we are concerned to 'blame' anthropogenic sources, then, as noted above, we should take 0.7 of the 28.5 μg/m^3 figure, i.e. 20 μg/m^3. This has the effect of lowering the central mortality estimates to 4667 for England and Wales, and to 7220 using the *New Scientist* assumptions of a higher urban population. In other words, the 'true' level of mortality could be about one-half that estimated in the *New*

Scientist article which appears to have included all sources of PM_{10} in the estimate.

In summary the 'best estimates' for PM_{10} mortality due to anthropogenic sources are:

England and Wales			
	Low	Mid	High
Low urban population	3014	4667	6320
High urban population	4663	7220	9777

For the UK, these estimates can be multiplied by 1.11.

Brunekreef (1995) reports acute mortality associated with PM_{10} of some 5000 and serious health effects in a 'few tens of thousands' of people per year in the Netherlands which appears to be consistent with the estimates here, and may suggest the mortality figures are understatements. The numbers reported here are also entirely consistent with those reported by the Energy Technology Support Unit (ETSU) for acute health effects from PM_{10}. The ETSU study utilizes a 5 × 5km grid map of PM_{10} concentrations obtained by extrapolating from nitrogen oxide concentration (ETSU, 1996).

9.6 PROBLEMS OF THE DOSE–RESPONSE FUNCTION

The dose–response function is mainly derived from data linking changes in PM_{10} concentrations to health effects in US cities. Transferring the use of such a dose–response function to calculate deaths attributable to total PM_{10} levels in urban areas of England and Wales is reliant upon a number of assumptions relating both the validity of the epidemiology underlying the DRFs and the validity of transferring the results. The main critical factors appear to be:

a. the argument that there is no threshold below which PM_{10} concentrations are harmless and are not a cause of mortality;
b. that it is a linear dose–response function, so that the relationship at one level of PM_{10} is the same at all levels;
c. that conditions in US cities and measurements taken there are comparable to British cities;
d. that there is some 'biological pathway' by which particulate matter affects health;
e. that the possible presence of confounding factors does not alter the relationship;
f. statistical artefact.

Thresholds

For (a), there has as yet been no evidence produced of threshold levels. Thus, Schwartz (1994) asks 'is there a threshold or other non-linearities in the concentration–response relationship?' (with regard to the historical link between smog and daily mortality in London). 'No evidence is seen for a threshold.' Schwartz (1994, p. 49) (with regard to data from Philadelphia). Similarly, '... studies ... identify no threshold between quintiles of range of observed exposures. In general, the linear and exponential functional forms adopted by most researchers do not suggest a strong attenuation of effects at low levels, and we adopt the conservative assumption of no threshold' (Desvousges *et al.*,1993, pp. 3–5).

Current regulatory limits relating to PM_{10} concentration include the US EPA standard of 50 $\mu g/m^3$ or the WHO 24-hour thoracic particle guideline of 70 $\mu g/m^3$. Both of these exceed levels which have been found to be significantly related to mortality in studies by Schwartz (1994), Desvousges *et al.* (1993) and Dockery *et al.*(1993). These limit values are therefore unlikely to provide any reasonable approximation to a threshold. Ostro (1995a) points out that the absence of an observed threshold may be the result of study design or of the fact that there is no threshold, but that the few studies that test for low level effects suggest effects continue to very low concentrations.

Linearity

For (b), if the concentration to mortality function is not linear, then the dose–response calculated for a particular level will not be applicable at other levels of PM_{10}. However, graphs in Schultz (1994, p. 49) and Dockery *et al.*(1993, p. 1757) would seem to indicate that this relationship probably is approximately linear.

Transferability

One implication of (c) would be the need to check age and health profiles of populations in US and UK cities to see if there is a higher predisposition to ill-health in one country.

The UK Royal Commission on Environmental Pollution (1994) notes the issue of the transferability of the DRF:

> . . . it has been suggested that PM_{10} may be responsible for as many as 10,000 extra deaths a year in England and Wales. Although there are not sufficient data about the origin, nature and ambient concentrations of particulates in UK cities to allow the

validity of this extrapolation to be tested, it seems to us that the health implications of particulates need to be taken very seriously (para. 3.28, p. 31).

The Royal Commission's implication is that the transferability of the DRF is acceptable, but that it is the data problem that raises the difficulties. While there undoubtedly are data limitations, as outlined above, and further detailed work is urgently required, it should not deter approximations of the kind suggested here.

Biological Pathways

The biological pathway by which particulate matter affects human health appears to be uncertain. Seaton *et al.* (1995) suggest that particulate clouds containing small acidic particles may both travel and persist in time, also penetrating indoors. Small particles may provoke alveolar inflammation which exacerbates lung disease and may also affect the coagulability of blood. The latter may affect cardiovascular disease, a health effect not accounted for here. Utell and Samet (1993) review the various epidemiological studies and argue that the biological mechanism is unknown. Ostro (1995a) reviews the evidence and suggests that pollution exposure is an additional burden of inflammation which may make worse the conditions of those already affected by respiratory infections. He further suggests that the available evidence is consistent with the requirements of tests for causality: the relationship is consistent, specific, produces a dose–response relationship and fits other known facts.

Confounding Factors

One potentially significant issue is the extent to which the dose–response functions adequately control for all variables affecting health status. It is usual to control for factors such as smoking and diet, but recent work has suggested that 'social status' may be an important factor in determining illness. One possibility, then, is that exposure to PM_{10} is correlated with social status and with illness. This needs careful testing with panel data covering data that include income, other measures of social status, and indoor and outdoor pollution concentrations. Ostro (1995a) notes that time series studies avoid such confounding factors since the population characteristics are fairly constant over time.

Statistical Artefact

Some of the datasets used in the various studies correspond closely to a Poisson distribution, i.e. variation in the observed values may correspond to what one would expect from random events. If so, it would be illicit to analyse the data further for some causal explanation. The variation that exists is explained by chance, not by some underlying causal factor such as air pollution. The importance of Ostro's consensus dose–response functions for premature mortality is signified by the fact that it has been used in a number of World Bank appraisals for air pollution control in various cities in developing countries (World Bank 1994a, 1994b, 1994c; see also Ostro 1994, 1995b). As such, significant expenditures could be affected by the results of the approach. The World Bank subjected Ostro's work to peer review – see McMichael *et al.*(1995) and Flanders *et al.*(1995). A large number of highly specific comments were made but the essential main points appear to be (a) that the work neglects long-term chronic effects, especially permanent impairment of lung function and the development of diseases such as asthma and chronic obstructive pulmonary disease. Studies based on essentially 'acute' data will probably not capture long-term health risks; (b) that it may not be appropriate to 'transfer' mainly North American dose–response functions to developing countries – the focus of the World Bank's interest – without further analysis of other factors, such as nutrition; and (c) that the statistical procedure used will not be accurate if the dose–response functions are non-linear and/or there is a threshold. Criticism (b) is not relevant to the current study, but clearly is relevant to extensions of the model to developing countries. Criticism (a) suggests that the procedures used may actually *understate* the health damage from air pollution generally and PM_{10} in particular. Criticism (c) is discussed above. Clearly, there are uncertainties, but the peer review process does not add to the uncertainties already identified.

9.7 VALUING STATISTICAL LIVES

Procedures for placing economic values on losses of statistical lives are well established and include (a) the hedonic wage approach; (b) contingent valuation; (c) contingent ranking; and (d) avertive behaviour approaches (Pearce *et al.*, 1994b). 'Official' valuations used by the Department of Transport in the UK for use in valuing accidents are based on a review of this literature, and, currently, the resulting values are:

1993 prices		1995 prices	
£744 057	=	£789 370	(at 3% inflation)

However, a more extensive review in Pearce *et al.*(1992) suggests that 1992 values should be £2 million for a statistical life, which would put the 1994/5 value at around £2.12 million. But is the value of a 'statistical life' (VOSL) the relevant magnitude in the case of pollution deaths? The reason for doubting it is that pollution-related mortality risks are likely to be highest for an older age group. Thus, Schwartz and Dockery (1992b) find that the risk of mortality is greater for people over the age of 65. Yet the literature on the economic value of a statistical life tends to assume that the extension to life expectancy of people at risk is of the order of 35–40 life years, whereas the relevant extended period for pollution cases is more likely to be 10–15 years (Cropper and Simon, 1994). Empirical work on the age-value of statistical life issue is very limited. Early work by Jones-Lee *et al.* (1985) reports results which suggest that valuations at age 60 may be around 70% of valuations at age 40. If so, and if £2.12 million is a 'consensus' VOSL, then the appropriate value would be £1.5 million. But Jones-Lee's own (1985) results suggest a VOSL for age 40 at about £3 million, so that £2.12 million as an average (1994 prices) could be appropriate for the at-risk groups in question. Jones-Lee (1993) finds no variation in VOSL with age. Finally, there is evidence that the willingness to pay to avoid 'contemporaneous risk' is less than the willingness to pay for 'latent risk': people are not indifferent to the way they might die. Risk of death from respiratory disease or cancer might therefore be valued more highly than risk of death in an accident, the main context in which VOSL estimates have been developed. A conservative approach is adopted here and a value of £1.5 million is used.

It is tempting to think that what is relevant is the 'value of a life year' and suggestions have been made to the effect that a VOSL like £1.5 million should be divided by average expected life years remaining. But, as Chestnut and Patterson (1994) point out, this assumes that utility is a linear function of life expectancy and it is not at all clear why this should be so. Indeed, valuing one's own life chances may be quite independent of the amount of time one expects to live. While the issue of the 'appropriate' value of a statistical life requires further attention, there is at the moment no evidence to suggest that such values decline markedly with age.

Applying the £1.5 million valuation figure to premature deaths from anthropogenic particulate exposure, then, produces the following results for England and Wales (adopting the low urban population estimate)

Lower bound:	3014 deaths x £1.50m =	£4.52 billion
Central estimate:	4667 deaths x £1.50m =	£7.00 billion
Upper bound:	6320 deaths x £1.50m =	£9.48 billion

These are substantial social cost burdens. Even at the much lower Department of Transport statistical life valuations of around £750 000 (1994 prices) the range is £2.26b to £4.74b with a central estimate of £3.50 billion.

Table 9.2 summarizes these estimates.

Table 9.2 Summary mortality cost estimates for particulate matter

	Lower bound £1994 billion	Central estimate £1994 billion	Upper bound £1994 billion
England and Wales only:	4.52	7.00	9.48
UK: base case	5.02	7.77	10.52

Notes: To obtain UK from England and Wales estimates, multiply by 1.11.

No account has been taken of the value of a statistical life to other people. This could increase the VOSL by 25–50% (Pearce and Knight, 1992) or as much as 100% (Schwab Christe and Soguel, 1995).

Additionally, the analysis here covers urban areas only. Annexe 2 reports some provisional estimates for rural premature mortality based on a rural mean concentration of 15 $\mu g/m^3$. These suggest an additional 1963 deaths in England and Wales and 2250 deaths for the UK. The effect of including these rural estimates would be to raise mortality costs by roughly 30%, to £9.9 billion in England and Wales and £11.2 billion in the UK.

9.8 ALLOCATING MORTALITY COSTS TO EMISSION SOURCES

How should the damage estimates be allocated between sources? As the quotation from the Royal Commission on Environmental Pollution notes, it is difficult to ascribe 'responsibility' for pollution in urban areas since what matters is both the source and its contribution to concentrations. If concentrations are proportional to emissions and if the sources are 'evenly spread' over urban areas, then responsibility could be allocated by emission source. But this is not a very tenable assumption.

The *UK Digest of Environmental Protection and Water Statistics* does not report sources for PM_{10}, but does report sources for black smoke. The Quality of Urban Air Review Group ('QUARG') sets out sources for both PM_{10} and black smoke *emissions* (QUARG, 1993a, b). These estimates are reproduced in Table 9.3. As can be seen, responsibility is quite different if PM_{10} is used rather than black smoke. As noted above, as far as *urban concentrations* are concerned, emissions from power stations and industry are likely to be relatively less important than transport-related emissions. Emissions from the domestic sector will contribute to urban concentrations and these are seen to be the dominant source at 47% of PM_{10} emissions. Walters (1994) states that 'Motor vehicles produce a substantial and increasing proportion of particulate emissions, particularly in urban areas, where vehicles may contribute over 90% of black smoke and 70% of fine particulates (PM_{10})'. QUARG (1993b) estimates that 94% of black smoke emissions in London come from road vehicles, but notes that this proportion may not be representative of other towns and cities where public transport facilities differ.

Table 9.3 Source contributions to smoke and PM_{10} emissions 1991

	PM_{10}	Black smoke
Cars: petrol	9	3
Cars: diesel	1	3
Total cars	10	6
LGVs: petrol	1	< 1
LGVs: diesel	1	3
Total LGVs	2	3
HGVs: large	5	2
HGVs: small	7	16
Total HGVs	12	18
Buses	2	6
Motorcycles	< 1	< 1
Total road vehicles	27	42
Domestic and commercial	47	36
Power stations	7	5
Other industry	18	15
Other (refineries, agriculture, aircraft and shipping)	1	2
Total %	100	100

Source: QUARG (1993b, Table 5.1).

Clearly, there is a further layer of uncertainty in seeking to ascribe responsibility for excess mortality between sources. Unpublished work by Eyre (1995) does suggest some 'urban – rural' ratios for various pollutants, including PM_{10}, i.e. ratios that account for the higher dose arising from urban sources than rural sources. For PM_{10} the ratio is put at 6.4, suggesting that transport sources can be weighted by 6.4 relative to, say, power station sources. It is less clear what weight should be attached to domestic sources which, as the QUARG data show, are dominant in terms of total UK PM_{10} emissions. As a working hypothesis, then, we weight the emissions from transport at 6.4, domestic sources at 3.0 and all other sources at unity. This produces the following 'percentage responsibility' factors when applied to the QUARG data:

Road vehicles:	27% of PM_{10} emissions × 6.4 = 1.728
Domestic and commercial sources:	48% of PM_{10} emissions × 3.0 = 1.440
Other:	25% of PM_{10} emissions × 1.0 = 0.250
	Sum of weighted percentages = 3.418

Revised weighted contributions:

Road vehicles:	1.728/3.418 = 50.5%
Domestic and commercial sources:	1.440/3.418 = 42.1%
Other:	0.250/3.418 = 7.4%

These allocation procedures clearly require a great deal of further attention. However, a fraction of about one-half for transport-related emissions seems to be in accord with general statements on the source responsibility of particulate concentrations in urban areas, and could be somewhat low.

The effects of applying these allocation rules to the economic value of mortality damage are shown in Table 9.4. They suggest that transport sources may account for around £3.5 billion of mortality damages in urban England and Wales each year (based on the low urban population estimates). This may be compared with an earlier estimate by Pearce *et al.* (1994b) which placed *all* pollution damage from transport sources at only £2.8 billion.

Table 9.4 Possible sectoral shares of particulate matter damage (£billion)

	Total damage	Due to transport	Due to domestic sector	Due to other
England and Wales				
base case, central estimate	7.00	3.54	2.94	0.52
United Kingdom				
base case, central estimate	7.77	3.92	3.26	0.59

Note: For transport share, multiply total estimates in Table 9.2 by 0.505; for domestic share, multiply by 0.42.

9.9 PARTICULATE MATTER AND MORBIDITY

The damage estimates so far relate to excess *mortalities* only. Rowe *et al.*,(1995) have assembled 'best estimates' of the relevant dose–response functions for morbidity. These are set out in Table 9.5. The assumption again is that such DRFs can be 'transferred' to the UK context. Certain simple adjustments could be undertaken, for example, for variations in the age structure of populations.

Table 9.5 Morbidity dose–response functions for PM_{10}

Morbidity effect	Low estimate	Central estimate	High estimate
RHA/100 000	6.6	12.0	17.3
ERV/100 000	116.0	237.0	354.0
RAD/person	0.29	0.58	0.78
LRI/child/per asthmatic	0.010	0.017	0.024
Asthma attacks per person	0.33	0.58	1.96
Respiratory symptoms/person	0.80	1.68	2.56
Chronic bronchitis/100 000 (risk of new case)	30.0	61.2	93.0

Notes:
Effect per 10 μg/m³ change in PM_{10}.
RHA = respiratory hospital admissions; ERV = emergency room visits; RAD = restricted activity days; LRI = lower respiratory illness (in children).

Source: Rowe *et al*. (1995)

Table 9.6 gives the resulting estimates of health incidence for England and Wales and the United Kingdom assuming that 44% of the population is 'urbanized' in the sense defined above. If this is an underestimate, then the totals need to be increased accordingly. The populations at risk are taken to be 22.782 million and 25.344 million respectively (see Annexe 1).

Table 9.6 Estimates of morbidity effects of anthropogenic PM_{10}

	Number of events or cases		
	Lower bound	Central estimate	Upper bound
RHAs			
England and Wales	3007	5467	7882
UK	3345	6082	8768
ERVs			
England and Wales	52 850	107 977	161 282
UK	58 789	120 112	179 407
RADs			
England and Wales	13.21m	26.42m	35.53m
UK	14.70m	29.39m	39.53m

Table 9.6 continued

	Number of events or cases		
	Lower bound	Central estimate	Upper bound
Child LRIs			
England and Wales	ne	ne	ne
UK			
Asthma attacks			
England and Wales	15.03m	25.42m	89.30m
UK	16.72m	29.39m	99.33m
Respiratory symptoms			
England and Wales	36.45m	76.54m	116.63m
UK	40.54m	85.14m	129.74m
Chronic bronchitis			
England and Wales	13 668	27 833	42 371
UK	15 204	31 016	47 132

Source: Table 9.5 and assuming overall urban populations of 22.78 million and 25.34 million for England and Wales and UK population, respectively. The general formula for any estimate N is $N = b.POP. (28.5 - 8.5)/10 = 2.b.POP$, i.e. 45.56$b$ and 50.69b, respectively, where 8.5 is the non-anthropogenic concentration, and the division by 10 allows for the coefficients in Table 5 being expressed per 10 $\mu g/m^3$. Ratio of lower and upper bounds to central estimate taken from Rowe *et al.* (1995).

Table 9.7 provides unit prices taken from Rowe *et al.*(1995). These unit prices cannot simply be transferred since they relate to various studies in the USA. Table 9.7 therefore makes various kinds of adjustments to them to reflect the differences in incomes between the two countries. The results of these adjustments are to reduce the US unit values by 10–25%. Improved adjustments could be made by looking more closely at medical costs in the US and the UK.

Table 9.8 assembles the resulting total valuations. Table 9.8 suggests that a few categories of morbidity effects dominate the overall picture, notably restricted activity days (RADs) (which are taken here to subsume the estimates for respiratory symptoms) and chronic bronchitis. The effect of computing morbidity effects is roughly to double the mortality costs in Table 9.2.

Combining mortality and morbidity effects produces the result that urban anthropogenic PM_{10} may cost the United Kingdom something of the order of £14 billion per year (see Table 9.9). Note, however, that these estimates are based on individuals' willingness to pay to avoid the illness. They say nothing about the costs to the health services. It is not always clear if 'cost of illness' estimates should be added to WTP measures. If they should, then the estimates here understate the true social costs of health damage. To illustrate, Action Asthma

(1990) estimate that the effects of asthma as a whole resulted in a cost to the UK National Health Service in 1988 of some £344 million in terms of general practice costs and costs to the hospital sector.

Table 9.7 Unit values for morbidity effects

	Unit value (EC/US) £1994			Adjusted unit value = Unit value $\times Y_{uk}/Y_{us}$* (central value only)	Adjusted unit value = Unit value $\times (Y_{uk}/Y_{us})^{e}$ ** (central value only)
	L	C	H		
RHAs (adjusted COI)	4900	9800	14 700	7450	8918
ERVs (adjusted COI)	185	370	555	280	337
RADs (WTP + adjusted COI)	25	50	75	38	46
Asthma (WTP)	9	25	40	19	23
Respiratory symptoms (WTP)	4	7	10	5	6
Chronic bronchitis (WTP)		147 000		111 720	133 770

Notes:
L = low, C = central, H = high.
COI = based on 'cost of illness' approach. WTP = willingness to pay approach.
Values in Rowe (1995) adjusted from 1992 to 1994 prices by multiplying by 1.05 and from $s to £s by dividing by 1.5.
* Ratio of UK to US GNP per capita in 1992 = 0.76. This adjustment is the equivalent of setting *e* in the third column equal to unity.
** *e* = 0.35, see Krupnick *et al.*(1993). The effect is to multiply the unit values in the first column by 0.91.

The uncertainties associated with the results relate to the following issues:

a. uncertainty surrounding the transferability and legitimacy of the underlying DRFs. Given their basis in meta analysis a judgmental view at this stage is that this is not likely to be a major source of uncertainty;
b. measurement of the population at risk;
c. uncertainties surrounding the unit values for a statistical life – (i) the unit value was adjusted downwards to reflect 'high age' valuations, but there is

little information on which to base this adjustment, and (ii) others' valuations of the life at risk have been excluded, biasing the unit value downwards;

d. the absence of dose–response functions for long-term pollution exposure. This could result in the estimates here being serious understatements of true damage.

These uncertainties need to be addressed further.

Table 9.8 Total damage estimates for PM_{10} morbidity effects

	Lower bound (£million)	Central estimate (£million)	Upper bound (£million)
RHAs			
England and Wales	26.8	48.8	70.3
UK	29.8	54.2	78.2
ERVs			
England and Wales	17.8	36.4	54.4
UK	19.8	40.5	60.5
RADs			
England and Wales	607.7	1215.3	1634.4
UK	676.2	1351.9	1818.4
Child LRIs			
England and Wales	ne	ne	ne
UK			
Asthma attacks			
England and Wales	345.7	584.7	2054.0
UK	384.6	676.0	2284.6
Respiratory symptoms			
England and Wales	218.7	459.2	699.8
UK	243.2	510.8	778.4
Chronic bronchitis			
England and Wales	1828.4	3723.2	5668.0
UK	2033.8	4149.0	6304.8
Totals (*)			
England and Wales	2826.4	5608.4	9481.1
UK	3144.2	6271.6	10546.5

Note: * Respiratory symptom costs are assumed to be subsumed in RAD costs, so that respiratory symptom costs are excluded from the totals.

Source: Tables 9.6 and 9.7; $e = 0.35$, that is, the final column of Table 9.7 has been used.

Table 9.9 Total costs of PM_{10} health damage in the UK

	Lower bound (£1994 billion)	Central estimate (£1994 billion)	Upper bound (£1994 billion)
England and Wales			
Urban morbidity	2.83	5.61	9.48
Urban mortality	4.52	7.00	9.48
Rural mortality	1.90	2.94	3.98
Total	9.25	15.55	22.94
United Kingdom			
Urban morbidity	3.14	6.27	10.55
Urban mortality	5.02	7.77	10.52
Rural mortality	2.18	3.38	4.58
Total	10.34	17.42	25.65

Note: Rural morbidity not estimated.

ANNEXE: A PROVISIONAL ANALYSIS OF RURAL PM_{10} DAMAGE

There exists no substantial dataset on PM_{10} concentrations in UK rural areas (but see ETSU, 1996). Harrison (1995) suggests that a mean rural concentration of 15 $\mu g/m^3$ is likely to be about right. Taking the rural population as being the residual from the at-risk urban population (see text), this suggests 56% of the population is exposed to 15 $\mu g/m^3$. Taking a background non-anthropogenic source as being 30% of actual concentrations in urban areas gives a background level of 8.5 $\mu g/m^3$. Applied to rural areas, then, the 'excess' exposure in rural areas is 15–8.5 = 6.5 $\mu g/m^3$. Arguably, the baseline in rural areas will be higher due to seasonal rural dust from soils etc. (Hefflin *et al.*,1994), which would imply that excess exposure will be less. On the other hand, concentrations may well understate true exposure due to rural dwellers commuting to urban areas where they are exposed to higher concentrations (see the evidence for Los Angeles in Brajer and Hall, 1992). Multiplying rural anthropogenic PM_{10} by total deaths in rural areas of 314 606, and using the dose response coefficient of 0.00096 gives an estimate of premature deaths in England and Wales of

$$6.5 \times 314606 \times 0.00096 = 1963$$

Extended to the UK an estimate for the UK would be:

$$\frac{\{58006 - 25343.9\}}{\{51277 - 22782.2\}} \times 1963 = 2250$$

Provisionally, then, we estimate that there are perhaps a further 2000 cases of premature mortality in rural areas of the UK due to PM_{10} exposure. We have made no estimate of rural morbidity due to PM_{10}. The social cost associated with this rural mortality would be £2.94 billion for England and Wales, and £3.38 billion for the UK.

NOTE

1. This paper was originally published in *Energy Policy*, **27**(7), July, 609–20.

REFERENCES

Action Asthma (1990), *The Occurrence and Cost of Asthma*, Action Asthma, Cambridge Medical Publications, Worthing.

AEA Technology (1995), *Air Pollution in the UK: 1993/1994*, Prepared by the National Environmental Technology Centre (NETCEN) for the UK Department of the Environment, Harwell.

Bentham, G. (1994), University of East Anglia, personal communication.

Bown, W. (1994), Dying from too much dust, *New Scientist*, March 12, 12–13.

Brajer, V. and Hall, J. (1992), Recent evidence on the distribution of air pollution effects, *Contemporary Policy Issues*, **X**, April, 63–71.

Brimblecombe, P. (1994), personal communication.

Brunekreef, P. (1995), *Quantifying the Health Effects for the Netherlands of Exposure to PM_{10}*, National Institute of Public Health and Environmental Protection, Bilthoven, Report 623710002 (In Dutch).

Chestnut, L. and Patterson, A. (1994), *Human Health Benefits Assessment of the Acid Rain Provisions of the 1990 Clean Air Act Amendments*, RCG Hagler Bailly, Bounder, Colorado for US EPA.

Cropper, M. and Simon, N.B. (1994), Are we valuing risks to life correctly?, World Bank, Washington DC, mimeo.

Desvousges, W *et al.* (1993), *Review of Health Effects Resulting from Exposure to Air Pollution*, Research Triangle Institute, Task Force on Externality Costing, Working Paper 1 (revised), November.

Dockery, D.W., Pope, D.A and Xiping, X. (1993), An association between air pollution and mortality in six U.S. cities, *The New England Journal of Medicine*, **329**(4), 1753–808.

Dockery, D.W., Schwartz, J. and Spengler, J. (1992) Air pollution and daily mortality: association with particulates and acid aerosols, *Environmental Research*, **59**, 362–73.

Energy Technology Support Unit (ETSU) (1996), Green Accounting Research Project – UK Case Study, mimeo, ETSU, Harwell, Oxfordshire, UK.

Eyre, N. (1995), Eyre Energy and Environment Consultants, personal communication.

Flanders, D., Haddix, A., Olson, D., Romieu, I., White, M. and Williamson, G.D. (1995), *Review of Urban Air Pollution Health Impact Methodology*, Center for Disease Control, Atlanta.

Harrison, R.(1995), University of Birmingham, personal communication.

Hefflin, B.J., Jalaludin, B., McClure, E., Cobb, N., Johnson, C., Jecha, L. and Etzel, R. (1994), Surveillance for dust storms and respiratory diseases in Washington State 1991, *Archives of Environmental Health*, **49**(3), 170–74.

Jones-Lee, M., Hammerton, M. and Philips, P. (1985), The value of safety: results from a national sample survey, *Economic Journal*, **95**, 49–72.

Jones-Lee, M., Loomes, G., O'Reilly, D. and Philips, P. (1993), *The Value of Preventing Non-fatal Road Injuries: Findings of a Willingness to Pay National Sample Survey*, Working Paper SRC/2, Transport and Road Research Laboratory, Crowthorne.

Krupnick, A., Harrison, K., Nickell, E. and Toman, M. (1993), *The Benefits of Ambient Air Quality Improvements in Central and Eastern Europe: a Preliminary Assessment*, Discussion Paper ENR93-19, Resources for the Future, Washington DC.

Maddison, D., Johansson, O., Littman, T., Pearce, D.W. and Verhoef, E. (1996), *Blueprint 5: The Social Costs of Transport*, Earthscan, London.

McMichael, A., Anderson, R., Elliott, P., Wilkinson, P., Ponce de Leon, A. and Simon, F. Soria (the 'London Review Group') (1995), *Review of Methods Proposed, and Used, for Estimating the Population Health Risks of Exposure to Urban Air Pollution*, London School of Hygiene and Tropical Medicine, London.

Ostro, B. (1994), *Estimating Health Effects of Air Pollution: a Method with an Application to Jakarta*, Policy Research Department, Working Paper 1301, World Bank, Washington DC.

Ostro, B. (1995a), Addressing uncertainties in the quantitative estimation of air pollution health effects, Paper presented to EC/IEA/OECD Workshop on the External Costs of Energy, Brussels, January 1995.

Ostro, B. (1995b), *Air Pollution and Mortality: Results from Santiago, Chile*, Policy Research Department, Working Paper 1453, World Bank, Washington DC.

Pearce, D.W. (1994), *Assessing the Health Costs of Benzene Exposure in the UK*, CSERGE, University College London and University of East Anglia, mimeo.

Pearce, D.W. (ed.) (1994b), *Blueprint 3: Measuring Sustainable Development*, Earthscan, London.

Pearce, D.W., Bann, C., Georgiou, S. (1992), *Social Costs of Fuel Cycles*, HMSO, London.

Pearce, D.W and Knight, I.(1992), *Valuing Non-Fatal Injury Costs*, Paper prepared for UK Department of Transport Seminar on Non-fatal Injuries, London, mimeo.

Pearce, D.W., Whittington, D. and Georgiou, S. (1994a), *Project and Policy Appraisal: Integrating Economics and Environment*, OECD, Paris.

Pope, C.A. and Dockery, D. (1992), Acute health effects of PM_{10} pollution on symptomatic and asymptomatic children, *American Review of Respiratory Disease*, **145**, 1123–8.

Pope, C.A., Schwartz, J. and Ransom, M. (1992), 'Daily mortality and PM_{10} pollution in Utah Valley, *Archives of Environmental Health*, **47**(3), 211–17.

Pope, C.A., Thun, M.J., Namboordi, M., Dockery, D.W., Evans, J.D., Speizer, F. and Heath Jr, C.W. (1995), Particulate air pollution as a predictor of mortality in a prospective study of US adults, *American Journal of Respiratory and Critical Care Medicine*, **151**, 669–74.

Quality of Urban Air Review Group (QUARG) (1993a), *Urban Air Quality in the United Kingdom, First Report*, Prepared for the Department of the Environment.

Quality of Urban Air Review Group (QUARG) (1993b), *Diesel Vehicle Emissions and Urban Air Quality, Second Report*, Prepared for the Department of the Environment.

Rowe, R., Chestnut, L., Lang, C., Bernow, S. and White, D. (1995), *The New York Environmental Externalities Cost Study: Summary of Approach and Results*, Paper presented to European Commission, International Energy Agency and Organisation for Economic Cooperation and Development Workshop on External Costs of Energy, Brussels, 30–31 January, 1995.

(UK) Royal Commission on Environmental Pollution (1994), *Eighteenth Report: Transport and the Environment*, Cm 2674, HMSO, London.

Schwab Christe, N. and Soguel, N. (1995), *The Pain of Victims and the Bereavement of their Relatives: a Contingent Valuation Experiment*, IDHEAP, University of Lausanne, Switzerland, mimeo.

Schwartz, J. (1991a), Particulate air pollution and daily mortality in Detroit, *Environmental Research*, **56**, 204–213.

Schwartz, J. (1991b), 'Particulate air pollution and daily mortality: a synthesis, *Public Health Reviews*, **19**, 39–60.

Schwartz, J. (1993a), Air pollution and daily mortality in Birmingham, Alabama, *American Journal of Epidemiology*, **137**, 1136–47.

Schwartz, J. (1993b), Particulate air pollution and chronic respiratory disease, *Environmental Research*, **62**, 7–13.

Schwartz, J. (1994), Air pollution and daily mortality: a review and meta analysis, *Environmental Research*, **64**, 36–52.

Schwartz, J. and Dockery, D. (1992a), Particulate air pollution and daily mortality in Steubenville, Ohio, *American Journal of Epidemiology*, **135**, 12–19.

Schwartz, J. and Dockery, D. (1992b), Increased mortality in Philadelphia associated with daily air pollution concentrations, *American Review of Respiratory Disease*, **145**, 600–604.

Schwartz, J. and Marcus, A. (1990), Mortality and air pollution in London: a time series analysis, *American Journal of Epidemiology*, **131**(1), 185–94.

Schwartz, J., Slater, D., Larson, T., Pierson, W. and Koenig, J. (1993), Particulate air pollution and hospital emergency room visits for asthma in Seattle, *American Review of Respiratory Disease*, **147**, 826–31.

Schwartz, J ., Spix, C., Wichman, H. and Malin, E. (1991), Air pollution and acute respiratory illness in five German communities, *Environmental Research*, **56**, 1–14.

Seaton, A., Macnee, W., Donaldson, K and Godden, D (1995), Particulate air pollution and acute health effects, *The Lancet*, **345**, 21 January, 176–8.

Small, K. and Kazimi, C. (1995), On the cost of air pollution from motor vehicles, *Journal of Transport Economics and Policy*, January, 7–32.

Utell, S. and Samet, J. (1993), Particulate air pollution and health: new evidence of an old problem, *American Review of Respiratory Disease*, **147**, 1334–35.

Walters, S. (1994), Effects on health of traffic-related pollution – a review of epidemiological studies, in C. Read (ed.), *How Vehicle Pollution Affects Our Health*, The Ashden Trust, London.

World Bank (1994a), *Indonesia Environment and Development: Challenges for the Future*, Environment Unit, Country Department III, East Asia and Pacific Region, World Bank, Washington DC, March.

World Bank (1994b), *Thailand: Mitigating Pollution and Congestion Impacts in a High Growth Economy*, Country Operations Division, Country Department 1, East Asia and Pacific Region, World Bank, Washington DC, February.

World Bank (1994c), *Chile: Managing Environmental Problems – Economic Analysis of Selected Issues*, Environment and Urban Development Division, Country Department 1, Latin America and the Caribbean Region, World Bank, Washington DC, December.

Xu, X., Gao, J., Dockery, D. and Chen, Y. (1994), Air pollution and daily mortality in residential areas of Beijing, China, *Archives of Environmental Health*, **49**(4), July/August, 216–222.

10. Assessing the social rate of return from investment in temperate zone forestry[1]

10.1 THE NATURE OF BENEFITS FROM FORESTRY INVESTMENTS

Forestry is a multiple output activity. The planting of forests produces a number of joint outputs and services. Outputs can be positive taking the form of benefits, or negative, i.e. forests may actually reduce the provision of a service compared to the displaced land use, creating a cost. Much depends on exactly where afforestation takes place. Thus:

- an afforested area supplies trees as timber and as a source of recreation;
- depending on the 'mix' of trees and the treatments applied to them, in place biological diversity may be increased compared to the number of species and/or total species biomass in the displaced land use;
- landscape values may be increased or decreased according to the preferences of those looking at the landscape;
- some watershed may be protected by afforestation through the prevention of soil erosion. Others may suffer from soil erosion from ploughing and road building activity;
- water run-off may be reduced by interception to the point where surrounding areas suffer a diminution of water supply, but flood peaks may be reduced once the forest is established;
- microclimates may be affected by afforestation, but considerable uncertainty surrounds these impacts;
- afforestation may increase the deposition of airborne sulphur oxides and nitrogen dioxide in the forested area, but, in so doing, will reduce the transport of these pollutants to other areas. This 'acidification stripping' process may then result in increases in waterborne pollutants in the forested areas through leaching, and the effects of acidification of soils;
- forests act as carbon sinks, and hence afforestation can reduce CO_2 emissions stored in the atmosphere, reducing the 'greenhouse effect';

- economic security for the nation may be advanced by afforestation because of reduced costs from interruptions in flows of imported timber;
- the decline of rural communities may be lessened through afforestation. The US Forest Service, for example, has as one of its objectives the maintenance of 'community stability'. This is particularly relevant to the many small communities in the west of the USA dependent upon public timber harvesting. For an evaluation of the 'worth' of this benefit see Boyd and Hyde (1989).

Other benefits widely attributed to afforestation include the creation or protection of rural employment and the saving of imports. These impacts are discussed separately below because they generally will not qualify as allowable benefits in the sense used in this chapter.

Only some of these outputs or services are marketed. Typically, only timber values are reflected in the assessment of rates of return to plantations. As is well known, such rates of return frequently fall below conventional 'discount rates' employed by private or public agencies. Hence afforestation invariably appears to be 'uneconomic'. However, it is the whole range of outputs that is relevant to economic assessment. Use of timber values alone to determine investment worth is in fact a purely commercial criterion.

Henceforth, we distinguish between commercial rates of return and economic rates of return, the latter encompassing the value of non-marketed outputs and services and other adjustments considered below.

The benefit of afforestation can be measured as the sum of:

timber values
recreational value
landscape value
biodiversity value
watershed protection or damage (and other ecological function values)
microclimate
air pollution value (other than CO_2)
water pollution values
'greenhouse' benefit – that is, value of trees as carbon stores
economic security
community integrity

This conceals an aggregation problem because individual components of the aggregate benefits may be inconsistent with each other. Thus a high timber value may be inconsistent with a high recreational value. There are trade-offs between the component values in the benefit equation. This issue needs to be borne in mind when aggregating benefits. Total benefits are symbolized by *B*. The costs of afforestation (land acquisition, planting costings, maintenance, thinning, felling etc), will be symbolized by *K*. If any of the above benefit flows are actually negative – e.g. if reduced water run-off is a cost rather than a benefit – then they will appear as such in the benefit side of the equation. That is, benefits are negative costs, and costs are negative benefits.

The overall comparison is thus between the benefits of afforestation and the costs of afforestation, or: Net benefits = B–K, ignoring, for the moment, the problem of time. Afforestation is judged potentially worthwhile if $B > K$, and potentially not worthwhile if $B < K$.

It is important to compute *B* and *K* relative to the alternative use of the land. The same exercise should therefore be carried out for such alternative uses. Typically these will be 'wilderness' or agriculture, but in the case of planned 'community forests', afforestation could be at the expense of derelict land, building or recreational land use.

The cost–benefit approach then justifies afforestation if:

$$[B_f - K_f] > [B_a - K_a]$$

where '*f*' refers to forestry and '*a*' to the alternative land use. More strictly, we require this condition to hold in circumstances where '*a*' is the highest alternative value of the land: afforestation must be compared to the next best use of the land.

10.2 MARKET FAILURE AND THE VALUATION OF FORESTRY BENEFITS

The fact that many of the outputs of forests are not marketed means that the use of purely commercial or 'free market' criteria to determine the amount of afforestation will result in an under-supply of afforestation as long as the non-marketed benefits are positive. This under-supply is an instance of market failure. Basically, markets do not supply the 'right' amount of afforestation. It must not be concluded from this that some form of public ownership will therefore necessarily produce the 'right' amount. Public ownership could introduce distortions of its own. Other forms of regulatory intervention may also introduce bigger distortions than those induced by market failure. If so, it may be a matter of opting for the 'least distorted' option, an instance of what economists call the 'second best' problem. There are no *a priori* rules for deciding the form of ownership or regulation. it is an empirical matter. For an evaluation of regulatory options for forestry in the USA, using cost–benefit principles, see Boyd and Hyde (1989).

But there are other forms of market failure. We cannot be certain that the use of resources is correctly valued if market prices are used, nor that outputs at market values are correctly valued. For inputs the basic rule is that they should be valued at their opportunity cost, that is, what they would have received had they been put to alternative use.

Labour

In the forestry context the resource that has attracted most attention in this respect is labour. Because afforestation tends to take place in rural areas where alternative employment outlets are few, it can be argued that the opportunity cost of forestry labour is very much lower than the wage rates actually paid. They might, for example be rates payable for labour on hill farms, or casual labour in the tourist industry, or, if the alternative to forestry employment is unemployment, the cost could be regarded as near zero. In the benefit–cost equation then, the labour component of K would be costed as this opportunity cost wage, or shadow wage.

The use of a shadow wage rate is disputed, and the dispute tends to centre on differing interpretations of how labour markets function. Some economists argue that the economic system functions so that, effectively, all markets 'clear'. There is then full employment in the sense that any new job must always take a worker from somewhere else in the system. In the technical language, there is no employment additionality. There may well be income additionality in that the forestry job pays more than the job it displaces. Indeed, one would expect this to be the case if people only move jobs for higher rewards. But if there is no employment additionality, it would be wrong to shadow price a forestry job at zero. Its proper shadow price would be the income in the displaced job. Moreover, if we think of afforestation as investment at the margin, tracing through the various transfers of jobs that enable the forestry job to be filled is likely to result in the shadow wage being very close to the actual wage paid. If, on the other hand, markets do not clear, then the creation of a job in the forestry sector does result in employment additionality, and lower shadow prices are justified (see Byatt, 1983).

Rather than evaluate what is in effect a fundamental disagreement in macroeconomic theory it seems better to adopt two approaches to labour valuation: (a) adopting the ruling wage rate in forestry, and (b) adopting some fraction of this to reflect a lower wage rate. A 1988 survey of 100 farms in Scotland (Dewar, 1998) produced an average of £0.62 per hour as the income from farming. However, non-farm activity was used to supplement the low rates of pay in farming. On average, 1227 hours p.a. were spent in farm activity and

957 hours in non-farm activity. Average farm plus non-farm income was £4964 p.a. But, if agriculture alone was the alternative occupation, then income averaged only £565 p.a., although only 5% of farmers relied on agricultural income alone. Subsidies supplied additional income as did work by other members of the household.

In terms of a 'shadow wage rate' these figures suggest that the maximum rate is around £5000 p.a., i.e. some two-thirds of the market wage. Depending on location, the shadow rate could be considerably less than this, but we set the shadow wage rate at 0.67 of ruling market rates.

Imports

The other shadow price that attracts a lot of attention in the forestry literature is the value of timber itself. Timber is an internationally traded good and the relevant shadow price for UK timber is therefore the price that it could secure if exported, or the price that has to be paid on world markets for the imports that would otherwise have to be secured.

Since the United Kingdom imports some 90% of its timber needs, international trade is particularly important. The shadow price of timber is thus its border price, i.e. its import or export price. Many commentators nonetheless feel that this price, which is the market price in the UK, still understates the true value of afforestation. They argue that the market fails in at least one of the following ways:

(i) The market fails to anticipate future scarcity of timber. Since gestation periods are long, the shadow price to be applied to afforestation now should be the expected real price in, say, 30 years' time allowing for future scarcity. This argument has been particularly powerful in the history of both UK policy and in the USA (Boyd and Hyde, 1989).

(ii) The market fails to reflect the importance of substituting for imports. There are two strands to this argument:
1. The market may not anticipate supply interruptions from trade embargoes, political disruptions of supply, etc.
2. The value of an avoided import is somehow higher than the market price paid for that import. This is the 'import substitution' argument.

Argument (i) is an argument for forecasting relative prices. A number of such forecasting exercises have been carried out for UK forestry (Pearce *et al.*, 1988; Pearce and Markandya, 1990; Arnold, 1991; Whiteman, 1991). The required adjustment to prices is then relatively simple.

Argument (ii)1 is a legitimate one for shadow pricing timber output. An evaluation of the chances of such embargoes and other supply interruptions suggest that a small increment in prices of 0.2–1.8% to reflect the shadow value of economic security would be justified.

Argument (ii)2 is illegitimate. A UK tree does not have a value higher than its border prices simply because it displaces an import valued at that border price. The theory of comparative advantage explains why import substitution arguments cannot be used to defend afforestation. The essence of the argument is (a) that free trade maximizes the well-being of those taking part in trade, (b) that, from a purely 'nationalist' point of view, protection of a domestic industry may be beneficial if the protecting country has monopoly power over the good being traded, and (c) where no such monopoly power exists, any tariff or other protective measure will reduce the volume of a nation's trade, making it worse off.

Applied to forestry in the UK, there is no monopoly of timber since the UK is very much a 'price taker', timber price being determined in world markets. No feasible afforestation programme in the UK could affect world prices. Hence protectionist policies towards forestry in the UK would reduce UK well-being. Subsidizing forestry on import substitution grounds is thus illegitimate.

Land

Valuing land acquisition for afforestation poses a problem because the land in question is typically used for agriculture which is in receipt of various forms of subsidy under the Common Agricultural Policy. That is, actual land prices will not be the same as those which would rule if the various forms of agricultural policy intervention did not take place. One study suggests that if all forms of support and trade distortion are removed, agricultural land prices might fall by as much as 46%. If so, land costs for afforestation should be recorded as 0.54 of the actual cost, (1986 as the base year). However, as agricultural support declines over time, agricultural land prices will converge on the free market prices, so the 'shadow price' of land will rise relative to the free market price. Put another way, the multiplier of 0.54 would decline over time. Harvey (1991) raises two further caveats to the use of the 0.54 multiplier. First, as land leaves agriculture it is likely to become the subject of an 'amenity' demand, i.e. a demand from people who simply wish to own land for amenity purposes. Hence the 46% price fall figure is likely to be too high. Second, there is an additional form of demand for land to be held in agriculture for amenity reasons. This is akin to an option or existence value (see Section 10.4), and effectively means that some element of the existing subsidy reflects this value. It is not clear that this form of value applies equally to afforested land regardless of the form of afforestation. It is likely to be true for broad-leaved forest, but less true for coniferous forests. The difference between the social value of agricultural land and the free market price is further narrowed by these considerations.

Accordingly, we suggest an upper limit of the social value of land used in future afforestation is taken to be 0.8 of the market value. Since this figure is likely to be on the high side, and certainly does not allow for the land price effects of any major expansion of forestry, a range of values between the limits of 0.5 and 0.8 is used.

10.3 BENEFITS AND TIME

Benefits and costs accrue over time. Time plays a particularly important role in afforestation economics because timber can take 30, 50 or 100 years to mature for an optimal rotation, depending on the type of wood, the geographical zone, soil type etc. Because economics adopts the standpoint that consumer preferences 'matter', preferences for having benefits now rather than later, and preferences for postponing costs rather than suffering them now, mean that benefits and costs are discounted. The rate of discount is in fact another shadow price. It is the price of consumption now in terms of consumption in the future.

Discounting is controversial because of its potential for shifting forward in time, frequently to another generation, the costs of actions undertaken for benefit now (e.g. the benefits of nuclear power versus the costs of disposing of radioactive waste). In the forestry context the problem is that the discounting of future benefits means that planting costs now figure prominently in the rate of return calculation while the benefits from a rotation in 30 years' time are downgraded significantly. To see this consider a rotation in year 30 yielding, say £100 000 of timber at projected prices. At the current UK 'target' discount rate of 8%, this would be valued at:

$$\frac{\pounds 100\,000}{(1.08)^{30}} = \text{approx } \pounds 10\,000$$

The application of discounting techniques means that afforestation is potentially justified if:

$$\Sigma\, d_t\, \{B_{ft} - K_{ft}\} > \Sigma\, d_t\, \{B_{at} - K_{at}\}$$

Where d is the 'discount factor' and is equal to $1/(1+r)^t$, r is the discount rate, t is time and Σ means 'sum of'. Various suggestions have been made for lowering the discount rate applied to afforestation, primarily because it appears unfairly to discriminate against any investment with a long gestation period (for an extensive discussion see Markandya and Pearce, 1988). The problem with adjusting discount rates downward is that there is no easily derived rule for the quantitative adjustment that is needed.

Moreover, if the rate is lowered for forestry why should it not be lowered for other investments?[12] If all discount rates were lowered then it can be shown that the effect could well be detrimental to the environment, the preservation of which is the main motive for advocating lower rates. The overall detrimental effect comes about because generally lower discount rates would alter the optimal balance between investment and consumption in the economy in favour of investment. In turn if investment is more polluting than consumption, then the net effect is to encourage more environmental decay (Krautkraemer, 1988). Many of the arguments for lowering discount rates are in fact arguments for valuing benefits more accurately and comprehensively. Even then, discrimination against forestry seems to remain. This suggests the possibility of lowering the rate for afforestation but not for other investments. This effectively was the situation in the UK whereby afforestation had to achieve a Treasury-approved rate of return lower than that on other projects – a minimum of 3% overall compared to 5% for other public investments. Current (1990) recommended discount rates are 6% on most public investments, with 8% for transport projects. The UK Treasury currently proposes that 6% be used for forestry if non-market benefits are to be included. In the cost–benefit analyses of this chapter we use the 6% rate with a lower 3% rate occasionally being also used for sensitivity purposes.

An alternative route is to apply the nation-wide general discount rate to forestry and to introduce a sustainability constraint. Although there are many interpretations of sustainable development a strong case can be made for interpreting it as non-declining per capita well-being over time, a condition for which is that the stock of overall capital in the economy should also be non-declining. Put more simply, it is a requirement to 'keep capital intact' and is more familiar in business as the need not to 'live off capital'. The precise rationale for this requirement need not detain us here.

Note that it would be improper to use the lower rate if it is designed to capture the non-market benefits of afforestation. This is because, as will be seen, the aim here is to derive estimates for the major non-market benefits and to add these to the timber benefits. Making these estimates and lowering the discount rate would be double counting. However, the 6% rate applies across the board to UK public services (except transport investments) and, for this reason, it is argued that the 6% rate and the integration of non-market benefits is legitimate.

In practice the constant capital stock rule could mean two things: maintaining a stock of all capital, man-made and 'natural; or maintaining a stock of 'natural' capital, i.e. environmental assets. In the former case it would be legitimate to run down environmental capital (e.g. deforestation would be legitimate) provided other forms of capital were built up. In the latter case, the existing stock of environmental assets must not be run down in the aggregate, but there can be substitution within that stock. On the narrower interpretation of sustainability, then, it could be argued that the UK's stock of forest should not be run down. Put another way, afforestation would be justified at least as compensation for loss of forests, but an expansion of the stock of land devoted to forestry would require additional arguments.

The sustainability argument is further complicated by substitution within the stock of existing environmental assets. Thus, forest stocks might be run down in favour of expanded farming. Two observations are in order. First, what constitutes acceptable substitution depends on valuation which is precisely why the approach of 'cost–benefit thinking' has been adopted. Second, in the UK context the issue is generally one of a longer-run decline in land devoted to farming, with afforestation being considered as one of the main alternative uses of some of the released land.

In fact some of the arguments justifying expansion of forestry are already represented in the benefits of afforestation for 'fixing' CO_2 emissions. The sum of benefits does not indicate to whom the benefits and costs accrue. UK forestry investment would typically be evaluated according to the benefits and costs to the UK. But the benefit of fixing CO_2 is not confined to the UK. It is a 'global public good'. The sustainability requirement, then, also needs a 'boundary'. If the boundary is the UK, then the only afforestation that would be justified on a sustainability constraint is that which holds the forest stock in the UK constant. But if UK afforestation is seen as a contribution to moves to restore the global forest stock, then the picture is rather different. The UK cannot adopt a stance that afforestation is good so long as it compensates for a global loss of forests, but there is an alternative approach which would credit UK forest expansion with the benefits of global CO_2 reduction.

It seems likely that nations will negotiate a near-global agreement on the containment of greenhouse gases. [This now exists as The Framework Convention on Climate Change 1992, David W. Pearce.] This agreement will state a 'target' global warming increase above which the world should not go because of the significant ecological disruption that would otherwise be judged to ensue. That upper limit target rate that is widely suggested is 0.1° C per decade of 'realised warming', together with 2°C absolute increase in temperature above pre-industrial levels. (Rijsberman and Swart, 1990). Any target can then be translated into 'allowable' greenhouse gas emissions. On the assumption that non-carbon greenhouse gases are severely curtailed – as the 1990 modifications to the Montreal Protocol on the protection of the ozone layer require – the allowable warming target of 0.1°C per decade appears to correspond to significant reductions in CO_2 emissions below current (1990) levels (IPCC, 1990). A rational international agreement will allow for carbon 'sinks' as the negative of an allowable emission, i.e. the creation of any carbon sink should constitute an 'offset' for any CO_2 emissions of equal amounts.

The offset idea is effectively the sustainability constraint – it embodies the underlying requirement that the total of CO_2 emissions should not exceed a fixed annual level. On this basis, afforestation secures a 'carbon credit' equal in value to the cost of reducing CO_2 emissions by other means, e.g. by substituting non-carbon fuels. This issue is explored further in Section 10.10.

10.4 THE NATURE OF ECONOMIC VALUE

Given that non-market value is potentially very important in justifying forestry expansion it is worth dwelling briefly on the components of economic value. Although different authors use different classificatory systems, the following seems most helpful. Economic values may be divided into:

- use values;
- non-use values.

Values can be divided into direct and indirect values. A direct use value would be, for example, timber harvesting and the use of thinnings. Recreational uses of forests is another (Willis and Benson, 1989). An indirect use value would be exemplified by an ecological function, such as watershed protection. Another use value is option value which reflects the willingness to pay for afforestation on the grounds that, while not used at present, the option to use the forest is valued.

Non-use values relate to economic values unassociated with any direct or indirect use values. Individuals may, for example, wish to support afforestation on the grounds that they think forests are valuable even though they will never personally make direct use of them. Motives for these 'existence' and 'bequest' values are debated but may include concern for future generations, the adoption of some 'stewardship' role with respect to nature, conferment of 'rights' to nature, and so on.

Table 10.1 shows the overall classification system. It also indicates the types of valuation methodology that are appropriate for the various components of 'total economic value'. These methodologies are not discussed further here. The following sections are devoted to drawing up a 'balance sheet' for the cost–benefit assessment of forestry expansion.

Table 10.1 Valuing forest benefits

	Total economic value			
Direct use benefits	Indirect use values	Option values	Existence values	Bequest values
Type of benefits				
T	B	B	B	B
R	W	R	L	
B	M	C		
S	G	L		
L	C			
	A			
	P			
	Valuation technique			
Market prices	Avoided damage costs	CVM	CVM	CVM
HPM	Preventive expenditures			
TCM	Value of productivity changes			
	Replacement costs			

Notes:
TCM = travel cost method
S = economic security
C = community integrity
L = landscape
W = watershed/ecosystem function
M = microclimate
G = greenhouse impact
HPM = hedonic pricing method
CVM = contingent valuation method
T = timber
R = recreation
B = biodiversity
A = air pollution
P = water pollution

10.5 THE COMPONENTS OF COST–BENEFIT ANALYSIS: TIMBER (T)

This section estimates the value of timber. Table 10.2 summarizes commercial rate of return and NPV data for afforestation under various yield classes and locations, excluding all grants.

Table 10.2 Commercial analysis of afforestation (timber benefits only)

		NPV	IRR
FT1	semi natural pinewoods/uplands	–798	3.2
	land value = 0.5	–975	3.0
	land value = 0.8		
FT2	semi natural broadleaves/lowlands	–2940	–
	land value = 0.5	–3839	
	land value = 0.8		
FT3	semi natural broadleaves/uplands	–1099	–
	land value = 0.5	–1276	
	land value = 0.8		
FT4	spruce/uplands	–4	6.0
	land value = 0.0	–288	5.4
	land value = 0.5	–458	5.1
	land value = 0.8		
FT5	community forests	–3173	2.6
FT6	native broadleaves/lowlands	–3384	1.0
	land value = 0.5	–4283	0.9
	land value = 0.8		
FT7	pines/lowlands	–1741	3.7
	land value = 0.5	–2605	3.2
	land value = 0.8		
FT8	fir, spruce, broadleaves/lowlands	572	7.1
	land value = 0.0	–819	5.0
	land value = 0.5	–1653	4.3
	land value = 0.8		

Notes:
NPV at £1989/90 per hectare, and IRRs; 6% discount rate.
FT: forestry type
LV: 0.5 refers to shadow price of land at 50% of market value
'–' under IRR means a negative IRR

In the table, various assumptions are made about the shadow price of land. In each case 80% of the market value is used. This is taken to be £3000 per hectare in the lowlands and £660/hectare in the uplands. If a different view is taken, by arguing that the amenity value factor in agricultural land prices applies equally well to forestry land, then the lower factor of 50% of market value might be used (see the discussion in Section 10.2). A shadow price of zero may also be applicable in some cases where the alternative value of the land is zero.

A once-for-all premium of 1% on timber prices reflects economic security. For forest types appropriate to those parts of the country where the shadow price of labour is less than the market wage, the cost of labour is taken to be 67% of its market value.

The internal rate of return columns in Table 10.2 are perhaps the easiest way of seeing the overall private profitability of timber production. At a 6% discount rate only the following are profitable or marginally profitable:

- mixed fir, spruce and broadleaves in the lowlands, assuming land has zero opportunity cost;
- spruce in the uplands provided land has zero opportunity cost.

Timber Prices

As noted above timber prices in commercial rate of return calculations should reflect future expectations. Similarly, the relevant price for an evaluation of UK afforestation is the price at which timber is imported to the UK. For this reason, world regional prices are the relevant ones for the evaluation exercise.

Arnold (1991) suggests various estimates of average annual price rises in the USA:

- 1–1.1 % p.a., mostly concentrated after the turn of the century Pulpwood prices rise more slowly than sawlog prices;
- 0.2–1.2% p.a. averaged across sawlogs and pulpwood, and perhaps higher with sawlog prices rising faster than pulpwood, if there is a high demand.

Contrary to the USA, the European picture appears to be more one of rising prices for pulpwood and falling prices for coniferous logs. The difference in the price trends in the two regions reflects the past application of recycling technology more intensively in Europe than the USA, and the consequent more limited scope for further market penetration or recycling. There has also been slower growth in the consumption of European sawn wood. Prices in the two regions are expected to converge. Expected technical change in the European processing industry and large supplies of roundwood are likely to keep prices down. Pearce *et al.* (1988) survey various price projections and conclude that a range of 0–2% p.a. in future real prices would embrace all reasonable assessments, and that projections at the lower end of the range are more likely to be realized. Overall, stable real prices define the lower bound of expected price changes with an upper bound of perhaps 1.5% p.a. Table 10.2 assumes constant real prices only. This is in keeping with the analysis of Sedjo and Lyon (1990).

10.6 THE COMPONENTS OF COST–BENEFIT ANALYSIS: RECREATION (R)

Benson and Willis (1991) provide estimates of the net benefits to recreationists of different types of forest plantation. The results arc shown in Table 10.3. It is a matter of local circumstance as to when recreation benefits are likely to accrue. It is assumed here that there are no benefits until year 16 and that thereafter they continue at the same level until the end of the rotation. The benefits are 'gross' in the sense that recreational benefits from the alternative use of land are not accounted for.

Table 10.3 Recreational consumer surplus by forest type

Recreational value	Uplands	Lowlands
Low	3	n.a.
Moderate	30	50
High	n.a.	220
Very high	n.a.	424

Note: £1989 per hectare/year

While recreational values are not translatable across continents, it would be surprising if they differed very much. Recent work in the USA suggests a present capital value per hectare of forest of around $1100, i.e. around £690. It is interesting to note that this is consistent with the moderate annual recreational values presented here for the lowlands.

Just as timber prices may rise in real terms over time, so recreational benefits may rise. USA work does suggest rising real values. Walsh surveys the US evidence on the growth of recreation demand (Walsh, 1986). Land-based recreation is forecast to grow by some 1.0% per annum. The 1% growth rate may in fact be too low for the UK (data from the General Household Survey indicates that all recreational activity surveyed has been growing at 3% per annum (participations per adult per year), while walking has grown at 2% p.a.).

Adopting a 1% growth rate for the increase in benefits from forest-based recreation is therefore conservative.

The final analysis in Section 10.13 shows the effects of including a rising value of recreational benefits.

10.7 THE COMPONENTS OF COST–BENEFIT ANALYSIS: WILDLIFE CONSERVATION (BIODIVERSITY) (B)

It is possible to rank desirable forest types in respect of wildlife values. These values are regarded as being a function of 'naturalness', diversity and rarity. Diversity is typically regarded as being most valuable if it is itself natural. The introduction of Sitka spruce does for example increase diversity, but conservationists tend to regard such gains as being at the expense of natural diversity. Most afforestation tends to increase diversity. The ranking that emerges from one study is: (a) new mixed 'native' woodland; (b) mixed broadleaves and conifers; (c) non-native broadleaves or conifers alone (Good *et al.*, 1991).

Wildlife impacts depend very much on the actual location of any new forest. Of particular value is planting which links existing woodland, making the connected area larger and thus increasing diversity. Of note is the finding that spruce is probably no better or worse than alternative non-native woodlands for wildlife diversity. The assumption is that afforestation displaces low value agricultural land which, in turn, is regarded as being of low wildlife conservation interest.

10.8 THE COMPONENTS OF COST-BENEFIT ANALYSIS: WATER RESOURCE IMPACTS (W)

Forests have a number of water-related ecological impacts on the surrounding watershed of forested areas. These are:

- impacts on water supply;
- impacts on water quality;
- impacts on air pollutant deposition;
- soil erosion;
- fertilizer impacts;
- pesticide impacts;
- harvesting impacts.

Water Supply

Afforestation involves evaporation losses mainly due to canopy interception: 20–50% of incoming rainfall may be intercepted with streamflow reductions of around 15%. At one well studied site, reductions in streamflow of about 15% were recorded where 60% of the site was planted with conifers. Current models predict a loss of flow of 15% in the wet uplands from a 75% afforested catchment. The economic importance of such reduced flows depends on the relationship between supply and demand for water. While some monetary estimates of loss have been made, e.g. in terms of additional water extraction or storage costs to water authorities, and reduced hydropower capacity, the data is not currently in a form that enables valuation of the various areas under discussion. The effects are negligible in the lowlands or will appear as a small cost.

Air/Water Pollution

Forests 'scrub' air pollutants so that afforestation has the effect of increasing deposition of various pollutants. Some pollutants are absorbed by leaf and stem surfaces; some, such as SO_2 and O_3 are absorbed through the stomata; and the effect on NO_2 and NO appears indeterminate. Co-deposition of NH_3 and SO_2 may produce a significant increase in the deposition of both gases. Deposition varies according to the type of forest. The economic significance is two-fold. By scrubbing the pollutants the forest may prevent them from incurring damage elsewhere, depending on the buffering capacity of the recipient soils. But by concentrating them in the forested area pollutant concentrations in drainage waters are increased. This impacts on acidification and aluminium content. Technically, the correct 'valuation' of this impact would compute the localized damage due to acidification from forests and then deduct the damage that would otherwise be done by the emissions that initially arise. That is, forests should not be debited with all acidification damage given that the source of the acidification is, say, power station emissions.

Acidification

Streams draining forested areas on sensitive sites may be more acidic and may contain more aluminium, although long-term studies have so far failed to detect an impact.

Erosion and Sedimentation

New planting may cause soil erosion and consequent increased sedimentation of watercourses. Chemical leaching may also occur. Costs to the water industry can be high, with one instance of £180 000 additional costs for a treatment plant to counteract the effects of ploughing for planting in the catchment area. Soil erosion may also be present throughout the rotation. Soil erosion is, however, common with intensive agricultural systems, and the overall effect may be beneficial.

Fertilizers

Fertilizer run-off from forest treatment appears to be of negligible significance as far as rivers are concerned, but can be important if run-off is to lakes and reservoirs. Impacts are likely to be very site-specific and again this is not likely to be bad in areas that were intensively farmed.

Table 10.4 Summary of water-related ecological impact by areas

	Uplands	Upland margins	Lowlands
Water loss			
ecological	–	–	–
economic	–	–	–
Erosion			
ecological	–	neg	+
economic	–	neg	+
Fertilizer			
ecological	neg	neg	+
economic	neg	neg	+
Pesticide			
ecological	neg	neg	+
economic	neg	neg	+
Deposition			
ecological	+ +	neg	neg
economic	+ +	neg	neg
Harvesting			
ecological	–	neg	neg
economic	–	neg	neg

Notes:
+ = a benefit
– = a cost compared to alternative land use
neg = negligible

Pesticides

Insecticides and herbicides are used on a relatively small scale in forestry but can affect water quality. Herbicide impacts can occur through reduced vegetative cover affecting streamwater chemistry.

Harvesting

Harvesting by clear felling modifies the microclimate, results in a sudden increase in debris and interrupts nutrient cycling. Nitrate in drainage waters may be increased. But there is no evidence that water treatment costs have increased as a result.

Hornung and Adamson (1991) conclude that ecological impacts are likely to be site-specific and that there is considerable scope for their mitigation through careful forest management. Impacts by forested area are summarized in Table 10.4. A distinction is made between ecological and economic impacts; significant ecological impacts could occur without them being 'valued' highly, and vice versa. More generally, one would expect them to be similar in magnitude.

10.9 THE COMPONENTS OF COST–BENEFIT ANALYSIS: LANDSCAPE EVALUATION (L)

Campbell and Fairley (1991) assess the role of forests in landscape evaluation. Aesthetic qualities include enjoyment, psychological well-being, child education and development, artistic and creative stimuli and a 'sense of security'. They indicate that there is a general consensus about what constitutes landscape value. These values contribute both to land and property values, and to option and existence value (of Table 10.1) not revealed in market prices. They also argue that the demand for landscape conservation is growing. Landscape value is highest with multipurpose non-monocultural forests. As with biodiversity, native woodlands are assigned the highest landscape value. Also echoing the biodiversity discussion, landscape value depends critically upon the location and design of forests, so that no general conclusion can be reached about non-site-specific values. Overall, however, the ranking for landscape values would appear to be very similar to that for biodiversity.

10.10 THE COMPONENTS OF COST–BENEFIT ANALYSIS: GREENHOUSE EFFECT (G)

Trees take carbon dioxide from the atmosphere and fix it in perennial tissue. The CO_2 is eventually released as the wood decays or is burned. Some uses of the wood 'lock up' the carbon for long periods, and this period of lock-up overlaps the next rotation of tree growing so that rates of accumulation of carbon exceed rates of decay. This net gain is not indefinite and is probably around 100 years plus, after which fixation is then matched by decay and there is no further increase in storage. In areas of organic-rich soils, an increase in CO_2 output from the soils as a result of increased composition of pre-existing soil organic matter, consequent on drying produced by tree growth, may have to be set against any carbon credit due to carbon fixing in tree biomass.

For a period of at least 100 years, then, afforestation produces a net gain in carbon fixing capacity and hence, a 'carbon credit' is due to afforestation on this basis. Carbon fixing by forests has thus to be seen as a means of postponing global warming. The extent of this effect can be modified by at least two further factors. If timber end-uses are changed then net fixation could be increased, e.g. by using more timber in durable uses. Second, there may be carbon losses from soil if afforestation occurs on peaty soils. These may offset, to some extent, the CO_2 fixation effects of afforestation.

Cannel and Cape (1991) provide figures for the equivalent carbon stored by different yield classes. Table 10.5 summarizes the carbon storage figures, allowing for decay rates in timber products.

Table 10.5 Carbon storage in forests

Area	Tree type	Storage (tonnes C/ha/p.a.)
Upland	Sitka spruce	1.7
	Scots pine	1.4
	Birch	1.0
Lowland	Scots pine	1.7
	Corsican pine	2.7
	Oak	1.5
	Poplar coppice	4.0

Note: C = tonnes CO_2 as carbon

What is the value of fixing a tonne of CO_2? There are two approaches that might be used:

- the damage-avoided approach would suggest that a tonne of fixed CO_2 is equal to the avoided damage that would be done if the carbon was not fixed;
- the offset approach would suggest that the value of carbon fixing is equal to the cost of offsetting CO_2 emissions by investing in CO_2 reduction technology. Since CO_2 removal is not currently feasible, this amounts to saying that the value is equal to the cost of substituting a non-carbon fuel for a carbon fuel at the margin.

Pursuing the damage-avoided approach, global warming damage estimates have been produced by Nordhaus (1991) and by Ayres and Walter (1991). They are highly speculative but suggest the following figures:

Per tonne CO_2 (carbon weight) (1990 $)

Nordhaus	$1.2 (minimum) – $10 (maximum)
Ayres and Walter	central guess = $30–35

Nordhaus' 'medium damage' scenario calculates an optimal reduction in greenhouse gases consistent with a benefit per tonne C of CO_2 reduction of $7, or around £4 per tonne. These figures relate to losses of GNP and Ayres and Walter's figures suggest that other costs may be significantly higher. We therefore suggest a value of £8 per tonne CO_2 carbon weight.

Calculating Carbon Fixing Credits for UK Forestry

Carbon fixing data were supplied by the Forestry Commission Research Station at Alice Holt. The carbon fixing functions allow for repeated rotations and for a 'typical mix' of end uses of wood. The end uses are significant because once felled, carbon is released from wood, but in varying degrees according to the uses made of wood. The end-use mix assumed here is:

Branches, lop and top	100% to waste, bark and fuel
Small diameter roundwood	51% to pulpwood 37% to particleboard 1% to medium density fibreboard 8% to fencing 3% to mining
Large diameter roundwood	13% to waste, bark and fuel 10% to pulpwood 23% to particleboard 1% to medium density fibreboard 14% to pallet and packaging 19% to fencing 13% to construction 5% to mining 2% to 'other'

Since we are not interested in detailed accuracy at this stage, the 'average carbon in fixed form' curves have been approximated by a generalized function of the form:

$$F = M(1 - e^{-gt}) \tag{10.1}$$

where F = average carbon in fixed form, i.e. a moving average of accumulated carbon fixation.

To obtain annual additions to carbon fixations, we require:

$$\frac{dF}{dt} = Mge^{-gt} \tag{10.2}$$

Equations (10.1) and (10.2) are estimated below for this option to illustrate the calculations.

$$M = 80 \text{ t.C/ha}$$

when

$$F = 60 \text{ t.C}, t = 60$$

Hence $60 = M(1-e^{-60g})$ from (10.1)

$$= 80(1-e^{-60g})$$

Therefore $0.25 = e^{-60g}$
Therefore $g = 2.3\%$ p.a. ($g = 0.023$).

Substituting in (10.2) we have:

$$\frac{df}{dt} = 80(0.023)e^{-0.023t}$$

$$= 1.84e^{-0.023t} \tag{10.3}$$

Note that dF/dt allows for carbon decay from the first rotation.

These gains need to be discounted. At 6%, for example, the right-hand side of equation (10.3) becomes:

$$1.84e^{-0.023t}e^{-0.06t}$$
$$= 1.84e^{-0.083t}$$

This takes a value of only 0.03 t.C/ha for year 50, so virtually all carbon 'credits' are captured by calculating present values up to the time horizon t = 50. The present value (PV) of this is then:

$$PV = \frac{50}{1} 1.84e^{-0.083t} dt$$

$$= \frac{(-0.0158 + 0.920)}{0.083} 1.84 = 20.04$$

Therefore, the relevant carbon credit is 20 tonnes C/ha.

Table 10.6 summarizes the resulting present values of 'carbon credits'; for example, FT1 – semi-natural pinewoods in the uplands – is estimated to achieve a PV of carbon fixed of 17.8 tonnes/ha. At £8/tonne this gives a carbon credit of 17.8 × 8 = £142.

Table 10.6 Summary carbon credits (damage approach)

Forest type	Carbon credit
FT1	142
FT2	187
FT3	200
FT4	210
FT5	213
FT6	246
FT7	167
FT8	254

Note: Present values, 6% discount rate £ per hectare.

The offset approach will produce different results. Anderson (1990) has made some preliminary estimates of carbon credits for a 'typical' forest and, after allowing for the decay of the wood products, suggests figures of £527–554 per hectare (present value at 6% discount rate). These figures are approximately twice those suggested by the damage-avoided approach. In the final summary cost–benefit we use the lower figures, but their conservative nature needs to be borne in mind.

10.11 THE COMPONENTS OF COST–BENEFIT ANALYSIS: ECONOMIC SECURITY (S)

Pearce and Markandya (1990) have evaluated the arguments for ascribing a credit to afforestation on grounds of economic security. Economic security refers to the benefits of avoiding the costs that would be imposed by import supply interruptions such as might occur with a trade embargo. Economic security does not refer to 'import savings'. While it is difficult to estimate the welfare gains from economic security, the Pearce–Markandya work suggests that the border price for timber might be raised by between 0.2 and 1.8% to reflect economic security, depending on demand conditions. Overall, adding 1% to border prices would seem justified. This premium is already allowed for in the timber valuations in Table 10.2.

10.12 THE COMPONENTS OF COST–BENEFIT ANALYSIS: COMMUNITY INTEGRITY (C)

Community integrity relates to the value that society puts on the conservation of rural communities. It is not to be confused with the benefits of creating rural employment (which may be zero as discussed earlier), but nonetheless has a link to employment. Essentially, some or all of what society spends to create rural employment in sparsely populated areas could be regarded as a reflection of willingness to pay for conserving rural communities and the rural 'way of life'.

10.13 SUMMARY OF COST–BENEFIT ANALYSIS

We now illustrate how the various quantified items in a cost–benefit assignment of afforestation can be brought together. Consider FT1: semi-natural pinewoods in the uplands.

Table 10.7 allows for timber, recreation and carbon fixing values, but assumes a zero timber real price rise. It does allow for rising recreational values relative to the general price level, and makes various assumptions about shadow wages and land prices. It omits the items for landscape (L), biodiversity (B), watershed (W), microclimate (M), non-CO_2 air pollution (A), and community values (C). At present, these have proved too difficult to value.

Assumptions

1 Land price: 50% and 80% of market value (£600).
2 Labour cost: 67% of market wage rates.

3 Timber price: constant in real terms, with single 1% premium to reflect economic security.
4 Recreation: moderate value for the uplands = £30/ha/yr low value for the uplands = £3/ha/yr.
5 Carbon: value of fixing one tonne carbon is £8.
PV of carbon fixed = 17.8% t; at £8/t, value = £142/ha.

Results

	NPV at 6% (89/90)	IRR
Timber value only		
land value 50%	–798	3.2
land value 80%	–975	3.0
Timber and recreation value		
land value 50% moderate recreational value	–483	4.1
land value 80% moderate recreational value	–661	3.8
land value 50% low recreational value	–768	3.3
land value 80% low recreational value	–946	3.1
Timber, recreational and carbon-fixing value		
land value 50% moderate recreational value	–344	4.5
land value 80% moderate recreational value	–522	4.1
land value 50% low recreational value	–628	3.7
land value 80% low recreational value	–806	3.4

The remaining costs can be treated similarly and the results are shown in Table 10.7.

Further analysis shows that the results in Table 10.7 are highly sensitive to assumptions made about land values and recreational values. Thus, FT8 (fir, spruce and broadleaves in the lowlands) shows a 4.3% IRR for timber alone if land is valued at 80% of market prices, but a 7.1 % IRR with zero shadow land values. This rises to 16.9% for zero land values, high recreational values and the carbon credit.

Certain conclusions may be drawn from the analysis on the assumption that the net effect of the unquantified items is not significant, or that they cancel each other out. Table 10.8 shows the circumstances in which forest expansion is justified at the 6% discount rate.

Obviously, trade-offs would be possible. Lower recreational values could be acceptable if the opportunity cost of land was also lower. It is important, however, to relate land price assumptions to the yield class assumptions higher than assumed yield classes might be obtained, but at the price of more expensive land, and vice versa.

Table 10.7 Representative cost–benefit appraisals

	Forest type							
	FT1	FT2	FT3	FT4	FT5	FT6	FT7	FT8
Timber	–975	–3839	–1276	–458	–3173	–4283	–2605	–1653
Recreation	314	547	261	268	2091*	547	476	412
Carbon	142	187	200	210	213	246	167	254
Total	–519	–3105	–815	20	–869	–3490	–1962	–987
IRR (%)	4.1	0.1	–	6.0	4.8	1.6	3.8	4.9

Notes:
£ 1989/90 Present Values, per ha.
r = 6%, land value = 0.8, shadow wages = 0.67, moderate recreational value.
* high recreational value assumed.

Table 10.8 Justification for afforestation

Forest type	Assumptions giving positive NPV at 6%
FT5 Community forests	Very high recreational values
FT4 Spruce in uplands	Moderate recreational values and land values at 0.5 market values
FT8 Fir, spruce, broadleaves in	High recreational value and land values at 0.8 market values
FT7 Pine in lowlands	Moderate recreational value and land values at 0.5 market values

It is important to note also that the case for justifying an expansion of the forest types in Table 10.8 depends also on assumptions about a range of environmental values. So, for example, an expansion of spruce in the uplands might not be justified for poorly designed, monoculture forests where landscape values might be negative, but might be justified where planting would result in well designed, multipurpose forests.

On the basis of the analysis above, options other than those listed in Table 10.8 do not have an immediate economic justification. These are: native broadleaves managed for timber, semi-natural pinewoods in the uplands, and semi-natural broadleaves in the uplands or lowlands. But it is important to note that these forest types are likely to have benefits which are currently unquantified, especially biodiversity conservation. Semi-natural pinewoods in the uplands, for example, with moderate recreational value and a shadow land price of 0.5, shows an overall quantified negative NPV of £344/ha. Society may well be willing to pay this sum to conserve the associated biodiversity. A similar argument applies to the other forest types.

NOTE

1. This paper was originally prepared as a report for the UK Forestry Commission. It was revised for shortened publication as Chapter 17 of R. Layard and S. Glaister's *Cost Benefit Analysis*, second edition, Cambridge University Press, 1994.

REFERENCES

Anderson, D. (1990), *The Forestry Industry and the Greenhouse Effect,* Report to the UK Forestry Commission and the Scottish Forestry Trust, Edinburgh.

Arnold, M. (1991), *The Long Term Global Demand for and Supply of Wood,* Oxford Forestry Institute, Oxford, mimeo.

Ayres, R. and Walter, J. (1991)The Greenhouse Effect: damages, costs and abatement, *Environmental and Resource Economics,* **1**(3), 237–70.

Benson, J. and Willis, K. (1991), *The Demand for Forests for Recreation,* University of Newcastle, Newcastle.

Boyd, R. and Hyde, W. (1989), *Forestry Sector Intervention: The Impacts of Public Regulation on Social Welfare,* Iowa State University Press, Ames.

Byatt, I. (1983), Byatt report on subsidies to British export credits, *World Economy,* **7**, 163–78.

Campbell, D. and Fairley, R. (1991), *Forestry and the Conservation and Enhancement of Landscape,* Countryside Commission for Scotland, Edinburgh.

Cannell, M. and Cape, J. (1991), *Forestry Expansion: International Environmental Impacts: Acid Rain and the Greenhouse Effect,* Institute of Terrestrial Ecology, Grange-over-Sands, Cumbria.

Dewar, J. (1991), *New Planting Methods, Costs and Returns,* Forestry Commission, Edinburgh, *Very Small Farms in Scotland: an Economic Study,* SAC Economic Report No. 10, February.

Good, J. *et al.* (1991), *Forests as Wildlife Habitat,* Institute of Terrestrial Ecology, Grange-over-Sands, Cumbria.

Harvey, D. (1991), *The Agricultural Demand for Land: Its Availability and Cost for Forestry,* Countryside Change Unit, University of Newcastle, Newcastle.

Hornung, M. and Adamson, J. (1991), *Forestry Expansion: The Impact on Water Quality and Quantity,* Institute of Terrestrial Ecology, Grange-over-Sands, Cumbria.

Intergovernmental Panel of Climate Change (IPCC) (1990), *Policymakers Summary of the Scientific Assessment of Climate Change,* Working Group 1, May.

Krautkraemer, J. (1988), The rate of discount and the preservation of natural environments, *Natural Resource Modelling,* **2**(2) (Winter), 1–20.

Markandya, A. and Pearce, D.W. (1988), *Environmental Considerations and the Choice of Discount Rate in Developing countries,* Environmental Department, World Bank, Washington, DC.

Nordhaus, W. (1991), To slow or not to slow: the economics of the greenhouse effect, *Economic Journal,* 101(407) (July), 920–37.

Pearce, D.W. and Markandya, A. (1989), *Environmental Policy Benefits: Monetary Valuation,* OECD, Paris.

Pearce, D.W. and Markandya, A. (1990), *Economic Security Arguments for Afforestation,* Department of Economics, University College London, mimeo.

Pearce, D.W. and Markandya, A. (1991), *Assessing the Returns to the Economy and to Society from Investments in Forestry,* Forestry Commission, Edinburgh.

Pearce, D.W., Markandya, A. and Knight, I. (1988), *Economic Security Arguments for Afforestation,* A Report to the Forestry Commission, Edinburgh, November.

Rijsberman, F.R. and Swart, R.J. (1990), *Targets and Indicators of Climatic Change,* Stockholm Environment Institute, Stockholm.

Sedjo, R. and Lyon, K. (1990), *The Long Term Adequacy of World Timber Supply,* Resources for the Future, Washington, DC.

Walsh, R. (1986), *Recreation Economic Decisions: Comparing Benefits and Costs,* Venture, State College PA.

Whiteman, A. (1991), *UK Demand for and Supply of Wood and Wood Products,* Forestry Commission, Edinburgh.

Willis, K. and Benson, J. (1989), Recreational values of forests, *Forestry,* **62**(2), 93–110.

11. Global environmental value and the tropical forests: demonstration and capture[1]

11.1 INTRODUCTION

In the Appendix to Robert Goodland's edited volume *Race to Save the Tropics* (Goodland, 1990) the very first precondition for saving the tropical forests is given as 'revamp orthodox economics'. I am not entirely sure what 'orthodox economics' is any more, but assuming it is what we generally teach in our universities, I want to take one step back from Goodland's assertion and beg the question: can orthodox economics save the tropical forests? I shall suggest that there is a perfectly respectable and cogent case for giving an affirmative answer to the question: yes, orthodox economics can save the tropical forests. It can do it by (a) demonstrating that a good deal of deforestation occurs because of economic distortions the removal of which would be self-rewarding without accounting for the effects on tropical forests, and (b) by demonstrating the global environmental values of the tropical forests, and, just as importantly, it can show how those global values can be captured by the developing countries. This sequence of 'demonstration and capture' now defines the most exciting and policy-oriented feature of environmental economics in the context of tropical forests. I shall argue that, while the local market and non-market values of tropical forests help correct the tilted playing field that favours forest clearance, global values are likely to be more important still.

But whether it *will* save the tropical forests is a different question. If the answer to that question is 'no' – and I shall suggest respectable and cogent reasons for that answer too – it does not follow that some other economics – 'new', 'unorthodox', 'green', 'alternative' or 'ecological' – will save the tropical forests either. Perhaps more alarmingly, if *all* economics fails us when it comes to saving the tropical forests, we cannot assume that some 'non-economic' approach will work either. The most telling proof of the falseness of that assumption is that the record to date is of forest management *unrelated* to proper economic considerations. Table 11.1 shows the sad story about deforestation to date.

Table 11.1 Rates of tropical deforestation in the 1980s (million hectares p.a.)

	Closed forest			Total forest	
	Late 1970s[1]	Mid-1980s[2]	Late 1980s[3]	1980s	Late 1980s[4]
Number of countries	34				90
S.America	2.7	3.3	6.7	6.8	6.2
C.America and Caribbean	1.0	1.1	1.0	1.6	1.2
Africa	1.0	1.3	1.6	5.0	4.1
Asia	1.8	1.8	4.3	3.6	
					3.9
Oceania	–	–	0.4	–	
Totals	6.5	14.9	13.9	17.0	15.4
Adjusted total[5]	n.a.	15.3	14.2	–	–
Percentage of remaining forest	0.6	n.a.	1.8	0.9	0.9
Assuming forest area of m.ha:			780	1910	1756

Notes and Sources:

1 Late 1970s data for the 34 countries covered in Myers (see below) from Food and Agriculture Organisation, *Tropical Forest Resources*, Rome 1981.

2 Various years to 1986, taken from World Resources Institute, *World Resources 1992–1993*, Oxford University Press, Oxford, 1992, Table 19.1. In turn, the estimates are based on FAO sources, including an update for some countries of the 1981 estimates, and some individual sources. Note that the estimates cover closed forests only.

3 N.Myers, *Deforestation Rates in Tropical Forests and Their Climatic Implications*, Friends of the Earth, London, December 1989. Myers' estimates cover 34 countries accounting for 97.3% of the extent of tropical forest in 1989.

4 Food and Agriculture Organisation, Rome. 1993 estimates.

5 Myers estimates that 40 other countries with small tropical forests suffered deforestation rates totalling 0.36 million ha.p.a. in 1989. We have 'grossed up' the World Resources Institute figures by the same factor (14.22/13.86) to ensure comparability.

11.2 THE RATE OF TROPICAL FOREST LOSS

The focus of worldwide attention on tropical forests has arisen because of the sheer diversity of functions which they serve, the uniqueness of primary forest in evolutionary and ecological terms, and the accelerating threat to their existence. Tropical forests are the homeland of many indigenous peoples; they provide the habitat for extensive fauna and flora (biodiversity), which are valued in themselves, and are valued for educational, crop-breeding and medicinal purposes; they supply hardwood timber, and other forest products such as fruit, nuts, latex, rattans, meat, honey, resins, oils etc; they provide a recreational facility (e.g. 'ecotourism'); they protect watersheds in terms of water retention, flow regulation water pollution, and organic nutrient cleansing; they act as a store of carbon dioxide so that, while no net gains in the flow of carbon dioxide accrue to climax forests, carbon dioxide is released, and a cost ensues, if deforestation occurs, while forests also fix carbon in secondary forests and in reforested areas; and finally they also provide a possible regional microclimatic function.

Global concern about the rate of tropical deforestation accelerated in the 1980s. But at what rate are the world's tropical forests disappearing? Data for all types of forest are approximate. Different sources use different definitions of 'tropical forest' and different definitions of 'deforestation'. Closed forest refers to dense forest in which grass cover is small or non-existent due to low light penetration through the forest canopy. Total forest area is larger in extent than closed forest and includes open forest where light penetration allows undergrowth. On some estimates, annual rates of deforestation for closed forests at the end of the 1980s appear to have been somewhere around 14-15 million hectares per annum (Table 11.1). If correct, this rate of deforestation would amount to some 1.8% of the remaining area of tropical forest (taken to be around 8 million km^2, or 800 million hectares). But not much should be read into the closed forest loss rate of 1.8% recorded in the third column of estimates: they are dramatically affected by disputed figures from deforestation in the Brazilian Amazon. More credence can be given to the final columns for total forest loss. These suggest that the pace of deforestation has not slowed. Although comparisons are difficult because of changing definitions, deforestation rates may have been running at far less, around 0.6% p.a., in the late 1970s. Using total forest area as the unit of measurement, deforestation rates appear to run at 15 million hectares per annum according to the 1993 assessment by FAO, or some 0.9% of the total remaining forest area of some 1756 million ha.

Such rates of loss cannot be extrapolated. As deforestation proceeds, the remaining forest is increasingly characterized by steep slopes or permanent and seasonal flooding which makes it unsuitable for conversion to agriculture and other uses. Sheer unsuitability for conversion may be the ultimate protector of a minimum stock of tropical forest, although even that cannot be safe from regional air pollution or global warming impacts. Nonetheless, a rate of approximately 1% p.a. is an alarming loss rate and appears to be almost a doubling of earlier loss rates, although those are very much 'guesstimates'.

11.3 APPLYING ORTHODOX ECONOMICS TO TROPICAL FOREST MANAGEMENT

The fundamental forces giving rise to tropical deforestation arise from two factors:

a. competition between humans and non-humans for the remaining ecological niches on land and in coastal regions. In turn, this competition reflects the rapidly expanded population growth of developing countries; and
b. 'failures' in the workings of the international and national economic systems. 'Failure' in this sense means the failure of these economic systems to reflect the true value of environmental systems in the working of the economy. Essentially, many of the functions of tropical forests are not marketed and, as such, are ignored in decision-making. Additionally, decisions to convert tropical forest are themselves encouraged by fiscal and other incentives for various reasons.

Of course, other factors are at work as well. In a comprehensive view we would need to add misdirected past policies by bilateral and multilateral aid agencies, corruption, the indifference of much big business to environmental concerns, the results of international indebtedness, and poverty itself (Brown and Pearce, 1994b). But, the analysis of spatial competition and economic failures takes us a very long way in explaining deforestation as a process (Brown *et al.*,1993).

Competition for Space

Most of the competition for space between man and Nature shows up in the conversion of land to agriculture, aquaculture, infrastructure, urban development, industry and unsustainable forestry. Table 11.2 shows land use conversions by world region between 1979 and 1991. The loss of the world's forests, rich sources of biodiversity, is apparent, especially in South America, but also in Asia and Africa. Indeed, the loss rates expressed as a percentage of 1979/81 forest cover are similar in these three regions: 3.8% in Africa, 4.9% in Asia, and 5.1% in South America. Unless the reasons for these conversions are understood, the outlook for the conservation of biodiversity is bleak. The conversions appear to be mainly to pasture, with cropland and 'other' land uses roughly cancelling each other out.

Population pressure is clearly a force of some considerable importance. Whereas humans compete only marginally for niche space in the world's oceans, they compete directly with other species for land and coastal waters space. The story about world population change is by now well known. Table 11.3 records World Bank projections for the next 160 years. World population is expected to stabilize at around 12 billion people towards the end of the next century, but this is more than twice the number of people on earth today. The fastest growth rate is in Africa, currently growing at 2.9% p.a. and heading for a population of 3 billion people towards the end of the next century, around five times the population of today. These figures suggest that sheer pressure of human beings on space will displace the habitat of other living species.

Table 11.2 Land conversions 1979/81–1991

	Area (million hectares)				
	Cropland	Pasture	Forest	Other	Total
Africa	+ 9	+ 8	–26	+11	+ 1
N. and C. America	– 2	+ 4	+ 2	– 4	0
S. America	+13	+21	–42	+11	+ 3
Asia	+ 6	+66	–26	–43	+ 3
Europe	– 2	– 3	+ 1	+ 4	0

Notes: Other land includes roads, uncultivated land, wetlands, built-on land.
Sums of rows and sums of columns should add to zero, but rounding and data imperfections produce small errors, especially for Asia and South America. The forest column suggests annual loss rates of about 9 million ha, significantly less than the loss rates shown in Table 11.1.

Source: Estimated from World Resources Institute (1994-5), Table 17.1.

Table 11.3 World population projections

	1990	2100	2150
World population (billions)	5.4	12.0	12.2
	Percentage increase		
Asia/Oceania	59.4	57.0	56.8
N. & S. America	13.7	11.0	10.8
Africa	11.9	23.9	24.5
Europe	15.0	8.1	7.9

Source: World Bank

But the picture is far more complicated than population growth alone. As a very rough indicator, the land 'lost' in Table 11.2 can be divided by the decadal population increase in those regions to obtain the following population-growth – land-conversion linkages: each (net) individual added to the population in the 1980s was associated with 0.16 hectares of land conversion in Africa, a similar loss rate of 0.13 hectares in Asia, but 0.75 hectares in South America. Thus, while South America's population growth rate is markedly less (2.1% p.a.) in the 1980s compared to Africa (2.9% p.a), each net addition to the South American population 'caused' around five times as much land loss as each net addition in Africa and Asia. Quite why these conversion efficiencies – the rate at which land can support rising populations – differ is not clear. A tempting answer is that South America has converted mainly to low density livestock pasture, but in fact Asia has the highest conversion to pasture with 92% of all land loss being to pasture, and only 47% in South America and 29% in Africa. Another explanation might be that South America is simply less efficient in terms of output per hectare, and hence requires a higher level of land per capita. In terms of crop yields, South America is certainly less efficient compared to Asia (2181 kg/ha for cereals against 2854 kg/ha for Asia) but is markedly more efficient than Africa (1168 kg/ha). The story is very similar for root and tuber crops. The picture is further complicated by the fact that the Asia statistics are dominated by China which has converted some 80 million hectares of land to pasture since 1980, so that any specific factors there affect this generalized picture. As we see later on, inefficiency of conversion may simply reflect the availability of 'unoccupied' land, i.e *de facto* open access land, especially forested land. The greater the area not 'occupied' the less the incentive to economize on the land that is converted. This may well explain part of the story since large parts of South America have large tracts of effectively open access land.

All this suggests an econometric approach in which forest loss, or land conversion, is regressed on those factors thought to influence rates of conversion. Brown and Pearce (1994b) report the results of a survey of various models that have been used to explain, statistically, conversion rates. Table 11.4 summarizes the results. They suggest that there is no absolutely conclusive link between any of the selected variables and deforestation. However, cautious conclusions might be:

a. the balance of evidence favours the niche competition hypothesis if that is expressed in terms of the influence of population growth on deforestation;
b. population density is clearly linked to deforestation rates;
c. income growth is fairly clearly linked to rates of deforestation, suggesting that deforestation has more to do with growth of incomes than with poverty – a result that runs counter to the popular interpretations of the causes of environmental degradation;
d. the evidence on the role of agricultural productivity change is finely balanced. One would expect growth in productivity to lessen the pressure on colonization of forests, i.e. the coefficient of association should be negative. The two studies finding this association are for South America and Indonesia. The two studies finding the opposite association are for Thailand and the Brazilian Amazon;

e. the link between indebtedness and deforestation is ambivalent. One study finds a positive link for tropical moist forests but not for other forests; another finds a positive link, and another finds no such link. Again, this ambivalence is at odds with the popular interpretations of the causes of environmental degradation.

Table 11.4 Econometric studies of deforestation

	Deforestation significantly related to:				
	Rate of population growth Δ	Population density	Income	Agricultural productivity	International indebtedness
Allen and Barnes 1985	+				
Burgess 1992		+	–		
Burgess 1991(a)	–		+		+
(b)	–				+
Capistrano (a)			+		
and Kiker (b)			+		–
1990 (c)	+		+		–
Constantino and Ingram 1991		+	–	–	
Kahn and McDonald 1994	–				+
Katila 1992		+		+	
Kummer and Sham 1991		+			
Lugo, Schmidt and Braun 1981		+			
Panayotou and Sungsuwan 1994		+	–		
Palo, Mery and Salmi 1987		+			
Perrings 1992(a)	+	+	+		+
(b)	–	+			
Reis and Guzman 1992				+	
Rudel 1989	+		+		
Shafik 1994					
Southgate 1994	+			–	
Southgate, Sierra and Brown 1989	+				

Notes:
Δ = rate of population growth; Pop den = population density; Y = income
Agprod = agricultural productivity; Debt = international indebtedness.
A minus sign means that an increase in the variable leads to a decrease in deforestation. A plus sign means an increase leads to an increase in deforestation. Blank entries mean either not statistically significant or not tested for.

Source: Brown and Pearce (1994b)

Surprisingly, few of the studies available at the time of this survey accounted for property rights regimes, despite the fact that property rights are cited as a main factor in environmental degradation generally, and in the theory of tropical forest loss in particular. The exception in the Brown and Pearce survey is the work of Southgate (1994) in which property rights in South America are seen to be an important explanatory factor. More recent work by Deacon (1994) underlines the importance of property rights. Deacon further relates these rights, or the lack of them, to government instability and lack of democratic participation.

Economic Failure

The economic theory of species extinction was developed mainly in the water context and very largely in terms of the fishery (see Clark, 1990). There it is comparatively straightforward to see that a combination of open access property rights (no-one owning the sea) and profitability (the difference between revenues and the cost of fishing effort) does much to explain overfishing and the loss of mammalian species. Once the theory is moved to land, the additional factor is the sheer competition for niche occupancy, and the theory needs to change, as Swanson (1994) has demonstrated. Rather than saying open access explains excess harvesting effort, the question is why nation states allow open access conditions to prevail. Put another way, why do governments not invest more in conservation land uses? There are three immediate reasons and they comprise the second major strand in the explanation for tropical forest loss: an economic theory of deforestation.

Figure 11.1 summarizes the essence of a theory of deforestation in terms of the 'orthodox' theory of externalities. Figure 11.1 can be interpreted as a simpler exposition of the general theory expounded by Sandler (1993). The horizontal axis shows the rate of land conversion (left to right) and its functional inverse, the level of biodiversity (increasing from right to left). M_{π} is a marginal private benefit (marginal profit) function showing that marginal profits decline as more land is converted. This is a result of rising conversion costs as the conversion frontier is spatially extended, and/or declining land productivity as land is developed along a Ricardian gradient. Of course, infrastructural developments – especially roads – will lower conversion costs and raise profit margins, so that M_{π} shifts outward (Schneider, 1992; Cervigni, 1993). Figure 11.1 is therefore fairly static in concept. Land conversion imposes 'local' externalities, especially where the conversion is from tropical forest to agriculture. These costs are fairly well documented – see Kumari (1994), World Bank (1991), Pearce *et al.*, (1993) – and consist of the deleterious effects of soil erosion, loss of local biodiversity and so on. In Figure 11.1 these are shown as MEC_{dom}.

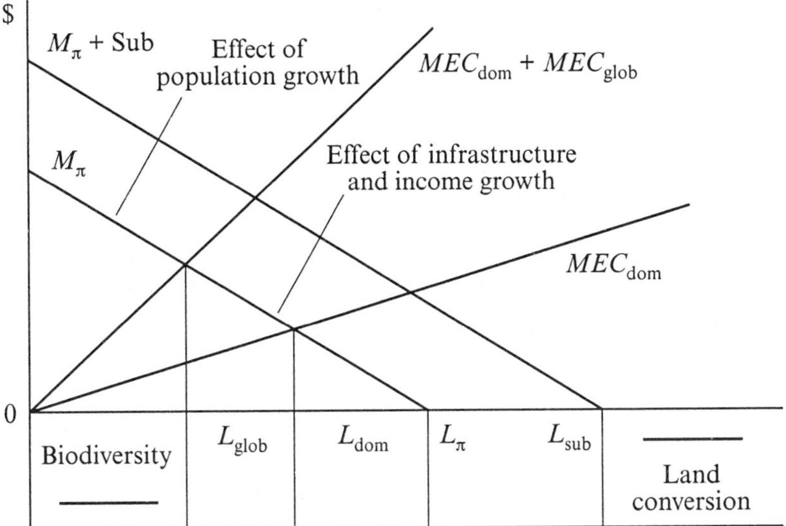

Figure 11.1 The causes of deforestation

Clearly, then, the local social optimum is L_{dom} compared to the private local optimum of L_π. But there are other externalities involved, since individuals outside the national territory suffer some of the consequences of deforestation: scientific knowledge is lost, as is any 'existence' or 'passive use' value. To the local externality, then, must be added a rest of the world externality or MEC_{glob}. The total externality is therefore $MEC_{dom} + MEC_{glob}$, and the 'global optimum' is L_{glob}. If it is possible to 'capture' the global externality, then less land conversion takes place and more biodiversity is 'saved'. Finally, forest sectors are rarely left to market forces: government intervention is the rule not the exception. Such interventions often have deleterious environmental consequences due to the artificial encouragement of deforestation. The most widely studied interventions are subsidies to livestock, credit and land clearance, and the under-pricing and under-taxation of logging concessions – see Binswanger (1989), Schneider (1992), Repetto and Gillis (1988). How far forest pricing *causes* accelerated deforestation through 'excessive' logging is disputed. Repetto and Gillis (1988) and Grut *et al.* (1991) argue that pricing and concession policies create 'rent seeking' activity, while the exchanges between Hyde and Sedjo (1992, 1993) and Vincent (1993) suggest that raising forest taxation will do little for slowing rates of logging.

The result of such policies, which are explicit or implicit subsidies to land conversion, is to shift M_π outwards to M_π + Sub, raising the private optimal level of land conversion to L_{sub}.

The relevance of Figure 11.1, beyond being a didactic device, is that it shows that many forms of 'failure' can be present at one and the same time. Indeed, the forms of imperfection are:

$L_\pi - L_{sub}$ = intervention or government failure
$L_{dom} - L_\pi$ = local market failure
$L_{glob} - L_{dom}$ = global market failure or 'global appropriation failure'

and these failures may be summed to arrive at the total potential disparity between globally optimal and domestically optimal levels of land conversion. Note that the domestic and global market failures get bigger as population grows.

Do these failures represent a failure of 'orthodox' economics? They certainly reflect a failure of the way in which economic systems actually work, but that is quite different to saying that economics itself has failed. Economics fails only if it cannot explain environmental degradation comprehensively, and only if it cannot elicit from a causal analysis the measures needed to correct the failures. In practice, there are mechanisms for dealing with all the failures (Pearce, 1995). Local market failures can be addressed through land tenure policies, by land use zoning, zoning with tradeable development rights, and taxation. Intervention failures require government reform and environmental conditionality in aid programmes. Global failures are more complex because of the need to create world-wide markets, but, in principle, development rights can be made tradeable at the international level, private sector flows can be 'tapped' for the capture of environmental benefit, various 'swaps' such as debt-for-nature swaps, can be employed, and there are also the projects to be funded under the Global Environment Facility's remit. All this suggests that we have a very reasonable idea of *why* the 'wrong' amount of land conversion occurs, and *how* to correct it. All that is necessary is the extension of 'orthodox' economics to the global level. The issue is not the failure of orthodox economics, but the practical judgement as to which causes are most important. Put another way, what do we know about the various distances on the horizontal axis in Figure 11.1. And what do we know about the dynamics of Figure 11.1: could it be, for example, that corrections to all the failures will quickly be swamped by population change? This is in part an issue of the economic value of alternative land uses and to that issue we now turn.

11.4 ECONOMIC FAILURES 1: LOCAL MARKET FAILURE

First, under-investment arises for the classic economic reason of 'market failure'. What this means is that the interplay of market forces will not secure the economically correct balance of land conversion and land conservation. This is because those who convert the land do not have to compensate those who suffer the local consequences of that conversion – extra pollution and sedimentation of waters from deforestation, for example. The corrective solutions to this problem are well known – a tax on land conversion, zoning to restrict detrimental land uses, environmental standards, and so on. From this it follows that we cannot rely on market forces to save the world's environmental assets as long as those assets are dispensable because of market forces. Notice, however, that the measures needed to correct this market failure do not result in zero deforestation. In the economist's language there is an 'optimal' rate of loss. It is less than what happens now, but it is not zero.

Panayotou (1993) provides a convenient listing of local market failures:

a. ill-defined or non-existent property rights;
b. missing markets;
c. high transaction costs inhibiting trade in conservation benefits;
d. publicness of conservation benefits;
e. market imperfections such as monopoly;
f. myopia and hence high discount rates;
g. uncertainty and risk aversion;
h. irreversibility.

Assessing just how important these factors are is difficult.

Many authors cite poor or perverse land tenure as a factor in deforestation. Poor tenure by existing occupants of forest land helps to explain reduced resistance to rival claims from those who wish to clear land. Mahar and Schneider (1994) note that only 11% of Brazilian Amazon land was titled in the early 1980s, creating an essentially 'open access' resource. Perverse land tenure applies when the colonizer has an incentive to clear because clearance is evidence of tenure. Countries where clearance is evidence of land tenure include Costa Rica, Honduras, Panama, Brazil, Ecuador. In Brazil, for example, the land settlement agency still determines the spatial extent of settlement rights by multiplying the cleared area by a factor of three (Mahar and Schneider, 1994). But few of the econometric studies surveyed in Brown and Pearce (1994b) tested for land tenure as a factor explaining deforestation. Southgate *et al.*'s (1989) study of Ecuador suggests a strong influence of tenure insecurity on deforestation. See also Deacon (1994).

Missing or incomplete local markets are endemic to the tropical forest context. Tropical forests yield many products for which there *are* markets, but the resulting market prices tend to reflect only the opportunity cost of labour and capital, not the true rents of the forest land (Panayotou, 1993). In turn, the effective zero or negligible rents perceived in the market place owe much to the absence of property rights discussed above. *Externalities* also arise from deforestation and trades or bargains to reduce them are scarce because of high transactions costs, poor information and the prevailing structure of interests and power. Thus, esturial fishermen do not bargain with upstream forest colonizers to reduce the effects of sedimentation on fisheries. Yet we know these effects can be important. Hodgson and Dixon (1988) show that a ban on logging upstream of Bacuit Bay, Philippines would have reduced fishery losses from sedimentation by 50%, and would have increased tourist revenues by a factor of four. In Ruitenbeek's study of the Korup rainforest in Cameroun (Ruitenbeek (1992), over 50% of the direct and indirect use values of the forest were accounted for by downstream fishery benefits. In contrast, and underlining the site specificity of many of the local benefits, Kumari (1994) found negligible fishery effects in moving from unsustainable to sustainable logging practices in the Selangor forest swamps in Peninsular Malaysia.

Public goods are also endemic to tropical forests. Public goods consist of non-excludable and jointly provided goods and services. Notable local public goods – i.e. those where the domain of value is limited to the relevant nation – include protection, micro climate, and biological diversity. Few of these have been the subject of economic valuation exercises. Pearce *et al.* (1993) estimate only modest watershed benefits from forest conservation in Mexico relative to other values.

Monopolistic markets may well work to the advantage of conservation if the monopoly relates, say, to mineral deposits in the forest area: restrictions on output to maximize profits may well reduce forest destruction compared to the competitive alternative. While Panayotou (1993) cites monopolized informal rural credit markets as a factor working *against* conservation, the effect may well be ambiguous. If smaller farmers cannot secure access to credit at non-inflated prices this may well reduce the incentive to invest in existing land areas compared to the alternative of colonizing new land. Exclusion from normal credit markets easily arises if ownership is a precondition of collateral for credit, as is often the case in agricultural areas (Pearce and Warford, 1993). But cheap credit has also been implicated in deforestation in the Amazon areas, controlled interest rates being an effective subsidy to land clearance. Econometric studies of deforestation have largely ignored credit markets as a factor in explaining deforestation.

Surprisingly little is known about the actual discount rates that forest zone farmers exhibit. Using both contingent valuation and asset choice analysis, Cuesta *et al.* (1994) estimate that 80% of farmers in Costa Rica have discount rates in the range 16–21% in real terms. While social discount rates can be of the order of 10% in developing countries, if per capita real consumption growth rates are high, the Costa Rica estimates suggest that private rates may well be at least twice the social rate. Moreover risk and uncertainty arising from insecure land and resource tenure are excluded in the Cuesta *et al.* study because the farmers in question owned their land. Even at these 'tenure-risk-free' discount rates, Cuesta *et al.* conclude that optimal soil conservation measures will not be undertaken without a conservation subsidy.

Overall, the evidence for local market failure is strong. How strong it is relative to other forms of failure remains an issue of judgement.

11.5 ECONOMIC FAILURES 2: INTERVENTION FAILURE

A second explanation for deforestation is 'intervention failure' or 'government failure' – the deliberate intervention by governments in the working of market forces. The examples are, by now, well known (Pearce and Warford, 1993) and include the subsidies to forest conversion for livestock in Brazil up to the end of the 1980s; the failure to tax logging companies sufficiently, giving them an incentive to expand their activities even further; the encouragement of inefficient domestic wood processing industries, effectively raising the ratio of logs, and hence deforestation, to wood product, and so on. What intervention does is to distort the competitive playing field. Governments effectively subsidize the rate of return to land conversion, tilting the economic balance against conservation.

Table 11.5 assembles some information on the scale of the distortions that governments introduce. Such distortions are widespread. The general rule in developing countries is for agriculture to be *taxed* not subsidized, but significant subsidies exist in several major tropical forest countries such as Brazil and Mexico. By comparison, OECD countries are actually worse at subsidizing agriculture. In 1992 OECD subsidies exceeded $180 billion (OECD, 1993). These subsidies work in two ways. Subsidies in developing countries will tend to encourage extensification of agriculture into forested area. Subsidies in the developed world make it impossible for the developing world to compete properly on international markets, locking them into primitive agricultural practices. While the removal of OECD country subsidies would appear to be a recipe for expanding land conversion in the developing world to capture the larger market, the demands of a rich overseas market are more likely to result in agricultural intensification and hence reduced pressure on forested land. Table 11.5 also shows that many developing countries fail to tax logging companies adequately, thus generating larger 'rents' for loggers. The larger rents have two effects: they attract more loggers and they encourage existing loggers to expand their concessions and, indeed, to do both by persuading the host countries to give them concessions. Persuasion involves the whole menu of usual mechanisms, including corruption.

Table 11.5 Economic distortions to land conversion

(a) Agricultural producer subsidies[1]		
Mexico	mid 1980s	+53%
Brazil	mid 1980s	+10%
S.Korea	mid 1980s	+55%
S.S.A	mid 1980s	+9%
OECD	1992	+44%
(b) Timber stumpage fees as percentage of replacement costs[2]		
Ethiopia	late 1980s	+23%
Kenya	late 1980s	+14%
Ivory Coast	late 1980s	+13%
Sudan	late 1980s	+4%
Senegal	late 1980s	+2%
Niger	late 1980s	+1%
(c) Timber charges as percentage of total rents		
Indonesia	early 1980s	+33%
Philippines	early 1980s	+11%

Notes:

1 Producer subsidies are measured by the 'producer subsidy equivalent' (PSE) which is defined as the value of all transfers to the agricultural sector in the form of price support to farmers, any direct payments to farmers and any reductions in agricultural input costs through subsidies. These payments are shown here as a percentage of the total value of agricultural production valued at domestic prices.

2 A stumpage fee is the rate charged to logging companies for standing timber. It is expressed here as a percentage of the cost of reforesting (b) and as a percentage of total rents (c).

Sources: Agricultural PSEs: Moreddu *et al.* (1990); OECD (1993); stumpage fees: World Bank (1992), and Repetto and Gillis (1988).

11.6 ECONOMIC FAILURES 3: GLOBAL APPROPRIATION FAILURE

Local market failure describes the inability of existing markets to capture non-market and other economic values of the forest within the context of the country or local area. But there are missing global markets as well. We can consider two such global markets which are highly relevant to tropical forests: the 'non-use' or 'existence' value possessed by individuals in one country for wildlife and habitat in other countries, and the carbon storage values of tropical forests. Global appropriation failure (or GAF for short) arises because these values are not easily captured or appropriated by the countries in possession of tropical forests.

Non-Use Values

Economists use methods of measuring individual preferences, as revealed through individuals' 'willingness to pay' to conserve biodiversity. The methodologies include contingent valuation (CVM), which functions through sophisticated questionnaires which ask people their willingness to pay, and other techniques such as the travel cost method, the hedonic property price approach and the production function approach. The economic values that are captured in this way are likely to be a mix of potential use value and non-use values. Use values relate to the valuation placed on the resource because the respondent makes use of it or might wish to make use of it in the future. Non-use values, or 'passive use values' as they are also called, relate to positive willingness to pay even if the respondent makes no use of the resource and has no intention of making use of it.

'Global valuations' of this kind are still few and far between. Table 11.6 assembles the results of some CVMs in several countries. These report willingness to pay for species and habitat conservation in the respondents' own country. These studies remain controversial. In the context of tropical forests and biological diversity this controversy has some justification. In particular, 'embedding' – the problem of valuing a specific asset rather than the general context of which the asset is part – is bound to be a major problem for assets that are remote from respondents or jointly produced with other assets (e.g. species within prized habitats) – see Schulze *et al.* (1994). While we cannot say that similar kinds of expressed values will arise for protection of biodiversity in other countries, even a benchmark figure of, say, $10 p.a. for the rich countries of Europe and North America would produce a fund of $4 billion p.a., around four times the mooted size of the fund that will be available to the Global Environment Facility in its operational phase as the financial mechanism under the two Rio Conventions and its continuing role in capturing global values from the international waters context, and perhaps 10 times what the Fund will have available for helping with biodiversity conservation under the Rio Convention. Clearly, a focal point for biodiversity conservation must be the conservation of tropical forests.

Table 11.7 looks at possible *implicit* prices in debt-for-nature swaps. How far the procedure of estimating implicit prices of this kind is valid is open to doubt, although it has been used by some writers – see Ruitenbeek (1992) and Pearce and Moran (1994). Numerous debt-for-nature swaps have been agreed. Table 11.7 sets out the available information and computes the implicit prices. It is not possible to be precise with respect to the implicit prices since the swaps tend to cover not just protected areas but education and training as well. Moreover, each hectare of land does not secure the same degree of 'protection' and the same area may be covered by different swaps. We have also arbitrarily chosen a 10 year horizon in order to compute present values (PV) whereas the swaps in practice have variable levels of annual commitment.

Table 11.6 Preference valuations for endangered species and prized habitats

		Valuation (US 1990 $ p.a per person)
	Species	
Norway:	brown bear, wolf and wolverine	15.0
USA:	bald eagle	12.4
	emerald shiner	4.5
	grizzly bear	18.5
	bighorn sheep	8.6
	whooping crane	1.2
	blue whale	9.3
	bottlenose dolphin	7.0
	california sea otter	8.1
	northern elephant seal	8.1
	humpback whales[1]	40–48 (without information) 49–64 (with information)
	Habitat	
USA:	Grand Canyon (visibility)	27.0
	Colorado wilderness	9.3–21.2
Australia:	Nadgee Nature Reserve NSW	28.1
	Kakadu Conservation Zone, NT[2]	40.0 (minor damage) 93.0 (major damage)
UK:	nature reserves[3]	40.0 ('experts' only)
Norway:	conservation of rivers against hydroelectric development	59.0–107.0

Notes:
1 Respondents divided into two groups one of which was given video information.
2 Two scenarios of mining development damage were given to respondents.
3 Survey of informed 'expert' individuals only.

Source: Pearce (1993)

Table 11.7 Implicit global willingness to pay in international transfers: implicit WTP in debt-for-nature swaps

Country	Year	Payment (1990$)	Area m.ha (PV)	WTP/ha (1990$)	Notes
Bolivia	8/87	112000	12.00	0.01	1
Ecuador	12/87	354000 }	22.00	0.06	2
	4/89	1068750 }			
Costa Rica:					
	2/88	918000	1.15	0.80	3
	7/88	5000000			
4 parks	1/89	784000			
	4/89	3500000	0.81	4.32	4
La Amistad	3/90	1953473	1.40	1.40	5
Monteverde	1/91	360000	0.014	25.70	6
Dominican R.	3/90	116400			
Guatemala	10/91	75000			
Jamaica	11/91	300000			
Philippines	1/89	200000}	9.86	0.06	7
	8/90	438750}			
	2/92	5000000			
Madagascar	7/89	950000 }	0.47	2.95	8
	8/90	445891 }			
	1/91	59,377			9
Mexico	2/91	180000			
Nigeria	7/91	64788			
Zambia	8/89	454000			10
Poland	1/90	11500	unrelated to area purchase		
Nigeria	1989	1060000	1.84	0.58	11

Notes:
A discount rate of 6% is used, together with a time horizon of 10 years. The sum of discount factors for 10 years is then 7.36.

1. The Beni 'park' is 334 000 acres and the surrounding buffer zones are some 3.7 million acres, making 1.63 million *hectares* in all (1 hectare = 2.47 acres). 1.63 x 7.36 = 12 million hectares in present value (PV) terms.
2. Covers six areas: Cayembe Coca Reserve at 403 000 ha; Cotacachi-Cayapas at 204 000 ha; Sangay National park at 370 000 ha; Podocarpus National park at 146 280 ha; Cuyabeno Wildlife Reserve at 254 760 ha;Yasuni National Park – no area stated; Galapagos National park at 691 200 ha; Pasochoa near Quito at 800 ha. The total without Yasuni is therefore 2.07 m.ha. Inspection of maps suggests that Yasuni is about three times the area of Sangay, say 1 m.ha. This would make the grand total some 3 m.ha. The PV of this over 10 years is then 22 m.ha. This is more than twice the comparable figure quoted in Ruitenbeek (1992).

Notes to Table 11.7 continued

3. Covers Corvocado at 41,788 ha; Guanacaste at 110 000 ha; Monteverde Cloud forest at 3 600 ha, to give 156 600 ha in all, or a present value of land area of 1.15 m ha. Initially, $5.4 million at face value, purchased for $912 000, revalued here to 1990 prices.
4. Guanacaste at 110 000 ha, to give a PV of 0.81 m.ha.
5. La Amistad at 190 000 ha, to give a PV of 1.4 m.ha.
6. Monteverde Cloud Forest at 2023 ha x 7.36 = 14 900 ha.
7. Area 'protected' is 5753 ha of St Paul Subterranean River national Park, and 1.33 m.ha of El Nido National Marine Park. This gives a PV of land of 9.86 m.ha.
8. Focus on Adringitra and Marojejy reserves at 31 160 ha and 60 150 ha, respectively. This gives a PV of 474 000 ha.
9. Covers four reserve areas: Zahamena, Midongy-Sud, Manongarivo and Namoroko.
10. Covers Kafue Flats and Bangweulu wetlands.
11. Oban park, protecting 250 000 ha or 1.84 m.ha in PV terms. See Ruitenbeek (1992).

Source: Pearce and Moran (1994).

Ignoring the outlier (Monteverde Cloud Forest, Costa Rica) the range of implicit values is from around 1 cent/ha to just over 4 dollars/ha. Ruitenbeek (1992) secures a range of some 18 cents to $11/ha (ignoring Monteverde) but he has several different areas for some of the swaps and he also computes a present value of outlays for the swaps. But either range is very small compared to the opportunity costs of protected land, although if these implicit prices mean anything they are capturing only part of the rich world's existence values for these assets. That is, the values reflect only part of the total economic value.

Finding a benchmark from such an analysis is hazardous but something of the order of $5/ha may be appropriate. If so, these implicit existence values will not save the tropical forests. On the other hand, debt-for-nature swaps clearly involve many free riders since the good in question is a pure public good and the payment mechanism is confined to a limited group. Looked at another way, $5 per ha p.a for saving say 25% of the world's remaining closed tropical forests would amount to a fund of 780 m ha x $5 x 0.25 = $1 billion p.a.

The only *inter-country* valuation exercise appears to be that of Kramer *et al.* (1994). This reports average WTP of US citizens for protection of an additional 5% of the world's tropical forests. One-time payments amounted to $29–51 per US household, or $2.6–4.6 billion. If this WTP was extended to all OECD households, and ignoring income differences, a broad order of magnitude would be a one-off payment of $11 – 23 billion. Annuitized, this would be, say, $1.1 to 2.3 billion p.a.

All these 'global' estimates are very crude, heroic even, but it is interesting to note that the hypothetical payments are not wildly divergent:

	$billion p.a.
Implied WTP (GEF)	$0.4
Implied WTP (DfN)	$1.0
Like Assets Approach	$4.0
Global CVM	$1.1–2.3

The disturbing feature of the valuations from the conservationist standpoint is that the world has effectively decided on its *actual* WTP for biodiversity conservation through the Global Environment Facility, and that actual WTP is markedly lower than the hypothetical WTP of the other estimates.

Carbon Storage

All forests store carbon so that, if cleared for agriculture there will be a release of carbon dioxide which will contribute to the accelerated greenhouse effect and hence global warming. In order to derive a value for the 'carbon credit' that should be ascribed to a tropical forest, we need to know (a) the net carbon released when forests are converted to other uses, and (b) the economic value of one tonne of carbon released to the atmosphere.

Carbon will be released at different rates according to the method of clearance and subsequent land use. With burning there will be an immediate release of CO_2 into the atmosphere, and some of the remaining carbon will be locked in ash and charcoal which is resistant to decay. The slash not converted by fire into CO_2 or charcoal and ash decays over time, releasing most of its carbon to the atmosphere within 10–20 years. Studies of tropical forests indicate that significant amounts of cleared vegetation become lumber, slash, charcoal and ash; the proportion differs for closed and open forests; the smaller stature and drier climate of open forests result in the combustion of a higher proportion of the vegetation.

If tropical forested land is converted to pasture or permanent agriculture, then the amount of carbon stored in secondary vegetation is equivalent to the carbon content of the biomass of crops planted, or the grass grown on the pasture. If a secondary forest is allowed to grow, then carbon will accumulate, and maximum biomass density is attained after a relatively short time.

Table 11.8 illustrates the net carbon storage effects of land use conversion from tropical forests; closed primary, closed secondary, or open forests; to shifting cultivation, permanent agriculture, or pasture. The negative figures represent emissions of carbon; for example, conversion from closed primary forest to shifting agriculture results in a net loss of 194 tC/ha. The greatest loss of carbon involves change of land use from primary closed forest to permanent agriculture. These figures represent the once and for all change that will occur in carbon storage as a result of the various land use conversions.

The data suggest that, allowing for the carbon fixed by subsequent land uses, carbon released from deforestation of secondary and primary tropical forest is of the order of 100–200 tonnes of carbon per hectare.

The carbon released from burning tropical forests contributes to global warming, and we now have several estimates of the minimum economic damage done by global warming, leaving aside catastrophic events. Recent work suggests a 'central' value of $20 of damage for every tonne of carbon released

(Fankhauser and Pearce, 1994). Applying this figure to the data in Table 11.8, we can conclude that converting an open forest to agriculture or pasture would result in global warming damage of, say, $600–1000 per hectare; conversion of closed secondary forest would cause damage of $2000–3000 per hectare; and conversion of primary forest to agriculture would give rise to damage of about $4000–4400 per hectare. Note that these estimates allow for carbon fixation in the subsequent land use.

Table 11.8 Changes in carbon with land use conversion (tC/ha)

	Original C	Shifting agriculture	Permanent agriculture	Pasture
Original C		79	63	63
Closed primary	283	–204	–220	–220
Closed secondary	194	–106	–152	–122
Open forest	115	–36	–52	–52

Note: Shifting agriculture represents carbon in biomass and soils in second year of shifting cultivation cycle.

Source: Brown and Pearce (1994a).

How do these estimates relate to the development benefits of land use conversion? We can illustrate with respect to the Amazon region of Brazil. Schneider (1992) reports upper bound values of $300 per hectare for land in Rondonia. The figures suggest carbon credit values 2–15 times the price of land in Rondonia. These 'carbon credits' also compare favourably with the value of forest land for timber in, say Indonesia, where estimates are of the order of $1000–2000 per hectare. All this suggests the scope for a global bargain. The land is worth $300 per hectare to the forest colonist but several times this to the world at large. If the North can transfer a sum of money greater than $300 but less than the damage cost from global warming, there are mutual gains to be obtained. (We have assumed here that there is no 'intrinsic production value' -i.e. some surplus of WTP over the price of developmental uses of forest land due to some feeling that forest resources *should* be used up. What evidence there is suggests such values are negligible – Lockwood *et al.* (1994).

Note that if the transfers did take place at, say, $500 per hectare, then the cost per tonne carbon reduced is of the order of $5 tC ($500/100 tC/ha). These unit costs compare favourably with those to be achieved by carbon emission reduction policies through fossil fuel conversion. Avoiding deforestation becomes a legitimate and potentially important means of reducing global warming rates.

11.7 CAN ORTHODOX ECONOMICS SAVE THE FORESTS?

Table 11.9 brings together some of the studies that have attempted to compare local and global benefits. They are necessarily incomplete, but they still suggest that global values, especially carbon storage, dominate local values. Non-timber products could be important, however.

Table 11.9 Comparing local and global conservation values (US$/ha)

	Mexico Pearce *et al.* (1993)	Costa Rica World Bank (1993a) (carbon values adjusted)	Indonesia World Bank (1993b) (carbon values adjusted)	Malaysia World Bank (1991)	Peninsular Malaysia Kumari (1994)
Timber	–	1240	1000–2000	4075	1024
Non-timber products	775	–	38–125	325–1238	96–487
Carbon storage	650–3400	3046	1827–3654	1015–2709	2449
Pharmaceutical	1–90	2	–	–	1–103
Ecotourism/Recreation	8	209	–	–	13–35
Watershed protection	<1	–	–	–	
Option value	80	–	–	–	
Non-use value	15	–	–	–	

Notes:
Adapted from Kumari (1994) but with additional material and some changed conversions. All values are present values at 8% discount rate, but carbon values are at 3% discount rate. Uniform damage estimates of $20.3 tC have been used (Fankhauser and Pearce, 1994), so that original carbon damage estimates in the World Bank studies have been re-estimated.

The economic valuation of forest functions is still in its infancy. Notable weaknesses in the current state of knowledge include, above all, our limited idea of global non-use values. But even on the basis of what we have, some lessons are beginning to emerge. The dominant of these is that global values may well dominate local values. If true, the implication is that imaginative schemes for international transfers will be needed to supplement (a) the correction of local market failures, and (b) domestic distortionary policies which contribute to deforestation. A further, more hazardous, implication is that reliance on some of the global and local use values (such as the potential for pharmaceutical plants) to justify conservation could be misplaced. Those values may not be large enough to correct the unbalanced playing field between conservation and development. If the focus *does* shift to global values – which is the focus of the

Global Environment Facility – then there is at least one major risk and at least one challenge.

The risk is that the threat of global warming will disappear as the science of global warming improves. If that risk is removed, that can only be good news for the global community and even better news for those countries at particular risk, for example, from sea level rise. But it will be bad news for the tropical forests since the evidence suggests that global carbon store values are of enormous importance for the tropical forests. Ironically, the good news, if it comes, is offset by the bad news for forests.

The challenge is to the economics profession, and to others, to 'demonstrate' global non-use values and to invent ways of capturing them. The time for 'global' contingent valuation studies has come, and it is important that they proceed rapidly. The further challenge, however, is to differentiate local and global benefits from conservation. At the moment there is an uneasy division between resource flows aimed at securing global public goods – warming reduction and biodiversity increase – and those aimed at securing local development benefits. The distinction is, in effect, that between the financial flows commanded by the Global Environment Facility and conventional development assistance.

11.8 APPROPRIATING GLOBAL VALUE

The previous sections have argued that orthodox economics is well on the way to demonstrating the economic value of tropical forests. While there are significant local conservation benefits, there is evidence to suggest that the global benefits dominate. This latter proposition remains uncertain since (a) the science of global warming is not finalized, so that the carbon storage benefits are probabilistic, and (b) investigations into global existence value have barely commenced. The former can only be resolved by waiting for the scientists. The latter requires a concerted research effort in economic valuation. This leaves the issue of appropriation: how are the economic values turned into cash, technology or commodity flows to make them 'real' to those who make land use decisions in the tropical forests?

The Sustainability Issue in Tropical Forests

The appropriation issue has first to be put into the context of sustainable land utilization. The essence of the land use decision in tropical forests is that, in many cases, there exists a supply of open access land beyond the existing frontiers of cultivation. Provided this land is available, there is no 'land constraint' and the absence of this constraint provides a major incentive for 'nutrient mining' whereby the soil and biomass nutrient stock in the forest is treated as an exhaustible resource, not a renewable one. Southgate (1994) suggests that some central and south American countries and the Caribbean have hit the land constraint, either because of natural barriers – Bolivia and Peru – or for other reasons – Uruguay, Costa Rica, Nicaragua, Honduras, El Salvador, Guatemala, Dominican Republic and Jamaica. In Haiti the extensive margin has actually gone beyond the zero rent point. Using a simple econometric model, Southgate shows that land conversion rates are less in those countries where the land constraint bites, and that increases in agricultural productivity substantially reduce the drive to extend the frontier. This offers one clue to policy design – increases in agricultural productivity may be the single most important measure for slowing the rate of deforestation in certain areas. If so, a good deal of rethinking is required with respect to conventional policy: saving biodiversity through forest protection policies not only does nothing to contain the drive to extend the frontier, it may actually exacerbate it. Similarly, the distinction between 'development' and 'environment' policies virtually disappears: some development policies become the most powerful means of protecting local and global environmental benefits. None of this should be allowed to divert attention from 'management failure' as a factor in deforestation; i.e. inefficiency arising from poor forest management.

Figure 11.2 illustrates the essential features. Profitability is shown on the vertical axis, and time on the horizontal axis. Forest clearance usually takes place through burning. The burn converts the major part of the nutrient stock, which is in the forest biomass, into ash which makes the nutrients available to the nutrient-deficient soil, clears pests and makes the land suitable for crops. But the nutrients are a stock resource, so that cropping reduces the stock over time and hence the productivity of the soil. This is shown by the strictly concave profit functions. Since there may be multiple users of the land the picture is complicated. Loggers may be there first, followed by crop farmers followed by ranchers (Schneider, 1992). For any *single* user the switchover point – the time at which the colonizer moves on to new land – will be determined by a comparison of the profitability of staying on the existing piece of land and the profitability of moving to the new land. Transport and other costs are likely to rise the further the frontier moves out, so that π_2 begins at a lower point of profitability than π_1. T_1 is then the switchover point. Since there are multiple users, the original land area may continue to be used beyond T_1, although, as long as new land is available to other users as well, they too will move before total exhaustion is reached at T_2. This means that some nutrients are left and regeneration is possible, albeit with a different diversity of biomass. The land is not 'dead' altogether, but its nutrient stock is potentially severely depleted.

However, if the second area is not available because the extensive margin has been reached, then there are incentives to invest in productivity-raising assets

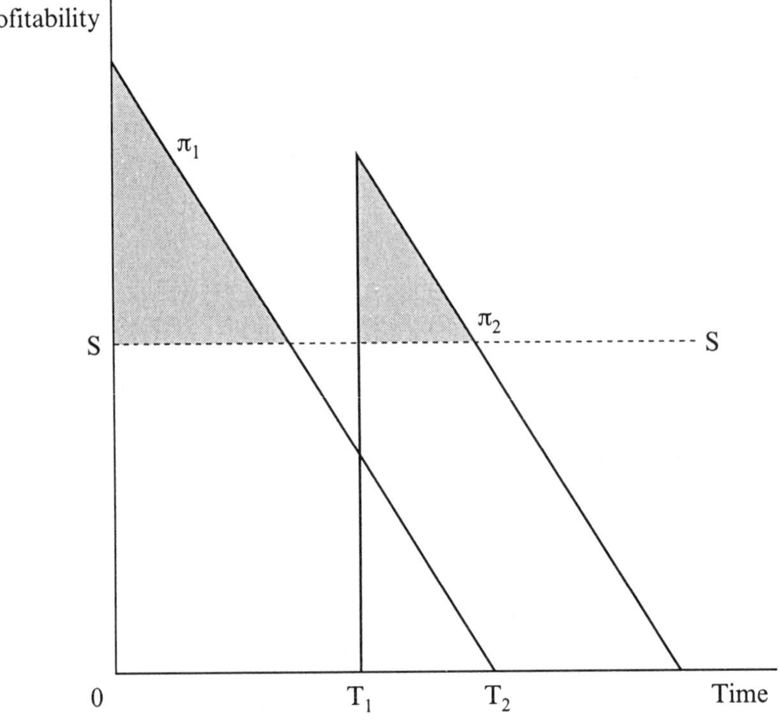

Figure 11.2 A simplified model of nutrient mining

– soil conservation, for example. But since we are trying to explain deforestation, the focus is on regions where, after nutrient mining in one area, a new area is cleared. From the colonizer's standpoint, it is the present value of the succession of future profits that matters. Nothing is lost by reinterpreting the concave functions in Figure 11.2 as discounted flows. These flows need to be compared to the 'sustainable' alternative, say agro-forestry with a focus on non-timber products and some internalization of the global externalities. For simplicity, we show this alternative as the line SS in Figure 11.2. The conservation issue is threefold in the case where no land constraint bites: (a) raising the height of SS in order to demonstrate that sustainable utilization may well be profitable in some cases; (b) raising the height of π_1 to reduce the incentive to move to area 2; and (c) compensating the colonizer for the forgone profits shown as the shaded area in Figure 11.2. Policy (a) is preferred if sustainable use alternatives are viable and the issue is one of information and demonstration. Policy (b) is preferred if sustainable use alternatives simply do not appear to be competitive. Policy

(c) is preferred where (a) and (b) cannot, for one reason or the other, be applied, i.e. both sustainable alternatives and on-site productivity improvements are not feasible. Policy (c) requires finding compensation mechanisms to enable colonists to capture the forgone profits shown as the shaded area in Figure 11.2.

Mechanisms for Value Capture

There are several ways in which global appropriation failure can be corrected through creating global environmental markets (GEMs). We distinguish between private and public ('official') ventures, and between those that are regulation induced and those that are spontaneous market initiatives. Public regulation-induced activity arises because of international agreements, such as the Biodiversity and Climate Change Conventions. Table 11.10 sets out a schema.

Table 11.10 A schema for global environmental markets

	Regulation-induced	Spontaneous market
Public/official ventures	Examples: government to government measures under joint implementation provisions of the Rio treaties: Norway, Mexico, Poland, GEF	Examples: government involvement in market ventures: Swiss Green Export aid; debt-for-nature swaps
Private sector ventures	Examples: carbon offsets against carbon taxes and externality adders.	Examples: purchase of exotic capital – Merck and Costa Rica

Regulation-Induced Trades

The existence, or threatened existence, of regulations acts as a stimulus to trade.

Government–government trades

The first joint implementation agreement has been agreed between Norway, Poland and Mexico, through the medium of the Global Environment Facility (GEF). Norway agrees to create additional financing (through the revenues from its own carbon tax) for GEF carbon-reducing projects in Mexico (energy efficient lighting) and Poland (converting from coal burning to natural gas) (Global Environment Facility, 1992). The US Environmental Defence Fund is understood to be developing a reforestation project in Russia. The US

Government announced the *Forest for the Future Initiative* (FFI) in January 1993 under which carbon offset agreements will be negotiated between the USA and several countries, including Mexico, Russia, Guatemala, Indonesia and Papua New Guinea. The aim is for the US Environmental Protection Agency to broker deals involving the private sector.

Private sector trades

The European Community Draft Directive on a carbon tax and other European legislation also provides an incentive to trade in this way, as does State regulation on pollution by electric utilities in the USA. While not strictly a private enterprise trade, in the *Netherlands*, the state electricity generating board (SEP) established a non-profit making enterprise in 1990. FACE (Forests Absorbing Carbon Dioxide Emissions) aims to sequester an amount of CO_2 equivalent to that emitted by one 600 MW power station. This is estimated to require some 150 000 hectares: 5000 ha in the Netherlands, 20 000 ha in central Europe and 125 000 ha in tropical countries. At the end of 1993 the actual area had risen to 180 000 ha with the additional area in tropical countries (see Table 11.11).

In the US case the offset deals are currently not directly linked to legislation, but several have occurred which are clearly a mix of anticipation of regulation and 'global good citizenship' (Newcombe and de Lucia, 1993). These include the *New England Power Co.*'s investment in carbon sequestration in Sabah, Malaysia through the reduction of carbon waste from inefficient logging activities. The forest products enterprise is run by Innoprise. New England Power estimate that some 300 000 to 600 000 tonnes of carbon (C) will be offset at a cost of below $2 tC. Rain Forest Alliance will assist in monitoring the project. New England Power regard the Innoprise project as the first of a series aimed at assisting with the Corporation's plan to reduce CO_2 emissions by 45% by the year 2000. *PacifiCorp*, an electric utility in Oregon, is considering reforestation projects and urban tree planting programmes in the US, and an international sequestration project (Dixon *et al.*,1993). Two pilot projects have been announced: (a) a rural reforestation project in Southern Oregon which funds planting subject to a constraint of no harvesting for 45–65 years, at an estimated cost of around $5 tC; and (b) an urban tree programme in Salt Lake City, Utah at a provisionally estimated cost of $15–30 tC sequestered. *Tenaska* Corporation is considering sequestration projects in the Russian boreal forests. Ultimately, some 20 000 ha of forests may be created in the Saratov and Volgograd regions at a cost of $1–2 tC. Russian partners in the venture include the Russian Forest Service, the Ministry of Ecology and others. Tenaska is also planning reforestation projects in Washington state to complement a project in Costa Rica (see Table 11.11).

While these investments are aimed at CO_2 reduction, sequestration clearly has the potential for generating joint benefits, i.e. for saving biodiversity as well through the recreation of habitats. Much depends here on the nature of the offset. If the aim is CO_2 fixation alone, there will be a temptation to invest in fast growing species which could be to the detriment of biodiversity. It is important therefore to extend the offset concept so that larger credits are given for investments which produce joint biodiversity – CO_2 reduction benefits.

The US Energy Policy Act of 1992 requires the Energy Information Administration to develop guidelines for the establishment of a database on greenhouse gas offsets, together with an offset 'bank'. The Keystone Center in the USA is also establishing an interchange of information with a number of electric utilities to explore the issues involved in establishing offset deals.

Global Good Citizenship

Several offset deals appear to have been undertaken quite independently of legislation or anticipation of regulation. Applied Energy Services (AES) of Virginia has also undertaken sequestration investments in Guatemala (agroforestry) and Paraguay and is in the process of setting up another project in the Amazon basin. The Guatemala project is designed to offset emissions from a 1800 MW coal-fired power plant being built in Uncasville, Connecticut. The intermediary for the project is the World Resources Institute and in Guatemala the implementing agency is CARE. The project involves tree planting by some 40 000 farm families, soil conservation techniques, and biomass conservation through fire prevention measures, etc. Carbon sequestration is estimated to be 15.5 m.tons of carbon. The $15 million cost includes $2 million contribution from AES; $1.2 million from the Government of Guatemala; $1.8 million from CARE, with the balance coming in-kind from US AID and the Peace Corps. The motivations for involvement vary. AES's involvement relates to its concern not just to offset CO_2 emissions, but to achieve the local development and environmental benefits the deal brings. Dixon *et al.* (1993) report the sequestration cost as $9 tC overall, but inspection of the data suggests it may be much less than this. $9 tC would be expensive for carbon sequestration alone, but there are other benefits from the scheme, including local economic benefits. In the Paraguay deal, AES has advanced money to the (US) Nature Conservancy for investment in some 57 000 ha of endangered tropical forest. The International Finance Corporation agreed to sell the land for $2m, well below the market price of $5–7 m. AES expects to sequester some 13 million tC at around $1.5 per tC to offset CO_2 emissions from the Barbers Point 180 MW coal-fired plant in Oahu, Hawaii. Local benefits include eco-tourism, scientific research, recreation, agroforestry and watershed protection. AES is also planning to offset emissions from a third power plant with support for indigenous peoples in Peru, Ecuador and Bolivia to secure title to their lands and to develop sustainable extractive activities.

Table 11.11 summarizes the private sector carbon offset deals to date.

Table 11.11 Private sector carbon offset deals

Company	Project	Other participants	Million tC sequestered or reduced	Total cost ($ million)	$ tC sequestered
AES	Agro-forestry Guatemala	US CARE; Govt. of Guatemala	15–58 over 40 years	15	(a) 0.5–2 (b) 1–4 (c)9
AES	Nature reserve Paraguay	US Nature Conservancy; FMB	13 over 30 years	6	(a)0.2 (b) 0.45 (c) <1.5
AES	Secure land tenure, sustainable agriculture Bolivia, Peru, Ecuador	Other utilities giving consideration to deal	na	2	na
SEP	Reforestation				
	Netherlands		0.9	20	(b) 22.7
	Czech Rep.		3.1	30	(b) 9.7
	Malaysia	Innoprise	6.3	15.7	(b) 2.5
	Ecuador		9.7	17.3	(b) 1.8
	Uganda		7.2	8.0	(b) 1.1
	Indonesia		6.8	21.7	(b) 3.2
Tenaska and others	Reforestation Russia	EPA; Trexler; Min.of Ecology; Russian Forest Service, etc.	0.5 over 25 years	0.5?	(a) na (b) 1 (c) 1–2

Tenaska	Forest conservation C.Rica + reforestation Washington state	Other utilities giving consideration	na	5+	na
PacifiCorp	Forestry Oregon	Trexler	0.06 p.a.	0.1 p.a.	(a) na (b) na (c) 5
PacifiCorp	Urban trees Utah	Trexler;TreeUtah	?	0.1 p.a.	(a) na (b) na (c) 15–30
New England PC	Forestry Malaysia	Rain Forest Alliance; COPEC	0.1–0.15	0.45	(a) na (b) 3–4.5 (c) na
New England PC	Methane recovery Appalachians	na	na	na	na
Wisconsin Electric Power Co; NIPSCO Industry; Edison Development Co.	Coal to gas conversion	Bynov Heating Plant, Decin Czech Republic	12 800 tpa?	1.5	(b)43

Notes:
(a) Assumes 10% discount rate applied to total cost to obtain an annuity which is then applied to carbon fixed per annum, assuming equal distribution of carbon sequestered over the time horizon indicated.
(b) Assumes no discounting.
(c) Cost per tC as reported in Dixon *et al.* (1993).

Source: Pearce (1994). CO_2 converted to C at 3.67:1. Dutch guilders converted to US $ at 1.75 DG per $.

Buying Down Private Risk

Newcombe and de Lucia (1993) have drawn attention to another potentially very large private trade which has global environmental benefits. Investment by the private sector in the developing world is invariably constrained by risk factors such as exchange rate risks, repayment risks, political risks and so on. In so far as this investment benefits the global environment, as with, say, the development of natural gas to displace coal, the existence of the risks reduces the flow of investment and hence the global environmental benefits. But these risks might be shared ('bought down') by having an international agency, such as the Global Environment Facility, provide some funds or services which help reduce the risk. Given the scale of private investment flows, the potential here is enormous. Nor is there any reason why it should not benefit biodiversity, either indirectly as a joint benefit of other investments, in for example, raising agricultural productivity and hence in reducing the pressure for land degradation, or directly through afforestation schemes.

'Exotic capital'

Financial transfers may take place without any regulatory 'push'. The consumer demand for green products has already resulted in companies deciding to invest in conservation either for direct profit or because of a mix of profit and conservation motives. The Body Shop is an illustration of the mixed motive, as is Merck's royalty deal with Costa Rica for pharmaceutical plants and Pro-Natura's expanding venture in marketing indigenous tropical forest products. There is, in other words, an incentive to purchase or lease 'exotic capital' in the same way as a company would buy or lease any other form of capital.

The deal between Merck & Co, the world's largest pharmaceutical company, and INBio (the National Biodiversity Institute of Costa Rica) is already well documented and studied (Gámez *et al.*, 1993; Sittenfield and Gámez, 1993; Blum, 1993). Under the agreement, INBio collects and processes plant, insect and soil samples in Costa Rica and supplies them to Merck for assessment. In return, Merck pays Costa Rica $1 million plus a share of any royalties should any successful drug be developed from the supplied material. The royalty agreement is reputed to be of the order of 1% to 3% and to be shared between INBio and the Costa Rican government. Patent rights to any successful drug would remain with Merck. Biodiversity is protected in two ways – by conferring commercial value on the biodiversity, and through the earmarking of some of the payments for the Ministry of Natural Resources.

How far is the Merck–INBio deal likely to be repeated? Several caveats are in order to offset some of the enthusiasm over this single deal. First, Costa Rica is in the vanguard of biodiversity conservation, as its strong record in debt-for-nature swaps shows. Second, Costa Rica has a strong scientific base and a considerable degree of political stability. Both of these characteristics need to be present and their combination is not typical of that many developing countries. Third, the economic value of such deals is minimal unless the royalties are actually paid and that will mean success in developing drugs from the relevant genetic material. The chances of such developments are small – perhaps one in one to ten thousand of plants species screened (Pearce and Moran, 1994). INBio has undertaken to supply 10 000 samples under the initial agreement. There is therefore a chance of one such drug being developed. But successful drugs could result in many hundreds of millions of dollars in revenues. Finally, there are two views on the extent to which deals of this kind could be given added impetus by the Biodiversity Convention. The Convention stresses the role of intellectual property rights in securing conservation and is sufficiently vaguely worded for there to be wide interpretation of its provisions. But it also appears to threaten stringent conditions concerning those rights and technology transfer and it remains to be seen how the relevant Protocols are worded. If so, parties to the Convention may find private deals being turned into overtly more political affairs with major constraints on what can be negotiated (Blum, 1993).

Other examples of direct deals on 'biodiversity prospecting' include California's Shaman Pharmaceuticals (Brazil and Argentina)and the UK's Biotics Ltd (general purchase and royalty deals), while Mexico and Indonesia are looking closely at the commercialization of biodiversity resources.

The demand for direct investment in conservation is not confined to the private sector. The demand for conservation by NGOs is revealed through debt-for-nature swaps, which are further examples of these exotic capital trades (for an overview see Pearce and Moran, 1994 and Deacon and Murphy, 1994).

Mixed private/public trades: resource franchise agreements

A great variety of trades involving both the public and private sectors is possible. For example consider the general area of resource franchise agreements (RFAs). The general principle of RFAs is that specific land uses in defined zones are restricted ('attenuated') in return for the payment of a premium. At one extreme, if all land uses other than outright preservation are forbidden, the premium equals the rental on the land that would arise in the 'best' developmental use. If some uses are restricted, the premium will tend to be equal to the differential rent between the unrestricted 'highest and best' use and the rental on the restricted use. The minimum supply price offered by colonizers and host governments will be this differential rent. The demand price will be determined by global willingness to pay for the benefits of attenuating land uses. This is the essence of the comparison made earlier between land prices and global warming damage estimates, for example. Payment of the premium would be, say, annual since an 'up front' payment could result in the host country reneging on the understanding after payment is received. To secure compliance, annual payments would be made in order that they can be suspended in the event of non-compliance. Such trades are not without their problems. The earlier example of carbon storage values compared land prices with the present value of global warming damage from a tonne of carbon dioxide. Two discount rates are embedded in this comparison: the farmer's and the world's. If payments have to be annual, the present values need to be annuitized. Since it is the farmer who has the property rights, his discount rate will dominate. The relevant comparison will be between annual willingness to pay and annual willingness to accept a premium. Another issue relates to the successional uses of land. The logger should effectively pay a price for land that reflects not just the logging value, but also a residual price of the land if it can be on-sold to ranchers or farmers. Markets need to work fairly well for the conservation and development values to be compared.

Several authors have suggested franchise type agreements – Sedjo (1991); Panayotou (1994); Katzman and Cale (1990). Such development rights could become tradeable, just as joint implementation schemes could become open to subsequent bargains leading to a full emissions trading programme. The potential buyers could range from local conservation groups through to international conservation societies, corporations, governments and so on, with motives ranging from profiting from sustainable use through to scientific research and good citizenship images. Panayotou (1994) suggests that corporations in developed countries could be given credit for buying into such tradeable rights, e.g. through relaxations on domestic regulatory obligations. Measured against the *status quo* this obviously has the disadvantage of 'trading' environmental quality between developed and developing country economies, a problem that has brought criticism on joint implementation proposals already. Nonetheless, the approach could be utilized in the event of tighter developed country restrictions being contemplated.

11.9 CONCLUSIONS

This paper has suggested that orthodox economics – the economics that tends to be practised now – has barely been tested in the fight to save the tropical forests. Moreover, it appears to have a huge potential. That potential rests on:

a. demonstrating that substantial economic value resides in the tropical forests;
b. showing how mutually profitable trades can emerge so as to capture that economic value.

None of this implies a diversion from policies aimed at correcting domestic market failures nor domestic intervention failures, nor management failure – the equivalent of 'X inefficiency' in forest management. Nor does it imply an exclusive focus on the developing world. The rich world has more than its fair share of gross distortions that destroy the rich world's remaining environmental assets. But the focus on developing countries is justified because (a) they possess the tropical forests which, in turn, have such an array of ecological, and therefore economic, benefits for the world in general; and (b), a critical point, the corrective measures needed can stimulate economic development as well as conserving resources.

But there are clear risks in resting conservation arguments *solely* on the economic values of conservation. A balanced approach would stress the incidental conservation benefits of other policies aimed at correcting economic distortions.

While the evidence is still limited, what there is suggests that those who argue for the conservation of tropical forests on grounds of *local* economic value alone – for example, non-timber products and sustainable timber benefits (Peters *et al.*, 1989) – may not have a strong case. The initial enthusiasm that greeted claims of high value sustainable forest use based on non-timber forest products (NTFPs) has waned somewhat in the face of (a) methodological doubts about such studies (Godoy and Lubowski, 1992, Southgate and Whitaker, 1994; (b) revised estimates of NTFP productivity; (c) wrong extrapolation from one forest type to another (Phillips, 1994; Godoy and Lubowski, 1992), and (d) doubts about the sustainability of NTFP exploitation itself (Peters, 1991).

Some of the global use benefits may also not be large enough to outweigh the developmental benefits of forest clearance. Simpson *et al.* (1994) suggest that pharmaceutical values, for example, are modest. The value of the 'marginal species' is likely to be very low due to (a) the high number of species, and (b) the substitution possibilities. Translated into per hectare values, we may be speaking of only a few dollars.

Two elements of global value stand out. The first is the carbon storage value of forests. This may well be several times the domestic value, and the issue then is how to capture that value through measures such as joint implementation and perhaps eventually a full greenhouse gas trading regime. The problem here is that the science of global warming is uncertain – giving rise to the good news/bad news paradox that, if warming turns out to be untrue (the good news), one of the major arguments for tropical forest conservation will disappear (the bad news). The second element is global existence value. The problem here is that research has barely started into demonstrating the scale of these values. Illustrative but very crude tests were used here: an extrapolation of contingent valuation results for unique species and habitats would suggest modest individual willingness to pay for conservation which, if extrapolated, would nonetheless generate a huge new flow of finance. Implicit prices in debt-for-nature swaps could also result in reasonable estimates of global WTP. The one global CVM study we have also suggests sizeable annual funds if translated into actual WTP. The unnerving feature of these rough implied estimates and the global CVM is that they are well above the actual WTP as revealed in the GEF replenishment. Is this provisional evidence of hypothetical bias? Or is it the case that the institutions simply have not developed to the point where individuals feel confidence that their true WTP will be translated into conservation action?

Finally, if global values are going to save the tropical forests there has to be an imaginative use of a wide range of instruments, from debt-for-nature swaps to tradeable development rights to joint implementation and private green image investments. The challenge remains: demonstrate and appropriate. Orthodox economics should be given a chance to save the tropical forests: the unorthodox is without appeal or practicality. And the non-economic approaches have failed.

NOTE

1. Originally read to the conference *Forestry and the Environment: Economic Perspectives II* Conference at Banff National Park, Alberta, Canada, 12–15 October 1994, and subsequently published in W.Adamowicz *et al.* (1996), *Forestry, Economics and the Environment*, CAB International, Reading.

REFERENCES

Allen, J. and Barnes, D. (1985), The causes of deforestation in developing countries, *Annals of the Association of American Geographers*, **75**(2), 163–84.

Binswanger, H. (1989), *Brazilian Policies that Encourage Deforestation of the Amazon*. Working paper 16, Environment Department, World Bank, Washington DC.

Blum, E. (1993), Making biodiversity conservation profitable: a case study of the Merck.INBio Agreement, *Environment*, **35**(4), May, p. 16.

Brown, K. and Pearce, D.W. (1994a), The economic value of non-market benefits of tropical forests: carbon storage, in J. Weiss (ed.), *The Eonomics of Project Appraisal and the Environment*, Edward Elgar, London, 102–123.

Brown, K. and D.W.Pearce (eds) (1994b), *The Causes of Tropical Deforestation: The Economic and Statistical Analysis of Factors Giving Rise to the Loss of the Tropical Forests*, University College Press, London, and University of British Columbia Press, Vancouver.

Brown, K., Pearce, D.W. Perrings C. and Swanson T. (1993), *Economics and the Conservation of Global Biological Diversity*, Global Environment Facility, Working Paper No.2, Washington DC.

Burgess, J. (1991), *Economic Analyses of Frontier Agricultural Expansion and Tropical Deforestation*, MSc dissertation presented to University College, London.

Burgess, J. (1992), *Economic Analysis of the Causes of Tropical Deforestation*, London Environmental Economics Centre, Discussion Paper, 92-03, November 1992.

Capistrano, A. and Kiker, C. (1990), *Global Economic Influences on Tropical Broadleaved Forest Depletion*, The World Bank, Washington DC.

Cervigni, R. (1993), *Biodiversity, Incentives to Deforest and Tradeable Development Rights*, Centre for Social and Economic Research on the Global Environment (CSERGE), Working Paper GEC 93-07, University College London.

Clark, C. (1990), *Mathematical Bioeconomics: The Optimal Management of Renewable Resources*, second edition, John Wiley, New York.

Constantino, L. and Ingram, D. (1990), *Supply–Demand Projections for the Indonesian Forestry Sector*, FAO, Jakarta.

Cuesta, M., Carlson, G. and Lutz, E., (1994), *An Empirical Assessment of Farmers' Discount Rates in Costa Rica and Its Implication for Soil Conservation*, Environment Department, World Bank, Washington DC.

Deacon, R. (1994), *Deforestation and the Rule of Law in a Cross Section of Countries,* Resources for the Future, Washington DC, Discussion Paper 94–23.

Deacon, R and Murphy, P. (1994), *The Structure of an Environmental Transaction: the Debt-for-Nature Swap*, Resources for the Future,Washington DC, Discussion Paper 94–40.

Dixon, R., Andrasko, K., Sussman, F., Trexler, M. and Vinson, T. (1993), Forest sector carbon offset projects: near-term opportunities to mitigate greenhouse gas emissions, *Water, Air and Soil Pollution*, Special issue.

Fankhauser, S. and Pearce, D.W. (1994), The social costs of greenhouse gas emissions, in *The Economics of Climate Change*, OECD, Paris, 71–86.

Gámez, R., Piva, A., Sittenfield, A., Leon, E., Jimenez, J. and Mirabelli, G. (1993), Costa Rica's Conservation Program and National Biodiversity Institute (INBio), in Reid *et al.*(1993).

Global Environment Facility, (1992), *Memorandum of Understanding on Norwegian Funding of Pilot Demonstration Projects for Joint Implementation Arrangements Under the Climate Convention*, GEF, Washington DC, mimeo.

Godoy, R. and Lubowski, R. (1992), Guidelines for the economic valuation of nontimber tropical-forest products, *Current Anthropology*, **33**(4), 423–33.

Goodland, R. (1990), *Race to Save the Tropics: Ecology and Economics for a Sustainable Future*, Island Press, Washington DC.

Grut, M., Gray, J. and Egli, N. (1991), *Forest Pricing and Concession Policies: Managing the High Forests of West and Central Africa.* Technical Paper No.143, World Bank, Washington DC.

Hodgson, G and Dixon, J. (1988), *Logging Versus Fisheries and Tourism in Palawan*, East West Center, Occasional Paper No.7, Honolulu, Hawaii.

Hyde, W and Sedjo, R. (1992), Managing tropical forests: reflections on the rent distribution discussion, *Land Economics*, **68**(3), 343–50.

Hyde, W and Sedjo, R. (1993), Managing tropical forests: Reply, *Land Economics*, **69**(3), 319–321.

Kahn, J. and McDonald, J. (1994), International debt and deforestation, in Brown and Pearce (1994b), 57–67.

Katila, M. (1992), *Modelling Deforestation in Thailand: the Causes of Deforestation and Deforestation Projections for 1990–2010*, Finnish Forestry Institute, Helsinki, mimeo.

Katzman, M. and Cale, W. (1990), Tropical forest preservation using economic incentives: a proposal of conservation easements, *BioScience*, **40**(11), December, 827–32.

Kramer, R., Mercer, E. and Sharma, N. (1994), Valuing Tropical Rain Forest Protection Using the Contingent Valuation Method, School of the Environment, Duke University, Durham, NC, mimeo.

Kumari, K. (1994), An environmental and economic assessment of forestry management options: a case study in Peninsular Malaysia, Chapter 6 of K. Kumari *Sustainable Forest Management in Malaysia*, PhD Thesis, University of East Anglia, UK.

Kummer, D. and Sham, C.H. (1994), The causes of tropical deforestation: a quantitative analysis and case study from the Philippines, in Brown and Pearce (1994b), 146–58.

Lockwood, M., Loomis, J. and T. de Lacy, (1994), The relative unimportance of a non-market willingness to pay for timber harvesting, *Ecological Economics*, **9**, 145–52.

Lugo, A., Schmidt, R. and Brown, S. (1981), Tropical forest in the Caribbean, *Ambio*, **10**(6), pp. 318–24.

Mahar, D. and Schneider, R. (1994), Incentives for tropical deforestation: some examples from Latin America, in Brown and Pearce (1994b), 159–71.

Moreddu, C., Parris, K. and Huff, B. (1990), Agricultural policies in developing countries and agricultural trade, in I. Goldin and O. Knudsen (eds), *Agricultural Trade Liberalization: Implications for Developing Countries*, OECD, Paris, 115–57.

Newcombe, K. and Lucia, R. de (1993), *Mobilising Private Capital Against Global Warming: a Business Concept and Policy Issues*, Global Environment Facility, Washington DC, mimeo.

OECD (Organisation for Economic Cooperation and Development) (1993), *Agricultural Policies, Markets and Trade: Monitoring and Outlook 1993*, OECD, Paris.

Palo, M., Mery, G. and Salmi, J. (1987), *Deforestation in the Tropics: Pilot Scenarios Based on Quantitative Analyses*, Metsatutkimuslaitoksen Tiedonantaja nro. 272, Helsinki.

Panayotou, T. and Sungsuwan, S. (1994), An econometric study of the causes of tropical deforestation: the case of Northeast Thailand, in Brown and Pearce (1994b), 192–210.

Panayotou, T. (1993), *Green Markets: The Economics of Sustainable Development*, Institute for Contemporary Studies Press, San Francisco.

Panayotou, T. (1994), *Financing Mechanisms for Environmental Investments and Sustainable Development*, Harvard Institute for International Development, Harvard University, mimeo.

Pearce, D.W. (1993), *Economic Values and the Natural World*, Earthscan, London.

Pearce, D.W. (1994), Joint implementation: a general overview, in C.P. Jepma (ed.) *Joint Implementation*, Kluwer, Dordrecht, 15–33.

Pearce, D.W. (1995), New ways of financing global environmental change, *Global Environmental Change*, **5**(1), 27–40.

Pearce, D.W., Adger, N., Brown, K., Cervigni, R. and Moran, D. (1993), *Mexico Forestry and Conservation Sector Review: Substudy of Economic Valuation of Forests*, Centre for Social and Economic Research on the Global Environment (CSERGE) for World Bank Latin America and Caribbean Country Department.

Pearce,D.W. and Moran, D. (1994), *The Economic Value of Biodiversity*, Earthscan, London and Island Press, Washington DC: in association with the International Union for the Conservation of Nature (IUCN).

Pearce, D.W. and Warford, J. (1993), *World Without End: Economics, Environment and Sustainable Development*, Oxford University Press, Oxford and New York.

Perrings, C. (1992), *An Economic Analysis of Tropical Deforestation*, Environment and Economic Management Department, University of York, UK, mimeo.

Peters C., Gentry, A. and Mendelsohn, R. (1989), Valuation of an Amazonian rainforest, *Nature*, **339**, 655–6.

Peters, C. (1991), *Environmental Assessment of Extractive Reserves: Key issues in the Ecology and Management of Non-Timber Forest Resources*, Draft Report to Environment Department, World Bank, Washington DC.

Phillips, D. (1994), The potential for harvesting fruits in tropical rainforests: new data from Amazonian Peru, *Biodiversity and Conservation*, **2**, 18–38.

Reis, J. and R. Guzman, (1992), *An Econometric Model of Amazon Deforestation*, paper presented at the Conference on Statistics in Public Resources and Utilities, and in the Care of the Environment, Lisbon, April, 1992.

Repetto, R. and Gillis, M. (1988), *Public Policies and the Misuse of Forest Resources*, Cambridge University Press, Cambridge.

Rudel, T. (1989), Population, development, and tropical deforestation: a cross national study, *Rural Sociology*, **54**(3), 3–38. Reprinted in Brown and Pearce (1994b), 96–105.

Ruitenbeek, J. (1992), The rainforest supply price: a tool for evaluating rainforest conservation expenditures, *Ecological Economics*, **1**(6), July, 57–78.

Sandler, T. (1993), Tropical deforestation: markets and market failure, *Land Economics*, **69**(30), 225–33.

Schneider, R. (1992), *An Economic Analysis of Environmental Problems in the Amazon*. Report 9104-BR, Latin America Country Operations Division, World Bank, Washington DC.

Schulze, W., McClelland, G. and Lazo, J. (1994), Methodological issues in using contingent valuation to measure non-use value. Paper to US Department of Energy and Environmental Protection Agency Workshop of *Using Contingent Valuation to Measure Non-market Values*, Herndon, Virginia.

Sedjo, R. (1991), *Toward a Worldwide System of Tradeable Forest Protection and Management Obligations*, Resources for the Future, Washington DC, mimeo.

Shafik, N. (1994), Macroeconomic causes of deforestation: barking up the wrong tree, in Brown and Pearce (1994b).

Simpson, D., Sedjo, R. and Reid, J. (1994), *Valuing Biodiversity: an Application of Genetic Prospecting*, Resources for the Future, Washington DC, Discussion paper 94-20.

Sittenfield, A. and Gámez, R. (1993), Biodiversity prospecting in INBio, in Reid *et al.*(1993).

Southgate, D. (1994), Tropical deforestation and agricultural development in Latin America, in Brown and Pearce (1994b), 134–45.

Southgate, D., Sierra, R. and Brown, L. (1989), *The Causes of Tropical Deforestation in Ecuador: a Statistical Analysis*, London Environmental Economics Centre, International Institute for Environment and Development (IIED), London.

Southgate, D. and Whittaker, M. (1994), *Economic Progress and the Environment: One Developing Country's Policy Crisis*, Oxford University Press, Oxford.

Swanson, T. (1994), *The International Regulation of Extinction*, Macmillan, London.

Vincent, J. (1993), Managing tropical forests: Comment. *Land Economics*, **69**(3), 313–18.

World Bank (1991), *Malaysia: Forestry Subsector Study*. Report 9775-MA. World Bank, Washington DC.

World Bank (1992), *World Development Report: Development and the Environment*, Oxford University Press, Oxford.

World Bank (1993a), *Costa Rica: Forestry Sector Review*. Report 11516-CR. World Bank, Washington DC.

World Bank (1993b), *Indonesia: Forestry, Achieving Sustainability and Competitiveness*. Report 11758-IND, World Bank, Washington DC.

12. The economics of African wildlife utilization[1]

12.1 INTRODUCTION

Two questions need to be answered in respect of wildlife conservation:

a. how much wildlife should be conserved? and
b. what is the most effective and sustainable way of conserving wildlife?

The economic approach to answering the first question involves some comparison of the costs and benefits of conservation. In answering the second question the emphasis is on the design of incentive systems that ensure that those whose lives are affected by conservation have a motivation to abide by a conservation agreement rather than to threaten it. No economist would suggest that the economic approach is all-embracing: there are clearly many factors that have to be taken into account in conservation decisions. Nonetheless, the economic approach offers policy insights that often contrast with conventional wisdom.

In this paper we offer a brief overview of the economic approach, looking first at an elementary model of conservation economics, then at the economic benefits and costs of conservation, and finally at the ways in which benefits and costs must be allocated to ensure that any conservation effort is sustainable. Much more detail can be found in the rapidly growing literature on the economics of biodiversity conservation – see McNeely (1988), Dixon and Sherman (1990), Perrings *et al.* (1995), Barbier *et al.*(1994), Shah (1995), Pearce and Moran (1994), Swanson (1995a, 1995b).

12.2 AN ECONOMIC MODEL OF WILDLIFE CONSERVATION

Conserving wildlife in a sustainable fashion logically implies that the underlying causes of wildlife loss are understood and addressed by policy measures. The economic theory of species extinction casts considerable light on the causal processes at work. The theory has its origins in the theory of the fishery

(Gordon, 1954) and has been extended to cover wild species in general (Clark, 1973a, 1973b, 1990).

Two sets of factors may give rise to extinction. The first is the property rights regime. Regimes may be 'open access', common property, single private owner, or single state owner. Open access differs from common property in that the former regime has no owners and hence no rules for restricting or managing access to the resource. Common property regimes involve sets of rules and regulations limiting access and harvest rates, these rules being enforced by communal law or communal custom. Under single ownership, access is restricted to any outsider not part of the ownership regime, and the community in question is now a private organization or the nation state. As a general rule, the greater the restrictions on access the less the harvest effort applied to the resource and hence the more likely it is that resource stocks will be large. With open access, however, effort is unconstrained until the newest new entrant finds that resource stocks have depleted to the point where his effort is only just rewarded by the extra revenues obtained from the sale of the resource: the 'zero rent' point. In itself, then, open access does not generate extinction of the resource because further entry beyond the open access equilibrium does not occur. As long as the costs of harvest are positive, some of the resource is left intact, though with low sustainable yields. Nonetheless, population dynamics are ill understood and hence the risk of extinction is higher the lower are the stocks. It is quite possible, therefore, for open access to create the conditions in which harvest levels give rise to stock levels that are below minimum viable sizes. This will be especially true in contexts where minimum viable size is influenced by family or group dynamics, as is the case for some land-based animals. Removing critical family members may render the remaining population non-viable.

Common property regimes are far more likely to protect the resource against extinction, although common property tends itself to be vulnerable to external influences, including human population growth which places pressure on the regime to continue managing the resource in the interests of the whole community. Moreover, rapid population change is the context in which wildlife conservation has to be discussed. The in-built dynamics of population change mean, for example, that the developing world's current population of 4.5 billion people will grow to at least 7.3 billion in 2100 regardless of any policies adopted now to slow that rate of change (Bongaerts, 1994; World Bank, 1994a). That is, we are looking at a minimum of a 50 per cent change in developing country populations over the next 100 years.

On the traditional model of species extinction particular combinations of cost of effort and resource price will also make the open access situation more risky still. High prices for the harvested resource – elephant ivory or rhinoceros horn for example – make it profitable to harvest the resource. Low costs of exploitation combined with high prices mean high profit levels and these encourage depletion. This 'high price, low cost' combination appears to fit certain land-based species well, e.g. elephants. Ivory prices can be very high and the use of vehicles and high velocity rifles makes costs low. The open access nature of the range which many of these species occupy also means that detection rates for illegal harvesting will tend to be low. Even if the penalties are severe, including death itself, the expected value of the financial gains from poaching can exceed the cost of the penalty multiplied by the probability of being caught.

The first cause of extinction on this model, then, is the property rights regime, with open access having the highest risk of extinction for the species, and common property having a far lower but non-zero level of risk. Species attracting exotic demand, such as for ivory, and being subject to advances in technological change which reduce effort costs are particularly at risk.

The second cause of extinction in the traditional model arises in the single owner, profit-maximizing context. Extinction under single ownership can be the outcome of deliberate planning, i.e. so-called 'optimal extinction'. The essential condition for dynamic profit maximization is that the growth rate of the species stock should equal the single owner's discount rate. The growth rate of the resource is effectively the rate of return on the resource. It then follows fairly obviously that if this rate of return is less than the rate of return the single owner can get by investing elsewhere (his 'discount rate' is equal to the opportunity cost of capital, i.e. what he can get by investing elsewhere) the resource will be run down to zero. It will pay to 'mine' the resource to extinction.

Again, the analysis is suggestive since slow growth species will almost automatically be at risk on this model: their 'own rate of return' will be low. And this is how it tends to be in practice. Elephants, rhinoceros and whales are endangered while most (but not all) species of deer or seals are not.

Until recently, it was assumed that this traditional model was applicable to land-based species without much adaptation. Hence the analysis has tended to be in terms of property rights regimes, the price/cost ratio, and the discount rate/own growth comparison. For an application to the African elephant, see Barbier *et al.* (1990). But Swanson (1994) has set out the important adjustment required to the model once the resource in question is land-based, an adjustment that radically alters the policy implications.

Swanson's argument is rooted in the fact that land-based biological resources are assets that are subject to human management: they are part of an asset portfolio. Moreover, whereas fisheries can be argued to have low opportunity costs – there are few competing uses of the seas – this is categorically untrue of land-based biodiversity. This is because land-based biodiversity depends on a base resource, the land itself, and this land does have alternative uses. The most obvious conflict is between land for conservation and land for 'development' uses such as agriculture. The critical point here is that whereas marine resources may be depleted because their growth fails to exceed the harvester's discount rate, in the land-based case they may be depleted because the returns from conservation fail to compete with the returns from land conversion to agriculture, roads, urban expansion, etc.

The second feature of the Swanson model is that whereas marine resources have a (generally) fixed carrying capacity, this is not true of land-based resources. Carrying capacity is no longer a 'given': it is something that is determined by choices about the level of base resources allocated to biodiversity.

There are two ways of seeing the differences between the traditional and the Swanson models. The first consists of a contrast between the conditions for maximizing profits from a given use of the base resource, the sea in the case of fisheries, and the land in other contexts. In the traditional model what is being maximized is the difference between revenues from the sale of the fish and the costs of harvesting them. In the Swanson model what is being maximized is the difference between the proceeds of sale and the *sum* of the costs of 'harvest' and the foregone return to the alternative use of the land. Put another way, the net benefits of land-based conservation have to be greater than the total opportunity costs of conservation, that is, the foregone net returns from developing the land. This is also the condition set out by Pearce and Moran (1994) in their review of the rates of return to biodiversity conservation.

In equation form, the fundamental equation for the conservation of wildlife becomes:

$$[B_C - C_C - (B_D - C_D)] > 0$$

where

B_C = the benefits of conservation
C_C = the direct costs of conservation (e.g. monitoring, policing)
B_D = the benefits of some alternative use of the land, i.e. 'development'
C_D = the costs of the alternative use of the land.

In the fisheries context the element $(B_D - C_D)$ is small or even zero: that is, the opportunity cost of conservation is low. In the land-based context, however, this element is significant, and will be increasingly significant as population grows, placing more pressure on land for conversion to agriculture, urban expansion, roads and so on.

What the basic equation underlines then is that wildlife is competing with other uses of the land and unless wildlife is invested with economic value it will be depleted, providing the essential economic rationale for the sustainable use approach to wildlife conservation.

The second way of viewing the difference between the two models of the extinction process is to look at the policy implications. Taking the elephant example again, the traditional model blames high prices for ivory for the decline of elephant populations. The Swanson model suggests the very opposite, that is, that ivory prices need to be kept high to encourage investment in sustainable management of elephant populations. Thus the Southern African range states invested in elephant conservation and operated a (largely) controlled and authorized trade in elephant products. They were also the states where elephant populations grew dramatically. States that 'underinvested' in elephants, including even a country like Kenya where the tourist value of the elephant was high, were the ones that lost elephants to poachers.

The insights from the Swanson model are therefore important. It is not enough to take the property rights regime as given, as in the traditional model. For the property rights regime is a matter of choice and management. It is incorrect to cite open access, say, as a 'cause' of environmental degradation, for the question should be why open access is allowed to prevail. Put another way, why has an open access state not invested in changing the rights regime so as to allocate the base resource – land of suitable characteristics – to wildlife conservation?

12.3 THE IMPLICATIONS OF THE ECONOMIC MODEL

Once it is understood that wildlife is competing with alternative uses of the land many things fall into place.

First, population growth becomes immediately relevant because population growth simply intensifies the conflict as humans demand 'niches' to occupy as residences or as locations for economic activity. As noted above, acting on population change is about long-run benefits given that there is considerable momentum in demographic change. It is nonetheless important that the context becomes one of coping with the currently unavoidable increase in population rather than coping with several billions in addition.

Second, if markets in the 'products' of wildlife are non-existent, the rate of return to conservation will almost certainly fail to compete with the rate of return to the alternative uses of land. Hence it is in the creation of markets for wildlife products that hope for conservation resides. This conclusion still offends some traditional conservationists and their argument would be that wildlife should not have to compete. The alternative economic use of designated conservation land should simply be declared unlawful. The problem with this approach is that it invariably leaves the incentives for converting the land entirely unaltered. This results in increasing frustration over time, and in the inevitable and familiar problem of erosion of protected areas. Put another way, since the demand for the developmental use of land is unaltered, that demand will still exert a formidable pressure on conservation land. The only ways out of this impasse are either to compensate those who lose from conservation, or to provide positive incentives for them to participate in conservation.

Third, and following on from the second observation, community participation and the sharing of conservation benefits with local communities becomes an integral part of any sustainable conservation plan. It is not just that participation is right in itself, but that it is a condition for successful economic intervention. Ascribing economic value to wildlife is not enough: those who otherwise have an incentive to thwart conservation plans must be able to capture at least some of that value. Otherwise, their incentive structure remains unaltered. This is important in the context where, from the community's standpoint, wildlife has no economic value, and doubly important when it has negative economic value because it destroys crops or threatens human lives and livestock. That applies as much to snow leopards in Nepal as it does to elephants. Capturing value involves the establishment of property rights in the wildlife resource, e.g. that the local community collects revenue from the sustainable utilization of wildlife whether that utilization is consumptive or otherwise. Note also has to be taken of the needs of local communities since wildlife cannot substitute for other assets at all times: an obvious example is the need for draught cattle in subsistence communities, so that 'blanket' removal of cattle would deprive farmers of a 'technology' that cannot be provided by wildlife.

Finally, not only do bans and moral outrage leave the fundamental forces causing wildlife loss largely unaffected, they also serve to 'disinvest' value in biodiversity: they take economic value away, when what is required is the investment of economic value in conservation through more and better markets for the sustainable output of conservation practices. Part of the problem with the conservationist argument that calls for 'the killing of demand' for wildlife products is that it ignores the supply side of the picture, the competition for land.

In summary, the economic analysis of wildlife conservation suggests a several tiered approach to policy:

a. invest wildlife with economic value;
b. ensure that this economic value is capturable, i.e. that institutions and markets exist which turn this economic value into a flow of real benefits;
c. ensure that part at least of this flow of real benefits accrues to those whose livelihoods are affected by the continued existence of the wildlife and who would benefit from the sacrificed land use;
d. avoid, wherever possible, conservation practice which bans or prohibits the utilization of wildlife products. Such bans take economic value away from the wildlife and render it an asset with limited economic value and thus less capable of competing against alternative land uses;

e. where such bans appear to be essential, ensure that compensation is paid to those who lose.

It would be naive to think that any one of these steps of a conservation programme can be easily implemented. In the real world all kinds of forces conspire to limit the conferment and appropriation of the economic value of wildlife. Poole and Leakey (1996), for example, cite the conflicts between development of a prawn farm in the wetlands of the Tana delta in Kenya and a lodge development in Amboseli National Park in excess of local carrying capacity. Ignorance, corruption and mismanagement will play their part in limiting rational economic solutions, as will the political compulsion of accommodating population growth and migration, water flow diversion, mining and electric power developments.

12.4 RATES OF RETURN TO WILDLIFE CONSERVATION

With the basic equation established, it is possible now to look at its components. We begin with the opportunity cost side of the picture ($B_D - C_D$) and estimates of the *commercial* returns to wildlife utilization, i.e. a component of ($B_C - C_C$). Commercial returns will tend to be very different to the wider *economic* returns to wildlife: the latter should be estimated on the basis of total willingness to pay for conservation, an issue addressed later on.

Policy Distortions

The first observation about opportunity cost is that the effects of various government interventions in the workings of agricultural and other markets are sometimes to exaggerate the opportunity cost of conservation, sometimes to under-estimate it. The most obvious ways in which this can happen are via subsidies to the development alternative and taxation of sustainable use of wildlife. Suppose agriculture is subsidized, then this will increase the profitability of agricultural land use and decrease the profitability of wildlife utilization. But if agriculture is taxed, the effect is to make agricultural conversion of land less attractive. In terms of the basic equation, taxes on alternative land uses reduce the size of ($B_D - C_D$), subsidies increase it. Similarly, taxes on the wildlife sector reduce the value of ($B_C - C_C$).

In the African context, agriculture is generally heavily taxed. African farmers have been taxed via controls on producer prices, setting maximum prices for output and hence lowering profitability; by export taxes; and taxes on agricultural inputs. Less obvious taxes include overvalued exchange rates, which have the effect of lowering the prices farmers get for exports. Under various structural adjustment policies in the 1980s African economies have sought to reduce these rates of taxation, either by relaxing controls on producer prices or by exchange rate reform, although usually not both together (World Bank, 1994b). In general, the central and most west African states increased implicit taxation through exchange rate overvaluation, and decreased explicit taxation (price controls). Only a few (Malawi, Burundi, Guinea and Madagascar) decreased both forms of taxation. Chad, Guinea Bissau, Sierra Leone and Zambia increased both forms of taxation. The remainder increased explicit taxes and reduced implicit taxes.

While agricultural taxation is the general rule for agriculture in the developing world, there are instances of subsidies that conflict with profitable wildlife conservation. Muir and Bojö (1994) note the heavy protection of beef production in Zimbabwe through state investment in marketing and processing. But direct subsidies to beef prices ended in the mid-1980s and beef prices were kept down thereafter to ensure wider political appeal. Other incentives for preferring cattle to wildlife include the role that cattle play culturally and as a savings asset. This attachment to cattle numbers as opposed to quality is instanced by the failure of Lesotho's livestock trade-in programme which aimed to substitute better quality but fewer livestock for existing livestock.

Overall, then, there are some financial incentives that favour agriculture and discriminate against wildlife, but the prevailing picture is one of a sector that is generally very highly taxed. If so, conservation needs to do even better than it has done to compete.

Measuring Returns less Opportunity Costs: Macro Approaches

While a great deal of effort has gone into measuring wildlife benefits, there appears to be less information about the true opportunity costs of conservation. Table 12.1 shows two estimates for Kenya and Kruger park, South Africa. It is important to determine the correct basis for comparison. Much of the pressure on land in Africa is, and will be, for food. Hence it is legitimate to compare livestock versus wildlife or crops versus wildlife. But there are various 'mixes' that also need to be considered, such as mixed wildlife and cattle systems. In turn, some wildlife utilization is consistent with consumptive uses of wildlife, while most wildlife is consistent with non-consumptive uses such as eco-tourism. The two studies in Table 12.1 give very different results. Land in Kruger Park is in fact mostly unsuitable for dryland cropping so that livestock is, effectively, the only realistic alternative land use. Wildlife would appear to more than pay its way in Kruger Park. In contrast the Kenya study suggests that Kenya is paying a very high price for its wildlife-based tourism, despite gross revenues of \$400–450m p.a. One major adjustment in the study is the halving of these gross revenues on the grounds that wildlife tourism is not the only purpose for the visits and that the different purposes are largely separable. The resulting $42m net gain contains a premium for foreign exchange earnings. Wells' estimates for the value of the wildlife sector in South Africa contains a wide range for the same reason that it is not easy to allocate revenues to sectors when the revenues have a multipurpose characteristic. Note that Wells' estimates dwarf those for Kenya and this seems unlikely. Wells' numbers refer to GDP but appear to be gross tourist expenditures, i.e. gross revenues rather than value added. It is clear that considerable research needs to be undertaken to extend and refine the estimates of both the value of the wildlife sector and its opportuniity.

Table 12.1 Estimates of macro benefits and opportunity cost of wildlife

Country	Author	GDP from wildlife tourism/forestry per annum	Foregone GDP = Opportunity cost per annum
Kenya	Norton-Griffiths and Southey (1995)	$ 42m	$203m
S.Africa (Kruger Park)	Engelbrecht and van der Walt (1993)	<$110m	$ 6m
S.Africa	Wells (1995)	$254m–$2174m	?

Measuring Returns less Opportunity Costs: Micro Approaches

A substantial number of studies exist on the commercial returns to alternative land uses at the micro level. Methods of appraisal vary, somewhat confusingly. Particularly valuable are the assessments prepared by Barnes for Botswana and those by Namibia's Department of Environmental Affairs which use net present value and internal rate of return measures. Others use financial returns to land, rates of return on capital and even profits per unit weight of animal. Table 12.2 reports some of the estimates using either internal rate of return or some measure of return on capital.

The Namibian conservancies relate to areas covering a number of privately owned ranches which come together to jointly manage wildlife which ranges across the boundaries of the individual ranches. Various revenue sharing schemes operate. Barnes and de Jager (1995) compare the rates of return to these conservancies with farm-scale operations. The conservancies are essentially multiples of the farm-scale units, so that the main difference is scale (say, 100 000 ha against 10 000 ha) and scale permits some different species to be accommodated and some different charges to be applied. Both financial and 'economic' rates of return are shown (FIRR and EIRR), the economic rate of return being assessed in terms of some 'shadow pricing' of inputs. This concept of an economic return is narrower than the wider economic value concept to be introduced shortly. Barnes and de Jager use an 8% discount as the cut-off rate for both financial and economic assessments. On this basis, the game viewing conservancy is financially profitable and both conservancies are economically profitable. Moreover, over the period of their operation the conservancies have increased wildlife numbers, diversity and biomass by fairly dramatic amounts (44% diversity of species increase and 70–85% increase in numbers/biomass). The Savé Valley scheme in Zimbabwe will also operate as a conservancy. Project documentation suggests rates of return on capital of 11% and 22% for different parts of the project (Savé Valley, 1994).

Table 12.2 Rates of return to wildlife

		FIRR	EIRR
1	Namibia		
	Farm scale		
	Southern mixed sheep/game	5.8%	ne
	Northern mixed cattle/game	3.9%	ne
	Northern game viewing	4.2%	ne
	Conservancies		
	Northern mixed cattle/game	7.3%	**12.9%**
	Northern game viewing	**10.0%**	**19.5%**
	Upmarket Tourist Lodge, Caprivi	**10.0%?**	
2	Botswana		
	Upmarket Tourist Lodge, Ngamiland	**17.5%**	**27.5%**
	Small-scale game harvesting (biltong, skins, trophies)	**21%**	**28%**
	Ostrich farming	**19%**	**14%**
	Crocodile farming	**18%**	**14%**
	Safari hunting	**16%**	**45%**
	Game ranching (meat, hunting, live animals)	6%	7%
	Cattle	5%	na
3	South Africa		
	Northern Cape Province*		
	excluding land rental		
	all operations	**106%**	ne
	game sales	**142%**	ne
	hunting	**47%**	
	cattle	**32%**	
	including land rental		
	all operations	**–41%**	ne
	game sales	**–35%**	ne
	cattle	**–32%**	ne

Table 12.2 continued

4 Zimbabwe		
Survey of 89 private ranches **		
cattle only	1.8%	**13.1%**
mixed cattle/wildlife	2.6%	ne
wildlife only	**10.5%**	**21.5%**
Communal areas: CAMPFIRE		
Southeast lowveld ***	see text	
cattle/wildlife	$Z 5.7	
cattle only	$Z 4.1	
5 Zambia		
Luangwa Valley (LIRDP, multipurpose including wildlife)	–14% to + 11%	

Notes:
Bold numbers indicate rates of return in excess of some cut-off discount rate.
* Excludes capital costs and hence overstates the true rate of return. Rate of return is expressed on operating expenses only.
** Return on capital investment.
*** Z$ per hectare. See Child (1990).

Sources: Namibia – Swanson *et al.* (1995), Barnes and de Jager (1995); South Africa – Crowe *et al.* (1996); Zimbabwe – Jansen *et al.* (1992), Child (1990); Zambia – Barbier (1992); Botswana – Barnes and Pearce (1991), Barnes *et al.* (1992).

Jones (1995) and Ashley and Garland (1994) indicate that extending the rights to wildlife utilization possessed by commercial farmers in Namibia to communal farmers could generate major financial gains for the communal lands. They simulate various communal arrangements, ranging from a private investor operating a tourist facility in a communal area, through various revenue sharing arrangements, to communities developing their own community enterprise.

The South African case study (Crowe *et al.*, 1996) suggests that game hunting and sales will bring systematically higher financial returns than cattle. Nonetheless, any new venture that would have to purchase or lease land would profit from neither – see the results when the land value is imputed. The case study in question is of a private estate where the land was acquired long ago.

The Zimbabwe CAMPFIRE projects have been the subject of a benefit–cost appraisal (Jansen, 1992). The CAMPFIRE projects operate on communal land and involve a revenue sharing arrangement with local districts. Jansen's study of three districts – Nyaminyami, Guruve and Mahenye – shows the importance of the general macroeconomic framework for the profitability of such ventures, e.g. failure to correct exchange rate policy threatens the wildlife sector. The same goes for protection of the wildlife against poachers and control of rates of immigration to the relevant areas. In all three case study areas, failure to secure a better economic and management climate for the projects leads to rapidly decreasing shares for the districts, to zero in two cases but to around $Z600 per household per annum in the Mahenye case. The economics of CAMPFIRE thus appear fragile and there is a clear need for careful management and improved revenue sharing to retain local community incentives (Muir and Böjo, 1994). Much the same conclusion applies to the Luangwa Valley community-based projects where some 60% of revenues accrues from wildlife, especially safari hunting (Barbier, 1992).

What can be concluded from Table 12.2? First, the presence of economic distortions, such as overvalued exchange rates, means that both financial and shadow priced rates of return should always be estimated, as would be standard in a project appraisal (Child, 1990). However, even when valid from a national point of view, wildlife still has to pay its way financially. The second conclusion of Table 12.2 is that some ventures appear to work well but some, especially when properly costed, do not make acceptable rates of return. Third, if the choice is between cattle and wildlife, the evidence suggests that wildlife is better, with mixed wildlife/cattle systems being somewhere in between. But such a ranking of options still does not guarantee the financial viability of privatized wildlife. In some cases the land might be better used for neither wildlife nor cattle.

The ambiguity of the financial conclusions, allied with some suspicion from Table 12.1 that some wildlife has a high opportunity cost, focuses attention on the wider economic value of wildlife. That is, are there economic values that are not being captured in the assessments of rates of return?

12.5 THE ECONOMIC BENEFITS OF WILDLIFE

The financial and economic rates of return considered so far will in fact understate the true *economic value* of wildlife conservation. Economic value is measured in terms of the *willingness to pay* (WTP) for uses of wildlife. In turn, WTP generally exceeds the price actually paid in the market place: some people are always willing to pay more than the actual prices (the difference being their 'consumer's surplus'), while those willing to pay less than the ruling price are excluded from the market. What matters for economic value is the summation of the WTPs of different groups, the 'total economic value' (TEV).

Consider the case of a tropical forest. TEV comprises use and non-use values. Conservation is consistent with some sustainable uses of the forest, including sustainable timber harvesting. Direct use values are fairly straightforward in concept but are not necessarily easy to measure in economic terms. Thus minor forest products output (nuts, rattan, latex etc.) should be measurable from market and survey data, but the value of medicinal plants for the world at large is more difficult to measure, although a number of estimates exist (Pearce and Puroshothaman, 1995; Mendelsohn and Balick, 1995).

Indirect use values correspond to the ecologist's concept of 'ecological functions'. A tropical forest might help protect watersheds, for example, so that removing forest cover may result in water pollution and siltation, depending on the alternative use to which the forest land is put. Similarly, tropical forests 'store' carbon dioxide. When they are burned for clearance much of the stored CO_2 is released into the atmosphere, contributing to greenhouse gas atmospheric warming and hence to economic damage. Tropical forests also store many species which in turn have ecological functions – one of the values of biological diversity.

Option values relate to the amount that individuals would be willing to pay to conserve a tropical forest for future use. That is, no use is made of it now but use may be made of it in the future. Option value is thus like an insurance premium to ensure the supply of something the availability of which would otherwise be uncertain. While there can be no presumption that option value is positive it is likely to be so in the context where the resource is in demand for its environmental qualities and its supply is threatened by deforestation.

Existence value relates to valuations of the environmental asset unrelated either to current or optional use. Its intuitive basis is easy to understand because a great many people reveal their willingness to pay for the existence of environmental assets through wildlife and other environmental charities but without taking part in the direct use of the wildlife through recreation. To some extent, this willingness to pay may represent 'vicarious' consumption, i.e. consumption of wildlife videos and TV programmes, but studies suggest that this is a weak explanation for existence value. Empirical measures of existence value, obtained through questionnaire approaches (the contingent valuation method), suggest that existence value can be a substantial component of total economic value. This finding is even more pronounced where the asset is unique, suggesting high potential existence values for tropical forests and for particular species of wildlife. Some analysts like to add bequest value as a separate category of economic value. Others regard it as part of existence value. In empirical terms it would be hard to differentiate them.

Hence, total economic value can be expressed as:

$$\begin{aligned} \text{TEV} = {} & \text{Direct Use Value} + \text{Indirect Use Value} \\ & + \text{Option Value} + \text{Existence Value} \end{aligned}$$

While the components of TEV are additive, care has to be taken in practice not to add competing values. There are trade-offs between different types of use value and between direct and indirect use values. For example, the value of timber from clear felling cannot be added to the value of minor forest products, but timber from careful selective cutting will generally be additive to forest products.

Estimating African Wildlife Benefits

A number of studies exist which attempt to estimate the WTP for wildlife, but there are comparatively few exercises relating to African wildlife, all of them for Kenya. Table 12.3 assembles the estimates.

Table 12.3 Willingness to pay for African wildlife

Study and approach	Resource	Willingness to pay
Brown (1989): contingent valuation, foreign visitors	African elephant in Kenya	US$ 182–218m p.a.
Moran (1994): contingent valuation, foreign visitors	Protected areas in Kenya	US$ 450m p.a.
Brown *et al.* (1994): contingent valuation and travel cost approach	Game parks in Kenya	US$ 52-86 per visitor day (CVM); US$ 77–134 per visitor day (TCM)
Navrud and Mungatana (1994): contingent valuation and travel cost approaches	Lake Nakuru, Kenya	US$ 7.5m (CVM); US$ 13.7–15.1m (TCM)

What is the value of such exercises? First, consider Moran's estimate of $450 million per annum economic value for Kenya and compare it to the opportunity costs of conservation as estimated by Norton-Griffiths and Southey in Table 12.1. It exceeds the opportunity cost by a factor of two, whereas Table 12.1 suggests that the financial returns to Kenya are less than the opportunity costs. The two assessments are quite consistent: financial returns can be less than opportunity cost while economic value can be greater than opportunity cost. The pessimism of the former conclusion is offset by the latter finding, but only if ways are found to 'capture' this broader economic value.

Second, and allowing for the uncertainty inherent in all these estimates, Kenya should be seeking to exploit this broader economic value by more careful pricing for entry to game parks, as indeed it has now been doing. For the willingness to pay estimates are basically telling us what the demand curve for wildlife conservation is like. This in turn means that it is possible to identify the price at which revenues to Kenya would be maximized. Such a charging policy would need to take account of carrying capacity measures, i.e. the 'optimal' price cannot be one that increases visitor demand if that demand already threatens wildlife, as has been the case in some Kenya reserves.

Third, the Brown *et al.* (1994) and Navrud and Mungatana (1994) studies show that revenue maximizing prices would actually involve increases in prices and hence fewer visitors. Despite this, revenues would rise. The additional benefit would be less stress on animal populations. Pricing can be differentiated between residents where demand tends to be more responsive to price of park entry and foreigners where demand is fairly non-responsive to prices. This has been the policy in Kenya game parks in recent years.

Fourth, while the studies quoted have not sought to find willingness to pay among foreigners who do not visit Africa, there is a strong likelihood that this 'existence' value is high. The only study that indicates this directly is for tropical forests (Kramer *et al.*, 1996) and it suggests that US households would be willing to pay $24–31 as a one-off payment to conserve 5% of existing rainforests, or a total of $2.2 to 2.8 billion across all 91 million US households. Only 11% of respondents had previously visited a rainforest and a further 8% planned to visit one, suggesting that around 80% of the respondents were expressing an existence value, i.e. a willingness to pay unrelated to use. Capturing this 'global value' is now the focus of many innovative schemes, ranging from debt-for-nature swaps, through to the Global Environment Facility, transferable development rights and other franchise agreements, and joint implementation. For a survey see Pearce (1995).

12.6 INCENTIVE SYSTEMS

The economic model introduced at the outset emphasized the importance of building incentive structures into wildlife management policy. The essential message was that the gazetting of areas for conservation will, of itself, do little to sustain wildlife since it tends to leave the pressures on those areas unchanged. Indeed, such 'command and control' policies build up frustrations over land use. There is a growing body of evidence that suggests this is borne out in practice. In most cases, it is rights of ownership or use that generate the incentives. The Namibia case studies (Table 12.1) show this clearly. The success of private ranches in Kenya in conserving the black rhinoceros is well known (Poole and Leakey, 1996).

Norton-Griffiths (1996) reports that Kenya has lost 44% of its wildlife over the past 18 years, 48% from outside the protected areas and 31% from within protected areas. Thus, while protected area status clearly confers some conservation, loss rates with protection are still markedly high. More to the point, out of eighteen pastoral areas only two – Kajiado and Laikipia – have approximately the same amount of wildlife as they had eighteen years ago. Yet these two districts practise financial incentives for conservation: wildlife extension and incentive payments for group ranch owners exist in Kajiado, and private management of wildlife in Laikipia. Kenya is now moving towards the conferment of user rights to wildlife for landowners generally through such innovations as revenue sharing agreements, wildlife enterprise development funds. Nonetheless, as Poole and Leakey (1996) show, this process is characterized by frequent disputes and by political interference at local and national level. Policies of what might be called 'decentralization and appropriation' necessarily create 'economic rents' – financial surpluses – and there can be no surprise that these attract 'rent seekers' who can quickly dissipate and destroy rents for local communities.

Probably the most famous incentive-based system for communal lands wildlife is the CAMPFIRE programme in Zimbabwe. As noted above, revenue sharing arrangements probably require improvement to sustain local community involvement. The loss of ivory revenues has not helped, one of the incidental effects of the outright regulatory approach adopted in the CITES ban. Gibson and Marks (1995) point to a further risk in community-based schemes generally, the inability to control local hunting across all species. Thus, while the use of local people as scouts in the Zambian ADMADE scheme reduced the hunting rate for large mammals, hunters simply switched tactics to take smaller mammals and to the use of less detectable snares. Strong cultural traditions also perpetuated hunting. Significantly, however, and in keeping with the CAMPFIRE analysis, many local people did not see the programme as being particularly beneficial to them because of the low 'pay-outs' to communities under the scheme.

Improving the financial prospects of wildlife conservation requires action both by the 'owner' countries, by the donor community, and by NGOs. Owner states, for example, need to look carefully at the comparative economics of land use and, where appropriate, provide incentives for land conversion to wildlife utilization. Such incentives are unlikely to be financial given the state of the economies in question, but they can take the form of relaxed planning regulations and a general 'political' statement in favour of wildlife utilization. Once established, careful consideration needs to be given to the appropriate pricing strategy for game park and reserved area entry: given the buoyant state of demand for wildlife experiences, setting prices to maximize revenues is an important first step. Such measures need to be carefully integrated with far better 'revenue sharing' arrangements whereby local communities secure a share of the proceeds. At the donor level the appreciation is growing that wildlife-based developments can serve a number of ends: the purely developmental in which the 'best' use of land is selected, poverty alleviation through revenue sharing schemes, and participation since local communities need to be involved in the design and management of projects. Some projects should also benefit from global benefit assessment, i.e. from demonstrating that the wildlife and habitat so conserved has a global value over and above its purely developmental value. The extent to which biodiversity is a global good is disputed in the literature (Cervigni and Pearce, 1995), but the existence of the Biodiversity Convention and the activities of the Global Environment Facility indicate at least partial acceptance of the global dimension. More importantly for the future are likely to be NGO, donor, owner and private sector ventures in which local and overseas private funds are put into wildlife conservation as an economic opportunity. Donors might wish to underwrite risks to encourage private sector finance. NGOs can supply management expertise and funds of their own.

This brief review of incentive systems suggests several provisional conclusions:

a. wildlife on private ranches appears to generate financial returns significantly higher than those to cattle, the usual alternative, indicating that the incentive for private investors is positive, though some studies suggest some limited rates of return when compared to the general opportunity cost of capital;
b. economic returns, in the sense of adjusted financial returns, are even higher, suggesting that national governments have a clear incentive to encourage wildlife schemes;
c. the real difficulties lie with the community-based schemes. Experience has been varied but the ingredients for successful schemes appear to be known. The difficulty is putting them into practice;
d. future directions for conservation initiatives are likely to include more and better partnerships between all stakeholders, from the local communities through to NGOs and donors and, especially, the private sector.

12.7 CONCLUSIONS

The 'sustainable use' of wildlife, as opposed to its outright preservation through 'command and control' policies, has a clear economic rationale. That rationale is based on the fact that wildlife competes with human appropriation of the land for food supply, infrastructure, and other economic development. Stripped of its economic value, wildlife cannot compete – the competitive playing field is too heavily tilted against it. Of course, preservation policies, whereby areas are gazetted and humans are given limited and prescribed access, remains an integral part of some policy for the conservation of wildlife. But far greater emphasis has to be given to economic uses of wildlife in terms of both consumptive and non-consumptive uses.

Some conservation policies have perverse effects, although these are unquestionably not the intention of those who advocate and frame such policies. Forbidding the use of wildlife products can simply 'disinvest' economic value, i.e. make the resource valueless (or less valuable) from an economic point of view. Since much wildlife is also a nuisance, both in terms of disease, interference with crops, and even danger to human life, the effect of taking economic value away is to lose the potential for a conservation relationship between wildlife and local community. One answer to such problems is to invest economic value in wildlife by creating markets for its use and then, critically, sharing the resulting revenues with local communities. Another solution lies in privatization where the landowner collects the revenues and hopefully shares them with local communities or, at least, provides employment. The clue to such arrangements lies in positive incentives, not threats of fines or worse for failing to conserve. Moreover, traditional preservationist approaches leave all the pressures on land unaffected: people are simply excluded from access to land and nothing happens to change the demand for that land. The classic wildlife–development conflict is therefore not avoided by simply declaring an area a conservation area.

The evidence of the financial rates of return to wildlife utilization is fairly extensive, though not always in a form that makes assessment easy. Where it has been standardized in terms of different 'models' of revenues and costs, the evidence suggests that, on many occasions, privatized wildlife pays far better than the usual alternative of cattle, but that on some occasions neither option would meet a standard financial test of worthwhileness. Put simply, owners might be better off with money in the bank. In so far as private owners have altruistic motives borne of a conservation ethic, as many do, the non-monetary returns may more than compensate for the forgone financial gains of using money elsewhere. Experiences with community-based schemes seem variable and the available assessments do not always seem very clear in their implications. In the long run wildlife will have to pay its way on a more secure footing than this.

Economic appraisal, as opposed to financial appraisal, suggests several things. First, simply adjusting the flows of revenues and costs for their 'shadow prices' tends to increase the rate of return to wildlife use investments. Such adjustments at least include modifications for overvalued exchange rates and for the 'true' cost of labour, which tends to be significantly less than the market cost in an unemployment context. While from the private landowner's point of view actual wage rates have to be paid, society's benefits are better measured by the shadow prices. This suggests at least that the wildlife sector should be better treated by national governments, e.g. with favourable tax regimes.

The second form of economic appraisal assesses not the flow of costs and revenues, but the total willingness to pay for wildlife. Only a few studies have been carried out for Africa but they all suggest substantial willingness to pay for conservation, particularly from tourists. The relevance of these exercises is that they are, in effect, tracing out the demand curve for wildlife. This then permits an assessment of the effects of charging different levels of price for wildlife viewing and consumptive uses. Several of the economic studies have been used to find the revenue maximizing price for entry to reserves and game parks. The effects suggest that Africa underprices its wildlife.

The wider economic studies also suggest that there has to be a greater effort to tap the 'global value' of African wildlife, i.e. the amount that individuals will pay to visit Africa, to conserve the option of future visits, and even simply to conserve wildlife even if there is no chance of the individual ever visiting reserves for real. The Global Environment facility exists to 'capture' such global value, but its resources are modest. This suggests a full exploration of the panoply of global financing mechanisms that exist or that could exist, from debt-to-nature swaps to carbon offsets. With imagination, the economic approach has the potential to assist in the desperately important task of conserving Africa's unparalleled environmental heritage.

NOTE

1. This paper was originally prepared for a 1996 seminar on wildlife utilization organized by the UK Overseas Development Administration (now the Department for International Development).

REFERENCES

Ashley, C. and Garland, E. (1994), *Promoting Community Based Tourism Development: Why, What and How?* Research Discussion Paper No.4, Directorate of Environmental Affairs, Ministry of Environment and Tourism, Windhoek.

Barbier, E. (1992), 'Community based development in Africa', in Swanson, T. and Barbier, E. (eds), *Economics for the Wilds: Wildlife, Wildlands, Diversity and Development*, Earthscan, London, 103–135.

Barbier, E., Burgess, J., and Folke, C. (1994), *Paradise Lost? The Ecological Economics of Biodiversity*, Earthscan, London.

Barbier, E., Burgess, J., Swanson, T. and Pearce, D.W. (1990), *Elephants, Economics and Ivory*, Earthscan, London.

Barnes, J. and de Jager, J. (1995), *Economic and Financial Incentives for Wildlife Use on Private Land in Namibia and the Implications for Policy*, Research Discussion Paper No.8, Directorate of Environmental Affairs, Ministry of Environment and Tourism, Windhoek.

Barnes, J. and Pearce, D.W. (1991), *The Mixed Use of Habitat*, Centre for Social and Economic Research on the Global Environment, University College London, mimeo, partially reprinted in Swanson and Barbier (1992), Chapter 2.

Barnes, J., Burgess, J. and Pearce, D.W. (1992), Wildlife tourism, in Swanson, T. and Barbier, E. (eds), *Economics for the Wilds: Wildlife, Wildlands, Diversity and Development*, Earthscan, London, 136–51.

Bongaerts, J. (1994), Population policy options in the developing world, *Science*, **263**, 771–6.

Brown, G. (1989), *The Economic Value of Elephants*, London Environmental Economics Centre, Discussion Paper 89-12, London: International Institute for Environment and Development (IIED).

Brown, G., Swanson, T., Ward, M. and Moran, D. (1994), *Optimally Pricing Game Reserves in Kenya*, Centre for Social and Economic Research on the Global Environment (CSERGE), University College London and University of East Anglia, UK, mimeo.

Cervigni, R. and Pearce, D.W. (1995), *North South Resource Transfers, Incremental Cost and the Rio Environment Conventions*, Centre for Social and Economic Research on the Global Environment, University College London, mimeo.

Child, B (1990), Assessment of wildlife utilization as a land use option in semi-arid rangeland of Southern Africa, in Kiss, A. (ed), *Living with Wildlife: Wildlife Resource Management with Local Participation in Africa*, Technical Paper 130, Africa Technical Department Series, Washington DC: World Bank, 155–76.

Clark, C (1973a), Profit maximisation and the extinction of animal species, *Journal of Political Economy*, **81**(4), 950–61

Clark, C. (1973b), The economics of overexploitation, *Science*, **181**, 630–34.

Clark, C. (1990), *Mathematical Bioeconomics*, second edition, Wiley, New York.

Crowe, T., Smith, B., Little, R. and Hugh High, S. (1996), Sustainable utilization of game at Rooipoort Estate, Norther Cape Province, South Africa, in C.Freese (ed.), *The Commercial, Consumptive Use of Wild Species: Implications for Biodiversity Conservation*, World Wide Fund for Nature, Washington DC.

Dixon, J. and Sherman, P. (1990), *Economics of Protected Areas: a New Look at Benefits and Costs*, Earthscan, London.

Engelbrecht, W. and van der Walt, P. (1993), Notes on the economic use of Kruger National Park, *Koedoe*, **36**(2), 113–119.

Freese, C. (ed.) (1996), *The Commercial, Consumptive Use of Wild Species: Implications for Biodiversity Conservation*, World Wide Fund for Nature, Washington DC.

Gibson, C and Marks, S (1995), Transforming rural hunters into conservationists: an assessment of community-based wildlife management programs in Africa, *World Development*, **23**(6), 941–57.

Gordon, H.S. (1954), The economic theory of a common property resource: the fishery, *Journal of Political Economy*, **62**, 124–42.

International Institute for Environment and Development (IIED) (1994), *Whose Eden? An Overview of Community Approaches to Wildlife Management*, IIED, London.

Jansen, D. (1992), *The Economics of CAMPFIRE: the Lessons to Date*, quoted in Muir and Böjo (1994).

Jansen, D., Bond, I. and Child, B. (1992), *Cattle, Wildlife, Both or Neither: Results of a Financial and Economic Survey of Commercial Ranches in Southern Zimbabwe*, World Wide Fund for Nature, Multispecies Animal Systems Project Paper No.27, Harare.

Jones, B. (1995), *Wildlife Management, Utilization and Tourism in Communal Areas*, Research Discussion Paper No.5, Directorate of Environmental Affairs, Ministry of Environment and Tourism, Windhoek.

Kramer, R., Mercer, E. and Sharma, N. (1996), Valuing tropical rainforest protection using the contingent valuation method, in Adamowicz, W., Boxall, P., Luckert, M., Phillips, W., and White, W. (eds), *Forestry, Economics and the Environment*, CAB International, Wallingford, 181–194.

McNeely, J. (1988), *Economics and Biological Diversity*, International Union for the Conservation of Nature, Gland, Switzerland.

Mendelsohn, R. and Balick, M. (1995), The value of undiscovered pharmaceuticals in tropical forests, *Economic Botany*, **49**(2), 223–8.

Moran, D. (1994), Contingent valuation and biodiversity: measuring the user surplus of Kenyan protected areas, *Biodiversity and Conservation*, **3,** 663–84.

Navrud, S. and Mungatana, E. (1994), Environmental valuation in developing countries: the recreational value of wildlife viewing, *Ecological Economics*, **11**, 135–51.

Norton-Griffiths, M. (1996), personal communication.

Norton-Griffiths, M. and Southey, C. (1995), The opportunity costs of biodiversity conservation in Kenya, *Ecological Economics*, **12**, 125–39.

Pearce, D.W. (1995), *Blueprint 4: Capturing Global Value*, Earthscan, London.

Pearce, D.W. and Moran, D. (1994), *The Economic Value of Biodiversity*, Earthscan, London.

Pearce, D.W. and Puroshothaman, S. (1995), The economic value of plant based pharmaceuticals, in Swanson, T. (ed), *Intellectual Property Rights and Biodiversity Conservation*, Cambridge University Press, Cambridge, 127–38.

Perrings, C., Maler, K.-G., Folke, C., Holling, C. and Jansson, B.-O. (1995), *Biodiversity Conservation*, Kluwer, Dordrecht.

Poole, J. and Leakey, R. (1996), Decentralization and biodiversity conservation in Kenya, in Lutz, E. and Caldecott, J. (eds), *Decentralization and Biodiversity Conservation*, World Bank, Washington, mimeo.

Savé Valley, Bubiana and Chiredzi River Conservancies (1994), *The Lowveld Conservancies: New Opportunities for Productive and Sustainable Land Use*, Savé Valley Conservancy, PO Box 170, Chiredzi, Zimbabwe.

Shah, A. (1995), *The Economics of Third World National Parks*, Edward Elgar, Cheltenham.

Swanson, T. (ed.) (1995a), *The Economics and Ecology of Biodiversity Decline*, Cambridge: Cambridge University Press.

Swanson, T. (ed.) (1995b), *Intellectual Property Rights and Biodiversity Conservation*, Cambridge: Cambridge University Press.

Swanson, T.,Barnes, J. and de Jager, J. (1995), 'Conflicts in wildlife conservation – the role of property rights in their resolution: the Southern African conservancies', in Swanson, T., Fernandez Ugalde, J. and Luxmoore, R. (eds), *Survey of Wildlife Management Regimes for Sustainable Utilisation*, Faculty of Economics and Politics, Cambridge University and World Conservation Monitoring Centre, Cambridge, mimeo.

Wells, M. (1995), *The Economic and Social Role of Protected Areas in the New South Africa*, Overseas Development Institute, London, mimeo.

World Bank (1994a), *Population and Development: Implications for the World Bank*, World Bank, Washington DC

World Bank (1994b), *Adjustment in Africa*, World Bank, Washington DC.

13. Packaging waste and the polluter pays principle: a taxation solution[1]

(with Kerry Turner)

13.1 THE PACKAGING PROBLEM

There is some consensus among policy-makers that packaging waste, as with other solid waste, presents a priority environmental problem in Europe, and elsewhere, although packaging waste does not show up in any public opinion poll in the UK as a priority environmental issue – see Pearce and Turner (1991). This concern is revealed in measures by various European countries to secure: (a) source reduction of packaging; and (b) increased recycling of packaging waste. For example, Germany has implemented a dual waste management system whereby: (a) designated packaging is returnable to retailers; unless (b) a private sector recycling scheme that meets certain collection and recycling targets is in operation. The European Commission introduced a directive on packaging and packaging waste in 1993. Table 13.1 gives broad estimates of packaging waste arising in the European Community: there is extensive uncertainty about the true magnitudes.

Table 13.1 Estimates of packaging waste in the European Community

Sector	Total [a]	Non-recycled [a]	Recycled [a]	Percentage of waste recycled
Domestic	25.0	22.5	2.5	10
Commercial	15.0	12.5	2.5	17
Industrial	10.5	6.0	4.5	43
ALL	50.5	41.0	9.5	–

Note: [a] In million tonnes.

Source: European Commission.

Economic analysis would suggest that too much packaging waste will be produced in a market system in which any environmental damage from packaging waste is not reflected in the prices of packaged products. This is market failure:

prices fail to reflect full social cost. Additionally, the product mix of packaged products will not be optimal. This is because individual products contain varying raw materials content per unit of product. The packaging for beverages, for example, has different environmental impacts according to the material used to package the produce.

Market failure in the packaging context particularly means that the receiving capacity of the environment is underpriced. Thus, the costs of landfill, incineration and composting are not reflected in packaged product prices. In this paper we show how product prices should be corrected for this component of market failure. The end result is a packaging tax or levy on the product. We also show how this can be translated into a raw materials levy. The study is confined to: (a) the UK and Japan; (b) beverage containers only; and (c) the disposal cost component of market failure. The formal model shows how additional components of environmental damage can be integrated into an extended analysis. Finally, we emphasize the simplicity of the approach. Policy-makers require 'transparent' procedures, not complex models.

13.2 THE PRINCIPLES OF A PACKAGING TAX

Two main market-based instruments (MBIs) – product charges and materials levies – have been suggested in order to reduce packaging waste and litter disamenity, as well as to encourage an extension of recycling activities. A third option, a deposit-refund system (DRS), has also been suggested and implemented in some countries. Under this system packaging producers would incur a charge on their products which would be passed on to the customers. The consumer is able to recover the charge (deposit) on return of the package (usually a beverage container) to an authorized recycling point. Evidence to date suggests that actual DRSs impose net costs on society. Schemes have led to only relatively small reductions in the volume and cost of waste disposal and have also been expensive to operate and have pushed up product prices. DRSs may have a more important role in the control of hazardous wastes (batteries and household or garden products such as insecticides and solvents). In this context DRSs offer the assurance that more material will be disposed of in a controlled manner through an authorized outlet. There is also the likelihood that actual schemes do not mimic the ideal systems proposed by economists – see Bohm (1981). For current purposes we make no distinction between levies, charges and taxes. In practice, it might be convenient to regard a levy as something that the packaging industry may impose on itself, and a tax as something that governments may impose. A charge may then be a generic term for a tax or levy.

A materials levy is an example of an input tax and would be imposed on the raw materials used to manufacture packaging, with due account being taken of existing rates of recycling and reuse. The size of the levy needs to be related directly to the environmental damage done by the production and consumption of the packaging, or to the costs of restoration of the environment. This is important since the proportional link between the size of the charge and damage done is fundamental to the polluter pays principle (the PPP, see OECD, 1975). A product charge, by contrast, is an output tax – a charge on the packaging end-product itself. The tax would be related to the potential waste disposal and pollution impact. In a later section we show how a product charge is simply converted into a materials levy.

A number of general criteria can be listed against which the product charge and the materials levy can be evaluated.

1. The chosen MBI should be compatible with national or European Community regulatory objectives and existing legislation. In the latter case, the scheme would need to represent minimum requirements for countries newly embarked on a policy course and not be in breach of the Treaty of Rome and the Internal Market provisions. Additionally, the MBI would have to be recognized as a credible substitute for regulatory legislation.
2. The MBI should have both low bureaucratic and low compliance costs.
3. The costs to the consumer should be minimized both in the sense of any resulting price rises and consumer participation costs.
4. The impact of the MBI should not be significantly regressive, i.e. should not confer a disproportionate burden on the least well-off in society.
5. Given that source separation (especially door-to-door collection) recycling schemes carry a heavy collection cost burden, sufficient to make such schemes financially unprofitable, the revenue-raising properties of a given incentive system could be important. Revenue-raising is not typically regarded as a requirement for an effective MBI since their purpose is the modification of behaviour, but given recycling schemes' general lack of profitability we add this feature to the other criteria.

13.3 THE MODEL

The nature of the external costs from packaging needs to be determined. Using the cost–benefit 'with/without' principle we have the following:

1. without packaging, we would not have its waste disposal costs which are borne by society, not producers or users;
2. without packaging we would not have packaging litter;

3. without packaging we would save: (a) the energy/materials costs of packaging; and (b) the externalities associated with the energy/materials content of packaging (air and water pollution, for example);
4. without packaging we would reduce resource scarcity, e.g. the scarcity value of energy.

Items 1 and 2 are relevant to the design of a packaging tax but, we argue, 3(a), 3(b) and 4 are relevant only in certain circumstances. Since there is a fashion for 'cradle-to-grave' energy and materials analysis of producer and consumer products, we need to discuss the rationale for these conclusions.

Consider the costs of energy used up to produce packaging. These are private costs, i.e. they are part of the costs of production of packaged goods. As such, they are already 'internal' to the decision to produce and consume packaging and are therefore reflected in the price of packaging materials in the market place. Energy and materials costs are not therefore additional costs to be debited to packaging materials; they are already included in their price in the market place. But the 'external' costs associated with energy and materials use are potentially relevant since these characterize market failure. The external costs of energy use (e.g. CO_2, SO_x emissions) would be relevant if these were not tackled anywhere else in the policy system. In such circumstances, the packaging tax should reflect the environmental damage done by energy used in the manufacture and transport of packaging. However, such external costs are typically not neglected in environmental policy in developed economies. For example, sulphur oxide and nitrogen oxide emissions are the subject of agreements under the auspices of the Economic Commission for Europe (ECE) and the Large Combustion Plants Directives of the European Community. Carbon dioxide taxes have been introduced in some European countries.

If these externalities are regulated to an 'acceptable' level then it would be wrong to argue that the same externality should be regulated again through a packaging tax. This would amount to double taxation, which is inefficient.

The externalities involved in the processes of packaging production may still be relevant if it can be argued either: (a) that society fails to regulate them optimally; or (b) that even the optimal externality should be regulated. Thus, on argument (a) we could still modify a packaging tax for the energy content of the packaging because society fails to control enough pollution from the use of energy. In response, however, we point out that if society has failed optimally to regulate this source of externality, the answer is to correct the inefficiency by regulating or taxing energy consumption directly, not through a packaging tax. Much the same argument applies to argument (b) which requires that the optimal amount of pollution should nonetheless be taxed (what Pezzey (1988) calls the 'extended' polluter pays principle). It will be more efficient to tackle the externality directly, e.g. through a carbon tax or sulphur tax, than through a tax on the final product.

The appraisal of natural resource availability and scarcity (item (4)) involves a combination of physical science, materials science and economic considerations. It is a complex process because scarcity is not the only influence in resource prices and prices often do not fully reflect scarcity, especially if the term 'resource use' encompasses the full range of environmental functions (amenity provision, waste assimilation and life-support) as well as raw materials supply. Absolute physical scarcity is unlikely to be a significant problem for the exhaustible resource-based materials currently in use in packaging, i.e. aluminium, oil (plastics), paper and glass. The user cost of current resource extraction (i.e. the losses incurred in the future due to current extraction of exhaustible resource stocks) is therefore likely to be very small and probably negligible. The exception to this rule would be the scarcity of final disposal sites themselves. If 'holes in the ground' become scarce either through physical non-availability (as in some cases in the USA, and more forcefully in the Netherlands and Germany) or through social non-acceptability, then a landfill user cost (LUC) might legitimately be added to the marginal external cost (MEC) tax. Effectively, thus, the general pricing rule for packaging becomes:

$$P = MPC + MEC + MLUC \tag{13.1}$$

where:

P = the price of packaging;
MPC = the marginal private cost of production of packaging;
MEC = the marginal external cost (disposal costs plus litter);
$MLUC$ = marginal landfill user cost.

In light of the previous discussion this can be expanded to:

$$P = MPC + MDC + MLC + MLUC \tag{13.2}$$

where:

MDC = marginal disposal cost;
MLC = marginal litter cost.
$MLUC$ will be related to MDC as follows:

$$MLUC = MCD_T/(1 + r)^T \tag{13.3}$$

where T = time T, the point at which some replacement disposal route has to be found to replace exhausted landfill sites.

Equation (13.2) thus becomes generalized as:

$$P_t = MPC_{t'} + MDC_{t'} + MLC_{t'} + MDC_T(1 + r)^{-T} \tag{13.4}$$

If *MDC*, *MLC* and *MLUC* are not already incorporated into the price of packaging through regulation, the tax t that is needed is:

$$t = MDC + MLC + MLUC \tag{13.5}$$

To illustrate how equation (13.5) can be estimated in practice, we consider a product tax in the context of beverage containers. We concentrate on beverage containers as the product tax seems workable in this case. Later work will expand the analysis to packaging in general. A formula for a product tax is:

$$t_i = \frac{W_i}{L_i}(1 - r_i)(MDC + MLC) \tag{13.6}$$

where:

t_i = tax on the ith container in cents or pence per 100 litres (l);
W = weight of container, i.e. we assume external costs are related to weight, not volume, in kg/100 l;
L = litres per container, so that W/L is weight per litre of beverage;
r = recycling rate as a fraction (e.g. 20% = 0.2);
MDC = (marginal) costs of waste disposal (pence per kilogram);
MLC = (marginal) costs of litter which could be measured by litter pick-up costs.

We omit further discussion of MLUC.

An incidental result is that trippage k, i.e. the number of times a given container is directly reused as with refillable bottles, and recycling are related as follows:

$$r = 1 - (1/k) \tag{13.7}$$

and hence:

$$k = 1/(1 - r) \tag{13.8}$$

Equation (13.6) therefore becomes:

$$t_i = \frac{W_i}{L_i k_i}(MDC + MLC) \qquad (13.9)$$

Equation (13.9) behaves as we require, i.e.

$\delta t/\delta W > 0$ as the weight of the container goes up the tax goes up; as the weight goes down (lightweighting) the tax goes down;
$\delta t/\delta K < 0$ as recycling goes up the tax goes down;
$\delta t/\delta C > 0$ where $C = MDC + MLC$, i.e. as damage costs rise the tax rises.

Thus the tax/levy achieves source reduction, recycling and a lower environmental impact via changes in the container mix.

We can readily convert our product tax into a raw materials tax (t_j) by dividing the tax, t_i, in equation (13.9) by W_i/L_j to give:

$$t_j = \frac{1}{k_i}(MDC + MLC) \qquad (13.10)$$

and if *MLC* is ignored:

$$t_j = \frac{MDC}{k_i} \qquad (13.11)$$

Equations (13.10) and (13.11) have the virtue of extreme simplicity. This is important in devising any new tax.

13.4 AN ESTIMATE OF A PACKAGING TAX FOR THE UK

Table 13.2 provides an estimate of a beverage containers tax for the UK. The trippage or recycling figures deserve some comment. Two forms of recycling can be accounted for in the formula: reuse rates, as with refillable bottles; and scrap collection rates independent of any reuse. Thus, a glass bottle might be credited with both being refillable and with the fact that much glass cullet is recycled and made into new bottles. Other containers are not refillable so that the trippage rates shown in Table 13.2 are recycling rates converted to trips using equation (13.7). Actual milk bottle trippage in the UK was 13.8 for the pint bottle. For disposal costs, no single database exists that is national, comprehensive, extensive and current.

Table 13.2 Some estimates of a UK tax on liquids containers

		Type of container							
					Glass bottle				
		PET plastic	Aluminium can		One-way	Returnable			Carton
(1)	Weight (kg/100 l)	3.0	5.1		36	45			2.8
(2)	Trips	1.05	1.05	1.11	1	7	10	14	1
(3) = (1/2)	Weight/trips	2.9	4.9	4.6	36	6.4	4.5	3.2	2.8
(4)	Disposable cost (pence/kg)	<...	...	...	...	2.0	...	...	...>
(5) = (4/3)	Tax (pence/100 l)	5.8	9.8	9.2	72	12.8	9.0	6.4	5.6
(6) = (5/1)	Virgin materials tax (£/tonne)	19.3	19.2	18.0	20.0	2.8	2.0	1.4	20.0

Average financial costs of landfill disposal in the UK in the late 1980s ranged from £1 to £6/tonne for non-metropolitan areas and in excess of £15/tonne for metropolitan areas such as London. These approximate financial costs undoubtedly underestimated the true economic costs of disposal, i.e. the full economic price for landfill encompassing all relevant costs such as pretreatment of waste and proper pollution containment measures. A more careful study of landfill disposal costs in 1989 put the average figure at between £14 and £21/tonne (Taylor, 1989). We have taken £20/tonne as our approximate landfill disposal cost estimate (the primary disposal route for waste in the UK), excluding any user cost element.

Table 13.2 shows that a UK beverage containers tax can be estimated simply on the basis of disposal costs, trippage rates and container weight. On this analysis the ranking in terms of the lowest-to-highest product tax rates is:

1. cartons; 2. PET; 3. returnable bottles with $k = 14$; 4. aluminium cans.

The high ranking of cartons and plastics is perhaps counter-intuitive from an environmentalist viewpoint. However, inspection of the low weight-to-product ratio explains the ranking. If the basis was switched to packaging volume, it is possible that rankings would change. In terms of raw materials the tax ranking (lowest first) is:

1. glass ($k > 1$); 2. aluminium; 3. plastics; 4). paper

13.5 A PACKAGING TAX FOR JAPAN

Table 13.3 repeats the exercise for Japan. Compared to the UK, recycling rates are seen to be important, reflecting Japan's limited waste disposal options. Cartons and aluminium cans score best in terms of tax burden attracted. The reusable glass bottle attracts twice the aluminium can/carton tax despite the high trippage rate (20 compared to a little over one-half of this for the UK). The clue to this disparity lies in the heavier weight of the Japanese beverage bottle, reflecting in turn the concentration of bottle sales in vending machines where stronger bottles are required.

Table 13.3 An estimate of a beverage containers tax for Japan

	Type of container						
	Cans			Glass bottle		Carton	
	PET	Steel	Aluminium	One-way	Returnable	Aseptic	Milk
Weight (kg/100 l)	4.4	13.2	5.64	91.6	122.0	2.73	3.01
Trips	1	1.82	1.82	1.96	20	1.02	1.02
Weight/trips	4.4	7.25	3.10	46.7	6.1	2.67	2.95
Disposal cost (yen/kg)	<...	...	23.9	...	...	...	....>
Tax (yen/100 l)	105	173	74	1116	146	64	70
Virgin materials tax (1000 yen/tonne)	23.9	13.1	13.1	12.2	1.2	23.4	23.3

A 2% trippage rate for cartons is assumed since a small amount of carton recycling takes place. Trippage rates for 200 ml bottles were quoted as being anything from 5 to 30, but we have used 20 as a fairly generous assumption. For aluminium a recycling rate of 45% is quoted by MITI, and 40% for glass cullet. We have applied these rates to aluminium cans and glass cullet, respectively, but recycling rates specific to beverage containers are not available. MITI has established the following recycling rate targets for cans and cullet for 1995 – 60% and 55%. If achieved, this will change the tax rates as follows: steel cans, 126 yen/100 l; aluminium, 54 yen/100 l; one-way glass, 985 yen/100 l.

13.6 CONCLUSIONS

The polluter pays principle lays down that both producers and consumers should pay the full social costs of their actions. It has been argued in this paper that the full social costs (particularly environmental damage costs) are not currently reflected in the prices of packaged products. This market failure means that the receiving capacity of the environment is underpriced and the full costs of packaging waste and litter disamenity ought to be reflected in packaged product prices.

Either an input package tax (a virgin materials levy) or an output packaging tax (a product charge) could be imposed to correct for market failure. These market-based instruments offer a more cost-effective solution to the problem of packaging waste and litter than regulatory legislation. We have demonstrated how a product charge can be readily converted into a materials levy. We have also questioned the necessity of imposing a full cradle-to-grave environmental audit on packaging production and consumption processes in order to calibrate a taxation system. Only the external costs of packaging are relevant in the economic–environmental audit. But some of these costs, e.g. ambient air and water pollution costs, are already at least partially internalized by national and European Community environmental protection legislation. Thus there is the danger of a mis-specification of targets and instruments in this packaging context, with the end result being the double counting of pollution damage costs (polluter pays twice).

It turns out that a relatively simple tax or levy system can be directed at the packaging waste and litter problem. The simplicity of the system is important on at least two counts:

1. it is readily understandable and could thus be more easily assimilated and adopted by the decision-makers;
2. its bureaucratic and compliance costs should be relatively low. The levy or tax can be properly related to environmental damage impacts by the incorporation of average costs for waste disposal and litter collection costs (proxy for the full pick-up and disamenity costs of litter) into the computations (see Table 13.2). User cost elements are also relevant but are more difficult to estimate in the UK context.

NOTE

1. Originally published in *Resources, Conservation and Recycling*, **8**(2), January 1993.

REFERENCES

Bohm, P. (1981) *Deposit-refund Schemes*, Johns Hopkins University Press, Baltimore, MD.

Organization for Economic Co-operation and Development (1975), *The Polluter Pays Principle*. OECD, Paris.

Pezzey, J. (1988), Market mechanisms of pollution control: 'polluter pays', economic and practical aspects, in R.K. Turner (ed.) *Sustainable Environmental Management: Principles and Practice*, Belhaven Press, London

Taylor, R. (1989), The true costs of landfill: energy recycling is a strong competitor. *Warmer Bulletin,* **21**, 15.

14. The social incidence of environmental costs and benefits[1]

14.1 INTRODUCTION

Is concern for the natural environment the exclusive concern of the relatively privileged classes of society? Certainly the popular, and often the academic, literature has presumed the existence of 'environmental elitism'. As one outspoken economist (Beckerman, 1974, p. 49) has put it: '. . . the heart of the matter is that the anti-growth movement and the excessive concern with the environment is basically middle class'. This sentiment can be found echoed in endless academic articles and in popular works. It is partly founded on a casual empiricism, a kind of armchair observation that it is the articulate and well clothed who participate in public inquiries to preserve some part of the countryside against a new motorway or coalmine, and who have the money and capacity to organize protest movements that have become increasingly professional. Perhaps more rigorously, it reflects an attempt to explain the emergence of the environmental movement in the 1960s and 1970s. The explanation would be along the following approximate lines. Any individual ranks his or her wants and attends first to the necessities of life. Thereafter, as incomes grow and as working hours are reduced, there is both the capacity and the time to consider 'social' goods, such as the environment.

In turn, the growth of incomes is perhaps seen as an indicator of the 'success' (or, at least, the persistence) of societies dedicated to expanded material wealth. This leaves the perennial radical youth with causes that sound increasingly hollow. They can point to excesses of capitalism or growth societies, but a cause for something is far more identifiable and 'the environment' and 'ecology' become the positive objects of concern to be embraced by a group in search of a cause. The common element remains wealth, since it is not the poor who embrace the cause, only the poor who have chosen to be so by making deliberate exits from the comfortable society they were born into.

Of course, this form of picture thinking is consistent with the fact that the pursuit of material wealth has reduced the availability of natural environments. It would be difficult to argue that, say, wilderness areas are now more and not less abundant than they were, or that less species are endangered than a hundred years ago, or that resources are not being depleted (whatever one's view of the time-scale). Environmental concern can therefore be a legitimate concern about a legitimate problem. The issue, however, is whether that concern is confined to a biased group of society. If it is, then, arguably, any social policy which has some concept of distributive justice inherent in it should consider attaching less weight to environmental concern than these apparent expressions of concern would seem to dictate.

Quite simply, the environmental movement may conceal or obscure other socially more desirable concerns such as the redistribution of income, or inner-city decay, or whatever. It would seem to matter, therefore, that we learn whether environmentalism is an elite concept.

One of the most interesting features of the early arguments about the desirability of economic growth was that they took place against the backdrop of assumptions about the elitist nature of environmental concern. The furthest that anyone went in attempting to justify the assumption was in embracing the kind of casual argument offered above in our characterization of the elitist theory. At no stage did it seem to occur to the participants in that debate that what was required was empirical observation of the kind that would be called for on any other issue. The purpose of this paper is to survey, critically, the attempts that have been made, all in recent years, to add a quantitative and analytical content to the debate. In short, we wish to know what evidence exists for the supposition of environmental elitism.

14.2 WHAT IS ENVIRONMENTAL ELITISM?

The debate over the class bias of environmentalism is confused by the fact that few people have asked exactly what elitism means and how we might test for its existence. Elitism may mean one or more of several things. It may refer to the class composition of the environmental protest movement. Since protest and achievement are not necessarily the same thing, it seems more fruitful to look at who actually benefits from environmental change and who bears the costs of that change. Taking benefits first, it is possible to consider them in physical terms (e.g. units of sulphur dioxide (SO_2) concentration reduced) or in monetary terms (i.e. by looking at the money value of the reduced damage and seeing how this is apportioned among income groups). For costs, it is necessary to see what the cost of the abatement programme is and how this cost is distributed among income groups.

The obvious difficulty with the physical measure of benefit is that we have no direct way of relating any physical change, correlated to income groups, to the way those groups perceive the change. The fact that group X 'gains' more than group Y in terms of a sulphur dioxide reduction does not mean that the gain is worth more to group X. It becomes essential to seek their monetary evaluation of that change.

The problem with seeking a monetary evaluation of benefits lies mainly in the absence of satisfactory techniques for measuring those benefits. We shall return to this issue later. As far as the burden of costs is concerned, any analysis is replete with difficulties since few environmental projects are 'earmarked' for specific taxes (although this should become increasingly common as pollution charges are introduced) and the tax itself will have forward shifting effects in that part of the cost, at least, will be passed on in the form of increased product prices. It then becomes necessary to trace the incidence of those price changes on income groups. To make things more complex, there may be associated employment changes, and so on. Tracing through the entire pattern of incidence is clearly involved.

It seems reasonable to concentrate on two aspects as far as acceptable indicators are concerned. First, can we adduce any evidence to the effect that the poor are likely to have more environmental quality than they want? If so, any environmental programme will involve them in being worse off compared to their desired position and the rich better off. The emphasis in over-providing environmental quality to the poor is justified by the fact that no specific harm is entailed by charging citizens less for the environment than they are willing to pay. However, as Dorfman (1977, p. 337) states: 'The harm inheres in compelling some citizens to pay more for government programmes than they would be willing to but for the coercive powers of the government.' Second, since the general argument is that environmental concern increases as income levels increase, we can use an explicit measure – the income elasticity of demand – to assess whether the 'demand' for environmental quality increases more or less proportionately as income increases. We shall require that the income elasticity be greater than unity before an environmental good can be deemed 'elitist' in this sense. This means that a percentage point increase in income should be associated with more than a percentage point increase in the demand for the good. Later we consider whether the empirical literature on the demand for environmental goods has established the case of the income elasticity being greater than unity. Note that we select a value of unity as the cut-off point. Freeman (1972) refers to income elasticities greater than zero as being evidence of a 'pro-rich' distribution since benefits rise with income. He refers to an elasticity greater than unity as 'strongly pro-rich' and an elasticity greater than zero but less than unity as 'mildly pro-rich'. Where the elasticity is between zero and unity, however, benefits will decrease as a proportion of income. We therefore prefer the use of the value of unity as the cut-off point. Moreover, if all goods with an income elasticity greater than zero are to be deemed 'pro-rich', virtually all goods would fall into this category and the concept of 'pro-richness' would seem to be rather redundant.

14.3 SOME ANALYTICS

Baumol (1972, 1974) and Baumol and Oates (1975) have established the fundamentals of an analytical framework within which the distributional issue can be considered in terms of the first criterion noted above, namely, whether an environmental good has any attributes such that it will be oversupplied to the poor. Environmental quality tends to be a public good, or, at least, has public good characteristics attached to it. By a public good we mean a good which, if supplied to one individual, is automatically supplied to others such that the consumption of that good by any one individual does not reduce the consumption of it by anyone else. Examples to fit this polarized definition are rare, but it is a convenient device for analysing the implications of the 'publicness' of the environment.

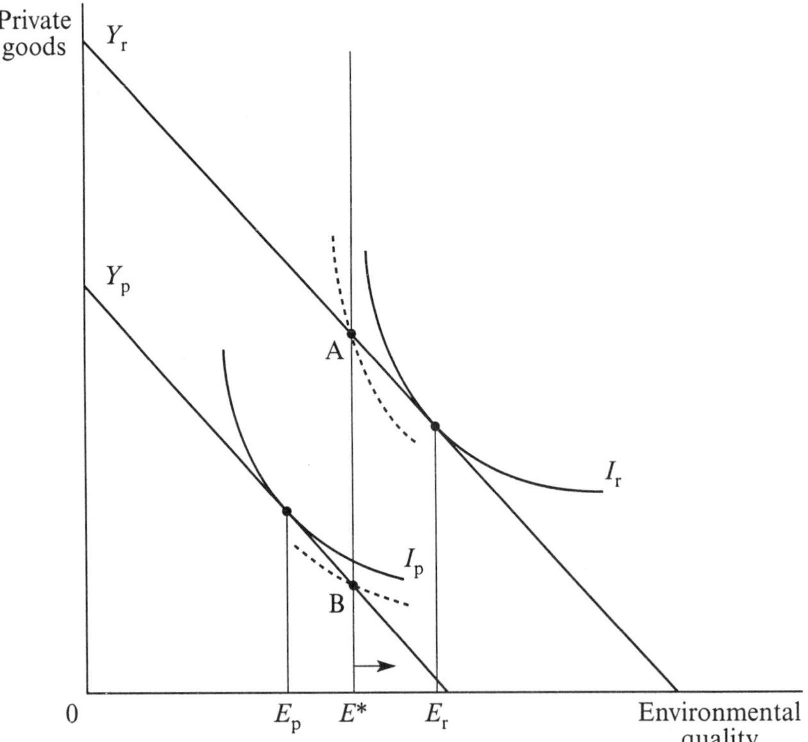

Figure 14.1 The allocation of private goods and environmental quality for different income groups

Figure 14.1 shows two general goods, a private good on the vertical axis and the public good (environmental quality) on the horizontal axis. The two stylized consumers of the goods are shown as poor (P) and rich (R) respectively. Their incomes are shown by the two parallel lines Y_p and Y_r which are drawn such that the consumers face the same relative prices for the two goods (the slopes of the income lines are equal) but, obviously, R has a higher income line than P. The corresponding indifference curves are placed on the diagram to show the amounts of the public good that each group would ideally demand, E_p and E_r respectively. Now, given that the essence of a public good is that it must be supplied in equal amounts to each group, it is clear that we cannot supply E_p to the poor and E_r to the rich. Assuming that the poor have some power, perhaps in the political process, some compromise is reached, let us say at E^*. That is, an amount of environmental quality is supplied which is less than the amount desired by the rich and more than the amount desired by the poor.

Reference to the indifference curves will show that the indifference curve for R cuts Y_r at A from above. The marginal rate of substitution between the two goods is greater than the ruling price (given by the slope of Y_r). For the poor, the indifference curve cuts Y_p from below at B, so the relevant marginal rate of substitution is less than the relative price. In simple language, the rich value the environment at E^* more than the price they pay and the poor value it at less. The benefits are therefore biased in favour of the rich. Furthermore, any programme designed to increase environmental quality would move E^* to the right, thus reinforcing the analysis. On these grounds, then, one might conclude that environmental benefits are class biased in favour of the rich.

The immediate problem with Figure 14.1 and the analysis associated with it is that the publicness of the environmental good is too extensive. That is, it assumes that rich and poor are somehow 'locked in' to some quantity of the good between E_p and E_r. This will be true for 'global' public goods such as reductions in, let us say, cumulated carbon dioxide (CO_2) in the atmosphere or reductions in the risk of some global environmental catastrophe (although, even here, one suspects that some would lose relative to others).

But most environmental goods take on the features of local public goods – they affect a specific geographical environment. An example would be airport noise. If it is possible to move away from the noise 'footprint' then it should be possible to escape the noise if one does not like it. If this is true we would expect patterns of mobility to emerge, reflecting the different willingness to pay of the groups in question. In terms of Figure 14.1 we would expect the rich to demand more of the public good, say peace and quiet, by moving outside the airport noise 'footprint'. Since the poor are assumed to have marginal valuations less than the price they are being asked to pay they can be expected to stay in the noisy areas. Indeed, if the housing market is perfect and everyone is free to move according to their valuations of their environment, we should have a whole spectrum of people who will in fact equate their marginal rates of substitution to the prices relevant to the location in which they find themselves. The inequality of marginal rates of substitution noted in Figure 14.1 would disappear and everyone would consume exactly that amount of the public good they desire. At this other extreme, then, environmental quality does not become an 'elitist' good in the strict economic sense used for Figure 14.1, for now each group, rich and poor has as much of the environmental good as it desires. The fact that the rich end up living in the unpolluted areas and the poor in polluted areas does not constitute 'elitism' because the poor are not being forced to secure more of the public good than they desire. It will be recalled that this was the first test suggested for the existence of elitism.

As Baumol and Oates (1975) note, neither the extreme of the global public good, nor the pure case of perfect adjustment to localized public goods through mobility, describes reality. Any number of imperfections exist in the housing market that make it difficult to argue that, even if we did observe the poor and rich living in the polluted and unpolluted areas, respectively, this would reflect an adjustment procedure of the kind noted above. Moreover, the fact that the poor may well actually consume less environmental quality than the rich tells us little about whether they wish to change their situation. Significantly, in the Baumol–Oates analyses it is either assumed that the marginal rates of substitution at the desired levels of the public good (E_p and E_r) are the same or that the rate of substitution by the poor is less than that for the rich (this is much more explicit in Baumol, 1972). If that is true, then whether they face equal or different price levels for securing an improvement in their environment,[2] the rich will always tend to consume more and the poor less of environmental quality in order to be in equilibrium. Nonetheless, these remain assumptions about the rates of substitution and not observed facts. To reverse the argument, if the poor have a higher rate of substitution than the rich, it is easy to show that Figure 14.1 could be drawn to show the poor securing too little environmental quality and the rich too much (I_p would be steeper than I_r) In short, the analytics tell us little because they make assumptions about marginal rates of substitution – i.e. valuations of the environment – rather than giving us empirical evidence as to what these valuations are.

14.4 THE PHYSICAL INCIDENCE OF POLLUTION

It can be argued that one piece of indirect evidence that a migratory process of the kind described above has taken place is that the poor tend to live in polluted areas and the rich in unpolluted areas, relatively speaking. This much seems borne out by the work of Freeman (1972) and Berry (1977). We survey this literature shortly. For the moment, consider the implications of such a finding. We could argue that this outcome is the result of voluntary movements which aim to adjust to the different levels of pollution in different localities. As such, we could be close to the second type of solution referred to – one in which each group consumes the localized public good to the level it desires. No one is under- or over-provided with the good and hence no elitism exists. It is, however, quite possible to argue the opposite. The pro-rich pattern of environmental quality may well reflect some migratory process, but, by and large, the poor are not as able as the rich to move locality in response to environmental variables. Hence, although they occupy the poor areas, we do not know that their valuation functions are such as to indicate an unwillingness to pay for environmental improvement in their areas. Quite simply, the migratory process is assumed to have taken place because of differences between the two groups in their marginal rates of substitution, whereas it could be the simple difference in income levels that determines the move, leaving the poor 'locked in' to polluted areas but with a marginal rate of substitution in excess of the price of improving their environment. This excess of valuation over price does not 'trigger' action simply because the poor are constrained in their capacity to move.

Evidence of the pro-rich geographical distribution of environmental quality is not therefore necessarily evidence that an increase of environmental quality would not have a higher value to the poor than would a similar incremental change for the rich in their relatively unpolluted areas. Nonetheless, it does suggest some prima facie evidence that some sort of adjustment mechanism has taken place. It is therefore worthwhile reviewing the evidence on the geographical incidence of pollution.

Early work by Freeman (1972, pp. 262–9) suggests an inverse relationship between air pollution and income class. Looking at three United States cities, Freeman found that an index of suspended particulates in the ambient environment was very closely correlated with the inverse of income levels within the cities. The same was true of an index of sulphation (SO_x). Interestingly, the relationship did not hold across the cities. That is, the index of suspended particulates for low income families in Washington was actually below that for the highest income groups in St. Louis. The index of sulphation (SO_x) was also systematically lower in Kansas City for all income groups than it was for the highest income group in either St. Louis or Washington. Also of interest was Freeman's finding that in each city the average black family was exposed to more air pollution (on these two measures) than the average family, of whatever colour, in the lowest income group.

Harrison (1975) considers the physical benefits in terms of carbon monoxide (CO), nitrogen oxides (NO_x), and photochemical oxidants (O_x) reductions arising from a US automobile emission control programme. The programme in question concerns the amendments made to the US Clean Air Act of 1970. Although that programme has been modified several times it does not significantly affect the results of interest here, namely, the distribution of the reductions in the pollutants by income group. Interestingly, Harrison found no relationship between these reductions and income group. The range was 9.9–11.4 p.p.m. of carbon monoxide for income groups ranging from under \$3000 p.a. to over \$25 000 p.a. While the biggest change benefited the highest income group, the smallest change benefited the third highest income group, and the benefits to low income groups exceeded those of the next three income groups. The same was true of NO_x and O_x. This initially surprising result (since low income groups are concentrated in central city areas which secured the greatest pollution reductions) is explained by Harrison by the fact that the low income groups are dominant in both metropolitan and non-metropolitan areas. Air quality benefits are low in the latter areas, thus cancelling out the high benefits to low income groups in the metropolitan areas. This does not alter Harrison's conclusion, but goes some way to explaining the initially counter-intuitive result.

He also points to the fact that the rich will secure some of the city centre benefits by commuting to work there, shopping and seeking entertainment in these localities, whereas the poor are less likely to do so. Finally, if rents are bid up through air quality improvement, some transfer of the benefits from the poor will take place as income is transferred to landlords, the richer class.

Once the results are disaggregated to consider urban areas only, the improvement programme is seen to be distinctly pro poor (i.e. in the initial position it is the poor who have the highest air pollution concentration and therefore they stand to gain most, in physical terms, from an abatement programme).

The most extensive study on the income distribution of pollution is that by Berry (1977) for the United States. He covers many pollutants and a number of cities, looking at several in some considerable detail. In terms of assessing the 'social burden' of pollution the study confined itself to air pollution, noise, and solid waste. Water quality was omitted because of the difficulties of relating water quality to urban area residents, the issue being that it is the users of rivers and watercourses who are affected, not necessarily residents. Further, drinking water standards are controlled by national health standards. Lastly, the comparisons are between central city residents and not the residents of entire metropolitan areas.

A detailed study of Chicago produced some interesting results. Table 14.1 shows the results for particulates and sulphur dioxide. The 'primary standards' referred to are the federal standard of 75 $\mu g/m^3$ annual geometric mean. The secondary standard is 60 $\mu g/m^3$. The table is to be read thus: 38% of the city centre's population were in the income class \$10 000–\$17 500 and were simultaneously exposed to particulate pollution levels which exceeded the primary standard. This is more than half the number of persons in that income bracket (percentage in the income bracket is given in parentheses). As a further example, 18.7 + 0.97 = 19.67% of the population were in the income bracket \$10 000–\$20 000 and were exposed to particulate levels between 60 and 75 μg/m³.

Table 14.1 Exposure to air pollution in Chicago

	Particulates				Sulphur dioxide	
Mean family income (\$000)	Primary standards		Exceeds secondary standards only		Exceeds secondary standards only	
> 20	1.19	(100.0)	0.00	(0.0)	0.00	(0.0)
17.5–20.0	1.93	(65.0)	0.97	(32.5)	0.07	(2.5)
10.0–17.5	38.09	(63.3)	18.71	(31.0)	0.15	(0.3)
7.5–10.0	29.26	(97.5)	0.74	(2.5)	0.37	(1.2)
< 7.5	5.20	(93.3)	0.37	(6.7)	0.00	(0.0)

Source: Berry (1977)

The interesting result is that it is middle income groups who bear the 'burden' of particulate pollution, although nearly 30% of the population in the \$500–\$10 000 p.a. class (nearly 100% of that income group) were exposed to particulate levels which exceed the primary standard.

Note, too, that the entire income group above \$20 000 lived in the most polluted areas, as did over 93% of the lowest income group. The result shows clearly that there is no obvious inverse linkage such as that suggested by Harrison for metropolitan areas as a whole.

Asch and Seneca (1978) confirm Berry's findings in their own analysis of air pollution in 23 states. They conclude that 'exposure to particulate matter is relatively higher in cities with low-income characteristics... While this is not surprising, the consistency of the relationship, even at the rather broad level of (city) aggregation and over the wide geographical coverage of 23 states, is noteworthy' (Asch and Seneca, 1978, p. 282). Extending their analysis to nitrogen dioxide (NO_2) and sulphur dioxide as well as particulates for three cities, Chicago, Cleveland and Nashville, Asch and Seneca consider intracity variations. Their findings largely confirm those found for the interstate comparisons: the distribution of physical pollution is essentially regressive, i.e. the poor 'suffer' most. They record, however, considerable variation between cities despite the consistent regressive pattern. For example, the percentage of families in the lowest income group exposed to pollution levels which violate federal standards was 58% in Chicago and 78% in Cleveland.

Further, however, one third of families in the \$15 000–\$25 000 upper income bracket lived in areas where federal primary standards are violated.

These findings of 'regressive' incidence relate to a single point in time since the analysis is cross-sectional. Asch and Seneca (1978) report limited evidence to suggest that changes in air quality over time may, however, be progressively distributed, i.e. the rich have suffered more than the poor from the changes which appear to have reduced pollution in low income areas but to have increased it in high income areas. The evidence is fragmentary and held only for particulates, the correlations with sulphur dioxide being statistically insignificant.

Similar, counter-intuitive, results exist in Berry's study for exposure to atmospheric mercury and arsenic, to which middle income groups are most exposed. Zinc most affects high income groups, lead most affects low income blacks, while cadmium most affects lower income whites. Pesticide poisoning tends to be correlated with the presence of rats, and this shows up worst in low income black areas.

Berry also considers solid waste, although it is not altogether clear what 'solid waste pollution' means. It is clear in the case of junked automobiles or industrial or residential demolition, but the fact that a family may generate solid waste for disposal by the refuse collection agencies does not translate readily into 'exposure' to any risks from that waste. However, insofar as there is risk and/or aesthetic 'damage', Berry pinpoints two Chicago subgroups most at risk. These are apartment-dwelling high income whites and high-density apartment dwelling low income blacks. It is unclear from the study just how far the former group's exposure is dominated by solid waste generation itself.

In a comparison of twelve city areas, the results tended to accord more with the pro-rich hypothesis about environmental quality. Thus, 'in all areas, the very poor are most likely to be concentrated in the areas with the most serious particulate problems' (Berry, 1977, p. 572). Similar, though less forceful, conclusions are reached for sulphur dioxide concentrations (four-city comparison only) and nitrogen dioxide (three-city comparison only). Low income groups were also those primarily affected by noise levels, although airport noise most affected middle income white groups.

By and large, Berry's work must be taken to confirm the view that, generally speaking, it is the poor who bear the physical burden of pollution, although the detailed Chicago results are quite ambiguous in this respect. Further, the subsequent study of twelve city centres was extremely limited by data and, in most cases, no more than a few cities were compared.

14.5 ESTIMATING INCOME ELASTICITIES

We saw that the geographical incidence of environmental disamenity could be used to support the argument that an adjustment mechanism of the kind discussed earlier was taking place, with the rich moving location to avoid local public 'bads' and the poor residing in the polluted areas. The preceding evidence suggests that the geographical incidence of environmental quality is, with some exceptions, basically pro-rich, provided attention is confined to urban areas. Nonetheless, we also argued that serious imperfections in the housing market make such observations consistent with the hypothesis that the poor might be willing to pay more than the rich for improvements in their environment. Since we have found no categorical evidence one way or the other, we need to consider whether income elasticities can be adduced for environmental amenity.

The most obvious source for such elasticities lies in the wealth of house price depreciation studies that have been carried out, mainly for air pollution and noise nuisance. These studies are surveyed in Pearce and Edwards (1979) for noise and Pearce (1978) for air pollution. The essential idea is to relate the price of housing to a series of attributes, such as room size, number of rooms, availability of a garage, proximity to schools, and so on. One attribute can then be a measure (or more than one) of environmental quality. Noise indices or ambient concentrations of sulphur dioxide, particulates, etc., can be included as 'negative' attributes. A multiple regression equation is formed with house prices being regressed on the attributes such that the coefficients that emerge can, in the view of many, be regarded as the 'prices' that individuals attach to the attribute. It may then be possible to link these prices to incomes to obtain an income elasticity of demand. The formal demonstration is given in the appendix to this chapter.

Using an approach of this kind, Nelson (1978) estimates the income elasticity of demand for air quality to be unity. Harrison and Rubinfeld (1978) use a different approach to that outlined in the appendix. Essentially, they do not postulate a supply function, but rather assume that air quality is independent of the valuation of that air quality by householders. Effectively, the supply curve is completely inelastic with respect to price. This permits them to argue that the inverse demand curve is all that is needed and income elasticities can be obtained directly from this procedure. Again, it is interesting that the income elasticities they secure are unity (or as near unity as to make no difference).

These results suggest that income elasticities for environmental quality – or at least for air pollution improvements – are about unity, thus offering some confirmation for the elitist hypothesis established at the outset. Unfortunately, it is far from clear that these results are actual findings from the studies. Instead, they may be artifacts of the way in which the models are constructed. That is, it may well be that an income elasticity of unity is 'built in' to the model. If so, it should occasion no surprise that the models generate such a result. The view that these are not genuine elasticities has been put by Edwards (1978) (see also Pearce *et al.* 1979). Essentially, Edwards shows that the underlying utility functions used in hedonic models are homogeneous. For a function to be homogeneous simply means that, if we take an equation such as (A14.2) in the appendix to this chapter, multiplication of each attribute, Z_i, by some constant, say 'b', would alter the entire value of the function V by a factor b^k, where k is the 'degree of homogeneity'. If the value of V does not change at all, the function is said to be homogeneous of degree zero since the value of V is multiplied by $b^0 = 1$.

Now, homogeneity of some order is essential to the specification of hedonic functions such as those shown previously. If they are not homogeneous, the prices of the attributes will depend on the actual level of utility of the individual. But if this occurs, we shall not be able to associate a unique price with each level of an attribute: the price will change as the level of utility changes. Note that one might 'escape' this problem by arguing that individuals with the same level of income are likely to have similar utility levels. Segmenting the study to include only them would therefore enable the homogeneity problem to be overcome. While this is true it also means that no income elasticity can be derived since it is precisely the manner in which valuations change with respect to changes in income that we need in order to estimate an income elasticity.

Given that the underlying utility functions must be homogeneous we now need to know why this homogeneity is likely to generate income elasticities of unity. The formal proof is not straightforward and is given by Edwards (1978). Suffice it to say that the implied income elasticities of demand for all attributes of houses are unity as long as the underlying utility function is homogeneous.

Essentially, hedonic models cannot be used to estimate income elasticities. It is perfectly in order to constrain the elasticity to be equal to unity in specifying the model, but then it is self-evident that the assumption cannot be a result.

It follows that perhaps the richest potential source of data on income elasticities – house price depreciation studies of pollution – is not, after all, suitable for deriving income elasticities. The 'findings' in some studies that the income elasticity is unity is more than suspect since it is argued that the very specification of the underlying utility function for hedonic models to be specified is such that the income elasticity will necessarily be unity.

14.6 OTHER EVIDENCE ON INCOME ELASTICITIES

If house price studies are ruled out of court as a source of information on income elasticities, very little is left. Very few social surveys have been carried out which incorporate data on incomes and valuations of pollution. Those that have are not easy to interpret in terms of the information we require. Harris (1979) has processed data from the UK Building Research Establishment on a questionnaire relating to noise reductions from urban traffic. His tentative conclusion is that the implied income elasticities are very low, of the order 0.2–0.4, which would make peace and quiet a non-elite good since a 1% rise in income would be associated with a less than 1% rise in expenditure (or 'willingness to pay') on noise abatement.

The opposite conclusion is suggested by Walters (1975) in his review of the data on noise at Heathrow and Gatwick airports. This data relates to house price differentials but these were not estimated by multiple regression techniques such as those used in the hedonic approach. Rather, the differentials were estimated by estate agents on the basis of what they thought would happen if certain noise levels prevailed. A significant factor is also that no independent data was used for income. Instead, Walters argues that the house price itself is a reasonable proxy for 'permanent' income – a kind of present value of future income streams to the household. If this can be justified, some kind of income elasticity can be obtained by simply writing

$$\text{Income elasticity } = E_y = \frac{D_2 / D_1}{HP / HP_1}$$

where D_2 = percentage house price depreciation for the higher income group for a given level of noise
D_1 = depreciation relevant to lower income group
HP_1 = lower house price
HP = HP_2 (higher house price) – HP_1

Note that *HP* now stands as a proxy for income and *D* is regarded as an exact valuation of noise (Walters' justification for the use of *D* in this way is roughly synonymous with that of the hedonic literature). The empirical results are given in Table 14.2.

If the procedure is correct, it will be seen that (a) 'income' elasticities are: generally at least 2 and rise above 3; (b) they are higher the greater is 'income'. There is no discernible trend of elasticity with noise level.

The basic problem with the Walters' approach is that house price is not a good proxy for the present value of expected income streams. This would only be justified if the income elasticity of demand for housing was itself unity. But reference to various studies shows that, while this was once a consensus view, it no longer is. As such, Walters' calculations must be regarded as suspect.

A further experiment is reported by Weisbrod (1978) in which surveyed groups were asked to vote 'yes' or 'no' to a programme of increased government action against polluters. Support for anti-pollution programmes was generally found to be better in better educated groups, becoming lower the older the population, and positively related to income up to an income level of $35 000, after which support was actually less than in the lowest income group (other factors being held equal). As Weisbrod himself notes, the statistical significance of the income variables used was low and it is unclear how much faith can be placed in the results. Nor is it clear why, even if they are correct, support for anti-pollution programmes should fall off with high incomes.

Table 14.2 Implied elasticities for peace and quiet: Heathrow and Gatwick

	Noise and number index (NNI)					
	35–45		45–55		55+	
House price (income)	H	G	H	G	H	G
£3000–£6000	–	2.09	2.17	1.60	2.10	–
£6000–£10 000	1.89	2.60	3.15	2.62	3.20	–

Source: Data from Walters (1975, p. 91). Elasticities are computed by the author.

The studies by Gianessi *et al.* (1977a, 1977b) and also Peskin (1978) take earlier national monetary estimates of air pollution damage in the United States (Waddell,1974). They then allocate these to geographical areas via the use of information on local emissions of a given pollutant. Effectively, this assumes proportionality between emissions and damage, but the use of a population density variable makes some allowance for pollution concentration. Pollution within a given geographical area is assumed uniform due to data limitations. Table 14.3 shows the results of meeting the requirement of the Clean Air Act of 1970 (as was the case with Harrison's study, Harrison, 1975).

The interesting feature of Table 14.3 is that benefits as a proportion of income fall as income rises, indicating an income elasticity of demand of less than unity. In fact the income elasticity for the low end of the income range (up to $6000) is of the order of 0.35, rising to 0.87 for the middle incomes and falling back again to about 0.60 for the upper incomes. This evidence therefore provides no support for the idea that environmental goods are 'elitist'. Of course, the problem lies not only with the difficulties of allocating damage to income sources but also in the fairly arbitrary estimates of damage produced in the Waddell (1974) study and which are used here.

These estimates are a mixture taken from many different sources and generalizing, for example, on one house price depreciation study for St. Louis by applying the depreciation estimates nationwide.

For our estimates of income elasticity to be meaningful we must have some assurance that the damage estimates represent willingness to pay on the part of the income groups, and since the Waddell estimates preceded most of the hedonic price literature we have no guarantee of this at all. Indeed, even if it was legitimate to generalize across a whole nation from single-city studies, it remains the case that hedonic price estimates have themselves been the subject of severe theoretical criticism which leaves them subject to the charge that they may not be, in the slightest, accurate reflections of willingness to pay (see Harris, 1978; Maler, 1977; Pearce and Edwards, 1979).

Table 14.3 Benefits of compliance with the US Clean Air Act of 1970

	Income class ($000)									
Source of benefit	< 3	3–4	4–5	6–8	8–10	10–12	12–15	15–20	20–25	25+
Industry and government	6.3	4.0	3.2	2.8	2.7	2.4	2.3	2.0	1.7	1.0
Household	1.7	1.1	0.9	0.7	0.7	0.6	0.6	0.5	0.5	0.3
Total	8.0	5.1	4.1	3.5	3.4	3.0	2.9	2.5	2.2	1.3

Source: Gianessi *et al.* (1977a).

Harrison and Rubinfeld (1978) have also shown that the money estimates obtained in hedonic approaches are very sensitive to the specification of the model. Nonetheless, it remains the case that the Gianessi study fails to provide any support for the view that environmental goods are elitist. We need to reconsider this view when we look at net benefits, i.e. estimates of benefits minus estimates of the distributional burden of the costs of the programme for the Clean Air Act.

Dorfman (1977) reports some results from an analysis of the (US) National Wildlife Federation Survey about environment. This survey included the question: 'Would you be willing to accept a $X per year increase in your family's total expenses for the clean-up of the natural environment?' Various levels of expenditure were given and these were correlated in the Dorfman study with income levels. The pooled data produced a function of the form:

$$\text{Percentage willing to accept cost} = 98 - 14.3 \log P$$

where P is the willingness to pay. Dorfman interprets this as a demand curve and computes demand curves for three income levels. No income elasticity is derivable from the Dorfman paper since actual data are not reported (merely being shown in graphical form). Nonetheless, Dorfman (1977, p. 336) concludes that clean environment is a superior good and that at any stated price more people at higher income levels are willing to buy it than at lower incomes.

14.7 THE INCIDENCE OF ENVIRONMENTAL ABATEMENT COSTS

So far we have looked at the evidence on the social incidence of environmental benefits. Clearly what matters ultimately is the distribution of net benefits. We may therefore now turn to the incidence of abatement costs. Here the issue is more complex in that, while benefit estimates are in themselves suspect, the 'hardness' of cost data is offset by the difficulty of tracing through the incidence of any pollution tax or general tax for financing an abatement programme.

The Gianessi *et al.* (1977a) study considers the cost side of the 1970 Clean Air Act proposals (see above for the benefit aspects). Three sources of costs were identified. Industrial abatement costs were assumed to be passed on *in toto* to final consumers and were allocated to consumers, and thereby to income groups, according to the consumption of the relevant goods by those consumers. This effectively means that the abatement costs are not borne in the region where the actual expenditures may take place since the 'cost' is embodied in the final product which is sold nationally. Household costs, mainly the costs of automobile pollution abatement, were distributed according to automobile ownership and were therefore largely borne in the region where the actual expenditure took place. Government abatement costs were assumed to be met by taxation and were therefore prorated according to average family tax burdens. The results show that some 8.2% of incomes for the below $3000 income levels would be accounted for by the costs of pollution control. This falls systematically with income to 2.7% for the $20 000–$25 000 income group and under 2% for the above $25 000 income group. In short, if we construe the abatement cost burden as a 'tax' this tax is definitely regressive: lower income groups bear a larger burden in proportion to their income than do higher income groups.

This picture of the regressiveness of cost burdens is borne out by Dorfman (1977) and Dorfman and Snow (1975). Dorfman looked at planned pollution control expenditures (not just air pollution) for 1972, 1976 and 1980 and found that, while the cost burden was roughly equally shared in 1972, it became distinctly regressive by 1980. This regressiveness is accounted for largely by the automobile abatement programme which can, effectively, be seen as a poll tax for any automobile-owning family.

The fact of more automobile ownership per family in higher income groups does not offset this overriding tax element. Industrial abatement costs were also seen to be regressive, suggesting that the poor buy the more polluting products. Federal abatement expenditures were found to be progressive. Essentially the same picture is given by Dorfman and Snow (1975), who rely on much the same data and methodology as Dorfman (1977).

Harrison (1975) also finds a regressive pattern for automobile emission control costs. His estimates differ significantly from those of Gianessi *et al.* (1977a), however. In general, Harrison's results are very much lower, which, according to Gianessi *et al.* is due to a failure to allow for the higher fuel cost of unleaded fuel in a realistic fashion. For the record, the two sets of calculations are shown in Table 14.4 in terms of the percentage of incomes taken up by automobile emission control. (The data from Gianessi *et al.* are actually for household abatement, but this is almost entirely accounted for by automobile emissions costs.)

Yan *et al.* (1975) showed that air pollution abatement could bring about price changes which, using input–output tables, could be demonstrated to affect mainly the middle income groups, thus indicating some counter-evidence for the regressiveness of abatement costs. The preceding evidence suggests that, even if the benefits of pollution-control programmes are not pro rich, the incidence of the costs of the programmes are likely to be. As such it becomes important to estimate the net benefits from the programmes.

Table 14.4 US automobile emission costs as a percentage of income, 1980

Income class ($000)	< 3	3–5	5–7	7–10	10–15	15–25	25+
Gianessi *et al.* [a]	4.8	3.4	2.75	2.35	1.9	1.45	0.7
Harrison	1.5	1.4	1.2	1.0	0.8	0.8	0.8

14.8 THE SOCIAL INCIDENCE OF ENVIRONMENTAL PROGRAMME NET BENEFITS

Several attempts have been made to estimate the incidence of net benefits. Gianessi *et al.* (1977b) produce results which show that the overall net benefits of the 1970 Clean Air Act in the United States can be expected to be regressive as far as automobile emission control is concerned and progressive as far as control of government and industry pollution is concerned. Ignoring the two lowest income groups (up to $4000 p.a.) the net benefit picture overall reveals a slightly regressive pattern. If the estimates are credible, the salient feature is that the automobile abatement programme is not only regressive in its incidence but actually has absolute negative net benefits (i.e. a net cost) for all income groups. This would suggest that the US policy on automobile emission control has aimed for too high a level of environmental quality and that the programme entails a regressive tax incidence and is therefore also distributionally unfair. It would, in short, fail both equity and efficiency tests. Needless to say, however, much depends on the absolute estimates of benefits and, as we saw, these are not particularly reliable in the Gianessi *et al.* case.

Dorfman (1977) brings together his assessment of national environmental policy costs and benefits in the United States to secure some rough estimates of incidence. This he does by taking the benefit estimates from the National Wildlife Federation Survey (see above) and the cost estimates derived independently. His final outline results are shown in Table 14.5. Here the results are more in line with the first test suggested for 'elitism', i.e. the extent to which households are being asked to pay for more environmental quality than they want. We also saw above that the Gianessi *et al.* estimates for automobile emission control could be interpreted as suggesting that all income groups were being 'offered' more control than they were willing to pay for. If any reliance can be placed on these figures, they suggest that national environmental policy in the United States is fairly strongly 'pro-rich' in the first sense discussed at the outset of this paper.

Table 14.5 Dorfman's estimates of net benefits of US national pollution control, 1977

Income class ($000)	Average benefits ($)	Average costs ($)	Net benefits ($)
< 5.7	60	121	–61
5.7–11.4	214	205	+9
> 11.4	608	549	+59

Source: Dorfman (1977, p.337).

Collins (1977) reports some results for a study of the 1972 amendments to the (US) Federal Water Pollution Control Act. This act allows for subsidies to be paid to publicly owned waste-water treatment plants. Collins confines his analysis to a specific region – Iowa, Missouri, Kansas, and Nebraska. The subsidies can be construed as benefits to users but, of course, there will be offsetting taxes elsewhere. The objective was therefore to estimate the net burden by an income group. The results show that groups in receipt of incomes up to $5000 p.a. were net gainers, groups between $5000 and $25 000 were net losers, and groups over $25 000 were net gainers. Groups over $50 000 were substantial net gainers.

In short, no regressive pattern was found. Instead, the distribution revealed a redistribution from middle income groups to higher income groups, with low income groups also receiving some net gains. Certainly, if incomes below $10 000 are ignored, strong regressivity of the proposal emerges. Using a general equilibrium model in which input–output coefficients are allowed to change according to levels of sulphur emissions, Johnson (1976) assesses the impact of sulphur restrictions in fuel in Sweden. He concludes that the net incidence of these restrictions is regressive. Whether a tax or a standard is used to secure sulphur reductions the cost per household is positive for the lowest of three selected income groups and negative (i.e. there are net benefits) for the highest two income groups.

This finding is systematic whether the income groups exist in urban, rural, or forest areas. The model itself is of interest, although many economists will have difficulty accepting the use of an absolute value for the marginal utility of income. This magnitude is essential to the model because of the use of a theorem by Aaron and McGuire which argues that the benefits to an individual from a public good are approximated by the quotient of aggregate benefits to the individual's (or group's) marginal utility of income.

14.9 CONCLUSIONS

This paper has concerned itself with an overview of the salient literature on the social incidence of environmental costs and benefits. Some literature has been ignored, particularly one paper by Ricci *et al.* (1977) since it measures 'pro-richness' in terms of income elasticities for the polluting goods rather than for environmental quality itself, and it is not clear if the step from one to the other is straightforward. We have also ignored the radical literature which considers the issue of whether radical philosophies are inimical to, or embrace, environmental quality as an objective. The essential issue here is whether Marxist thinking on nature as an input to be used for man's benefit is 'anti-environmental', or whether, as some new radicals argue, environmental decline is itself a likely source of revolution. These issues are discussed in papers by England and Bluestone (1973) and Bookchin (1974). Finally, we have ignored a major issue relating to the issue of whether environmentalism is elitist within a global context, i.e. whether it is the concern of rich countries as opposed to poor countries. In this respect one may note the concern, and success, of the less developed countries (LDCs) in extending the concept of 'environment' to cover all aspects of the living environment and habitat, so that issues such as housing, water supply, electrification, etc., can be properly considered within the remit of the United Nations programme on environmental improvement. How one defines 'environment' is a matter of choice, and while we do not quarrel with the extended use of the word, we have concentrated here on the natural environment. An interesting survey of LDC attitudes to environmental improvement is provided by Walter (1975, 1978). It is significant that no 'blanket' conclusion emerges from that study.

Two further omissions deserve mention. We have concerned ourselves exclusively with the distribution of environmental benefits across income groups within a given time period. Arguably, the real issue in environmental policy concerns the distribution of benefits and costs over time, especially where long-lived pollutants are concerned. Finally, we have not concerned ourselves with any prospect of an environmental Armageddon brought about by excessive pollution. It need only be said that, if it occurs, such a catastrophe is not likely to be a respecter of persons.

The essential conclusions of the present survey are:

1. The publicness of environmental quality lends prima facie evidence for the fact that the relatively poor are likely to be 'offered' more environmental quality than they want.
2. The publicness of environmental quality should not, however, be exaggerated since, in many cases, environmental bads are localized, thus permitting at least the relatively rich to adjust by changing location. If this locational change takes place in a completely perfect fashion, it could be argued that each income group ends up in the individually most desired location. This may well be consistent with the rich living in unpolluted areas and the poor living in polluted areas.
3. The relocation model needs to be treated with some caution since it fails to deal adequately with the constraints which exist on mobility for low income groups. As such, conclusions about whether they are under- or over-provided with environmental quality must depend on assumptions about their willingness to pay for environmental quality or on actual evidence.
4. If the rich are located in unpolluted areas, this might be construed as indirect evidence for the relocation process described above. We saw that, while the evidence is far from conclusive, it suggests that such a geographical pattern may well exist.
5. There is some evidence to suggest that the poor are over-provided, or will be over-provided, with environmental quality relative to their wants in the United States. This may be true of the entire US programme on environmental quality and seems particularly true of the automobile emission control programme.
6. While such a conclusion holds for net benefits, it is far from clear that the gross benefits of environmental programmes are regressive. Evidence was suggested to support and to deny this proposition.
7. The evidence on the incidence of abatement costs seems to indicate that environmental quality programmes are regressive.
8. Evidence on income elasticities is almost entirely inconclusive. It was shown that house price studies could not be used to estimate income elasticities and that those results that have been reported must not be treated

as empirical findings of the models. Further, the benefit incidence of the Clean Air Act of 1970 in the United States suggests income elasticities of less than unity. Other studies report higher elasticities for noise abatement.

9. The overriding impression, however, is that the methodologies used to estimate such a complex issue as social incidence are such that much more information and study is required before any grand conclusion to the effect that the environment is an 'elite' good can be reached.

APPENDIX: ESTIMATING INCOME ELASTICITIES IN A HEDONIC MODEL FRAMEWORK

The house price differential, or 'hedonic', technique (see Freeman, 1974; Nelson, 1978) starts by assuming that the market value of a house (rent or sale price) is a function of the various attributes of the house. For the ith house, this can be written as:

$$V_i = V(Z_{i1},\ldots,Z_{im}) \qquad \text{for } i = 1,\ldots,n \tag{A14.1}$$

where V_i is the market valuation and the Z_{ij} represent the levels of each of m attributes embodied in the ith house. This function is assumed to be the outcome of a perfectly functioning, well-behaved market for housing. If the above conditions are satisfied, then it is possible to determine the equilibrium marginal price of each attribute by simply estimating equation (A14.1) over all n individuals, giving an equation of the form:

$$V = V(Z_1,\ldots,Z_m) \tag{A14.2}$$

The quantity

$$P_j = \frac{\partial V}{\partial Z_j} \tag{A14.3}$$

is then the marginal hedonic price of the jth characteristic.

Having derived the implicit price of the attribute it is then possible to estimate its demand function (in its inverse form) as

$$P_j = D(Z_{ij}, Y_i,\ldots) \text{ for } i = 1,\ldots,n \tag{A14.4}$$

However, since the supply of housing (and consequently of characteristics) is not price inelastic, the estimation of such an equation in isolation may cause simultaneous equation bias. It should therefore be necessary to specify a supply function of the form

$$P_j = S_j(Z_{ij}, T_i ...) \text{ for } i = 1,...,n \tag{A14.5}$$

where T_i is at least one supply shift variable for the ith house, for identification purposes. Equations (A14.4) and (A14.5) can then be estimated by some simultaneous equation technique to yield equations of the form

$$P_j = D(Z_j Y,...) \tag{A14.6}$$

$$P_j = S(Z_j, T,...) \tag{A14.7}$$

Equation (A14.6) can be rearranged to make Zj the dependent variable, i.e.

$$Z_j = \_(p_j, Y,...) \tag{A14.8}$$

This is now in the form of an explicit demand function for the jth characteristic, in terms of its implicit price and income.

The income elasticity is then simply derived as:

$$E^Y = \frac{\partial Z_i}{\partial Y} \frac{Y}{Z_j} \tag{A14.9}$$

To make the preceding section perfectly clear, it is worth looking at one example of the mathematical specification of the various functions and going through the practical steps involved in calculating the income elasticity.

A favourite specification for the hedonic price equation is a multiplicative function of the form

$$V_i = AZ_{i_1}^{b_1} Z_{i_2}^{b_2} ... Z_{i_m}^{b_m} e_i \tag{A14.10}$$

expressing the value of the ith house as the product of a constant term A, the levels of each of the m characteristics raised to constant powers b_j, and a log-normally distributed error term e_i.

This reduces to the familiar log-linear function

$$\log V_i = \log A + b_1 \log Z_{i1} + b_2 \log Z_{i2} + ... + b_m \log Z_{im} + \mathrm{u_i} \tag{A14.11}$$

where $u_i = \log e_i$ is normally distributed. The coefficients b_j can be estimated by least squares from data on house prices (rents) and their corresponding attribute levels over the sample $i = 1,..., n$ to give

$$\log \hat{V} = \log \hat{A} + \hat{b}_1 \log Z_1 + ... + \hat{b}_m \log Z_m \qquad \text{(A14.12)}$$

Estimates of the implicit marginal equilibrium prices of each of the attributes are then derived by partially differentiating (A14.10) with respect to the attribute levels. If, for instance, $Z_{kj}S$ is a measure of peace and quiet (e.g. the reciprocal of the ambient noise level) then the estimated hedonic price of peace and quiet is

$$\hat{p}k = \partial V \div \partial Z_k = \hat{b}_k V \div Z_k \qquad \text{(A14.13)}$$

In this particular case, the price depends on the value of the house and the amount of peace and quiet. Thus, for each of the n individuals (houses) in the sample we can calculate an implicit equilibrium price for peace and quiet as

$$\hat{P}_{ik} = \hat{b}_k V_i \div Z_{ik} \qquad \text{for } i = 1,..., n \qquad \text{(A14.14)}$$

This gives us a series of prices (over n houses) from which we can estimate the (inverse) demand function for peace and quiet. The actual specification of the demand function will depend on the form of the utility function assumed (as indeed does the original house price function).

Nelson (1978) uses a straightforward linear form. To avoid simultaneous equation bias he also specifies a (linear) supply function. The system looks something like this (for the ith house):

$$\text{Demand:} \qquad P_{ik} = a + bZ_{ik} + cY_i + d\ tastes_i + \varepsilon_i \qquad \text{(A14.15)}$$

$$\text{Supply:} \qquad P_{ik} = a' + b'Z_{ik} + c'\text{ population density } + d'\text{ accessibility}_i + \varepsilon_i' \qquad \text{(A14.16)}$$

The system can then be estimated by two-stage least squares. The (inverse) demand function then looks like:

$$p_k = \hat{a} + \hat{b}Z_k + \hat{c}Y + \hat{d}\ tastes + \hat{\varepsilon} \qquad \text{(A14.17)}$$

where from (A14.15) we should have

$$\hat{b} < 0$$

(since p_k is a marginal price and not total willingness to pay) and

$$\hat{c} > 0$$

This can be rearranged so that

$$Z_k = -\frac{\hat{a}}{\hat{b}} + \frac{1}{\hat{b}} p_k - \frac{\hat{c}}{\hat{b}} Y - \frac{\hat{d}}{\hat{b}} tastes \qquad \text{(A14.18)}$$

or, renaming the coefficients

$$Z_k = \alpha + \beta P_k + \gamma Y + \delta tastes \qquad \text{(A14.19)}$$

where

$$\beta < 0$$

and

$$\gamma > 0$$

as for a usual demand function.

The income elasticity is now derived as

$$E^Y = \partial \frac{Z_k}{\partial} Y \frac{Y}{Z_k} = \gamma \frac{Y}{Z_k} \qquad \text{(A14.20)}$$

or, evaluated at the mean of the sample,

$$E^Y = \gamma \frac{Y}{Z_k}$$

where Y and Z_k are the appropriate sample means.

Had equations (A14.15) and (A14.16) been log-linear instead of linear, the income elasticity would simply have been

$$\partial \log \frac{Z_k}{\partial} \log Y = \gamma \qquad \text{(A14.21)}$$

i.e. a constant (as is necessarily the case in constant elasticity demand functions). In either case, there is no direct way of performing statistical hypothesis or significant tests (e.g. is E^Y equal to unity or not?) on the estimated value, since the derivation of the elasticity involves the use of non-linear transformations. This invalidates the usual statistical methods.

NOTES

1. Originally published in *Progress in Environmental Planning and Resource Management*, Vol. 2, 1980 (John Wiley).
2. In Figure 14.1 the price of securing environmental change is assumed to be the same for each group. This is reasonable up to a point. However, the marginal cost of securing changes in heavily polluted areas is less than the marginal cost of securing a further improvement in an already fairly unpolluted area. To put it another way, the abatement cost function tends to be both increasing and at an increasing rate for pollution reduction. The price lines should be parallel for rich and poor as long as each is being given the same amount on environmental quality, since we have no reason to suppose that the cost of provision will differ between rich and poor areas. But it is arguable that provision of yet more environmental quality in the rich area, beyond the maximum achievable by the poor, could be at a higher and higher cost, thus bending the price line downwards and making it steeper.

REFERENCES

Asch, P. and Seneca, J. (1978), Some evidence on the distribution of air quality, *Land Economies*, **54**, 257–78.

Baumol, W. (1972), Environmental protection and the distribution of incomes, in *Problems of Environmental Economies*. OECD, Paris.

Baumol, W. (1974), Environmental protection and income distribution, in H. Hochman and G. Peterson (eds), *Redistribution Through Public Choice*, Columbia University Press, New York, pp. 93–104.

Baumol, W. and Oates, W. (1975), *The Theory of Environmental Policy*, Prentice-Hall, Englewood Cliffs, NJ.

Beckerman, W. (1974), *In Defence of Economic Growth*, Jonathon Cape, London.

Berry, B. J. (1977), *The Social Burdens of Environmental Pollution*, Ballinger, Cambridge, MA.

Bookchin, M. (1974), Ecology and revolutionary thought, in Roelofs (ed.), *Environment and Society*, Prentice-Hall, Englewood Cliffs, NJ. 187–94.

Collins, R. A. (1977), The distributive effects of Public Law 92-500, *Journal of Environmental Economies and Management*, **4**, 344–54.

Dorfman, N. and Snow, A. (1975), Who will pay for pollution control? *National Tax Journal*, **27**, 101–15.

Dorfman, R. (1977), Incidence of the benefits and costs of environmental programs, *American Economic Review, Papers and Proceedings*, **67**, 330–40.

Edwards, R. (1978), On the impossibility of estimating the social incidence of environmental disamenity through the use of house price depreciation models. Occasional Paper 78 02, Department of Political Economy, University of Aberdeen.

England, R. and Bluestone, B. (1973), Ecology and social conflict, in H.Daly (ed.), *Toward a Steady State Economy*, Freeman, San Francisco, CA, 190–214.

Freeman, A.M. (1972), The distribution of environmental quality, in A.Kneese and B. Bower (eds), *Environmental Quality Analysis*, Johns Hopkins Press for RFF, Baltimore, MD, 243–80.

Freeman, A.M. (1974), On estimating air pollution control benefits from land value studies, *Journal of Environmental Economics and Management*, **1**, 74–83.

Gianessi, L., Peskin, H. and Wolff, E. (1977a), The distributional effects of the uniform air pollution policy in the United States, in *Resources for the Future*, Discussion Paper D-5, Washington, DC.

Gianessi, L., Peskin, H. and Wolff, E. (1977b), The distributional implications of national air pollution damage estimates, in F.T. Juster (ed.), *The Distribution of Economic WellBeing*, Ballinger, Cambridge, MA, 201–26.

Harris, A. (1978), *Valuing Environmental Amenity – A Critique of the House Price Approach.* Occasional Paper 78-01, Department of Political Economy, University of Aberdeen.

Harris, A. (1979), Is quiet a luxury good – a survey approach, *International Journal of Social Economics*, **6**, 177–88.

Harrison D. (1975), *Who Pays for Clean Air*? Ballinger, Cambridge, MA.

Harrison D., and Rubinfeld, D. (1978), Hedonic housing prices and the demand for clean air, *Journal of Environmental Economics and Management*, **5**, 81–102.

Johnson, F.R. (1976), *Income Distributional Effects of Air Pollution Abatement: A General Equilibrium Approach.* Discussion Paper 76-5-3, Department of Economics and Commerce, Simon Fraser University, Vancouver, BC.

Maler, K-G. (1977), A note on the use of property values in estimating marginal willingness to pay for environmental quality, *Journal of Environmental Economics and Management*, **4**, 355–67.

Nelson, J.P. (1978), Residential choice, hedonic prices and the demand for urban air quality, *Journal of Urban Economics*, **5**, 357–69.

Pearce, D.W. (1978), Air pollution, in D.W. Pearce (ed.), *The Valuation of Social Cost*, Allen and Unwin, London, 54–67.

Pearce, D.W. and Edwards, R. (1979), The monetary evaluation of noise nuisance: the implications for policy, in T. O'Riordan and R. D'Arge (eds), *Progress in Environmental Planning and Resource Management*, Vol. I. Wiley, Chichester, 207–220.

Pearce, D.W., Edwards, R. and Harris, A. (1979), *The Social Incidence of Environmental Costs and Benefits*, UK Social Science Research Council, London.

Peskin, H.M. (1978), Environmental policy and the distribution of benefits and costs, in P.R. Portney (ed.), *Current Issues in US Environmental Policy*, Johns Hopkins Press, Baltimore, MD, 144–63.

Ricci, P., Perron, L. and Emmett, B. (1977), Environmental quality, expenditure patterns and urban location: effects on income groups, *Socio-Economic Planning Sciences*, **11**, 249–58.

Waddell, T.E. (1974), *The Economic Damages of Air Pollution*, US Environmental Protection Agency, Washington, DC.

Walter, I. (1975), *Implications of Environmental Policies for the Trade Prospects of Developing Countries – Analysis Based on an UNCTAD Questionnaire*. UN Conference on Trade and Development, Geneva.

Walter, I. (1978), Environmental attitudes in less developed countries, *Resources Policy*, **4**, 200–204.

Walters, A. (1975), *Noise and Prices*, Oxford University Press, Oxford.

Weisbrod, B. (1978), *Distributional Effects of Collective Goods: A Survey Approach.* Discussion Paper 484-78, Institute for Research on Poverty, University of Wisconsin, Madison.

Yan, C-S. *et al.*, (1975), Air pollution control costs and consumption pattern effects: a regional analysis, *Journal of Environmental Economics and Management*, **2**, 60–68.

15. A social discount rate for the United Kingdom

(with David Ulph)[1]

15.1 INTRODUCTION

Discussions about the appropriate discount rate to adopt for public decisions continue unabated. In the United Kingdom, Her Majesty's Treasury has conducted periodic reviews of the theoretical and applied literature in order to assess the appropriateness of 'official' discount rates recommended for public sector decision-making. The last such review was conducted in 1991 and produced two recommended rates: 6% in real terms for public sector projects and 8% in real terms as a required average rate of return. While no official review has taken place since 1991, this paper reports the results of a review of the latest evidence on social discount rates in the context of the United Kingdom. We argue that the 1991 'official' rates are well in excess of any reasonable and defensible discount rate. Our best estimate is 2.4% and a range of 2–4% probably sets the upper and lower bounds of what is a credible social discount rate. Given the very wide disparity between rates of 6-8% and 2-4%, the policy implications are formidable.

15.2 UK GOVERNMENT DISCOUNT RATE POLICY

UK Government policy on discount rates is set out in a guidance document from HM Treasury (HM Treasury, 1991) and is further elaborated in Spackman (1991). The essential features of current guidance are:

- the discount rate relevant to returns accruing to the public sector from projects in the public sector is 6% real terms;
- this rate reflects the opportunity cost of public sector investment in terms of the rate of return to the marginal private sector investment displaced;
- it is also argued to be close to the 'time preference rate';

- public sector agencies selling commercially should use 8% real as a required average rate of return (RRR) since average rates of return are thought to be above marginal rate of return in the private sector;
- a partial exception is made for forestry where management decisions involve the 6% rate, but the Forestry Enterprise is permitted to use 3% as an explicit subsidy.

15.3 SETTING DISCOUNT RATES: CONVENTIONAL CRITERIA

A discount rate is the rate of fall of the social value of public sector income or consumption over time. There are two *numeraires* here – public sector income and the consumption of the public. Hence the discount rate chosen will depend on which numeraire is chosen. Two approaches are usually considered when determining social discount rates:

a. the 'social time preference' (STP) approach;
b. the 'social opportunity cost' (SOC) approach.

The 'social time preference rate' is the rate of fall in the social value of consumption by the public, as opposed to public sector income. It is as well known in the literature as the 'consumption rate of interest' (CRI). SOC is usually identified with the real rate of return earned on a marginal project in the private sector. (Strictly, it is the social return on that project, but this is usually ignored, or some attempt is made to account for it through the estimation of the social costs and benefits of the project rather than through the discount rate.) In Spackman (1991) this rate is referred to as the opportunity cost rate.

Which is the correct rate? There are four observations to make. The first is that, in an economy without any distortions (such as taxes), the two rates are the same. Given that distortions exist in any economy, it would be extremely surprising if the two rates were the same (Baumol, 1986). Hence there is an apparent problem of choosing between them. Second, this choice is better understood if we recall that the two rates relate to different numeraires. It is widely accepted in the literature that the proper procedure is to look at each £1 of investment cost and classify the sources of the cost according to whether they come from consumption or investment. Then, the investment component should be converted into consumption-equivalent units through the 'shadow price of capital', call it v (Lind, 1982; Bradford, 1975). Finally, the resulting consumption equivalent flows should be discounted at the social time preference rate or consumption rate of interest (the CRI). A similar procedure should, in theory, be applied to the resulting benefit flows. Those that accrue as re-investment should be shadow priced at v to convert them to consumption units. Those that accrue as consumption have a consumption value of unity.

However we reconcile the CRI with the SOC there is still, in principle, no single discount rate that emerges as 'the' CRI. There are two reasons for this. The first is that while interest rates to help ensure an intertemporally efficient allocation of resources by reflecting the rate at which society either can or wants to trade off consumption today for consumption in the future, there are infinitely many intertemporally efficient paths. These differ from one another in how they actually transfer resources between people who are alive at different points in time. That is they differ in their intertemporal equity properties. Using a high interest rate today is implicitly to take the view that we do not wish to invest in a lot of capital and other resources which may improve the standard of living of people alive in later years. Which particular intertemporally efficient path we choose to pursue depends fundamentally on value judgements about intertemporal equity. But that means these same value judgements will therefore determine the discount rate, and we will see later on exactly how they enter into the various formulae. All economists can do is to give guidance on what seem 'reasonable' judgements, and the range of values for discount rates to which they give rise. While this point has long been understood, it has featured prominently in recent work by Howarth and Norgaard (1990, 1993).

The second reason why there is in general no such as thing as 'the' CRI is that there is no reason to think that either rate will remain constant over time. For projects of short duration this consideration is unlikely to be important, but for long-lived projects this is important.

What emerges from this procedure is a revised benefit–cost decision rule in which *both* the CRI and the SOC appear, but in which the CRI is the 'fundamental' discount rate. The SOC rate influences the value of v, the shadow price of capital – i.e. the conversion factor that converts investment flows to consumption flows. Estimating the shadow price of capital turns out not to be difficult. A simplified formula is given by Cline (1992). Suppose an investment is made of £1 and it yields an annual payoff of £A over a lifetime of N years. The present value of the consumption stream is:

$$v = \sum_t A(1+s)^{-1}$$

where s is the CRI. If the project has an internal rate of return equal to the rate of return on capital, r, the following equation also has to be satisfied:

$$-1 + \sum_t A(1+r)^{-t} = 0$$

Solving for the value of A in the second equation and substituting it in the first equation gives:

$$v = \frac{r}{1-(1+r)^{-N}} \cdot \frac{1-(1+s)^{-N}}{s}$$

As an example, suppose $r = 8\%$, $s = 2\%$ and $N = 15$, then

$$v = \{0.08/(1-1.08^{-15}\}.\{1-(1.02^{-15}/0.02\}$$
$$= \{0.08/0.68\}.\{0.26/0.02\} = 1.43$$

i.e. the shadow price of capital is 1.43. Notice that it is determined solely by the two discount rates, s and r, and the average lifetime of capital.

The complication with the 'CRI plus shadow price of capital' approach is not the shadow price of capital, but determining the likely proportions of public investment expenditures coming from displaced consumption and investment. A common procedure is to use the ratios I/GNP and C/GNP where I is investment, C is consumption and GNP is Gross National Product. In the UK these ratios would be 17% and 83%.

15.4 WHY IS THE SHADOW PRICING APPROACH NOT USED IN THE UK?

Spackman (1991, para. 31) acknowledges that the shadow pricing procedure is the theoretically correct one. He also agrees that public investment displaces *both* investment and consumption, so that it is not legitimate to argue for an opportunity cost rate alone. Spackman's rationale for not pursuing the shadow pricing approach is (a) that 'the problems of quantifying in practice how much a particular public expenditure is financed by diversion from investment and how much directly from consumption are formidable'; (b) that shadow pricing 'would be quite foreign, and not attractive, to most practical managers'; and (c) 'it appears in practice that, even where time preference and the opportunity cost of displaced investment might in principle conflict, this conflict, at least in present UK circumstances is not generally material' (Spackman, 1991, paras 33–35). In short, the justification for not going down this route is a mix of practicability and the belief that s and r in the equations above are in fact very close to each other.

In what follows we will therefore focus on the determination of the CRI in conventional cost–benefit analysis. Later we discuss arguments that might suggest a lower discount rate is appropriate because of the length of life of projects involving long-term welfare concerns, e.g. radioactive waste disposal. In all the discussion the presumption will be that the CRI is the appropriate rate.

15.5 THE CONSUMPTION RATE OF INTEREST

Whatever approach is adopted, it is necessary to estimate the CRI. It is universally accepted that the formula for estimating the CRI is:

$$s = \delta + \mu . g$$

where δ is referred to as the 'rate of time preference', i.e. the rate at which *utility* is discounted; μ is the elasticity of the marginal utility of consumption schedule; and g is the expected rate of growth in average consumption per capita (Pearce and Nash, 1981; Lind, 1982). In order to estimate s, then, we need estimates of δ, μ and g.

The Rate of Time Preference, δ

There is a great deal of discussion and controversy over what value(s) δ should take. Some of this controversy can be resolved by realizing that there are in fact two factors that enter into the rate of time preference. The first is the rate of 'pure' time preference, which we will denote by ρ. This is the rate at which to discount welfare arising to people in the future purely by virtue of the fact that this utility arises later. The second is any increase (or decrease) in the risk to life. We will let $\dot{L}$ be the rate of growth of life chances. If life chances get worse through time, then this makes for a higher rate of time preference, whereas if they get better then this an argument for a lower rate of time preference. Thus we have the following relationship:

$$\delta = \rho - \dot{L}$$

We discuss the two factors in turn.

Rate of pure time preference, ρ

Spackman (1991, para. 22) suggests that although these 'pure time preference' effects are largely subjective there is no evidence to suggest that they amount to more than a small annual rate of discount. A rate of 1 to 2% a year would amount to discounting marginal utility in 25 years time (roughly one generation) by 20 to 40%.

However a significant number of writers regard zero as the only ethically defensible value for the rate of pure time preference. As Broome (1992) puts it:

> A universal point of view must be impartial about time, and impartiality about time means that no time can count differently from any other. In overall good, judged from a universal point of view, good at one time cannot differ from good at another. Hence.... the [pure time] discount rate... must be nought (Broome, 1992, p.92).

On Broome's analysis, then, the focus of debate shifts to whether impartiality is itself justified. His argument here is that the doctrine of utilitarianism, which is often thought to underlie cost–benefit analysis, itself implies impartiality. 'The doctrine of impartiality – 'each to count for one, and none for more than one' – lies at the heart of utilitarianism' (Broome, 1992, p.95). So, on this view, standard project appraisal, as embraced by HM Treasury, implies utilitarianism; utilitarianism implies impartiality; impartiality implies zero utility discounting. Hence the proper value for the rate of pure time preference, is zero.

However, there are two objections to this view. The first is that all that underlies cost–benefit analysis is a commitment to intertemporal efficiency, with the particular path that is chosen being decided on some grounds of equity. This by no means commits one to utilitarianism as the particular principle for path selection.

The second is that the utilitarianism argued for by Broome (cardinal utilitarianism) has a major difficulty that was pointed out by Sen (1973). While utilitarianism is perfectly consistent with equality as long as all people have equal productive capabilities, when applied to an economy where people have unequal productivities, pursuing a utilitarian objective will lead to what many would regard as the extremely inegalitarian position of having resources taken from the least productive and given to the most productive. One way to correct this problem is to give greater weight in the social objective to those who are least productive. If we look at this from an intertemporal perspective, then there are two factors that tend to make future generations more productive than current ones: capital accumulation, and technical change. Therefore if we applied a strict utilitarian objective function to intertemporal resource allocation the effect would be to redistribute heavily away from the current 'unproductive' generation to the more 'productive' future generation. This would come about through having low interest rates which would encourage a great deal of investment and innovation. So, far from being impartial, utilitarianism would actually lead to re-distribution towards those generations that are likely to be better off. One way to mitigate this problem is to give less weight in the social objective to future generation – which is precisely what a positive rate of pure time preference would do.

Of course, this argument is not itself without problems: in particular, it does not tell us what the appropriate pure rate of time of preference should be. It is also far from obvious that all future generations will indeed be better off than current ones. Indeed, the more cataclysmic environmental prognostications would suggest that environmental degradation may be one of the main factors making future generations worse off than current generations. It remains the case, then, that there is no clear view about what the pure rate of time preference should be.

Changing life chance, $\dot{L}$

As pointed out above, one reason for a positive rate of time preference could be a belief that life chances get smaller over time. This factor seems more amenable to empirical investigation, and less prone to fundamental disputes about value judgements. Nevertheless, there is still disagreement about what precise risks are being discussed, and the various attempts to produce estimates of changing life risks differ in both methodology and in the particular risks being estimated. Thus some authors, such as Kula (1985, 1987), look at the increasing risk of death for an individual as they get older. While this will certainly be an important reason for an individual to favour early consumption over later, it is far from clear what role this should play in discussions about the discount rate. There are three problems: (i) there are factors other than increased probability of death that come into play in an individual's weighting of consumption in different periods – e.g. increased dependence on medical treatment in old age could operate in the opposite direction; (ii) if individuals have adequate opportunity to smooth out their consumption over their lives, it is far from clear why this should lead governments to weight consumption arising at different times in different ways; (iii) if we are dealing with very long-lived projects then the risks that are appropriate are not so much the increasing probability of death of a single individual as they age, but what is happening to the life chances of whole generations. This is the changing risk that Newbery (1992) tries to measure. Newbery's value of $\dot{L}$ = 1.0 can be compared to a value of 1.1 which can be obtained by looking at the UK death rate for 1991 and dividing it by population, i.e.

$$\dot{L} = \frac{\text{Total deaths}}{\text{Total populations}} = \frac{0.647\text{m}}{57.56\text{m}} = 0.011$$

Overall values for $\delta = \rho - \dot{L}$

Table 15.1 brings together various estimates for δ which is further decomposed into separate values for $\dot{L}$ and ρ. The highest estimate for $\dot{L}$ is 2.2% (Kula, 1985) based on individual survival probabilities averaged over a long period of time. For the reasons given above we do not regard this as the right interpretation of $\dot{L}$. Kula's own measure comparable to that of Newbery (1992) is 1.2% (Kula, 1987), while we derived a value of $\dot{L}$ of 1.1%. Thus we take a range of $\dot{L}$ as being zero to 1.2%, with a best estimate of 1.1%. For ρ Table 15.1 shows that only

Scott (1989) derives an estimate independent on the value of $\dot{L}$ and this is set at $\rho = 0.5$. Scott's overall estimate of δ is a fusion of $\dot{L}$ and ρ. Thus, we adopt a range for ρ of 0.5 and a central estimate of 0.3. Table 15.1 also records authors who regard the overall value of δ as being zero, but inspection of this literature suggest that some of them are rejecting positive values of ρ rather than positive values of $\dot{L}$.

Table 15.1 Estimates and views of the rate of time preference

Negative time preference Lowenstein (1987) Lowenstein and Prelec (1991)	$\delta < 0$	Arises when costs (benefits) are viewed as a sequence. Phenomena such as 'savouring' the best until last, and 'getting it over with' – costs preferred now to later, imply negative time preference. Methodology – surveys
Zero time preference Ramsey (1928) Pigou (1932) Broome (1992) and others	$\delta = 0$	$\delta > 0$ 'ethically indefensible' and due to 'weakness of the imagination' (Ramsey); a 'defect of telescopic faculty' (Pigou); $\delta = 0$ justified by impartiality (Broome), etc.
Positive time preference Scott (1977)	$\delta = \rho - \dot{L} = 1.5$ $\dot{L} = -1.0$	$\rho = 0.5$ fits data on UK savings behaviour 1855–1974, raised to 1.5 because of 'risk of total destruction of our society'
Scott (1989)	$\delta = \rho - \dot{L} = 1.3$	See above
Newbery (1992)	$\dot{L} = -1.0$	Consistent with 'perceived risk of the end of mankind in 100 years'
Kula (1985)	$\dot{L} = -2.2$	Based on survival probabilities in the UK 1900–1975, but revised in Kula (1987)
Kula (1987)	$\dot{L} = -1.2$	Based on average probability of death in 1975
This paper (1994)	$\dot{L} = -1.1$	Average probability of death in 1991

The Value of the Elasticity of Marginal Utility of Consumption, μ

The traditional assumption underlying the CRI is that the utility to be gained from the stream of consumption $C = \{C_0, C_1, \ldots C_t \ldots\}$ takes the additively separable form

$$W(C) = \sum_{t=0}^{\infty}(1+\delta)^{-t}U(C_t)$$

where δ is, as before, the discount factor, and $U(C_t)$ is the flow rate of utility accruing in period t from consumption in period t. The marginal utility of consumption is then

$$\frac{dU}{dC}$$

We normally assume that this is positive but strictly decreasing in consumption (diminishing marginal utility). Formally, we assume

$$U'(C) = \frac{dU}{dC} > 0$$

but

$$U''(C) = \frac{d^2U}{dC^2} < 0$$

The elasticity of the marginal utility of consumption, μ, then measures the percentage rate at which the marginal utility falls for every percentage increase in consumption. Formally

$$\mu = -\frac{C.U''(C)}{U'(C)} > 0$$

In general, the value of μ will depend on the level of consumption C. However, a widely used form of utility function is one for which μ is independent of the level of C. This is the iso-elastic utility function:

$$U(C) = \frac{a}{1-\mu}C^{1-\mu}$$

for which the marginal utility is

$$U'(C) = aC^{-\mu}$$

There are two approaches to obtaining estimates of μ.

The first is to regard $W(.)$ as reflecting the views of individuals about how they wish to transfer consumption across time. In this case we try to infer values of μ from observations on individual savings behaviour.

The second is to regard $W(.)$ as reflecting society's judgement about how we should transfer consumption across people at different times. In this case, we think of μ as telling us about how much more worthwhile it is to carry out transfer of income from a rich person to a poor person depending on how well-off the two are.

We now briefly discuss each approach in turn. But before doing so we need to note that a number of economists regard the marginal utility of income as unmeasurable. We discuss below the relevance of this observation for the estimates of μ.

Estimates of μ from observations on individual behaviour

As pointed out above, we can try to estimate μ from the observations on individual savings behaviour. We first explain how this can be done, and then point out how this discussion relates to the view that μ is unmeasurable.

An immediate point to note here is that if we adopt the widely used iso-elastic form of single-period utility function then the intertemporal utility function $W(C)$ is essentially a CES utility function, and μ can also be interpreted as the intertemporal elasticity of substitution. Given the definition of the elasticity of substitution, this means that we can infer values of μ from observations on how sensitive an individual's relative levels of consumption in different periods are to changes in the relative prices of consumption in different periods – i.e. to the rate of interest. Formally, if an individual maximizes lifetime utility subject to an intertemporal budget constraint, then the optimal consumption path satisfies the condition that at all times

$$\mu.\frac{\mathrm{d}C/\mathrm{d}t}{C} = \delta + r_t$$

where r_t is the (instantaneous) rate of interest at time t. So, assuming that we know the factors determining δ, we can in principle determine the value of μ from data which allow us to look at the relationship between the rate of growth of individual consumption and the rate of interest.

The advent of data sets and techniques that allow us to estimate savings behaviour from panel data or pseudo-panel data has enabled recent work on estimating μ. We report later in more detail on the findings by Blundell *et al.* (1994) which give the most authoritative UK estimates.

Now of course there is not a single consumption good in each period, but a whole vector of consumption goods, so consumption at time *t* is to be thought of as total consumption expenditure, and the single-period utility function is essentially an indirect utility function giving the maximum utility available from a given level of expenditure. We know from consumer theory that individual consumption behaviour within each period depends only on individual preferences and not on the particular utility function used to represent these preferences. Thus consumption behaviour within each period is completely unaffected by any monotonic transformation of $U(.)$. Such transformations will, in general, give very different values for the elasticity of the marginal utility of consumption. Thus μ cannot, in principle, be estimated from observations on individual consumption behaviour within each period, and, in this sense, μ is unmeasurable from observed consumption behaviour. Early attempts to estimate μ this way only 'work' because they impose a particular functional form for the single-period utility function. This explains the caution of Stern (1977) and others in interpreting empirical estimates of μ.

Notice, however, that while intertemporal consumption behaviour is also independent of the particular utility function used to represent preferences, the relevant utility function here is $W(.)$. Monotonic transformation of $W(.)$ leaves μ as defined above completely unaffected, since, as we have pointed out, in this intertemporal setting μ is essentially the intertemporal elasticity of substitution, and this is a property of individual preferences for consumption in different periods. Thus Stern's strictures about the non-measurability of μ do not apply to estimates obtained from savings behaviour.

Stern's survey

Stern (1977) is widely quoted in support of 'central' and 'consensus' estimates of the value of μ in the range 1–10. Indeed, his survey appears to have been influential in determining the adopted values of μ used by Spackman (1991), and hence in determining the official view of discount rates in the United Kingdom. Stern uses three approaches to investigate the value of μ:

a. analysis of complete demand systems;
b. von Neumann–Morgenstern utility functions; and
c. savings behaviour.

The theory underlying approach (a) has been addressed above. Assuming some credibility could be given to the estimates, Stern's own survey produces values of μ as low as 0.4 and as high as 10.3. Indeed, he states that:

> From estimates of demand systems .. we have found a concentration of estimates of [μ] around 2 with a range of roughly 0–10 (Stern, 1977, p.221).

This makes the selection of values such as 1.5 or 2 look reasonable, until it is recognized that the value of 10.3 is for South Korea in 1970. In fact, Stern quotes only two UK estimates; –2 from a judgement of Brown and Deaton in 1972, and 2.8 by the same authors based on the 'Rotterdam model'.

Kula (1985, 1987) used an earlier approach of Fellner's. Essentially, this approximates μ as

$$\mu = y_e / p_e$$

where y_e is the income elasticity of demand and p_e is the price elasticity of demand. Stern (1977) notes that this is not accurate, and that Fellner's own estimate is over-stated because of its use.

Approach (b) is analysed by Stern in the context of von Neumann–Morgenstern utility, i.e. behaviour under uncertainty. Once again, additive separability is assumed:

> In this case we have the Ramsey – von Neumann–Morgenstern theorems to support additivity (thus taking the expectation of U(.)), but they do not of course distinguish between U and $\phi(U)$ as measures of overall utility for the individual (Stern, 1977, p.216).

Deaton and Muellbauer (1980) note the same thing. As it happens, it is not clear what we would learn from the uncertainty approach even if it was credible, since the results suggest values of μ of minus infinity to plus infinity.

Finally, Stern looks at saving behaviour for approach (c). Maximizing a lifetime utility function subject to a constraint on saving behaviour, the resulting formula for μ is (see Hicks, 1965):

$$S/\mathrm{Y} = 1/\mu[1 - \rho/r)$$

i.e.

$$\mu = (1 - \rho/r)Y/S$$

where S is saving, Y is income, ρ is the utility discount rate and r is the rate of return on investment. Stern selects $S/Y = 0.1$, $r = 5\%$, and $\rho = 2.5\%$ to obtain $\mu = 5$. If $\rho = 0$, then $\mu = 10$.

Stern's savings behaviour approach thus suggests further evidence for the '0–10' range for μ, making values of 1.5 or 2 look 'reasonable'. But there are major problems. Scott (1989) notes one problem with the savings formula above. If incomes are expected to grow, then 'the formula used by Stern no longer holds' (Scott, 1989, p.233). The correct formula becomes (keeping to our notation):

$$S/Y = [1/\mu)(r - \rho) - y]/[r - y]$$

or

$$\mu = \frac{r - p}{S/Y(r - y) + y}$$

where y is now the expected growth rate of incomes from work. Keeping Stern's figures and putting $y = 0.025$ (Scott's estimate) shows that, once this formula is used, the value of μ becomes 1 to 1.3, not 5 as in Stern's model. Moreover, even if ρ = 0 the upper bound on μ is 1.82, not 10.

Scott's own savings approach simultaneously estimates values of ρ and μ. For the period 1951 to 1973 in the UK Scott obtains ρ = 1.3% and μ = 1.5. This is based on an assumed fit of these values to the equation:

$$r = \rho + \mu.g$$

where r = 4.4% and g = 2.2%. Notice that Scott's μ = 1.5% is nowhere near Stern's value of 5, but is in keeping with the maximum of 1.8% (see above).

Stern himself is very cautious about the uses to which his estimates of μ can be put, but declares that he prefers, 'if forced', the savings behaviour estimates to the demand system estimates, provided better models of savings behaviour are used. As already indicated, those models are now available and μ can be correctly measured within the context of such models.

Empirical estimates of μ: recent work

The range of estimates for μ for the UK would appear to be 0.7 (Kula) to 1.5 (Scott). However, both studies have their problems. As noted above, only studies adopting savings behaviour models are relevant. Thus, Kula's work cannot be used to justify estimates of μ. Scott's work is more relevant, but recent work by Blundell *et al.* (1994) is the most sophisticated analysis yet. For the UK it suggests μ = 0.83 (see Annexe). On this basis a value of μ = 1.5 is unquestionably at the upper end of the range. A value of μ = 1 is defensible and a value relevant to current UK conditions is μ = 0.8 – 0.9.

A 'thought experiment'

The other approach to estimating μ is to regard it as an ethical evaluator, i.e. an indicator of the rate at which consumption should be allocated through time. It is possible to sketch out the implications of different values of μ for egalitarian judgements. Consider two households, one with a consumption twice that of the other, i.e. $C_1 = 2C_2$. Then the ratio of the two marginal utilities of consumption will be

$$\frac{aC_1^{-\mu}}{aC_2^{-\mu}} = 2^{-\mu}$$

This says if we were to transfer 1 unit of consumption from household 1 to household 2, then the loss to household 1 would be worth only a fraction $2^{-\mu}$ of the gain to household 2. This indicates what views we implicitly hold about the desirability of such a redistribution. The figures below set out the implications.

$\mu =$	0.5	0.7	1.0	1.5	2.0	5.0	10.0
$2^{-\mu} =$	0.7	0.6	0.5	0.35	0.25	0.03	negligible

A value of $\mu = 5$ or above effectively means that the social value of an extra £1 to the higher income group is zero or close to zero, underlining the implausibility of such values which, in any event, we show below to have no foundation anyway. A value of $\mu = 1.5$, which is the one selected by Spackman (1991), still implies that the higher income group's extra £1 is valued at only 35% of £1 to the lower income group. As Newbery (1992) remarks, this is a strongly egalitarian judgement.

The Expected Rate of Growth of Per Capita Consumption, *g*

The final component of the STPR is *g*, the expected rate of growth of per capita consumption. There are several considerations relevant to determining *g*. First, if the population choose to substitute leisure for consumption, a value of *g* based on real per capita consumption growth will understate the relevant magnitude. Second, real consumption per capita may fail to reflect rising social costs of consumption, in which case *g* will be overstated. One way to 'smooth out' such considerations is to take very long-run rates of growth in real capita consumption. The relevant data are set out below for the UK:[4]

1885	real per capita consumption at 1985 prices	= £1185
1895		= £1331
1951		= £1891
1992		= £4660

With 1885 or 1895 as base year the resulting value of *g* is 1.3% p.a. If the focus is shifted to the post-war period 1951–1992, then the value of *g* is 2.2% p.a.

Estimates of the CRI

Bringing these estimates together, we can derive an estimate for the CRI (STPR). We offer lower and upper bounds as shown in Table 15.2.

Table 15.2 Estimates of the consumption rate of interest for the UK

Estimates	ρ	$\dot{L}$	μ	g	CRI
Lower bound	0	0	0.7	1.3	0.9
Best estimate	0.3	–1.1	0.8	1.3	2.4
Upper bound	0.5	–1.2	1.5	2.2	5.0

The best estimate that emerges is CRI = 2.4%. If, however, the post-war period is taken as the basis of g, and if, as suggested earlier, a value of $\mu = 1$ is defensible, then a value of CRI = 3.9% emerges (taking the maximum value of $\rho - \dot{L} = 1.7\%$). A range of 2–4% for the CRI would seem to be appropriate, and our own view would be inclined to the lower end of the range. While it is certainly possible to arrive at a figure reasonably close (5%) to the UK Treasury figure of 6%, it is very difficult to justify, since it involves taking upper bound figures on each of the components of the formula. To go much above 4.0% one would either have to (i) be very pessimistic about future survival probabilities for mankind, while at the same time being very optimistic about prospects for consumption growth in the meantime; or (ii) be prepared to discount future generations at a very high rate; or (iii) be very much more egalitarian than people seem to be in terms of the tax policies they are prepared to vote for.

We have seen that there is a great deal of controversy over what is the 'correct' CRI. This partly reflects the point made earlier that there is no conceptually correct single rate. Moreover there is no good reason to think that a single rate should prevail through time. But, with these caveats in mind, we find it impossible to support the continued use of rates in the region of 6% for the UK. Such rates are far too high.

ANNEXE: RECENT SAVINGS MODELS TO ESTIMATE μ

Blundell *et al.* (1994) use a 'pseudo-panel' constructed by taking a time series of repeated cross-sections to estimate a model which simultaneously explains the allocation of household income within and across time periods. The model thus integrates conventional demand theory with savings behaviour in a completely consistent fashion. The data source is the UK Family Expenditure Survey, and the sample consists of over 70 000 households over a 17 year period from 1970–1986.

An important feature of this period is that there is a very obvious structural break in the data at the start of the 1980s. In the 1970s the real interest rate was negative and the average real consumption growth was higher than the real interest rate but tracked the behaviour of the interest rate fairly accurately. At the start of the 1980s the real interest rate rose sharply and was now higher than real consumption growth, moreover real consumption growth no longer tracked the real interest rate. Obviously, people's inflationary expectations dramatically shifted at the start of the 1980s with the arrival of the Thatcher government, and it is important to allow for this.

Abstracting from details to do with the intra-period consumption patterns, the underlying single-period utility function used by Blundell *et al.* (1994) is

$$u(c) = F[V(c)]$$

where c is real consumption, and

$$V(c) = \frac{C^{-\theta} - 1}{-\theta}, \theta > 0;\ F(V) = \frac{V^{1+\rho} - 1}{1+\rho}$$

This implies

$$\mu \equiv -\frac{cu''(c)}{u'(c)} = (1+\theta) - \frac{\rho\theta}{C^{\theta} - 1}$$

The implications of this are that: if $\rho \to 0$ then we get the conventional iso-elastic formulation; as $c \to \infty$, $\mu \to 1 + \theta$; if $\rho > 0$ then μ decreases with c; if $\rho < 0$ then μ increases with c. Blundell *et al.* estimate both θ and ρ, allowing the latter to depend on demographics.

Their findings are:

1. It is extremely important to allow for a behavioural shift at the start of the 1980s through the inclusion of a 1980 dummy – the model gives a much better fit to the data when this is done.
2. It is very important to allow μ to vary. Restricting the utility function to be iso-elastic results in a much more poorly determined equation.
3. Although demographics have a significant effect on intertemporal consumption allocation, their effect is small.

For their preferred equation including the 1980 dummy estimates, $\theta = 0.54$ and ρ is negative. The estimated value of μ at the sample means is 0.83, and the estimates at different percentiles of the income distribution (setting demographics at sample mean) are given in the table below.

percentile (%)	10	25	50	75	90
μ	0.34	0.53	0.71	0.88	1.04

If we look at percentiles of the entire sample we get essentially the same table – figures change only in the second decimal, which illustrates the fact that demographics are not playing a key role.

NOTE

1. This paper is adapted from a report prepared for UK Nirex Ltd and titled 'Discounting and the Early Deep Disposal of Radioactive Waste'. I am indebted to UK Nirex Ltd for permission to reproduce some of the earlier report.

REFERENCES

Baumol, W. (1986), On the social rate of discount, *American Economic Review*, **58**, September, 788–802.

Blundell, R., Browning, M. and Meghir, C. (1994), Consumer demand and the life-cycle allocation of expenditures, *Review of Economic Studies*, **61**, 57–80.

Bradford, D. (1975), Constraints on government investment opportunities and the choice of discount rate, *American Economic Review*, **65**(5), 887–99.

Broome, J. (1992), *Counting the Cost of Global Warming*, White Horse Press, Cambridge.

Cline, W. (1992), *The Economics of Global Warming*, International Institute for International Economics, Washington DC.

Deaton, A. and Muellbauer, J. (1980), *Economics and Consumer Behaviour*, Cambridge University Press, Cambridge.

Hicks, J.R. (1965), *Capital and Growth*, Clarendon Press, Oxford.

Howarth, R.B. and Norgaard, R. (1990), Intergenerational resource rights, efficiency, and social optimality, *Land Economics*, **66**(1), 1–11.

Howarth, R.B. and Norgaard, R. (1993), Intergenerational transfers and the social discount rate, *Environmental and Resource Economics*, **3**, 337–58.

Kula, E. (1985), An empirical investigation on the social time preference rate for the United Kingdom, *Environment and Planning*, **17**, 199–212.

Kula, E. (1987), Social interest rate for public sector appraisal in the United Kingdom, the United States and Canada, *Project Appraisal*, **2**(3), 169–74.

HM Treasury (1991), *Economic Appraisal in Central Government: a Technical Guide for Government Departments*, Her Majesty's Stationery Office, London.

Lind, R.C. (ed.), (1982), *Discounting for Time and Risk in Energy Policy*, Johns Hopkins University Press, Baltimore.

Lowenstein, G. (1987), Anticipation and valuation of delayed consumption, *Economic Journal*, **97**, 666–84.

Lowenstein, G. and Prelec, D. (1991), Negative time preference, *American Economic Association, Papers and Proceedings*, **81**(2), 347–52.

Newbery, D. (1992), *Long Term Discount Rates for the Forest Enterprise*, Department of Applied Economics, Cambridge University, mimeo.

Pearce, D.W. and Nash, C.A. (1981), *The Social Appraisal of Projects: a Text in Cost–Benefit Analysis*, Macmillan, Basingstoke.

Pigou, A.C. (1932), *The Economics of Welfare*, Macmillan, London.

Ramsey, F.P. (1928), A mathematical theory of saving, *Economic Journal*, **38**, 543–59.

Scott, M.F.G. (1977), The test rate of discount and changes in base-level income in the United Kingdom, *Economic Journal*, **87**(346), 219–41.
Scott, M.F.G. (1989), *A New View of Economic Growth*, Clarendon Press, Oxford.
Sen, A.K. (1973), *On Economic Inequality*, Clarendon Press, Oxford.
Spackman, M. (1991), *Discount Rates and Rates of Return in the Public Sector: Economic Issues*, Government Economic Service Working Paper No. 112 (Treasury Working Paper No. 58), HM Treasury, London.
Stern, N. (1977), The marginal valuation of income, in M. Artis and A. Nobay (eds), *Studies in Modern Economic Analysis*, Blackwell, Oxford.

16. Current economic costs of not using risk assessment in environmental policy at the European Community level[1]

16.1 INTRODUCTION

How are risk assessment procedures used by the European Community? The general answer must be that, to date, they have been used sparingly and randomly. There is no evidence to support the view that the Community possesses a rational approach to its use of natural resources, where natural resources here are taken to mean both the natural resources 'in the ground' such as oil and gas, but also the receiving capacities of natural environments to deal with waste products. In this paper we (a) define risk assessment, (b) show how risk assessments contribute to the rational use of natural resources, and (c) try to measure some of the costs of the neglect of risk assessment in the European Community.

16.2 RISK ASSESSMENT

Environmental degradation involves risks for human beings in terms of health damage, and risks for ecological systems in terms of impairing their natural functions. Ecological risk may in turn have impacts, perhaps long-term ones, on human health and well-being. Risk in this context means a deleterious effect associated with some probability (which may be unknown) of it happening. Risk is thus a two-part concept comprising likelihood of occurrence and scale of effect. The process of measuring both likelihood and scale is *risk assessment*. When probabilities are not known, the context is said to be one of *uncertainty*. The distinction between risk and uncertainty is important since absence of knowledge about probabilities has given rise to the *precautionary principle* in European (and other) environmental policy. The precautionary principle requires that action be taken to avoid possible adverse environmental consequences even when the precise nature of risks is not known. *Risk management* is the set of procedures adopted for dealing with risky contexts. In the words of one very influential report:

> Risk assessment is the process by which the form, dimension, and characteristics of...risk are estimated, and risk management is the process by which the risk is reduced (US EPA, 1990).

Probability multiplied by scale of likely effect gives the overall risk arising from an action, where an action may include doing nothing. Environmental policies, then, are aimed at reducing risks, or, to introduce another term for the same thing, are aimed at reducing *expected damage*. Expected damages could be measured by numbers of premature fatalities and this is a common measure of risk. More elaborate health indicators would include expected fatalities and expected incidence of morbidity. Once ecological risk is introduced, the number of indicators multiplies and it is not easy to assess the importance of the effects. A specific form of risk assessment is *comparative risk assessment* whereby two or more risks are compared and then set against the expenditures being undertaken to reduce them. For example, if $100 is spent on reducing risk A by 1×10^{-6} and $100 is spent on reducing risk B by 1×10^{-5} and the risks are in the same units (e.g. lives saved), then expenditure on B is clearly more cost-effective.

If the perspective is anthropocentric, then one way of 'reducing' the multiplicity of heterogenous and non-commensurable effects is to apply weights to each effect. There is a very large number of ways of weighting impacts. One in particular is of relevance to the analysis of EC environmental policy. This involves the weights applied to each impact being expressed as *prices*, where, in turn, the prices reflect the *willingness to pay by individuals* for any benefit in question, or willingness to pay to avoid or prevent some deleterious effect, or cost. This concept of willingness to pay is most familiar in market contexts: prices in the supermarket, for example, reflect the interaction of forces of supply and demand. Demand is simply another way of speaking about consumers' willingness to pay.

Translated in this way, one specific form of risk assessment is *benefit–cost analysis* whereby the risks are 'monetized' (Pearce, 1986; Schmid, 1989). Avoided risks are then benefits and these can be compared to the cost of controlling the risk. In order to achieve this end a considerable number of analytical stages are required. For health risk assessment, for example, it is necessary to establish *dose–response functions* which link the ambient concentration of some pollutant with a health risk of, for example, mortality per 100 000 of the population thought to be at risk from such exposure. If the benefit–cost form of risk assessment is pursued, the resulting 'lives lost' because of the pollutant are valued at some *value of a statistical life* (VOSL). In turn the VOSLs are derived from observed human behaviour in the presence of risk, for example by seeing whether there are wage premia in risky industries which act as monetary compensation for the additional risks. Alternative methodologies include seeking willingness to pay to avoid risks by analysing answers to carefully constructed questionnaires ('contingent valuation'), and looking at expenditures on risk-reducing devices such as smoke alarms ('avertive expenditure approach') (Freeman, 1993). For morbidity the effects may be valued by contingent valuation or, less well founded in economic theory, by the costs of treating diseases (the 'cost of illness' approach). Note that the benefit–cost approach permits comparative risk assessments to be more wide ranging, e.g. by indicating that \$100 spent on B reduces risk by \$X compared to \$aX reduced risk if spent on A (where $a < 1$). Finally, benefits and costs occur over time and benefit–cost approaches all adopt the convention of *discounting* whereby \$1 of benefit or cost occurring in the future counts for less than \$1 of benefit or cost occurring now. The rationale for discounting is essentially that 'society' discounts, i.e. individuals simply prefer the present to the future.

16.3 RISK ASSESSMENT IN THE USA

Risk assessment has been formalized to a considerable extent in the USA. It is essential to have some idea of the experience there because of the thoroughness of risk assessment studies and because of the strange contrast between the USA and Europe whereby Europe has barely adopted any official investigation into relative risks.

In 1987 US EPA Administrator Lee Thomas asked EPA officials to rank 31 environmental risks of interest to the EPA. Administrator William Reilly followed up the resulting report, *Unfinished Business: a Comparative Assessment of Environmental Problems* (US EPA (1987), by seeking a review and analysis of its findings. The final report, *Reducing Risk: Setting Priorities and Strategies for Environmental Protection* (US EPA, 1990), is probably the most detailed and exhaustive analysis of environmental risks yet to be undertaken anywhere in the world. There is no comparable European analysis.

Not only did *Reducing Risk* not espouse the benefit–cost approach to risk assessment, it actually criticized notions of willingness to pay and discounting. It argued that people might attach zero willingness to pay (WTP) to a wetland say, even though it serves important ecological functions. On discounting it argued that it would

> not be a useful analytical tool for sustaining economic development over the long term. The standard practice of discounting future resource values is inappropriate, and it results in policies that lead to the depletion of irreplaceable natural resources (US EPA, 1990).

Both comments are surprising in a major treatise that took a year and a half to produce and which employed some of the best expertise available. If, for example, wetlands serve valuable ecological functions, then these should be reflected in high economic values. All ecological functions have economic value as extensive research into natural environmental systems has shown (Pearce and Moran, 1994). The remarks on discounting are more understandable but the implication that the discount *rate* should be zero is fraught with difficulty. Failure to discount means accepting a discount rate of zero which makes society indifferent between a benefit now and one in the future. Various arguments suggest that this may actually work to the detriment, not the benefit, of the environment (Pearce and Markandya, 1991).

Nonetheless, *Reducing Risk* is a major source of information for any agency seeking to understand the relative scale of risks attached to the various environmental stressors present in modern economies (Finkel and Golding, 1994). Its essential findings were:

a. that the public have different perceptions of risk compared to the 'experts', a fact already signalled in *Unfinished Business* three years previously;
b. ecological risks and risks to human welfare were ranked high, medium and low. High risk threats were habitat modification, loss of biological diversity, global climate change and stratospheric ozone depletion. Medium risks arose from pesticides, surface water pollution, acid deposition and airborne 'toxics'. Low risk issues were oil spills, groundwater pollution, radiation hazards, acid runoff to surface waters and thermal pollution;
c. significant health risks were identified as being related to ambient air pollution (particulates, lead, benzene, carbon monoxide, etc.); worker exposure to chemicals in industry and agriculture; indoor pollution; and drinking water pollution.

Given the extensive detail on all these risks, it is all the more surprising that its impact in Europe appears to have been negligible.

16.4 EUROPEAN COMMUNITY LAW AND THE ENVIRONMENT

The Treaty of Rome establishing the European Community made no reference to the environment. Despite this, the Community introduced environmental legislation from the early 1970s and four 'Environmental Action Plans' (EAPs) were implemented from 1973 to 1992. These programmes developed various principles which are common to the EAPs of which the relevant ones for current purposes are threefold:

> prevention is better than cure; significant damage to the 'ecological balance' should be avoided; the polluter should pay for preventive measures.

The EAPs offer no further guidance than this on how to appraise environmental policy. There is no mention of cost and no mention of benefit or risk reduction.

When the Treaty of Rome was amended in 1987 (the Single European Act) express provision was made for environmental issues, thus providing the Community with a legal basis for action on the environment. The Treaty on European Union (the Maastricht Treaty) added some further embellishments to the relevant Articles.

Article 130r(2) established that 'environmental protection requirements shall be a component of the Community's other policies'. Article 130r(1) established the objectives of EC environmental action as:

> preserving, protecting and improving the quality of the environment; protecting human health; ensuring the prudent and rational utilisation of natural resources.

While the third objective, introduced in the 1987 Single Act and modified slightly by the Maastricht Treaty 1992, appears to offer some approximation to a principle of risk assessment it seems clear that it is intended to refer to the use of resources in the more traditional sense, rather than to the ambient environment as a waste receiving resource. Krämer is of the view that 'natural resources' extends to flora and fauna, but he makes no mention of assimilative environmental functions (Krämer, 1995).

Article 130r(2) offers guiding principles for environmental action:

> preventive action is to be taken; priority should be given to rectifying pollution at source; the polluter should pay.

The Maastricht Treaty added the 'precautionary principle' to these guiding principles. The precautionary principle is discussed below.

Article 130r(3) requires action to take into account four factors:

> scientific data; conditions in the various regions of the EC; *the potential benefits and costs of action or lack of action*; the economic and social development of the EC and the balanced development of its regions. (Emphasis added.)

Literally interpreted, this article introduces a dramatically different note since it makes it clear that, whatever interpretation is placed on the measurement of benefits and cost, some comparison of them is required. This would appear to have been the original intention of the Commission, but the Intergovernmental

Conference of 1987 considered that the phrase was too narrow in scope when translated into other languages. Thus, the phrase 'benefits and costs' remains in the English version but is, according to Krämer (1995) translated as 'advantages and charges' in other linguistic versions. The term 'charges' is supposed to be wider in scope and encompassing 'in particular social costs', although from the English point of view, charges would seem to be a very odd translation of an all-embracing cost concept. By all accounts, then, the reference to benefit and cost appraisal imposes on the Commission an obligation to:

> weigh up the advantages and disadvantages of Community rules before drafting and adopting measures. This appraisal must include, *inter alia*, economic considerations (Krämer, 1995, p68).

While accepting that the phrase 'benefits and costs' need not imply a full, monetized cost–benefit analysis, *some* form of risk assessment is clearly mandated by this provision. The issue in question, then, is how the Commission has taken this requirement into account in formulating its own Directives. At best, it would appear to have done so in only the most loose manner.

16.5 THE PRECAUTIONARY PRINCIPLE

The Maastricht Treaty (The Treaty of European Union) of November 1993 added a further legal obligation for EC environmental policy which is relevant to risk assessment, namely the *precautionary principle* (PP). The PP had appeared in the Dublin Declaration of 1990 (The 'Environmental Imperative') which had elaborated principles for environmental action and had included 'preventive and precautionary action'. The Fifth Environmental Action Plan (5EAP) of 1992 repeated the reference to a 'precautionary approach', but, like the Dublin Declaration, did not define it. Finally, the Maastricht Treaty declared that:

> Community (environmental) policy ...shall be based on the precautionary principle and on the principles that preventive action shall be taken, that environmental damage should as a priority be rectified at source and that the polluter should pay. Environmental protection requirements must be integrated into the definition and implementation of other Community policies.

Again, no definition of the PP is provided. What then might the precautionary principle be?

If individuals are very averse to environmental risk, it suggests a precautionary approach. The insights from risk experiments go a long way to explaining the attraction of a precautionary approach, particularly where there are low probabilities and potentially high damages, where the risk is involuntary (i.e is 'imposed' by others), and where the risk is of loss rather than gain. The precautionary principle may take several forms. In its strictest interpretation it suggests that no action should be taken if there is any likelihood at all, however small, that significant environmental damages could occur. This likelihood may be independent on the scientific evidence. That is, unless there is certainty that there are no detrimental effects, actions should not be taken which, for example, release harmful pollutants into the environment. Perhaps the closest form of the strict PP in practice is the German *Vorsorgeprinzip* -widely translated as the precautionary principle – which is designed to secure *Umweltschutz*, environmental protection, although Krämer (1995) suggests that this is a peculiarly Anglo-American view since German legal writers look to Anglo-American law for its interpretation ! *Umweltschutz* is a constitutional obligation in some German states, but not yet a Federal obligation. As Boehmer-Christiansen shows, *Vorsorge* developed as a justification for state intervention as part of the social democratic movement and as a counter to the prevailing 1970s philosophy that limited environmental protection on cost grounds (Boehmer-Christiansen, 1994). *Vorsorge* requires that environmental risks be detected early (the research focus), that action be taken even without proof of damage when irreversibility is feared, that technology should be developed for preventive action, and that the state has the obligation of environmental protection. There appears to be no mention of cost in this interpretation of the *Vorsorgeprinzip*.

Construed in this way, the precautionary principle can be thought of as one approach to the 'zero-infinity' problem in which the probability of damage is small or unknown, but the consequences are potentially very large. As such, the precautionary principle can be held to apply to both risk and uncertainty contexts. This focus on small or unknown probabilities but major potential damage explains the incorporation of the precautionary principle in the United Nations Framework Convention on Climate Change negotiated in Rio de Janeiro in 1992. Climate change is as yet an uncertain scientific fact. Its consequences could be very large, and certainly so for low-lying countries.

A second interpretation requires that there be a presumption in favour of not harming the environment unless the opportunity costs of that action are, in some sense, very high. Opportunity cost here refers to the cost of taking the precautionary action measured in terms of what has to be surrendered. Taking an extreme example, the cost of global conservation might be the sacrifice of part of economic development generally. Put another way, no significant deterioration of the environment should occur unless the benefits associated with that deterioration heavily outweigh the costs of the deterioration. Effectively, this *safe minimum standards* approach says that the benefit–cost ratio of any project or programme which incidentally damages the environment should be high. While this formulation is somewhat vague, it can be contrasted with the typical cost–benefit rule to the effect that the benefit–cost ratio should be greater than unity. The UK Government's espousal of the PP certainly implies that it is applicable only where the costs incurred in adopting it are low:

> The precautionary principle applies particularly where there are good grounds for judging either that action taken promptly *at comparatively low cost* may avoid more costly damage later, or that irreversible effects may follow if damage is delayed (HM Government, 1990).

Clearly, on these interpretations, adoption of the precautionary principle could be expensive. If the benefits forgone are substantial and new information reveals that the measure turns out not to have been warranted, then there will be a high net cost to precaution. On the other hand, if new information reveals that precaution was justified, nothing is lost. This suggests that some balancing of costs and benefits still must play a role even in contexts where the precautionary principle is thought to apply.

If the PP is interpreted as implying something like safe minimum standards, then the question arises as to the need for economic valuation of environmental costs and benefits. As is well known, such procedures are controversial and some people may feel happier with decision rules which avoid valuation. But there is no escape from valuation, not least because whatever rule is adopted it will imply an economic value. If we adopt safe minimum standards, for example, it effectively says that the avoidance of environmental damage is worth the sacrifice of the economic benefits from the environmentally damaging activity. It is still necessary to have some idea of the cut-off point: when is the forgone cost so large that it justifies environmental damage?

A more sophisticated argument for ignoring the costs of precautionary action arises in the context of biodiversity conservation. The ecologist speaks of the resilience of ecological systems – the ability of those systems to withstand stress and shocks. While it is a disputed proposition in ecology, there is some evidence to suggest that resilience increases with system complexity, and complexity can be measured by biological diversity. In that way, the more diversity there is, the more resilience there is and hence the more sustainable the system is. How does this relate to measuring the costs of the precautionary principle? The connection is that ecological systems may not be 'smooth and continuous'. There may be discontinuities such that it is possible to 'nibble away' at a system without any evident effect until one trips over a threshold and the system itself collapses. If that is true, the PP can be interpreted as avoiding the thresholds. The only relevance for economic valuation would lie in determining where to settle in the system prior to the threshold. But the threshold itself would be determined by 'physical' concerns – ecological information, for example. If the situation is one of being in the region of a threshold, valuation could be irrelevant: all that is needed is to know where the threshold is so that precautions may be taken to avoid going beyond it.

Such an approach is persuasive but problematic. In the first place, life science seems ill-equipped to identify where the thresholds are. It is not then possible to say when valuation is relevant and when it is not. Society may be so far below any threshold that valuation remains important. If thresholds have been passed society should be witnessing system collapses. Some ecologists and environmentalists would identify with that position.

Finally, Krämer argues that the precautionary principle does not in fact translate into more than the preventive principle already enshrined in Community guidelines prior to the Maastricht Treaty. Thus:

> There seems to be no legal situation where Community action would not have been possible under the preventive principle, but is not now possible under the precautionary principle. ..If there is no legal added value to the insertion of the precautionary principle in the Treaty, then this principle should be read together with the preventive principle which it strengthens. The precautionary principle refers to the environmental policy as a whole, while the preventive principle refers in the wording of Article 130r(2) to the individual action (Krämer, 1995, p. 54).

If this is correct, the precautionary principle does not reflect any specific new departure for Community environmental policy. The reasons for doubting this lie mainly in the implied redundancy of the act of inserting the principle in the Maastricht Treaty: it is not easy to understand why the wording would have been chosen. Hession and Macrory (1994), for example, suggest that the principle may be the groundwork for Community provisions on strict liability and rules of evidence in environmental liability and licensing cases.

These excursions into the meaning of terms are essential for an understanding of the extent to which risk assessment is used in the European Community. Interpretations of what risk assessment might mean clearly vary. Moreover, it is far from clear that, by introducing the precautionary principle into the Maastricht Treaty, the Community has embraced consistent environmental objectives. For the Treaty now appears to call for some benefit–cost appraisal, albeit without defining what form this is to take, while at the same time invoking the precautionary principle. But the precautionary principle could be taken to imply that cost considerations are not relevant to environmental policy. Some interpretations of the German precautionary principle could be taken to imply this. If this is correct, the Treaty contains an internal contradiction.

On other interpretations, the precautionary principle is relevant only when probabilities are small or unknown and damage potentially large, as with climate change. In this case, the irrelevance of cost is confined to only those environmental risks taking on a 'zero-infinity' characteristic. In all other cases, cost is relevant to risk assessment. A variation of this view is that the precautionary principle is relevant only when there is some suspicion of irreversibility (Boehmer-Christiansen's view), i.e. when some threshold is exceeded.

A final interpretation is that the precautionary principle urges preventive rather than curative action and that benefit–cost comparisons of some form remain relevant in all contexts. This appears consistent with the US EPA's *Reducing Risk* approach, and with the safe minimum standards approach. It is also, incidentally, consistent with the concept of 'best available technology not entailing excessive cost' (BATNEEC) which is also embodied in Community Directives, since best technology refers to the environmentally cleanest technology available, whereas the 'NEEC' serves as a reminder that this cannot be introduced if it is too costly. Disputes remain, however, as to the meaning of BATNEEC (Pearce and Brisson, 1993).

In what follows we look in detail at one case study on packaging waste, and conclude that no form of risk assessment appears to have informed the resulting Directive. We then take a brief look at other Directives to see if they, too, reflect this pattern.

16.6 CASE STUDY 1: THE PACKAGING AND PACKAGING WASTE DIRECTIVE

The EC Packaging and Packaging Waste Directive was finalized in December 1994 (European Parliament and Council, 1994). The Directive has a chequered history. An earlier 1985 Directive (85/339/EEC) had already attempted to encourage recycling and re-use of beverage containers, but the Commission found the implementation of this Directive to be 'disappointing' with respect to the protection of the environment and some of the measures adopted were regarded as being in restraint of free trade. The early 1990s therefore saw further attempts to secure an effective Directive, but this time extended to all packaging. The thrust of the Directive was to be the qualitative and quantitative prevention of harm to the environment, the former through the proscribing of hazardous contents in packaging, the latter through source reduction and recovery targets.

With respect to qualitative prevention, the second draft of the Directive (1991) specified the substances to be avoided in packaging. Subsequent drafts dropped the naming of the chemicals in question.

On quantitative prevention, the first and second drafts of the Directive set a source reduction target such that, 10 years after its implementation, the per capita output of packaging waste in the European Union should not exceed 150 kg per annum (the estimated output in 1990). This requirement disappeared in the third and subsequent drafts probably because it was seen as unrealistic when viewed against the background of expected economic growth in the Union. The final draft, however, retains the general aim of minimizing packaging subject to maintaining the 'necessary level of safety and acceptance for the packed product' (Annexe II).

Recovery targets changed over the lifetime of the Directive's formation. Early drafts set 'recovery' targets (recycling, re-use, energy recovery) of 60% of all material within 5 years of national implementation of the Directive, with specific targets of 40% of *each material* being recycled. In the long term (10 years) these targets would be 90% and 60%, respectively. By the third draft the 'intermediate target' was modified so that countries could set their own dates for their achievement. In the final draft, the intermediate 5-year targets are the only ones quantified and become ranges of 50–65% for all recovery, 25–45% for overall recycling, and a minimum of 15% recycling for each material. The long-term quantified targets are abandoned in the final draft, but are replaced with the threat of higher, unspecified targets. The 90% recovery target in the early drafts effectively meant that only 10% of packaging waste could go to 'final disposal'. The meaning of 'final disposal' changed as the Directive developed. Early drafts seem clear that final disposal meant landfill *and* incineration: the Commission was known to oppose incineration as a waste management option. But energy recovery from incineration was countenanced since the drafts indicated that, provided the recovered material had a calorific value of 13 megajoules (MJ) per kg, this would count as 'recovery' within the meaning of the Directive, i.e. it would count as part of the 90% long-term recovery target. (This calorific value is roughly that of paper and board.) The confusion was whether this endorsement of incineration meant that packaging waste had to be separately collected before incineration, or whether leaving the waste in the general flow of waste which might then be incinerated was acceptable. The significance of this confusion is that early drafts of Article 5 of the Directive required Member States to exclude from the market all packaging for which there were no established 're-use and recovery channels'. It was therefore unclear whether incinerated mixed household waste containing packaging was an established channel. In the event, this Article disappeared in the final Directive.

In its final form, the Directive may be summarized as follows:

Objectives

To reduce the overall impact of packaging on the environment by reducing packaging at source, eliminating harmful materials in packaging waste, maximizing the recovery of packaging waste for re-use, recycling, composting and energy recovery, and minimizing the quantity going to final disposal (landfill).

To bring national policies on packaging and packaging waste closer together to remove obstacles to trade and competition.

Coverage

The Directive covers all packaging in the European Union – industrial, commercial, office, shop 'or any other level'.

Targets

Within six and one half years of adoption of the Directive (five years from implementation in national law): 50–65% of packaging, by weight, must be recovered where recovery includes any activity which confers economic value on the waste (i.e. recycling, re-use, energy); and 25–45% of packaging by weight must be recycled, with a minimum of 15% of each material (paper, aluminium, steel, plastics) being recycled. These targets are relaxed for Greece, Ireland and Portugal who must attain at least 25% recovery by the five-year deadline, or achieve the five-year targets for the rest of the EU by 2005. 'Substantially increased' targets will be set by the Council in 2005.

The Waste Hierarchy

The terminology used in the Directive is important. 'Prevention' in this context means reductions in the weight of packaging and in any materials harmful to the environment. Re-use involves refilling the same packaging container or using it again 'for the same purpose for which it was conceived' (Article 3.5). Recycling involves the reprocessing of waste packaging to produce the same packaging again or some other product. But recycling does not include energy recovery by burning the waste in incinerators with heat recovery. The Directive is clear in indicating that re-use and recycling are 'preferable in terms of environmental impact' to other forms of recovery and to disposal. This hints at the so-called 'waste hierarchy' which has gained credence in policy discussions on waste management. The waste hierarchy sets out a ranking of waste management options. The ranking, from best to worst, is:

Source reduction
Reuse
Recycling
Composting
Energy recovery
Landfill

The Directive's language makes it clear that the drafters of the Directive favour the waste hierarchy. Thus, source reduction is described as a 'first priority'; reuse and recycling 'should be considered preferable in terms of environmental impact'; reuse is described as something that member States 'may encourage'; recycling is described as 'an important part of recovery' but energy recovery is described only as 'one effective means of packaging waste recovery'. Yet, despite clearly embracing the waste hierarchy, without quite saying so, the Preamble to the Directive states that 'life cycle assessments should be completed as soon as possible to justify a clear hierarchy between reusable, recyclable and recoverable packaging'. Life cycle assessment (LCA) is a technique for measuring the environmental impacts of any product according to each stage of its 'life cycle', from the extraction of raw materials through to final disposal. The Preamble therefore suggests that no LCA has yet been carried out that would justify the lower ranking given to energy recovery compared to recycling and re-use.

Are there any reasons to suppose the waste hierarchy is not a sound ranking of waste management options? The major difficulty with assuming that it is a correct ranking is the assumption that recycling is necessarily better than energy recovery. The problem is that recycling can be very resource intensive. It is reasonable to suppose that the market in recycled products takes care of those materials that can be profitably recycled, i.e. where the costs of collection and reprocessing are less than the price of the recycled material plus any financial savings to reprocessors. Beyond this market-determined level of recycling, which would be the prevailing levels, further recycling would need to be justified in terms of its environmental gains being greater than the extra costs of increasing the levels of collection. One environmental gain is very clear and would justify going beyond market-determined levels of recycling. Every tonne of material recycled is a tonne that is not disposed of to landfill or incineration. Hence waste disposal authorities save the costs of disposal if that tonne is recycled. In the UK this saving is formally recognized through 'recycling credits' such that when a waste collection authority (or, for that matter, any agent) recycles material that would otherwise have to be disposed of it can claim the saved disposal cost from the disposal authority. The remaining question, then, is whether yet more recycling is justified because of environmental savings.

The fact of the matter is that there is no clear answer to this question. Recycling involves various additional costs. If the collection system is a 'kerbside' one whereby vehicles collect material separately, then additional collection costs may be incurred. Moreover, additional truck journeys increase the risks of vehicle air pollution, accidents, congestion and noise. Even if the same number of journeys are made by collection trucks, so that no additional transport costs are incurred, householders and business premises will incur costs of separating and storing differentiated waste. Finally, recycling may itself have environmental impacts. Recycled paper, for example, has to be 'de-inked' and this process can cause pollution problems. Virtanen and Nilsson, for example, found that waste paper recycling, while reducing a number of environmental impacts, led to *increases* in non-renewable energy consumption and hence in sulphur dioxide and nitrogen dioxide emissions, as well as in net carbon dioxide emissions, total suspended solids and biochemical oxygen demand (to water), and net solid waste (Virtanen and Nilsson, 1993).

All these problems get worse when the material to be collected is itself diffuse in nature. This is especially true of plastics of which there are many kinds and which are not substitutable for each other. Thus, while recycling *may* be environmentally preferable to disposal, it may not be. Virtanen and Nilsson, for example, suggest that a balance of energy recovery and recycling is likely to be better than an emphasis on ever more recycling. Yet the EC Directive makes it clear that its targets for the five-year horizon will be substantially increased later.

There is no evidence that the European Commission sought any rigorous justification for its belief in the waste hierarchy. But there is one study that was known to them and which may have influenced them. Schall has attempted a justification of the waste hierarchy for the USA (Schall, 1992). Using data from the New York City region, Schall argues that source reduction results in the following savings:

> around $100 per tonne of waste management costs avoided, plus around $170 per tonne of environmental impacts from the production of the products that eventually become waste.

The calculation here is fairly easy to understand. Every tonne of waste *not* generated means that the costs of disposal are avoided. Those avoided costs comprise the actual resource costs (capital, labour, etc.) of disposing of the waste plus the environmental costs of disposing of the waste – e.g. carbon dioxide and methane emissions from landfill, the environmental costs of transporting the waste, and so on.

These are formidable cost savings and would clearly establish source reduction as the most beneficial 'waste management' option. Schall's analysis takes no account of any costs incurred by business in achieving source reduction, however. On recycling, Schall's estimates suggest that instituting a raised recycling target would be about as expensive as the existing system of final disposal in the New York region. In this respect there is no real support for the ranking in the waste hierarchy, but, equally, it can be argued that the ranking is not contradicted either. Schall cites recycling as being 'no more expensive' than the existing disposal option.

A UK study (CSERGE *et al.*, 1993) has suggested that energy recovery is a highly desirable waste management option. This is because incineration can be an efficient way of recovering energy. The energy recovered, in the form of heat or electricity, displaces energy somewhere else in the energy system. If it is electricity, what is displaced is the least efficient fuel. In the UK this is coal burned in 'old' coal-fired power stations. But the displaced energy means less pollution from the displaced energy source. Hence, incineration has the potential for generating environmental benefits. Recent revisions of the report suggest that these displacement effects are very large, of the order of £10 (around $16) per tonne of waste. If this is correct, energy recovery is likely to be very attractive *vis-à-vis* recycling, contrary to the waste hierarchy.

Setting the Targets

The same problem of 'ad hocery' arises with respect to the targets set in the Directive for recycling. Even if the waste hierarchy is proven to be sensible, it is extremely unlikely that ever stricter targets for recycling make sense. The reason is essentially that the more recycling there is, the more costly it is to recycle one extra tonne of waste. In the economist's language, the 'marginal cost' of recycling rises the more recycling there is. There are at least two reasons why costs might be expected to rise. First, material that is most easy to collect will be collected first and this can be expected to be in centres of high population density where waste generation is geographically concentrated. Such locations also permit the efficient location of recycling plant, i.e. plant will be located so that transportation costs are minimized. As recycling targets increase, so what must be collected becomes geographically more diffuse and hence more expensive to collect. Costs will therefore rise. The second reason is that material uses are such that the uses of them become more and more diffuse. At an extreme, for example, lead in gasoline is not recyclable. Lead in car batteries is. This diffuseness also raises costs as the extra tonne of material to be collected comes from sources which are less 'pure' in terms of quality and less easily recovered. Again, the pressure will be for the extra costs of collection to rise.

To these cost factors must be added another factor but, this time, one that affects the price obtained for recycled materials. The more recycling there is the more material is supplied to the secondary materials market. In some cases, such as aluminium and paper, there are technical limits to the amount of secondary material that can be used in new products – in both cases this is a function of the lower strength of the recycled material. There are also what might be termed social limits: for example, health regulations forbid the use of secondary paper fibres in the manufacture of any container that is in contact with food or drink. In still other cases – paper again is a good example – there are limits set by the available technology. Paper mills need to be converted if they are to make significant increases in the use of secondary fibres. Given all these limits on the size of the market, the effect of increasing the amount of recycled material will be to depress prices, making even existing recycling business less profitable. Perversely, then, the very aim of helping the environment by 'forcing' increased recycling on to the secondary materials market may be counterproductive, with existing recycling activity being harmed.

To an economist these issues are obvious. It is difficult to believe therefore that they were not recognized by the European Commission in developing the Packaging Directive. There is some evidence that the issue was known and understood. But rather than seek some economic evaluation of sensible targets, it appears that the result was an emphasis on 'creating markets' for secondary materials. That is, the Commission became interested in ways of ensuring that there were markets for the excess supply of recycled material. Nonetheless, this initiative does not show through in the Directive. It is true that the target setting changes between early and final drafts of the Directive, but the firm target of 90% 'recovery' of waste in early drafts is consistent with the 50–65% 5-year target in the final draft once allowance is made for the focus in the early drafts on the 10-year horizon. The fact of price falls in face of increased recycling must also have been apparent from the early experience of the German *Duales* system which had been introduced in 1991 with the advent of the *Verpackungsverordnung*, the Packaging Ordnance. This Ordnance established the right of consumers to return their packaging waste to the point of purchase and from there to the producer of the product or the producer of the packaging. The resulting chaos was avoided by making this a threat if the industry did not itself institute a recycling system for the waste – the so-called Dual Waste Management System which is enabled under the Ordnance. The *Duales* system and the Ordnance are of wider interest because of the role they played in influencing the EC Directive, but for the moment the essential fact is that by substantially increasing the supply of recycled material in Germany, prices of materials fell, sometimes to such an extent that Germany exported the waste to other countries at low or even zero cost. This 'dumping' of waste affected recycling industries in other countries. Since this was the subject of official objections to the European Commission about the unfair trade aspects of the *Duales* system under Articles 30-36 and 85-86 of the Treaty, there must have been widespread understanding in Brussels of the effects of increasing supply by setting recycling targets.

How then should recycling targets be set? The strict answer is that they should not be set centrally at all. The proper approach is to ensure that the environmental costs of each waste management option are 'internalized', i.e. incorporated into the costs of waste disposal and recycling. This can be done by levies, charges or taxes and, indeed, such levies already exist or are planned for final disposal in several countries in the European Union: Austria, Belgium, Denmark, Netherlands, France, Italy and the United Kingdom (OECD, 1994). Once *prices* are corrected in this way, the market can then be left to determine how much will be recycled, how much incinerated, how much landfilled and so on. The EC Directive actually enables charges and other 'economic instruments' to be used if Member countries so wish (Article 15) but the logic of setting the charge first and then seeing what 'target' emerges is not recognized in the Directive. The role of economic instruments is simply to achieve the targets if that is how individual countries wish to proceed.

Notice also that rational target setting would be extremely unlikely, except by accident, to come up with the *same* minimum recycling target (15%) for each material. The fact is that different packaging materials have very different environmental impacts. Thus, organic materials generate methane and carbon dioxide in landfills, whereas inert materials do not. The energy used to produce each material varies, and hence so will the life cycle environmental impacts, and so on. This would clearly suggest different environmental impacts and hence different targets for the materials. The Directive's use of a common minimum target underlines the absence of rational target setting.

Setting targets *could* be rational provided a certain condition is fulfilled, namely that the costs and benefits of different target levels are assessed. A rational target would then be one where the maximum difference between benefits and costs is achieved or estimated. Beyond such a point, the extra cost of raising the target will be greater than the extra benefit of tightening target levels. This is how one would have thought Article 130R would be interpreted, i.e. targets would be informed by some sort of benefit–cost appraisal. But it is clear that the targets were not derived in this way.

Risk Assessment and the Packaging/Packaging Waste Directive

What then can be concluded from this analysis of the Packaging Directive? Some conclusions are:

a. Article 130R was in place throughout the period when the new Packaging Directive was being developed. It is just possible that the Commission regarded some US work as being in support of the 'waste hierarchy' implicit in the Directive. However, early drafts of the Directive are in fact far more explicit about the waste hierarchy. A 1992 draft, for example, refers to 'prevention first; recovery and in particular recycling second; final disposal only as a last resort'. It also declares that the ranking of re-use and recovery is not known in the absence of detailed LCAs. In short, the Commission had already embraced the waste hierarchy at the time the US work was becoming available.
b. At no stage was anything that resembles a benefit–cost test applied to the recycling targets in the Directive. Indeed, some of the target setting is clearly inconsistent with any benefit–cost comparison. For example, the likelihood of a benefit–cost test supporting common minimum standards for different materials is remote.

c. Other risk assessment procedures, including the precautionary principle, also appear to have played no role in establishing the context of the Directive. This is more understandable. Packaging waste carries only a negligible threat to human health in itself, although landfill and incineration do contain some health hazards. Nor can 'ecological risk' in the sense of the US *Reducing Risk* analysis be regarded as relevant. Indeed, the issue arises as to why the Commission or, for that matter, national governments generally, should have focused on packaging waste at all. Ecological risks and human health risks from such waste are low to non-existent. Earlier explanatory memoranda attached to the Directive indicated that the problems being addressed were the significant role of packaging in the overall volume of waste and the saturation of landfill sites. Neither assumption appears warranted. In the USA, for example, packaging as a share of total municipal waste fell from 29.5% in 1960 to 27.6% in 1988, a trend repeated in the UK. The 'landfill saturation' problem is true for some EU countries – Denmark, Netherlands and Germany (perhaps). It is not a general EU phenomenon.

There is, then, no evidence that rational assessment procedures were used to design the Directive and set the targets it contains. How costly has this neglect been? Here it is possible only to speculate. Consider, for example, the *Duales* system in Germany which exerted a clear influence on the EC Directive. The costs of the *Duales* have been put at around 4–6 billion DM per annum (annuitized capital costs and operating costs combined). Packaging waste in Germany is probably around 7 million tonnes per annum, and the Packaging Ordnance sets a target of diverting 64–72% of this to recycling, i.e. around 5 million tonnes. The cost of this diversion is therefore some 900–1200 DM per tonne of waste. This needs to be compared to the cost of landfill at some 200 DM per tonne to which might be added a 'scarcity premium' of some 500 DM per tonne because of the scarcity of landfill sites in Germany. Disposal costs will also rise in the future. But even allowing for these factors, the *Duales* system would appear to have added a net cost to German society (all the costs above are for pre-unification Germany).

16.7 CASE STUDY 2: THE HABITATS DIRECTIVE

Council Directive 92/43/EEC of 21 May 1992 relates to the conservation of natural habitats and of wild fauna and flora, the 'Habitats Directive'. The aim is to conserve biological diversity in the Union against the background of continuing decline in natural habitat. Since some habitats are under more serious threat than others, these are singled out for early attention. National conservation plans are to be prepared within two years of the implementation of the Directive. By the year 2000 a network of protected areas throughout the Community is to be established with a legal requirement for Member States to protect these areas in compliance with the Berne Convention on wildlife and natural habitats.

An explicit reference to burden sharing is made since it is recognized that such habitats are unevenly distributed across Member States and countries vary in their financial capacity to invest in conservation. Arguments that the Polluter Pays Principle make it the responsibility of countries to protect their own habitats regardless of financial capacity are rejected since the PPP 'can have only limited application in the special case of conservation' (Preamble). Hence, burden sharing, whereby richer states pay for the conservation of habitats in other countries, becomes a necessity, especially as the habitats are a 'common responsibility' of all Member States. Hence, 'a contribution by means of Community co-financing should be provided for within the limits of resources made available under the Community's Decision' (Preamble).

While the burden sharing arguments are themselves suspect (the PPP can in principle be applied to nature conservation), more relevant for current purposes is a comment made by the Economic and Social Committee in its general Opinion on the Directive, issued in October 1990. The Committee note, among other more general comments on the lack of clarity in the Directive, that:

> the lack of any estimates of the costs of implementation (which will have to be borne by the taxpayers, farmers and industrialists of the Member States) is a serious shortcoming. (Para 1.3)

and

> ..if it is to be effective it will require substantial funding. It would be appropriate to find funds for many of the rural habitats from the funding of the Common Agricultural Policy.. and for the urban habitats from the Community's development funds... (Para 2.9) (Official Journal of the European Communities, C31/1, Economic and Social Committee).

Risk Assessment and the Habitats Directive

The central point arising from this case study is the absence of costings for Community Directives. The listing of habitats in the Community and species to be protected constitutes a form of risk assessment, but, as seen earlier, all risk assessments should contain a cost reference. None was included in the Habitats Directive. The reference to burden sharing makes this omission all the more pertinent since, if applied, it would imply that some Member States would bear not just the unspecified cost of protecting their own habitats and species, but also some share of the equally unspecified costs of protecting the habitats of other

Member States. It is possible that the Habitats Directive was being formulated at a time when the reference to benefits and costs in 130r(3) was itself being debated. It could then be argued that there should be no expectation that the benefit–cost principle should have been applied. However, the discussion about the benefit–cost consideration was extant in 1987, five years before the Habitats Directive was finalized.

16.8 CASE STUDY 3: DRINKING WATER DIRECTIVE

Directive 80/778 – the Drinking Water Directive – fixes maximum concentrations of undesirable substances in drinking water. Amendments to the Directive are still being considered. Various representations have been made concerning the amendments with respect to the need for an appraisal of the costs and benefits of the standards in the Directive. By the end of 1993 no Member State fully complied with the Directive due to difficulties in reaching standards on nitrates, pesticides, coliforms and heavy metals. Widespread opinion suggested that some of the standards – e.g. for nitrates and pesticides – were unnecessarily restrictive (UK Royal Commission, 1995). The EC limit for individual pesticides (0.1 μg/l) and for total pesticides (0.5 μg/l), for example, does not correspond to WHO standards which are generally less stringent, are health-related, and are specific to specific pesticides.

The costs of complying with an amended Directive are thought to be considerable. In the United Kingdom, for example, the lead concentration limit can only be met by replacing lead pipes to water supplies in houses at a cost of billions of UK pounds. The benefits to human health are likely to be small since lead in water represents only a fraction of total lead intake by humans, but there could be other benefits from accelerated pipe replacements such as reduced leakage and increased pressure and flow.

There is no evidence that the Commission ever undertook a cost–benefit appraisal of the standards in the original Directive, but the origins of the Directive pre-date the benefit–cost requirement of 1987. However, some of the technical studies for the amendments are seeking to appraise benefits in qualitative terms and costs in money terms. This is perhaps a sign that 130r(3) is being taken a little more seriously. An interesting UK study suggests that people place high value on clean drinking water, with 98% of respondents citing 'safe to drink' as the most important feature of water standards, together with a surprising 88% citing treating sewage to EC standards (OFWAT, 1992). Average willingness to pay to improve the taste of drinking water was UK £29 per annum in areas with low water charges and UK £49 in high charge areas (Bolt, 1993). Aggregated across 20 million households these figures amount to a minimum of UK £580 million p.a., suggesting that a benefit–cost study might support the Commission's stance on improving quality since the total cost of meeting the Directive standards in the UK has been put at some UK£180 million p.a. (UK Government, 1992).

16.9 CASE STUDY 4: BATHING WATERS DIRECTIVE

The Bathing Waters Directive dates from 1976 and hence predates the benefit–cost requirement in the Single European Act and Maastricht Treaty. This Directive has been controversial and attracted very low levels of compliance until the mid-1980s when the Commission pursued Article 169 on infringements of Community law. By the end of 1993 some 25 judgements on infringements had been given by the European Court of Justice. It is known that the original 1976 Directive was drafted without the benefit of any form of risk assessment. Recent epidemiological work does suggest, however, that the EC standards may be consistent with modern risk assessments. Correlations between enteroviruses and total coliform counts have been found in waters exceeding the EC limits.

Nonetheless, even if the standards do coincide with modern 'no effect' thresholds, the Commission did not itself adopt any risk assessment procedure in evaluating progress under the 'old' directive, nor, more significantly, did it use risk assessment procedures in the proposed 1994 amendment to the Directive (6177/94). Yet the 1994 amendments should have been in compliance with the revised Article 130 of the Treaty. The aim of the 1994 proposals was to simplify and modernize the Directive. The Commission appears to have been aware of the potential criticism that no benefit–cost assessment had been undertaken, arguing that the revised Directive would 'on balance' reduce the financial burden on Member states (i.e. compliance costs are less), that clean bathing waters have financial benefits in the form of tourism, and that clean waters give rise to public health benefits. But no form of quantitative assessment of these impacts was available. In its Explanatory Memorandum, the Commission stated that:

> The assessment in financial terms of the improvement in the quality of the environment and public health is difficult to quantify. There is no reliable basis upon which an objective calculation to measure the value and security of a better environment can be made.

Elsewhere, the Commission explains that the incremental cost of the amended Directive, i.e. the compliance cost over and above the cost of the original Directive, would be zero.

The most exhaustive inquiry into the Directive is unquestionably that of the UK House of Lords (House of Lords 1994, 1995). Their analysis comes close to a benefit–cost assessment. They were themselves scathing in their criticism of the Commission for not pursuing some benefit–cost assessment. Thus:

> It is unacceptable that policy formulation has reached the stage of formal proposal from the Commission for revision of the bathing waters directive without the attachment of a menu of individually costed measures. The Committee deplores that a soundly based cost–benefit analysis has not yet been produced (House of Lords, 1994–5, para 25).

Compliance cost estimates for the UK were produced by the House of Lords committee. These are shown below and include some costs for the urban waste water directive (UWWD) which has as one of its effects the improvement of bathing waters:

Original BW Directive	UK£1.7 billion
Original UWW Directive	UK£7.3 billion

over 10 years. The costs of the proposed revisions depend on the extent to which various forms of treatment would be required. Under various scenarios:

A. secondary treatment and filtration of effluent and disinfection by UV radiation
B,C. different levels of secondary treatment, and UV radiation for discharges within a certain distance of bathing waters
D. insignificant new requirement,

the annuitised costs at 8% are:

A. £200–490m p.a.
B. £140–310m p.a.
C. £ 55–130m p.a.
D. negligible

Self-evidently, these estimates are not consistent with the view that the incremental cost of the revisions is zero (or that the proposal is 'cost neutral' as the Commission put it).

What of the benefits from a revised Directive? The House of Lords expert assessment was that there might be small gains in terms of reduced gastro-intestinal symptoms and eye, throat and ear infections. Their view was that the benefits of the enterovirus standard, the most costly part of the revisions, were zero. On the enterovirus standard the House of Lords states:

> it is hard to see how the Commission could have thought that the new standard would not entail costly capital expenditure.... (House of Lords, 1995, para 15).

16.10 CONCLUSIONS

The requirement for the integration of some form of risk assessment into EC environmental regulation is a recent phenomenon. It centres on one reference to comparing benefits and costs in Article 130r in the Single Act and on the introduction of the Precautionary Principle in the Maastricht Treaty. Even if the benefit–cost reference is construed broadly, it is clear that the Commission has rarely used any *formal* procedure for evaluating new regulations. Certainly, there are no signs of any consistent set of procedures for evaluating risks and costs. But it can be argued that the Commission is not under any formal obligation to adopt such procedures despite the wording of 130r. This is because the whole of 130r(3) is prefaced by saying that these issues shall be 'taken into account', i.e. no specific demonstration of an evaluation of advantages and disadvantages needs to be offered.

The absence of any risk assessment does not mean that the Commission promulgates irrational law. As we have seen, it could be argued that, fortuitously or otherwise, both the Bathing Water Directive and the Drinking Water Directive are consistent with either a precautionary approach or even a benefit–cost approach based on willingness to pay. Nonetheless, consistency with these principles appears to be more of an accident than the result of explicit design. In other areas, there are signs that Directives have been unduly influenced by prior national legislation and that no consideration has been given to the setting of targets and standards. This is certainly the case with the Packaging and Packaging Waste Directive.

Nonetheless, whatever the legal context, the more important issue is whether the Commission *should* adopt formal risk assessment procedures. The United States experience shows how difficult it is to pursue risk assessment and benefit–cost studies to their limit. Equally, that experience has been invaluable in showing how vast sums of public money can be spent to reduce risks only trivially. The US experience also shows the importance of designing procedures that account for the divergence between expert and lay opinion on risks, an area of policy analysis still in desperate need of more and better research. Above all, by not interpreting 130r more formally, the Commission could well be involving Member States in vast expenditures that could more profitably be used elsewhere. Allied to the need for risk assessment in some consistent form across Community environmental policy, is the need for procedures to establish priorities. It is difficult to avoid the impression that the Commission has pursued some issues to a point well beyond their deservingness for policy treatment.

NOTES

1. Originally prepared for a Mentor Group Round Table seminar in London, 1995.

REFERENCES

Boehmer-Christiansen, S. (1994), The Precautionary Principle in Germany – enabling government, in T. O'Riordan and J. Cameron (eds), *Interpreting the Precautionary Principle,* Cameron-May, London, 31–60.

Bolt, C.W. (1993), *The Cost of Quality: Establishing Willingness to Pay in a Regulated Monopoly,* OFWAT, Birmingham.

CSERGE, EFTEC and Warren Spring Laboratory (1993), *Externalities from Landfill and Incineration,* Her Majesty's Stationery Office, London.

European Parliament and Council Directive 94/62/EC of 20 December 1994 on Packaging and Plackaging Waste, *Official Journal of the European Communities,* L365.

Finkel, A. and Golding, D. (eds), (1994), *Worst Things First? The Debate Over Risk-Based National Environmental Profiles,* Resources for the Future, Washington DC.

Freeman III, A.M., (1993), *The Measurement of Environmental and Resource Values: Theory and Methods,* Resources for the future, Washington DC.

Hession, M. and Macrory, R. (1994), Maastricht and the environmental policy of the Community: legal issues of a new environment policy, in D. O'Keeffe and P. Twomey (eds), *Legal Issues of the Maastricht Treaty,* Wiley, London, 151–70.

HM Government, (1990), *This Common Inheritance: Britain's Environmental Strategy,* CM1200, Her Majesty's Stationery Office, London, para 1.88.

Krämer, L. (1995), *E.C Treaty and Environmental Law,* Sweet and Maxwell, London.

Office of Water Supply (Ofwat) (1993), Results of a MORI Poll.

Organisation for Economic Cooperation and Development (OECD), *Managing the Environment: the Role of Economic Instruments,* OECD, Paris.

Pearce, D.W. (1989), *Cost–Benefit Analysis,* Macmillan, London.

Pearce, D.W. and Brisson, I. (1993), 'BATNEEC: The economics of technology-based environmental standards, with a UK case illustration, *Oxford Review of Economic Policy,* **9**(4), Winter, 24–40.

Pearce, D.W. and Markandya, A. (1991), 'Development, environment and the social rate of discount', *World Bank Research Observer,* **6**(2), July, 137–52.

Pearce, D.W and Moran D. (1994), *The Economic Value of Biodiversity,* Earthscan, London.

Schall, J. (1992), *Does the Solid Waste Management Hierarchy Make Sense*?, School of Forestry and Environmental Studies, Yale University, Program on Solid Waste Policy, Working Paper No. 1, October.

Schmid, A. (1989), *Benefit–Cost Analysis,* Westview Press, Colorado.

Schmid, A.A. (1989), *Benefit–Cost Analysis: a Political Economy Approach,* Westview Press, Boulder.

UK Government, *This Common Inheritance: the Third Year Report,* Cm 2549, HMSO, London, 1992.

UK House of Lords, Select Committee on the European Communities, Session 1994–5, 1st Report, *Bathing Water,* HL Paper 6-I; and Session 1994–5, 7th Report, *Bathing Water Revisited,* HL Paper 6-I, London, HMSO.

UK Royal Commission on Environmental Pollution (1995), *Sixteenth Report: Freshwater Quality,* Cm.1966, HMSO, London.

United States Environmental Protection Agency (1987), *Unfinished Business: a Comparative Assessment of Environmental Problems,* EPA, Washington DC.

US Environmental Protection Agency (1990), *Reducing Risk: Setting Priorities and Strategies for Environmental Protection,* Report of the Science Advisory Board: Relative Risk Reduction Strategies Committee, US EPA, Washington DC

Virtanen, Y. and Nilson, S. (1993), *Environmental Impacts of Waste Paper Recycling,* Earthscan, London.

PART 4

Global Environmental Change

17. Competing paradigms for managing environmental change

17.1 ISSUE: ECOLOGICAL 'VERSUS' ENVIRONMENTAL ECONOMICS

We have always had competing paradigms for solving environmental problems. I take a paradigm to be some set of beliefs, assumptions, concepts and accepted procedures for approaching a scientific problem. Paradigms compete because their proponents see them as being mutually exclusive. Advocates tend to 'invest' in one paradigm and hence entrench themselves in a particular position, thereafter tending to be unyielding with respect to challenging paradigms, so-called 'paradigm isolation'. An emerging area of apparent competition between paradigms is that between environmental economics and ecological economics. Environmental economics tends to be further qualified as being neo-classical environmental economics.

We cannot be sure that the emerging paradigm from any battle of paradigms is right. It may be, but it may not be. This is because the 'winning paradigm' may win for reasons unrelated to its intrinsic merit: indeed, we appear not to understand why paradigms change (Kuhn, 1970). And if what emerges is a compromise it may also be wrong.

It is not entirely clear yet exactly what the differences are between these paradigms, but clear candidates for distinguishing them might be:

- a greater emphasis in ecological economics on the well-being of future generations, as typified in writings on sustainability and intergenerational equity;
- a raising of the profile of concern for irreversibility in the sense of irreversible loss of environmental assets such as species and habitats;
- a denial that there is substitutability between some or all natural assets and other assets such as man-made capital. This shows up in concepts like 'critical capital' (Pearce *et al.*, 1989);
- a greater focus on uncertainty about the results of depleting natural assets, combined with a belief that some of the consequences are large in scale;
- a belief that there are thresholds in the effects arising from the gradual depletion of natural assets.

Some features of the debate are worthy of note:

- These are matters of emphasis not absolute content. This is because all of them are entertained in environmental economics to one degree or the other. For example, the literature on the theory of economic growth considered sustainability of economic development paths long ago. What is potentially different is the combined emphasis on all of these.
- These features are not independent of each other. Non-substitutability, for example, explains partly why irreversibility is thought to matter: what is lost may not be substituted for by something else. Irreversible loss may explain thresholds, for example, as one keystone species is lost in a given ecosystem. Scale effects are similarly linked to thresholds. And so on.
- The discussion tends to take place at a fairly generalized level. If we take the substitution issue, for example, very little empirical evidence is offered for, or against, the idea of non-substitutability.
- There is a 'moral tone' to the ecological economics argument, a sense of righteousness. Sustainability is a moral issue, for example, reflecting one or more concepts of stewardship, species rights, obligations to future generations, etc. This moral tone is to be expected in such 'extraparadigmatic' disagreements as Norton (1995) calls them.
- Practitioners of environmental economics may reveal impatience with demands for a new paradigm since the old one has hardly been exploited in practice. Paradigm debates can be seen not just as an offence against vested interests, but as a self-defeating diversion from real-world conservation effort.

17.2 ILLUSTRATING THE PARADIGM DEBATE: ACID RAIN

We can illustrate the competing paradigms with any number of examples. Here we choose acid rain and later we consider global warming.

Figure 17.1 shows the concept of a 'critical load' (CL) – the level of pollution deposition above which damage occurs and below which no damage occurs. In the acid rain context, critical loads are calculated for soils, forests and aquatic ecosystems. A comparable concept for ambient concentrations is a 'critical level'. Note that it is a threshold. Critical loads or levels (CLs) tell us nothing about the nature of damage beyond critical loads. They are 'no risk' targets at which pollution (waste) just equals assimilative capacity of the environment. They are consistent with the precautionary principle since they do not carry risk of damage; with critical natural capital since, if adopted as a target, they imply a

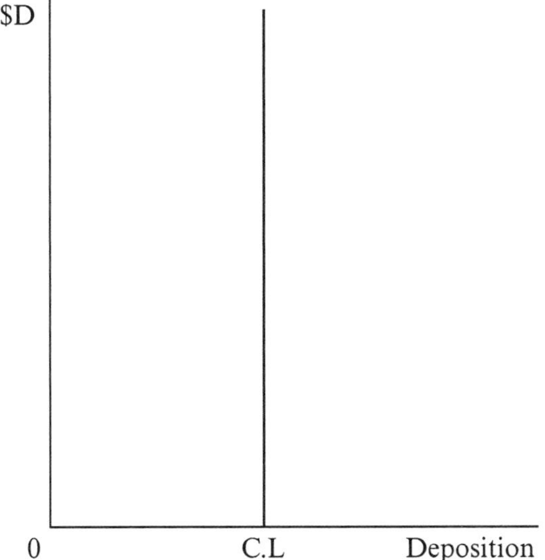

Figure 17.1 Critical loads and acid deposition

persistent conservation of the ecosystem to which they refer. They tend to assume non-substitutability since they imply that they are desirable targets: e.g. the absence of any reference to the nature of damage beyond CLs implies that the only acceptable target is CLs. Note that cost is not mentioned at all in the critical load concept. In practice cost is always relevant to political decisions and so Figure 17.2 introduces the idea of cost.

Figure 17.2 works with marginal abatement cost. Note the direction of the curve: higher costs of taking out more and more pollution. MAC1 is a 'conventional' cost curve relating to technologies of acid rain removal – e.g. flue gas desulphurization. But in reality control costs are lower due to energy conservation and fuel switching, so MAC2 tends to be more relevant. Note the possibility of no regrets opportunities which are usually defined as zero or negative cost activities. The diagram does not tell us where to go unless we believe in CLs, but it does tell us to exhaust no regrets options and to go somewhere between CL and the point where MAC2=0.

Why is cost relevant? This may seem a strange question but it is important because on some interpretations of ecological economics cost is in fact not referred to. This is because zero damage (CLs) are regarded as the only target consistent with:

sustainability (an issue we return to); or
rights of non-humans (otherwise they are harmed); or
Gaia (otherwise Earth is harmed); or
the 'essentiality' of ecosystems, or ecosystem health.

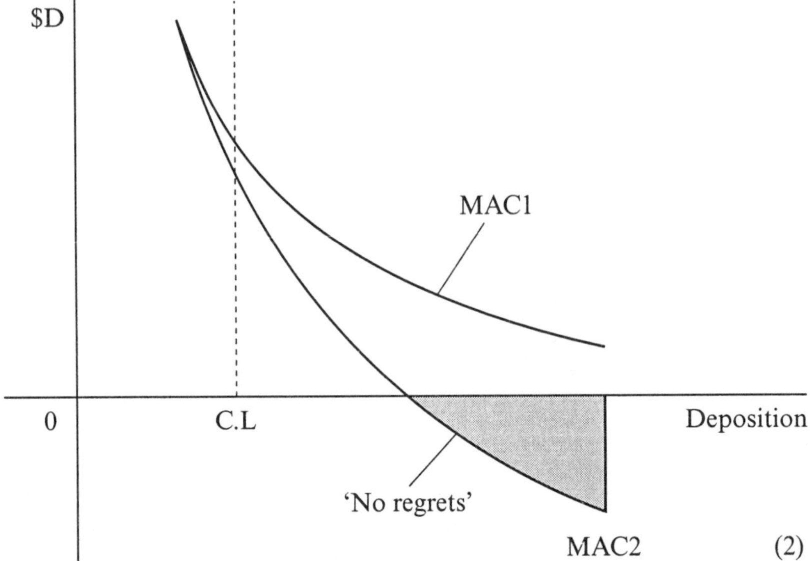

Figure 17.2 Critical loads and abatement costs

For example, in discussing the ecological economics paradigm Norton (1995) makes no reference to cost. The relevance of cost has to be presented in the terms of the alternative paradigm, i.e. in terms of ecological economics. Expressing it in terms of the other paradigm will not do since that amounts to saying ecological economists are not playing by the rules of environmental economists, when it is precisely the point that they do not wish to play by those rules. Is cost then relevant in the ecological economics paradigm? There are some good reasons for supposing that it is. First, costs represent real resources. Money is not just money, but merely the means of measuring real resources. In turn, those resources could have generated some benefits elsewhere, e.g. in controlling global warming, reducing water pollution, improving the health services, and so on. This is why cost for the economist = opportunity cost. We should always add the footnote that costs equal forgone benefits. Forgone benefits equal forgone human well-being, or even non-human well-being. And there may be 'rights' to that well-being. If so, rights are being traded against rights. Putting it this way

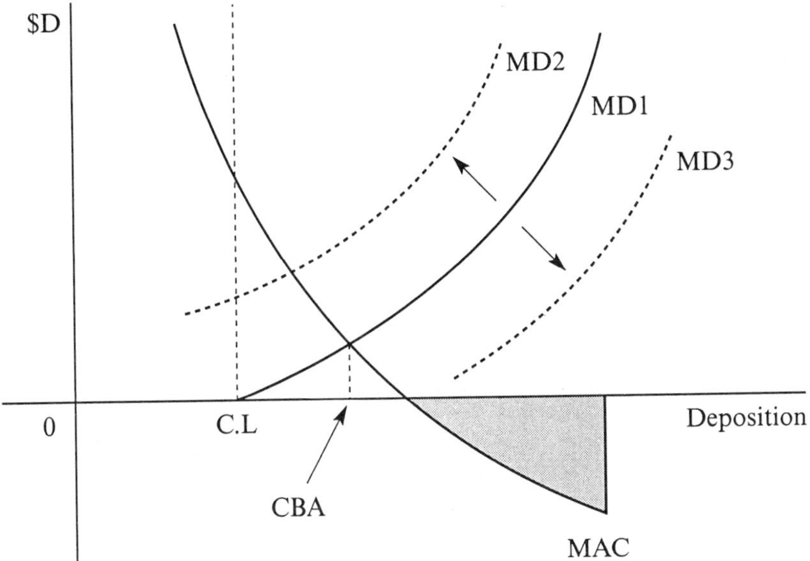

Figure 17.3 Acid rain: costs and benefits

is rather different to saying we are trading rights against cost or rights against money, yet that is exactly how many people argue.

Costs have 'moral invisibility', benefits are morally visible. Should we spend £X in saving one life, when the whole idea of trading lives against money appears abhorrent. Yet £X on one life is £X less on other lives. The one life is morally visible, the other lives are morally invisible. The trade-off is the whole basis of risk analysis which should always be net risk analysis. Unless we have some valid ethical reason for elevating the morally visible above the morally invisible, any paradigm for environmental conservation is logically obliged to take account of cost. What 'meta-ethical principle' exists that would produce a result in which cost is not relevant? (Note that recourse to win win solutions defines a context where the trade-off does not occur. Win win situations are therefore 'morally irrelevant'.)

If there is a trade-off, we must know what we are trading off. Hence we have to have some idea of a damage function. This need not be in terms of money.

Figure 17.3 introduces a damage function, again in marginal terms. If the damage function is in dollar terms we get the familiar 'CBA cross', i.e. the point where marginal costs and benefits are equal. MD1 moves to MD2 if there are secondary benefits, i.e. if by controlling a targeted pollutant other pollutants are 'incidentally' controlled. This has to be read carefully since it is not saying there

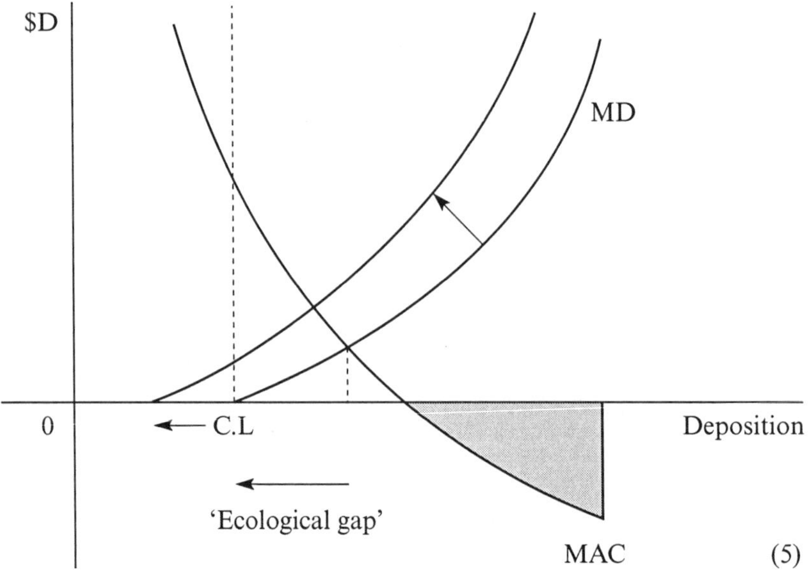

Figure 17.4 Ecological gap and acid deposition

is more damage at each level of deposition, but that the benefits of control exceed the avoided damage from the targeted pollutant. So, if we control SOx we may also control NOx and TSP and we get multiple benefits. Sometimes it works the other way: MD1 shifts to MD3. This might happen if we introduce flue gas desulphurization and make CO_2 emissions worse, for example. Or by controlling sulphur we alter the sulphur/nitrogen balance. Note that if MD2 holds, then more control is dictated by the CBA model. IF MD3 holds, then there is a need to inspect carefully the choice of technology.

We can use the concept of an 'ecological gap' (see Chapter 4) to characterize the apparent difference between ecological objectives (CL) and economic objectives (CBA). Is there common ground between the environmental economist and the ecological economist? We might show how consideration of dynamics could move the two paradigms together. In a dynamic context, the CL itself may depend on the extent to which CLs are exceeded in a previous time period. This is a classic example of a negative feedback. Such negative feedbacks may be very important in contexts where damage is cumulative, as much of it appears to be in the acid rain context. Essentially we are getting the picture shown in Figure 17.4. We see that this means the 'damage function' itself shifts upwards, again shifting the CBA optimum which, however, may never be such that the negative feedback mechanism is avoided. Over a very long period, then, CL may tend to zero: the resource itself becomes extinct. Yet at each instant of time, we are reassured that the situation as we see it is 'optimal'. We 'optimally' extinguish the resource, and we know that is possible from the resource economics literature. Of course, if this dynamic process does not characterize the problem then we may have little problem with the idea of an 'optimum'. What ecological economists are trying to tell us is that such dynamic processes are the norm not the exception.

17.3 ILLUSTRATING THE PARADIGM DEBATE: GLOBAL WARMING

We can apply the same analysis to climate change. Figure 17.5 shows climate change in terms of a rate of surface warming (the horizontal axis). The vertical axis once again shows damage in monetary terms. In this case the threshold is far more uncertain than it is with acid rain. This is because biological change will tend to occur with even minor changes in temperature and because there are 'cycles' of climate change anyway, regardless of any long run trend in rates of warming. Article 2 of the Framework Convention on Climate Change speaks of an 'ultimate objective' of stabilizing greenhouse gas emissions 'at a level that would prevent dangerous anthropogenic interference with the climate system'. But no-one is clear what this level is, or how the term 'dangerous' is to be interpreted. But some writers have argued that the rate of warming is perhaps more important than the absolute level of warming, and that rates in excess of 0.1 degree centigrade per future decade would constitute 'dangerous' interference. This target level comes in part from the lack of historical experience, i.e. mankind has no experience of environments with climate change as rapid as this. Current projected rates of warming are slightly less than 0.2 degrees centigrade per decade, shown here as 'business as usual' (BAU).

In terms of Figure 17.5 any rate of warming to the right of the 0.1 degrees threshold is 'unacceptable' uncertainty. The diagram also shows a marginal abatement cost curve for greenhouse gas emission control. On the basis of available evidence, it would seem that marginal control costs at the BAU level are below zero, although sceptics argue that if this was true such measures would have been implemented already. This explains the shape of the MAC curve. As with the acid rain case, this superimposition of control costs on physically determined thresholds tells us little about what to do. For example, suppose MAC appeared as in Figure 17.5? Then, given that the area under the MAC curve is total cost, the issue might be presented as one of unacceptable or acceptable costs. Choosing a point however looks decidedly indeterminate.

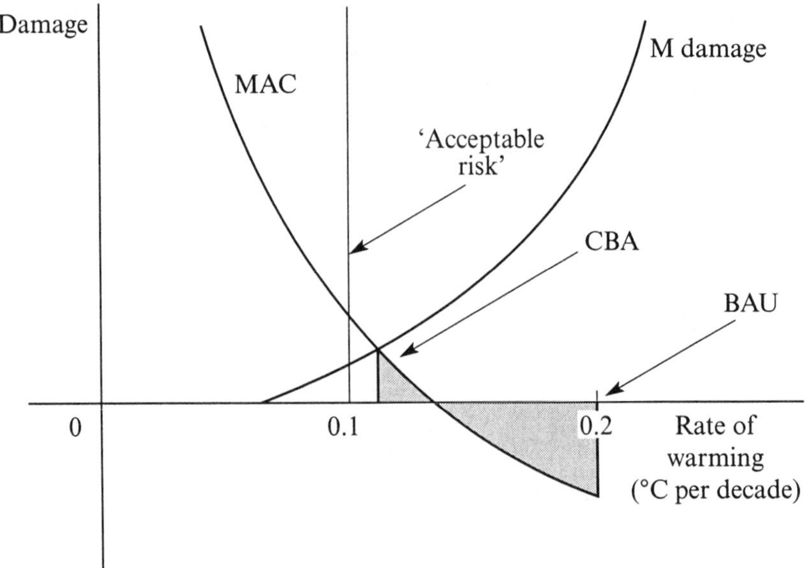

Figure 17.5 Global warming and the precautionary principle

Figure 17.5 imposes a hypothetical marginal damage curve on to the previous analysis. It has been deliberately constructed to show the CBA optimum lying in the zone of uncertainty. What is 'optimal' may therefore not be 'sustainable', just as we found with acid rain critical loads analysis. But if the 0.1 degrees threshold is a genuine threshold, then the cost–benefit optimum dictates longer-run non-sustainability. It also suggests a marked distinction between ideas of 'acceptable risk' and cost–benefit optima. Two reconciliations are possible. First, as with the acid rain case, we could argue that the ecological gap between the threshold and the CBA optimum will set up dynamic changes that will ultimately make the two converge in the long run. The second, and related conciliation, is to argue that the marginal damage curve effectively becomes vertical at the threshold. CBA and thresholds solutions would then be the same. Obviously, what matters is both the rate of dynamic change in ecosystems, about which very little indeed is known (indeed, how could it be known if 0.1 degrees is a threshold based on past 'experience'?), and the rate of discount relevant to the climate change context. This is equally problematic since social discount rates are invariably chosen for well-defined groups of individuals, e.g. a nation. The social discount rate for the world as a whole is unknown.

17.4 EQUITY AND EFFICIENCY

Our diagrams have been presented in terms of economic efficiency. What happens if 'winners' and 'losers' are differentiated according to

a. time,
b. space.

Differentiation in Time

The issue here is that the cost of control/benefit of non-control is borne by the current generation and damages from non-control/benefits of control are borne by future generations. This characterizes acid rain if we think of future generations suffering loss of environmental assets. Weighing costs and benefits seems 'unfair' since the two groups are very different, and indeed, one group may not be able to 'vote'. Ecological economists would argue this position strongly.

How damaging is such an observation for environmental economics? The issue is once again the meaning of cost. For costs borne today to control pollution are potential forgone investments in assets that future generations will inherit. Put another way, control costs could come out of current savings, not consumption. What matters, then, is a comparison of the benefits to future generations from increased investment now, versus the benefits to future generations of diverting those funds to pollution control. A comparison of rates of return to the uses of funds is required and the 'intergenerational' problem does not obviate this. What evidence do we have on this? The interesting thing is that the evidence suggests the UK has been running down environmental assets to finance current consumption: we have been 'cheating our children' (see Chapters 6 and 7).

An offsetting factor is that generations are represented because of overlapping generations, so we should not exaggerate the intergenerational issue.

Differentiation in Space

What happens if the costs of control are borne by one set of people and the damages by another? In the global warming case the rich currently pollute more than the poor in per capita terms, and the rich have the burden of control. But since rich and poor may suffer from global warming there is a shared interest in controlling it, though not a shared interest in equal burden sharing. Cost does not go away as the driving factor. For if we devote resources to controlling global warming out of obligation to the future poor what may be sacrificed is the resources used to conserve environments for the current poor. And we are seeing just that: Eastern Europe instead of Africa and reductions in foreign aid budgets, not increases.

In the acid rain context it is interesting that the rich pollute the rich and the poor pollute the rich as well, so the rich have an interest in paying to control their own pollution and the pollution from the poor. Indeed, bilateral bargains exist whereby the 'victim' pays the polluter not to pollute. Some Scandinavian countries for example, pay the Baltic states to reduce acidic pollutant emissions, and Japan is already making concessional transfers of technology to China because of the emergence of transboundary pollution problems there.

17.5 CONCLUSION

Paradigm challenges are fun, but we need to be careful:

- the history of paradigm fights tends to suggest that one side wins, and we have no guarantee that the 'right' side will win since the 'rightness' of the paradigm may not be the factor determining victory;
- paradigm fights divert attention from the purely pragmatic issue of getting on with solving problems now using the prevailing paradigm. Even if the prevailing paradigm is in some sense 'wrong', using the wrong paradigm to solve problems may be less damaging than doing nothing because no-one is sure what paradigm to use;
- the ecological and environmental economics paradigms in both the acid rain and climate contexts may not be as far apart as people think: a focus on dynamics might help;
- and cost has everything to do with it.

REFERENCES

Kuhn, T. (1970), *The Structure of Scientific Revolutions*, University of Chicago Press, Chicago.

Norton, B. (1995), Evaluating ecosystem states: two competing paradigms, *Ecological Economics*, **14**, 113–127.

Pearce, D.W., Markandya, A. and Barbier, E. (1989), *Blueprint for a Green Economy*, Earthscan, London.

18. The economics of global warming[1]

18.1 INTRODUCTION: GLOBAL WARMING SCIENCE

The Intergovernmental Panel on Climate Change (IPCC) has now produced its 'Second Assessment of Climate Change 1995' and this has appeared as three large volumes together with a separate volume with purports to contain summaries of the three volumes and intended for policy-makers (IPCC, 1996a, 1996b, 1996c, 1996d).

I propose not to dwell long on the scientific findings (Working Group I) since I am not qualified to judge the science. Nor will I be concerned more than superficially with the scenario projections for fossil fuel use: these are clearly important, but deserve a separate treatment (see World Energy Council, 1996a).

By now, most people will be aware that the scientists have gone about as far as they are likely to, given the IPCC remit (on which more below), in confirming that earth surface warming is taking place at some rate greater than natural variability, and that the 'balance of evidence' is that this accelerated warming is due to 'a discernible influence on climate' through the release of greenhouse gases. The actual phrasing in Chapter 8 of Working Group I, is:

> Taken together, these results [from studies of geographical, seasonal and vertical patterns of temperature change] point towards a human influence on global climate. Our ability to quantify the magnitude of this effect is presently limited by uncertainties in key factors, such as the magnitude of longer-term natural variability and the time-evolving patterns of forcing and response to changes in greenhouse gases, aerosols and other human factors (IPCC, 1996a, p. 412).

The actual phrasing in the Policy-makers' Summary begins with the same caution on 'our ability' etc. but ends with:

> The balance of evidence suggests that there is a discernible human influence on global climate (IPCC, 1996d, p. 22).

For some there will be no real distinction between the original and summary statements. Others, however, may consider that the summary statement conveys more certainty than the Chapter 8 statement, and it appears that it was the Summary statement that was seized upon by the media to the effect that the IPCC scientists had now confirmed global warming as being a real and human-induced phenomenon. (For an expression of concern over the difference in interpretations see World Energy Council, 1996a.) Whatever the correct interpretation it seems fair to say that (a) the science is still uncertain, (b) that the degree of uncertainty is disputed, and (c) that care needs to be taken in reaching conclusions based on reading IPCC documents: it matters whether it is the Policymakers' summary that is used or the original chapters, a point we return to. As far as the science is concerned, the correct decision-making context is one of how to behave under uncertainty. We return to this point since it circumscribes the economics of global warming. As a working assumption at least, we assume that global warming is 'confirmed' but that there is uncertainty about rates of change.

Taking the mid-range projections, IPCC I now projects 2°C average temperature increase by 2100 (uncertainty range 1–3.5°C) – a 30% reduction on the 1990 forecasts – and mean sea level rise of 50 cm (range 15–95 cm) by 2100 – a 25% reduction on previous forecasts (IPCC 1996d, p.23). It is important to understand, of course, that these rates of warming will not end in 2100 which is simply an arbitrary benchmark, just like '2xCO_2' concentrations is an arbitrary benchmark. But let us focus on the 2100 figures since this is what most of the literature does.

18.2 THE FEASIBILITY OF PREVENTION

We can make an admittedly crude distinction between 'prevention' and 'adaptation' and I take the latter to include mitigatory measures such as improved sea defences. Recall that Article 2 of the Framework Convention on Climate Change calls for

> stabilization of greenhouse gas concentrations in the atmosphere at a level that would prevent dangerous anthropogenic interference with the climate system. Such a level should be achieved within a time frame sufficient to allow ecosystems to adapt naturally to climate change, to ensure that food production is not threatened and to enable economic development to proceed in a sustainable manner.

The reference to stabilization tends to imply preventive policies and the reference to 'natural adaptation' also suggests prevention rather than managed adaptation. But is prevention feasible? Much depends on the *level* at which concentrations are to be stabilized, and this in turn depends on what level is consistent with the avoidance of 'dangerous interference', something that requires resolution using some assessment of damage at least, but more importantly some measure of the resilience of ecosystems to climate change, i.e. their ability to recover from climate shocks *and* to adapt in the face of further warming. Note also that stabilization of concentrations does *not* mean that warming ceases. Lags in the system will continue to cause warming and sea level rise and therefore, presumably, some forms of damage.

Table 18.1 repeats the central estimates from IPCCI. It is to be read as follows: if CO_2 concentrations are to be stabilized at 450 ppmv around 2075, then CO_2 emissions, worldwide, would have to return to their 1990 levels by the year 2030. If stabilization is at 550 ppmv in 2140, then emissions would have to return to their 1990 levels by 2110, and so on. The emissions in question are CO_2 only and are aggregate emissions. In per capita terms, the current annual average emissions are 1.1 tC per capita from fossil fuels and 0.2 tC for deforestation. Average developed and transitional economy fossil fuel emissions are 2.8 tC and for developing economies the figure is 0.5 tC. Taking world averages first, if the world's population is going to be 10 billion in 2100 compared to 6 billion now, then the scenario in which stabilization occurs at 550 ppmv would imply per capita emission levels in 2110 of about 6/10 =0.6 of today's emissions, a 40% cut. Thus, in 2030 we can expect world population to be 8.5 billion people. For per capita emissions then to be the same as in 1990 (1.3 tC) we compute $8.5*1.3*E = 7.8$ where 7.8 mtC is 1990 gross carbon emissions. $E = 0.7$, i.e. a 30% cut. The corresponding per capita emission cuts are shown in Table 18.1 for each stabilization scenario. (The population projections used are those of IIASA and these do not correspond to those used in the IPCC reports. The invariance of the per capita emission cuts for the higher concentrations arises from IIASA's estimation that the world population will peak at 11.5 billion, and may even decline after that.)

Table 18.1 Atmospheric CO_2 concentrations and world emission profiles

CO_2 concentrations stabilization (ppmv)	Year	'Return point' of emissions relative to 1990	Per capita emission cut at the return point relative to 1990
359	1990		
450	2075	2030	30%
550	2140	2110	40%
650	2190	2150	50%
750	2215	2175	50%

Source: Read off Figures 2.5 and 2.6, Chapter 2 of IPCC (1996a). Unfortunately, the numerical estimates are not shown in the IPCC chapter. Implied population projections are taken from IIASA (1996).

On the face of it, per capita reductions of 30–50% in CO_2 emissions do not appear infeasible. The problems lie more in the facts that (a) these emissions must decline even further after the 'return point', in every scenario case by a further 50% in aggregate and hence more than this in per capita terms at least until 2100 when the IIASA forecasts suggest a stabilized world population, and (b) some allowance has to be made for *growth* in emissions in developing economies, making the required per capita reductions in the developed world even larger. Have we any benchmark against which to judge the *political* feasibility of such reductions, assuming the technical feasibility is established? The omens are not good. A number of publications have noted that most Annex 1 Climate Change Convention Parties will not achieve even their year 2000 targets. The World Energy Council, for example, estimates that between 11 and 13 Annex 1 countries, out of 23, could exceed their 1990 emission levels in 2000 by 10% or more (World Energy Council, 1996b). Now it is arguable that this fairly widespread 'implementation failure' reflects the scientific uncertainty surrounding climate change when the Rio agreement was established, and that this uncertainty has now been reduced. The effect should then be to galvanize countries into real action. But the extent to which the uncertainty has really been reduced is at least questionable, as we saw above, and the issue then arises of whether governments will see the appropriate response to uncertainty being one of dramatic action now or some combination of other measures, including, one has to say, 'wait and see' policies. One does not have to agree with *The Economist* (1996) that the existing implementation failure by Annex 1 countries reduces the Climate Convention to 'farce' to appreciate that the prevailing focus on preventative policies is not going to be sustainable.

18.3 PARADIGMS FOR DECISION-MAKING

We have argued that making decisions about climate change involves determining the 'appropriate' level of abatement and adaptation in a context of scientific and economic uncertainty. Early in the proceedings of Working Group III I offered the IPCC Secretariat a diagram which attempts to encapsulate the 'competing paradigms' for such contexts. This diagram is reproduced here in slightly modified form as Figure 18.1. Figure 18.1 shows various paradigms. The first, of course, is business as usual (BAU), which means doing nothing and hence continuing to warm the Earth at about 0.2°C per decade. A 'no regrets' policy is identified here as doing all those things that have 'negative cost' and which Chapter 9 of IPCC III identifies, albeit in a somewhat haphazard manner. The cost–benefit outcome is clearly identified as the point where marginal control costs equal the marginal damages avoided (*plus* the marginal secondary damages avoided (secondary benefits) on which more below, but for convenience the intersection in Figure 18.1 is shown with marginal climate damages only). The precautionary principle (PP) is identified with the avoidance of rates of

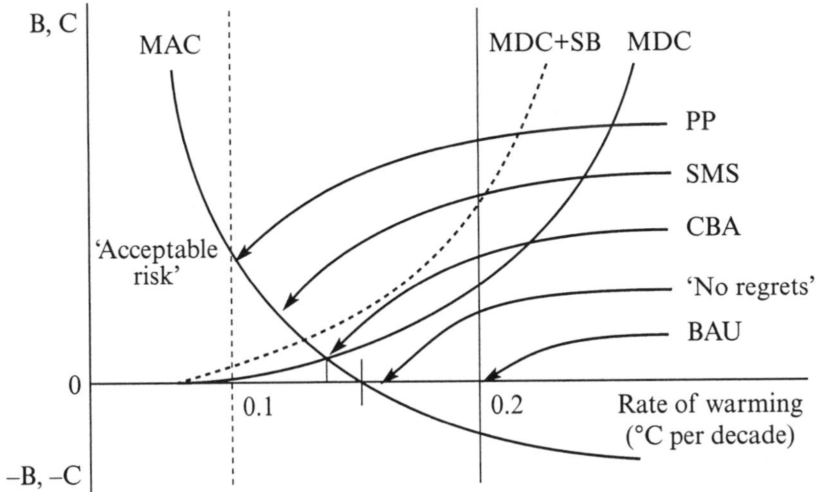

Figure 18.1 Alternative global warming control paradigms

warming in excess of some threshold, shown here as 0.1°C. 'Safe minimum standards' (SMS) is a rule which requires precaution combined with a presumption that 'conservation' is the preferred option *unless* the opportunity costs are 'too high'. Since the meaning of 'too high' costs is indeterminate, we show SMS in terms of a lighter arrow pointing somewhere between PP and CBA.

The elements of this diagram are repeated in Figure 5.10 of IPCC (IPCC 1996c, p.160), but with the horizontal axis reversed and therefore with the damage and cost curves reversed. But there are some other important differences. First, Figure 18.1 shows the abatement cost curve beginning *below* the horizontal axis, reflecting the potential for 'negative cost' control options. The IPCC diagram does not show this. Second, the IPCC diagram identifies a 'precautionary approach' with some point where the marginal damage curve is assumed to be a 'worst case' outcome and the intersection of the marginal damage curve with marginal control costs determines the appropriate level of control. In terms of Figure 18.1 here, however, we identify the precautionary approach with the avoidance of warming values above some threshold, illustrated here by 0.1°C which a number of writers have used as a benchmark (for example, Krause *et al.*, 1990). Indeed, the IPCC approach is not really consistent with the way the precautionary principle has been interpreted in practice: the IPCC approach still equates marginal costs and benefits, whereas the precautionary approach in practice has tended not to mention costs as a determining factor at all (see Chapter 17). The IPCC approach is also curious in identifying the cost–benefit approach as being equivalent to the equation of *expected* costs and benefits (i.e. the probability weighted value of benefits and costs). But there is nothing in cost–benefit analysis that justifies this assumption.

Third, the IPCC diagram makes no reference to 'secondary benefits', the benefits that would accrue in *non-climate* terms from controlling greenhouse gases, and which arise, for example, from the fact that other pollutants and damage-creating effects are produced 'jointly' with greenhouse gases (e.g. conventional air pollutants). Figure 18.1 shows this explicitly, although these secondary benefits appear here as 'secondary damages' from greenhouse gas-creating activities, and there is a quite explicit discussion of secondary benefits in Chapter 6 of IPCC III. More on this shortly because, for some reason, this and other aspects of the discussion on damages, have been systematically ignored by the critics of the cost–benefit approach to climate change.

Now the point of developing Figure 18.1 for IPCC was simply to show that there are competing paradigms for control, that levels of control *up to and including* the CBA optimum should be uncontroversial, and that there are respectable paradigms for going beyond the CBA optimum *but these paradigms all imply costs*. Of course, the CBA optimum *could* coincide with some point inside the 'acceptable risk' area. If so, there should be no debate at all: whichever paradigm we adopt we will get the same policy answer. The fact that there has been so much debate about the cost–benefit paradigm means that this likelihood is perhaps remote and that the diagram as we show it is not an unfair representation of reality.

Why stress the costs elements of all paradigms? The emphasis is not there to suggest that the precautionary or SMS approaches are 'wrong', but to make it clear to everyone that these approaches necessarily imply foregone benefits, i.e. costs either now or in the future. To economists such an observation is so self-evident that they may be surprised to see it being emphasized. But the fact is that in much of the IPCC discussion this obvious fact of a finite world was either not understood or was understood and conveniently ignored. The essential point is that cost is not just money. Cost is a foregone set of opportunities. Moreover, those foregone opportunities can accrue to the current generation – they have to go without something now in order to combat global warming, or they can accrue to future generations, for example in the form of less social capital, less educational capital and even less non-climate environmental capital than they would have otherwise received. Looking at the discussions on equity and discounting and future generations in the IPCC documents and more so in the surrounding commentaries, one could be forgiven for thinking that future generations are the only ones who matter, and that future generations stand only to gain and not to lose from climate change control. The same asymmetry of understanding pervades the philosophical discussions about the 'rights' of future generations, as if cost has nothing to do with rights. One could readily argue that all costs are potential losses of rights since costs necessarily imply a foregone opportunity and that may well mean the opportunity to exercise a right (see Chapter1).

It remains the case that IPCC III failed to explore the competing claims of these paradigms, almost certainly because of the way the volume was devised and executed, with so many different authors that interaction and consistency of theme was sacrificed. It is perhaps this that explains why much of the criticism was focused on the cost–benefit paradigm. Perhaps unwittingly IPCC III does give the impression that it sets more weight on that paradigm than on the others. I think the cost–benefit approach does offer important insights, but in itself cost–benefit does not offer any single answer regarding how to behave under uncertainty as Chapter 2 of IPCC III makes clear in an albeit rather brief discussion. Yet this is the context. A fundamental weakness of the IPCC III report, then, is its failure to be even handed about the competing paradigms, its failure to alert readers to the cost implications of all the paradigms, its failure to link cost and the criteria for more 'absolutist' approaches to climate change such as the rights of future generations, and perhaps its failure to offer better guidance on how to behave under uncertainty.

18.4 THE COST–BENEFIT PARADIGM

Let us take the cost–benefit paradigm and explore it a little. If we take a generous view – and such generosity does stretch credibility somewhat since many of the criticisms had nothing to do with rational argument or even a reading of what was written – it could be argued that what the critics of IPCC III were upset about was the implication that climate change is not a high priority issue because the benefits of control do not exceed the costs. It is possible to have some sympathy with this view simply because the outcome of the IPCC process is so confused and so confusing that it is difficult to get an overall picture of the cost–benefit balance. It categorically does not surface from a reading of the Policymakers' Summary of IPCC III, not least because some of that summary is a political artefact: the summary of Chapter 6, for example, is not a summary at all and was disowned by the main authors of Chapter 6. This perhaps underlines the earlier point that great care has to be exercised in reading the summaries of any of the IPCC volumes. Unfortunately, the alternative is to wade through very hefty volumes in an effort to distil what was actually said.

The July 1995 version of the IPCC Working Group III Policy Makers' Summary (PMS) referred to damages of 1–2% of GDP for developed economies and 2–9% for the developing countries. The overall 'net damages' are put at 1.5–2.0% of GDP. It referred to marginal damage estimates of \$5–125 per tC for carbon emitted now, i.e. the damage done by an extra tonne of carbon. These numbers are taken from IPCCIII Chapter 6. The PMS made no reference to the *benefits* of control. The final published version deletes the numbers for 'per GDP' damage and refers to them as being 'a few percent of world GDP'(IPCC, 1996c, p. 10). It retains the \$5–125tC marginal damage estimates. Again, no reference is made to benefits despite the careful exposition of the concept of secondary benefits in Chapter 6 and that chapter's deliberate distinction between global warming damages and climate change control benefits.

In the July 1995 PMS draft it was stated that costs of control 'may ultimately exceed 1–2% of GDP' for the OECD countries, who would be the ones having to pay, initially anyway. In the final version the 'costs of substantial reductions below 1990 levels [of emissions] could be as high as several per cent of GDP'. The range of annual costs for stabilizing emissions at 1990 levels is minus 0.5% to plus 2% of GDP at some point in 'the next several decades'. Costs in bottom-up studies are thought to be lower and figures are quoted for percentage reductions of 20% plus in emissions at zero or negative cost (IPCC 1996c, p.14). It is also interesting that the PMS on *costs of control* refers to secondary benefits and says they 'may be substantial' (IPCC 1996c, p. 12). But (as far as I can see) Chapter 9 does not discuss secondary benefits at all. Chapter 6 does, but the PMS for Chapter 6 makes no reference to them. Again, one has to express serious reservations about the IPCC process for producing summaries.

But why were the percent-of-GDP damage numbers deleted before the final version of IPCC III? Perhaps to avoid the very confusion that both the IPCC and the critics had generated for themselves, i.e. the comparison of costs of control 'ultimately exceeding 1–2%' (elsewhere in the PMS) and the 1.5–2% of damages in the July version (from Chapter 6). Without further thought it is easy to see that a comparison of 1–2% costs of control and 1–2% damages avoided would suggest to the unwary that costs are about equal to the benefits and hence that little should be done. But that comparison was false anyway, as we show shortly. The same false comparison may also explain, in part, why some critics sought to exaggerate the social costs of climate change, but that is another story which my colleagues and I have dealt with at length elsewhere (Fankhauser *et al.*, 1996).

Why can't costs and benefits be compared? They can, but it takes a little analysis to get there.

First, the '%GDP' figures were never comparable anyway. This point is a little complex and it is easy to see why some readers were confused. Yet Chapter 6 of IPCC III discusses the reasons why the comparison is misleading. The damage figures are for $2 \times CO_2$, ie they relate to some year in the future at which time the atmospheric concentrations of CO_2 have doubled. The $2 \times CO_2$ figure is a benchmark, nothing else. For if global warming goes unchecked, concentrations will more than double and damage will accordingly get bigger than the levels associated with $2 \times CO_2$. Suppose $2 \times CO_2$ occurs in 2050. Then annual damages before 2050 will be less than the 1.5–2.0% of GDP and damages after 2050 will be more than this. The costs of control figures (the minus 0.5 to 2%) relate to emissions stabilization, not to avoiding $2 \times CO_2$. The 'several per cent' relates to an unspecified 'substantial reduction' below the 1990 levels. The damage figures for $2 \times CO_2$ also have to be interpreted carefully for they relate to the damage from $2 \times CO_2$ *as if* it occurred now and related to the world economy as it is now. And just to make things worse, even if benefits are the same as avoided damages, all the damages in any year cannot be reduced because of time lags in the system: if global warming is for real it is too late to do more than reduce *some* of the damage.

Second, *even if* the various percentages were comparable, they are *total* damages and costs. From a comparison of total damages and costs we cannot conclude that nothing should be done, for there may be some level of action less than that addressed by these cost estimates where benefits exceed costs. The proper comparison should be between the *marginal* costs and benefits, i.e. the cost and benefit of reducing an extra tonne of carbon. If the cost–benefit paradigm is pursued (and no-one believes it is the only way of making comparisons, as the discussion of competing paradigms above showed), warming controls should be pursued as long as the marginal cost of abatement is less than the marginal benefit of abatement.

Third, what should be compared is costs and *benefits*, not costs and avoided damages. Benefits exceed avoided damages because warming control policies yield other benefits besides climate change. Thus, control of CO_2 from traffic produces benefits in the form of reduced air pollution, noise, congestion, accidents, etc. This point is made crystal clear in Chapter 6. As we saw, the summary of Chapter 6 does not mention it.

Any policy-maker reading the PMS only will get no sense of these confusions because they are simply not addressed in the PMS. One cannot lay the blame for this degree of confusion at the door of the critics alone, although some less obsessive behaviour on their part about trying to inflate the damage figures, might have opened their eyes to the massive potential for misinterpretation. A significant part of the problem just 'grew' because of the procedure of using so many different authors to address a very complex problem at such length. The wood has got lost because of the trees.

Can anything be rescued? One way to reclaim the need for action is to compare *marginal* benefits and costs. Chapter 6 gives estimates of marginal *damages* ranging from \$5–125 tC and this range is retained in the PMS. Suppose a fairly low figure of \$20 tC is taken as the estimate. This is still not the marginal *benefit* of control. To get benefits we need to add the 'secondary' benefits of carbon control, and these come to perhaps another \$20 tC, taking a low figure from the ranges reported in Chapter 6. So we have a fairly conservative \$40 tC of benefits from preventing one tonne of carbon.

We now need the marginal costs of control. Many of the available estimates are recorded in Chapter 9 of IPCC III, although not always in convenient form. But one thing is clear, there are many, many investments than can be made in carbon sequestration, fuel switching and energy conservation a long way below \$40 tC. Even without the inclusion of secondary benefits, there are many options below \$20 tC.

Why didn't IPCC say so? Part of the problem lies in the constitution of IPCC. IPCC cannot in fact make policy recommendations. It can only record the 'state of the art' and leave it up to policy-makers to infer the policy implications. A careful reading of IPCC III will therefore produce the very result that the critics wanted in so far as they want the cost–benefit implications to favour positive action. But saying benefits exceed costs is tantamount to a policy recommendation and so, if IPCC recognized the inference, they could not make it explicit. Unfortunately, the PMS never even hinted at the inference and, indeed, actually produced the impression that the opposite is the case. The final versions of the PMS are no improvement and are arguably worse.

Would the problem be solved by making damages so large that almost any control cost figure would become irrelevant? This seems to have been the thinking behind the critics' attacks. The guise for this ploy was the 'value of statistical life' (VOSL). Had the VOSL been given its proper name – personal willingness to pay for risk reductions – some of the heat might have gone out of the debate. As it is, the critics chose to refer to this concept as 'the value of life' a phrase that actually does not occur in Chapter 6 of IPCC III and which, in fact, Chapter 6 warns against the use of (see Box 6.1). All individuals, communities and nations clearly trade risks against resources. No society places human life outside the realms of economics, nor could it unless the world had infinite resources (in which case global warming would not be a problem, nor would health care or unemployment). To see how people trade risk and resources one can look at what they are willing to pay to avoid risks and what they are willing to accept by way of compensation to tolerate risks. This is how the economic literature has proceeded. Not surprisingly, since both money measures of risk are constrained by income, those with larger incomes tend to place higher monetary values on risk reduction. Suppose the willingness to pay of each of 100 000 people is \$*x* to eliminate a risk of 1/100 000. Statistically, the risk amounts to one person dying. Hence the value of this *statistical* life is 100 000 × \$*x*. The terminology is unfortunate but well established: it is easy to see how the unwary will go from statistical risks to statistical lives and then to a concept like the 'value of life'. But there is an element of valid concern. If risk has a lower value in country A than country B, would it not be rational to shift the burden of risk to country A? And if IPCC was to embrace a benefit–cost comparison for the benefit of policy-makers, would not the low risk values in developing countries mean that the developed world should do little to curtail global warming?

This is an equity issue and Chapter 6 of IPCC III actually addresses it, and one wonders just how many of the critics actually read Chapter 6 since none of them refer to this discussion. The risks to life in developing countries could be weighted more heavily than in developed countries. Chapter 6 shows how this can be done. The simplest procedure would be to value risks equally across the world on the grounds that we should be no less concerned at reducing risk in the developing world than in the developed world. That is not how the world *actually* behaves (think of foreign aid budgets), but as a moral principle it is a fair one. Chapter 6 does not actually use a common risk value since it reports the literature, but it would make little difference to its results if a common average was used. That should have ended the debate, but it is still not good enough for some of the critics, for they have argued that the *highest* number should be used. If, therefore, a developed country 'statistical life' is 'worth' $2 million, so should the developing country statistical life. But the logic of valuing risks at the highest number is deeply flawed. For the risk values used in developed and developing countries are *averages* within countries. If different values are averaged in one country, they must be averaged across countries. If they are averaged across countries, Chapter 6's results remain. But if the highest average is used for the whole world, then the highest number should be used within any country. The single individual with the highest aversion to risk would dictate the value to be attached to risk for the entire world population at risk.

The mistake made by the critics was to use up their energy in a misleading campaign to make the damages bigger than Chapter 6 makes them appear to be. Their optimal strategy should have been to comb the report for the evidence on the existence of net benefits of control, assemble it and distribute it since they can make appeals for policy where IPCC cannot. Few environmental campaigns have been more ill conceived, and few more counterproductive. For one of the incidental outcomes of this campaign was in making some contribution to the confusion embodied in the policy-makers' summaries.

18.5 NEW ESTIMATES OF GLOBAL WARMING DAMAGE

Fankhauser *et al.* (1996) report some revisions to the IPCC III estimates. For example, using purchasing power parity estimates rather than conventional exchange rates produces a range of damages of 1.1–1.8% of world GDP compared to 1.4–1.9% for $2 \times CO_2$. Equity weighting produces a range of results with the largest increase in damages arising when strong aversion to inequality is built into the analysis, as one would expect. It remains problematic as to why one would use such high aversion factors for climate control measures if they are not to be used for all expenditure decisions, otherwise serious misallocation of resources would arise with say investment in malaria control losing out to investment in greenhouse gas emission control.

Perhaps more problematic for the critics of the cost–benefit approach is the neglect in IPCC III of damage estimates that incorporate adaptation. The reality is, of course, that damages will not occur without people taking mitigating action. At the time of writing IPCC III Chapter 6 few studies incorporated these effects. One set of studies will shortly be produced, but relating only to the USA (Mendelssohn and Neumann, 1997). Table 18.2 reports the results and compares them to the USA figures from earlier studies. Most of the new results are for market effects, so caution needs to be exercised in arguing that the estimates show a marked reduction in damages. But a significant point is that the market impacts are shown not even to have the same sign as previous studies: global warming turns out to be marginally beneficial to the USA's market economy.

Table 18.2 Changes in US damage costs with and without adaptation

	Mendelssohn/ Neumann	Other studies
Market effects		
Agriculture	+11.3	–8.4 to –17.5
Timber	+3.4	–0.7 to –3.3
Water	–3.7	–7.0 to –15.6
Energy	–2.5	–7.9 to –9.9
SLR	–0.1	–7.0 to –9.0
Fishing	–0.4 to + 0.4	na
Total market effects	+ 8.4	–31.0 to –55.3
[% GDP]	[+0.2%]	[–0.7% to –1.3%]
Non-market effects		
Water	–5.7	
Recreation	+4.2	–1.7
Mortality/morbidity	na	–5.8 to – 37.4
Air pollution	na	–3.5 to 7.3

Note: 1990 economy, $billion; + 2.5°C; + = a benefit; – = a cost

18.6 CONCLUSIONS

How far one should go in combating global warming depends on

a. how one treats the available evidence on costs and benefits, and the suggestion here is that the evidence as embodied in IPCC III justifies significant action;
b. how one treats uncertainty, on which IPCC III is effectively not very forthcoming, and on which cost–benefit has little to say beyond urging more rather than less precaution;
c. how one treats the equity issue – see Fankhauser *et al.* (1996);
d. how adaptation affects damages. The hint so far is that it may substantially reduce their size.

NOTE

1. Originally given as a talk to the British Institute of Energy Economics, Shell Mex House, The Strand, London, October 1996.

REFERENCES

Fankhauser, S., Tol, R., Pearce, D.W. and Vellinga, P. (1996), *Extensions and Alternatives to Climate Change Damage Valuation: On the Critique of IPCC Working Group III's Damage Estimates*, Centre for Social and Economic Research on the Global Environment, University College London and Institute for Environmental Studies, Free University of Amsterdam, mimeo.

Intergovernmental Panel on Climate Change (IPCC) (1996a), *Climate Change 1995: The Science of Climate Change: Contribution of Working Group I to the Second Assessment Report of the Intergovernmental Panel on Climate Change*, Cambridge University Press, Cambridge.

Intergovernmental Panel on Climate Change (IPCC) (1996b), *Climate Change 1995: Impacts, Adaptations and Mitigation of Climate Change – Scientific-Technical Analyses: Contribution of Working Group II to the Second Assessment Report of the Intergovernmental Panel on Climate Change*, Cambridge University Press, Cambridge.

Intergovernmental Panel on Climate Change (IPCC) (1996c), *Climate Change 1995: Economic and Social Dimensions of Climate Change: Contribution of Working Group III to the Second Assessment Report of the Intergovernmental Panel on Climate Change*, Cambridge University Press, Cambridge.

Intergovernmental Panel on Climate Change (IPCC) (1996d), *IPCC Second Assessment: Climate Change 1995*, World Meteorological Organisation and United Nations Environment Programme.

International Institute for Applied Systems Analysis (IIASA) (1996), The human race slows to a crawl, *Options*, Summer, 12–15.

Krause, F., Bach, W. and Kooney J. (1990), *Energy Policy in the Greenhouse*, Earthscan, London.

Mendelssohn, R. and Neumann, J. (1998), *The Impacts of Climate Change on the US Economy*, Cambridge University Press, forthcoming.

World Energy Council (1996a), *Climate Change 1995: The Intergovernmental Panel on Climate Change Second Assessment Report Reviewed*, Report No.5, World Energy Council, March, London.

World Energy Council (1996b), *Climate Change Negotiations: COP-2 and Beyond*, Report No.6, September, World Energy Council, London.

19. The role of carbon taxes in adjusting to global warming[1]

19.1 INTRODUCTION

In August 1990, Working Group 1 of the United Nations Intergovernmental Panel on Climate Change (IPCC) published its assessment of the scientific evidence on global warming (Houghton *et al.*, 1990). Referring to the greenhouse effect as a natural phenomenon, the Working Group was none the less of the opinion that: emissions resulting from human activities are substantially increasing the atmospheric concentrations of the greenhouse gases: carbon dioxide, methane, chlorofluorocarbons (CFCs) and nitrous oxide. These emissions will enhance the greenhouse effect, resulting on average in an additional warming of the Earth's surface. The main greenhouse gas, water vapour, will increase in response to global warming and further enhance it.

Scientific opinion continues to differ on the extent to which global warming is 'real', although the IPCC report poses a formidable challenge for anyone choosing not to believe it. From the economic standpoint, the uncertainty is unlikely to alter the appropriate policy stance, provided certain conditions are met. These are:

a. that if warming occurs it will impose significant damage;
b. that the damage is irreversible;
c. that the initial costs of controlling greenhouse gas emissions are low,
d. that greenhouse gas controls bring incidental or joint benefits besides the containment of global warming.

While the evidence about these conditions is itself disputed, even the central projections of global warming in the IPCC scenarios take the world into rates of warming, and, eventually, levels of warming outside the known tolerances of ecosystems in which mankind has a stake. If so, there is genuine uncertainty which alone should dictate a cautious stance in policy terms (Pearce, 1990).

Moreover to all intents and purposes, global warming is irreversible. Damages ought therefore to attract a higher weighting than comparable costs, either (a) through the inclusion of damage costs over very long time horizons (technically, to infinity) – in which case the issue of the choice of the appropriate discount rate arises, or (b) through some premium on costs for aversion to irreversible damage – reflecting some assessment of intertemporal equity.

The evidence on costs supports divergent views, from grave doubts over the economic ability of the developed world to cut back emissions sufficiently to avoid potential catastrophes, to judgements that cut-backs actually have acceptable rates of return even without counting the benefits of reduced warming. For a pessimistic view on costs see Manne and Richels (1990). For a critique of Manne and Richels, see Williams (1989), and for an optimistic view see Lovins (1989). For a comprehensive survey of substitution technologies and their costs see Barbier *et al.*, (1991).

However, most analysts seem agreed that the *initial* tranche of cuts that may be called for by an international convention on greenhouse gases could be secured cheaply. Later tranches would indeed be more expensive, particularly when the costs of aiding developing country greenhouse gas substitution are added to industrialized countries' costs.

Finally, there are incidental benefits to greenhouse gas control. The two basic technological responses are (a) substitution of low carbon fuels for high carbon fuels (e.g. natural gas for coal, nuclear energy for both, etc.), and (b) energy conservation in the sense of reductions in the ratio of carbon-based energy to economic activity. Both technological responses have the effect of reducing conventional air pollutants such as nitrogen oxides, sulphur oxides and suspended particulates (dust and smoke). Hence, the benefits of reduced concentrations of these pollutants can be counted in as benefits to CO_2 reduction policies. Since carbon-reduction measures would also need to target transportation, yet further benefits accrue in the form of reduced accidents, congestion and other road costs. One Norwegian study (Glomsrod *et al.*, 1990) suggests that while a hypothetical carbon tax might cost 2.75% of forgone GNP in the year 2010, 70% of that cost would be recouped in ancillary benefits.

This combination of uncertainty, irreversibility, probable initial low control costs, possible very high damage costs in the absence of action, and potentially high joint benefits from control, suggest that the policy stance on global warming should be fairly aggressive. At the end of 1990 such a stance was being adopted by European and Scandinavian countries, together with Canada, Japan, Australia and New Zealand. All these countries have targets for CO_2 reductions, usually aiming for a return by 2000 or 2005 to CO_2 emission levels pertaining in 1990. Significantly, while few of these countries have openly discussed detailed measures for attaining targets, there is widespread agreement that targets cannot be achieved by information campaigns and political persuasion. Put another way, it is highly likely that most nations will begin their policy on global warming by increasing expenditures on energy 'save it' campaigns, and increasing energy conservation standards in buildings, vehicles and energy appliances. Some, such as the United Kingdom, will also place significant faith in privatized electricity generators to adopt natural gas as opposed to coal-fired generating technology, thus lowering carbon emissions. The carbon content of the three main fuels is coal: 25.1 grammes carbon per 1000 BTUs; oil 20.3 and gas 14.5. Substituting gas for coal can therefore nearly halve emissions in new power stations. But, after these initial policies, emission reduction will very quickly require other instruments of control. The two economic candidates are a carbon tax and tradeable carbon emission permits. Tradeable permits are not discussed here, but this should not be taken as a sign of their irrelevance. As we shall see, however, taxes have some practical advantages over permits.

The remaining sections look at the virtues and problems of a carbon tax. The approach is more 'political economy' than economics because international negotiators are already at work on the design of a 'carbon convention'. While there is a desperate need for more and improved analytical studies of carbon taxes, there is also a great need for those studies to relate to real-world contexts. For once, negotiators appear to be ahead of the economists.

19.2 ADVANTAGES OF A CARBON TAX

There are major advantages of a carbon tax over the general alternative of regulating emissions through conventional command and control policies.

a. While most taxes distort incentives, an environmental tax corrects a distortion, namely the externalities arising from the excessive use of environmental services. A carbon tax would be set on the basis of the carbon content of fossil fuels. Given the widespread use of these fuels, any tax would inevitably be revenue raising, even though the tax works best if it is avoided through the introduction of low or zero carbon technologies. Governments may then adopt a fiscally neutral stance on the carbon tax, using revenues to finance reductions in incentive – distorting taxes such as income tax, or corporation tax. This 'double dividend' feature of a pollution tax is of critical importance in the political debate about the means of securing a 'carbon convention.' Industry will resist any new tax. Politicians are understandably nervous about introducing such taxes. But the corporate and public acceptability of such a tax is greatly enhanced if the tax is introduced as part of a 'package' of fiscally neutral measures. From a social standpoint the double dividend feature is also important. Estimates suggest that every £1 of tax raised by taxes on effort and enterprise gives rise to deadweight losses of 20–50 pence (Ballard *et al.*, 1985). Thus a fiscally neutral £1 carbon tax would amount to an effective tax of 50–80 pence. Finally, fiscal neutrality becomes an almost essential adjunct of a carbon tax set at any 'reasonable' rate (see later). This is because revenue raised may be so significant as to alter completely fiscal stances by governments. A $100 per ton carbon tax in the USA, for example, might result in government revenues equal to 3% of GNP. Such rates of tax must, therefore, be accompanied by revenue redistribution if they are not to dictate reversals of fiscal policy (unless that is independently intended) (Poterba, 1991).

b. The double dividend feature of a carbon tax could be extremely important in the international context. Current (early 1991) expectations are that the main features of a carbon convention will be in place by the time of the United Nations Environment Conference in Rio in mid 1992. [Negotiated in 1992, David W. Pearce] By then, targets allocated to countries should be known. Two broad scenarios are possible. Either individual countries will be left to determine their own measures to achieve the target, or some commonality in the use of policy instruments will be sought. The former is more likely, in keeping with traditional reservations about national sovereignty. But the latter has some attractions in the context of either carbon taxes or tradeable permits. Some mechanism will have to be found for persuading at least the developing world to sign up to any agreement. Given the pervasive use of fossil fuels and their critical role in the development process, few countries are likely to sign. Rationally, they will do so only if the net benefits to them from containing global warming are positive. For some countries, this may hold true (the Maldives, for example). For most, the perception – real or imagined – will be that the costs are too great. Some form of side payments will therefore be needed from the developed world if the developing world is to be party to the agreement. And their cooperation is highly important, if not initially then within, say, the first decade given their rates of growth of energy use. An internationally levied carbon tax has the potential to raise revenues which could be reimbursed on the basis of some criteria of deservingness. This extension of the fiscal neutrality concept to the international sphere could therefore solve both the allocational problem and the problem of non-cooperation. Tradeable permit systems could also be devised so as to induce cooperation, by 'overissuing' permits to the developing world so that the developed world enters the resulting market to buy them back. The prospects of such an international tax are perhaps remote given the suspicions which national governments will have of any such new institution emerging with revenue raising powers. The new Global Environmental Facility at the World Bank perhaps offers a modest prototype, although its revenues are unrelated to energy use and its disbursements are for conservation investments generally. Some commentators observe a 'revenue dilemma': if carbon taxes are high enough to induce behavioural change, no nation will surrender sovereignty to a new institution to raise such taxes. If they are low enough to induce the surrender of sovereignty, they will not have the desired incentive effects (Schelling, 1991).

c. Environmental taxes have the potential to minimize compliance costs for industry, and hence for consumers who will bear some portion of the tax. This minimum cost result derives from the fact that a tax common to all polluters will give rise to varying rates of abatement determined by individual marginal costs of pollution abatement. High marginal cost polluters will therefore pay the tax rather than abate, concentrating abatement measures in low cost polluters. The overall effect, then, is to minimize control costs (Baumol and Oates, 1971, 1988). Simulations suggest that use of taxes (or tradeable permits) can reduce compliance costs by 50% or more (Tietenberg, 1990).
d. Carbon taxes act as a continuous incentive to adopt ever cleaner technology and energy conservation. Standards tend to be 'technology-based', and therefore encourage technology switches up to the point judged by the regulator to be the 'best available'. But, unless standards are continually revised and set slightly above the best available technology, there is no incentive for the polluter to go beyond the standard. A tax, on the other hand, is always present as long as carbon-based fuels are used. There is some evidence to suggest that this dynamic efficiency aspect of environmental taxes is important (Tietenberg, 1990). In the CO_2 context, dynamic efficiency takes on an extra dimension because, unlike, say, sulphur, CO_2 is difficult to dispose of even if it is removed from stack gases. Proposals include injecting the 'captured' CO_2 in gas or oil fields, or to the deep ocean. Incentives to develop disposal technologies are therefore of particular relevance.
e. Carbon taxes can be easily modified as new information comes to light. Regulations, on the other hand, are difficult to change in a flexible manner. Again, the particular circumstances of the greenhouse effect are relevant here. The science is changing rapidly and we should therefore seek a policy instrument capable of responding to successive revisions of data and science. The experience of the Montreal Protocol (on protecting the ozone layer) is relevant here – the scale of the threat from chlorofluorocarbons has been revised upwards several times. The international community has revised the Protocol fairly rapidly, but revisions are easier for a treaty involving action by relatively few countries. For a more wide-ranging carbon convention, the fine-tuning of the policy instrument will be critical.

19.3 THE DISADVANTAGES OF A CARBON TAX

No policy measure is problem free. Probably the most widely discussed disadvantages of a carbon tax are as follows.

a. The target, in this case a set percentage reduction in projected CO_2 emissions, may not be achieved unless the relevant elasticities are known with reasonable certainty. Estimates of elasticities of demand for energy vary widely. Since a carbon tax will vary by carbon content of fuel, it is necessary to know inter-fuel substitution elasticities as well as the standard income and price elasticities. Some commentators therefore fear that a carbon tax will be a 'hit-and-miss' affair, inducing hostile reaction from industry and consumers as it has to be adjusted in an iterative fashion. It is not clear how serious an objection this is. As noted previously, flexible adjustment is very likely to be an essential feature of an efficient policy instrument anyway. Combining these 'learning' adjustments with others reflecting *ex post* elasticities is unlikely to be a major obstacle to a carbon tax.
b. Carbon taxes themselves will impose a deadweight loss which has to be set against the gain from the reduced externality from global warming. If the taxes are to have any incentive effect on energy conservation and inter-fuel substitution they must be non-marginal and therefore cannot be estimated reliably by partial equilibrium approaches: general equilibrium approaches are required. Partial equilibrium approaches can at best indicate the effect of 'small' carbon taxes. Poterba (1991) provides some approximate estimates of partial equilibrium welfare losses for a $5 per ton carbon tax in the USA and shows that they are very small relative to GNP, of the order of $280 million for total deadweight loss, or around 0.01% of US GNP. The efficiency costs of a 'small' carbon tax are small. Whalley and Wigle (1991) report general equilibrium estimates of welfare changes from substantial carbon taxes of the order of $450 per ton carbon. Their model suggests that the USA (and Canada) would lose around 1.2% of GNP if the tax is consumption-based, 4.3% if the tax is production-based, and a startling 9.8% of GNP if the tax is globally-based – i.e. internationally imposed, with revenues being redistributed on a per capita basis throughout the world. The Whalley/Wigle hypothetical carbon target – a 50% reduction in global carbon use relative to a base case – is, however, out of bounds as far as actual international negotiations are concerned.
c. The incidence of a carbon tax is widely regarded as one of its main defects. Interestingly, none of the available analyses of the incidence issue hypothesizes the correct policy context. As noted previously, many countries are committed to carbon targets. If a tax is adopted as the means of securing a target, then its incidence has to be analysed relative to the alternative non-tax instrument. If this is some form of command-and-control measure, then those measures also impose costs on producers and consumers, with a corresponding structure of incidence by social group, region, etc. Models are available for analysing the social costs of regulatory measures, including environmental policy (Jorgensen and Wilcoxen, 1990; Ketkar, 1984;

Klaassen *et al.*, 1987) but these appear not to have been used to estimate the net effect of a carbon tax on either incidence, or, for that matter, deadweight losses to the economy. Ignoring the issue of proper policy context, we might expect a carbon tax to be regressive since lower income households spend a larger proportion of their income on fuel than do higher income households. In the UK, for example, the lowest decile of gross income households spend 13.2% of income on fuel. The highest decile spends 3.5%. Johnson *et al.*, (1990) show that adjusting for household composition results in a more equal distribution of absolute fuel expenditures. Put another way, increases in fuel prices will have a disproportionate effect on low income groups. The regressive incidence is worsened with consideration of the effects of rising prices on particular social groups, such as pensioners.

The study simulates the effect of introducing 15% VAT on energy in the UK (to which, however, there has been a long-standing Treasury opposition) and shows that: (i) government revenues would be £1.7 billion; (ii) fuel consumption would be reduced by 4%; (iii) a tax rate of 75% would be needed to cut fuel consumption by 20% off 1988 levels; and (iv) the tax paid by the poorest decile of households would rise by about £1 per week, and £2 per week for the richest decile. The average rise is £1.50 per week. These figures translate into increases of tax paid (as a percentage of spending) of 1.8%, 0.4% and 0.7%, respectively.

Using input–output tables and the same consumer expenditure simulation model as IFS, Symons *et al.* (1990) show that a 20% reduction in CO_2 emissions from current levels would require a tax of around £60 per tonne of carbon in the UK. This tax rate, they suggest, would raise government revenues of some £17 billion. The indirect tax burden rises by nearly three times for the lowest decile of households, and by around 80% for the highest decile. If the proceeds of the carbon tax are used to eliminate VAT on all other goods, then the lowest decile household suffers a 160% increase in indirect tax burden and the highest decile only 20%.

Simulations of a £60 per tonne carbon tax with compensation measures to poorer households – minimum weekly expenditure levels of £45, benefit increases of £12 to pensioner households, and increased child benefit of £6 per child – show that one effect of compensation is greatly to reduce the carbon reduction level. Instead of 20% reduction on existing levels, only 11% is achieved due to compensating expenditures on carbon-containing goods and on fuel by the targeted households. However, inequality is actually reduced by this measure. Johnson *et al.* (1990) analyse several different tax reform packages to compensate for their hypothesized 15% VAT on energy. That work suggests that designing a fair compensation policy is far from easy, but should be feasible, especially if measures are taken to overcome the lack of take-up of means-tested benefits.

d. While the issue of social incidence is important in political assessments of carbon taxes, political resistance is due more to concerns about 'new taxes' – an especially sensitive issue in the UK in light of political repercussions from the introduction of the per capita community charge – and impacts on competitiveness. These concerns partly explain the willingness of some countries to make the focus of the carbon tax debate Brussels rather than national capitals. The European Commission is known to favour the introduction of EC-wide carbon taxes. Central introduction would do much to lessen concerns overcompetitiveness. How far such a carbon tax needs to be 'harmonized' is open to debate. Given that greenhouse gases are 'uniformly mixed accumulative pollutants' and that damage may be reasonably uniform across EC nations (the 'public bad' case) some authors have suggested that little is to be lost from harmonization (Mohr, 1990). The general political debate about carbon taxes and competitiveness has also been marked by little recognition that alternative means of control will also have cost impacts and hence potential implications for competitiveness.

19.4 THE NATURE OF A CARBON TAX

A carbon tax is most likely to take the form of a specific excise tax on the carbon content of fuels. In this respect it needs to be distinguished from generalized energy taxes such as *ad valorem* taxes (VAT) or a tax per million BTUs. The tax would vary for each of the three main fuels – oil, coal and gas – because their carbon content varies. The tax could be production or consumption based, but virtually all the discussion in the literature relates to a consumption-based tax. A production tax would become an extraction tax and, if internationally applied, would benefit 'carbon exporters' such as OPEC and work against net carbon importers such as Japan and the EC. If the objective is to curtail carbon consumption in the EC, say, then the tax would have to be consumption-based. Table 19.1 provides some simple illustrations of how the tax might affect fuels consumed by the electricity supply industry (ESI). A tax of £60 per tonne carbon is assumed in line with the computations in Symons *et al.* (1990), and is broadly consistent with widely discussed international taxes of $100 per ton carbon. The resulting price increases are seen to be substantial. Moreover, to allow for rising energy demand, the tax rates would need to be increased through time.

Barrett (1990) has conveniently assembled estimates of carbon taxes from various studies. These are shown in Table 19.2, together with some additional studies not included in Barrett (1990). Comparing the various studies is difficult since the basis for the hypothesized taxes is not always clear. Barrett converts the various estimates on two bases: tax per ton and tax as a percentage of the price of internationally traded crude oil (taken to be $20 a barrel). The same convention is adopted in Table 19.2.

Table 19.1 Illustrative estimates of the effect of a £60/ton carbon tax on the ESI

	Coal	Oil	Gas
Carbon content tons C/unit of fuel	0.667 tonne	0.130 bbl	0.016 10^3 ft = 0.0016 therm
Carbon emissions/bn BTU	(0.25)	(0.20)	(0.15)
£60 tonne/C tax as per unit fuel	£40.0 tonne	£58.5 tonne	9.6p/therm
ESI purchase prices 1989	£45.9 tonne	£61.0 tonne	19.5p/therm
Increase in price due to carbon tax	87%	96%	49%

Note: 1 tonne oil = 7.5 barrels.

Source: ESI purchase prices from *Digest of United Kingdom Energy Statistics*, HMSO, London, 1990, Table 69.

Table 19.2 Carbon tax studies and their results

Study	Carbon tax ($ ton C)	Percentage of oil price	Percentage reduction in CO_2	Region
Nordhaus (1990)	$3	2	9% in 2050	World
Manne and Richels (1990)	$250	158	75% in 2100	World
Cline (1989)	$158	100	57% in 2050 or 21% off 1985 by 2050	World
Edmonds and Reilly (1983)	$123	78	40% in 2050	World
Howarth *et al.* (1989)	$623	103	26% in 2050	World
Whalley and Wigle (1990)*	$460	300	50% off trend emissions	World
IEA (1989)	$72	44	12% in 2005	OECD
Bye *et al.* (1989)	$126	75	20% in 2000	Norway
Barker and Lewney	$145	92	18% in 2005	UK
(1990)	$516	327	33% in 2005	UK
Barrett (1990)	$34	32	20% in 1988	UK
	$59	57	35% in 2005	

Table 19.2 continued

Study	Carbon tax ($ ton C)	Percentage of oil price	Percentage reduction in CO_2	Region
Symons *et al.* (1990)*	$96	62	20% off 1988 by 2005	UK
Ingham and Ulph (1989)	$87-205	57-128	20% in 1988 by 2005	UK manufacturing
Manne and Richels (1989)	$300	190	85% in 2100 or 20% off 1985 by 2100	USA
Chandler and Nicholls (1990)*	$82	53	20% reduction in baseline	USA
CBO (1991)	$28	18	Stabilise 1990	
	$113	72	levels by 2000 10-20% off 1990 level by 2000	USA
Nordhaus and Yohe (1983)*	$20	13	6.7 below baseline,	USA
	$100	65	27% below baseline.	
	$200	130	43% below baseline.	
	$300	195	54% below baseline.	
Williams (1989)*	$160	104	63% below baseline.	Sweden
	$250	162	74% below baseline.	
Kram and Okken (1989)	$40	26	28% below baseline.	Netherlands

Notes:
For further detail see Barrett (1990).
* Refers to studies not included in the Barrett survey.

19.5 CONCLUSIONS

While Barrett cautions against straightforward comparisons of the results, there are several interesting features of Table 19.2. First, carbon taxes of the order of $100 per tonne carbon, or around a 65% increase in the price of a $20 barrel of oil, would appear to be adequate to secure the widely discussed 'first tranche' targets of stabilization at 1990 levels by 2000/2005, and some of the models suggest this may be sufficient to achieve the 'Toronto target' of 20% reductions in 1988/1990 levels by 2005. Some of the very high tax scenarios, which have clearly had an influence on the United States administration's stance on international CO_2 negotiations, would appear to be unduly alarmist.

Second, the tax estimates all generally assume that no other measures are taken prior to the introduction of a tax. In reality, countries will try to look for politically 'soft' measures before embracing carbon taxes (e.g. 'save energy' campaigns). The effect of this may be ambiguous, however. If the soft policies do not work – and past evidence suggests strongly that they will not – then valuable time may be lost and the resulting tax increases will be higher than necessary. Or, if the soft measures do work, there may be less for a carbon tax to do by way of securing emissions cutbacks. On balance, the former risk seems more likely than the latter benefit.

Third, while there are many reasons for varying estimates of impact, the underlying energy elasticities are likely to be crucial. It is significant that a number of the studies complain of the absence of up-to-date assessments of elasticities of demand by region. That suggests at least one research priority. Fourth, few of the studies actually consider the 'double dividend' feature of a carbon tax. Given the revenue implications of some of the hypothesized taxes, this is surprising. Thus, Poterba (1991) computes the government revenues arising from a \$100 tonne/carbon tax. Illustrative cases are: UK \$18.8 billion or 2.3% of GNP; France \$1.2 billion or 1.3% of GNP; Japan \$32 billion or 1.1% of GNP: and USA \$164 billion or 3.4% of GNP. The fate of these revenues is therefore crucial to any real-world discussion of carbon taxes.

NOTE

1. Adapted from The role of taxes in adjusting to global warming, *Economic Journal*, **101**, July 1991, 935–48.

REFERENCES

Ballard, C., Shoven, J. and Whalley, J. (1985), General equilibrium computations of the marginal welfare costs of taxes in the United States,' *American Economic Review*, **75**, 128–38.

Barbier, E., Burgess, J. and Pearce D. W. (1991), Slowing global warming: Options for greenhouse gas substitution, in Dornbusch and Poterba (1991).

Barker, T. and Lewney, R.(1990), *Macroeconomic Modelling of Environmental Policies: the Carbon Tax and Regulation of Water Quality*. Department of Applied Economics, University of Cambridge, mimeo.

Barrett, S. (1990), *Economic Instruments for Global Climate Change Policy*, Environment Directorate, Organisation for Economic Cooperation and Development, Paris.

Baumol, W. and Oates, W. (1971), The use of standards and prices for protection of the environment, *Swedish Journal of Economics*, **73**, 42–54.

Baumol, W. and Oates, W. (1988), *The Theory of Environmental Policy*, 2nd edition, Cambridge University Press, Cambridge.

Bye, B., Bye, T. and Lorentsen, L. (1989), *SIMEN: Studies of Industry, Environment and Energy Towards 2000*, Discussion Paper No. 44, Central Bureau of Statistics, Oslo.

Chandler, W. and Nicholls, A. (1990), *Assessing Carbon Emissions Control Strategies: a Carbon Tax or a Gasoline Tax*? ACEEE Policy paper No. 3, Battelle Memorial Institute, Washington D.C.

Cline, W. (1989), *Political Economy of the Greenhouse Effect*. Institute for International Economics, Washington DC, mimeo.

Congressional Budget Office (CBO) (1991), *Reducing The Deficit: Spending and Revenue Options*. Congressional Budget Office, Washington DC.

Dornbusch, R. and Poterba, J. (eds) (1991), *Global Warming: Economic Policy Responses*, MIT Press, Cambridge, MA.

Edmonds, J. and Reilly, J. (1983), Global energy and CO_2 to the year 2050, *Energy Journal*, **4**, 21–47.

Glomsrod, S. *et al.* (1990), *Stabilization of Emissions of $C0_2$: a Computable General Equilibrium Assessment*, Central Bureau of Statistics, Oslo.

Houghton, R., Jenkins, G.J. and Ephraums, E. (1990), *Climate Change: the IPCC Scientific Assessment*, Cambridge University Press, Cambridge.

Howarth, D., Nikitopoulos, P. and Yohe, G. (1989), *On the Ability of Carbon Taxes to Fend Off Global Warming*, Department of Economics, Wesleyan University, Middletown, CT, mimeo.

Ingham, A. and Ulph, A. (1989). *Carbon Taxes and the UK Manufacturing Sector*. Department of Economics, University of Southampton, mimeo.

International Energy Agency (IEA) (1989), *Policy Measures and Their Impact on CO_2 Emissions and Accumulations*, IEA Paris.

Johnson, P., McKay, S. and Smith, S. (1990), *The Distributional Consequences of Environmental Taxes*, Institute for Fiscal Studies, Commentary No. 23.

Jorgensen, D. and Wilcoxen, P. (1990), Environmental regulation and US economic growth, *RAND Journal of Economics*, **21**, 314–40.

Ketkar, K. W. (1984), Environmental protection policies and the structure of the US economy, *Applied Economics*, **16**, 237–56.

Klaassen G. *et al.* (1987), *The Macroeconomic Impacts of the EC Large Combustion Plants Directive Proposal*, Institute for Environmental Studies, Free University of Amsterdam.

Kram, T. and Okken, P. A. (1989), Integrated assessment of energy options for CO_2 reduction, in P. Okken, R.J. Swart and S. Zwerver (eds), *Climate and Energy: The Feasibility of Controlling CO_2 Emissions*, Kluwer, Dordrecht:.

Lovins, A. (1989), Abating global warming – at a profit,' *Rocky Mountain Institute Newsletter*, **5**.

Manne, A. and Richels, R. (1989), *CO_2 Emission Limits: An Economic Analysis for the USA*, Department of Economics, Stanford University, mimeo.

Manne, A. and Richels, R. (1990), *Global CO_2 Emission Reductions: the Impacts of Rising Energy Costs*, Department of Economics, Stanford University, mimeo.

Mohr, E. (1990), *EC Fiscal Harmonization, Environmental Taxes and Charges: Theory and Policy*, Kiel Institute of World Economics, mimeo.

Nordhaus, W. (1990), *To Slow or Not to Slow: The Economics of the Greenhouse Effect*, Department of Economics, Yale University, mimeo.

Nordhaus, W. and Yohe, G. (1983), Future carbon dioxide emissions from fossil fuels, in Changing Climate, National Academy of Sciences, Washington DC.

Pearce, D.W. (1990), *Global Environmental Change: The Challenge to Industry and Economic Science*, the 35th Fawley Foundation Lecture, University of Southampton, Southampton.

Poterba, J. (1991), Tax policy to combat global warming: on designing a carbon tax, in Dornbusch and Poterba (1991), 71–97.

Schelling, T. (1991), Economic responses to global warming: prospects for cooperative approaches, in Dornbusch and Poterba (1991), 197–221.

Symons, E., Proops, J. and Gay, P. (1990), *Carbon Taxes, Consumer Demand and Carbon Dioxide Emission: A Simulation Analysis for the UK*, Department of Economics, University of Keele, mimeo.

Tietenberg, T. (1990), Economic instruments for environmental regulation, *Oxford Review of Economic Policy*, **6**, 1–17.

Whalley, J. and Wigle, R. (1991), The international incidence of carbon taxes, in Dornbusch and Poterba (1991), 233–62.

Williams, R. H. (1989), *Low Cost Strategies for Coping with CO_2 Emission Limits*, Centre for Energy and Environmental Studies, Princeton University, December 1989, mimeo.

Index